Something to Fear

Something to Fear

FDR and the Foundations of
American Insecurity, 1912–1945

Ira Chernus and Randall Fowler

University Press of Kansas

© 2023 by the University Press of Kansas

All rights reserved

Published by the University Press of Kansas (Lawrence, Kansas 66045), which was organized by the Kansas Board of Regents and is operated and funded by Emporia State University, Fort Hays State University, Kansas State University, Pittsburg State University, the University of Kansas, and Wichita State University.

Library of Congress Cataloging-in-Publication Data

Names: Chernus, Ira, 1946– author. | Fowler, Randall, author.
Title: Something to fear : FDR and the foundations of American insecurity,
    1912–1945 / Ira Chernus and Randall Fowler.
Other titles: FDR and the foundations of American insecurity, 1912–1945
Description: Lawrence, Kansas : University Press of Kansas, 2023. |
    Includes bibliographical references and index.
Identifiers: LCCN 2023000415 (print) | LCCN 2023000416 (ebook)
    ISBN 9780700635641 (cloth)
    ISBN 9780700635658 (ebook)
Subjects: LCSH: Roosevelt, Franklin D. (Franklin Delano), 1882–1945. | United
    States—Foreign relations—1933–1945. | National security—Political aspects—
    United States—20th century. | Rhetoric—Political aspects—United States—
    History—20th century. | United Statesl—Politics and government—1901–1953. |
    World War, 1939–1945—United States. | Propaganda, American—History—
    20th century.
Classification: LCC E806 .C497 2024 (print) | LCC E806 (ebook) | DDC
    973.917–dc23/eng/20230126
LC record available at https://lccn.loc.gov/2023000415.
LC ebook record available at https://lccn.loc.gov/2023000416.

British Library Cataloguing-in-Publication Data is available.

Printed in the United States of America

10 9 8 7 6 5 4 3 2 1

The paper used in this publication is acid free and meets the minimum requirements of the American National Standard for Permanence of Paper for Printed Library Materials Z39.48-1992.

To those who labor for genuine peace and security in America and throughout the world.

Contents

Acknowledgments

Ira Chernus

This book has been so many years in the making, it is hard for me to recall all the people who have helped me along the way. I got significant aid from many scholars, including Fredrik Logevall, Frank Costigliola, Robert McMahon, Martin Medhurst, Walter Hixson, David Zietsma, and Michaela Hönicke Moore. To all the others, who remain unnamed here, I offer my sincere apology.

As always, I thank my colleagues in the Department of Religious Studies at the University of Colorado, Boulder, for not merely tolerating but appreciating my rather unorthodox area of research. Dillon Webster and Scott Brown were very helpful editorial assistants. Parts of the research were supported by a yearlong fellowship in the Center for Humanities and Arts and a short-term grant from the Graduate Committee on Arts and Humanities at CU-Boulder.

I was graciously invited to present parts of this work in lectures at Arizona State University, the University of Regina, and Princeton University; graduate students in the Department of Religion at Princeton offered particularly incisive questions and comments that enriched my thinking. Rick Shenkman gave me the opportunity to share some of my ideas with a wide public audience by inviting me to blog on History News Network. Librarians at the Franklin D. Roosevelt Library in Hyde Park, New York, were most helpful in guiding me to material and answering all my inquiries.

I owe an enormous debt of thanks to Randall Fowler, who took over this project at a rather advanced stage, when I no longer felt able to continue it. Randall took full responsibility for seeing it through to completion, and he did that in an excellent way. I am sure he has an outstanding academic future ahead of him.

Finally, I feel more gratitude than I can ever express to my spouse,

Kathy, who supported me and this project at every step of the way, from its inception to its publication.

Randall Fowler

There are many people to whom I owe a debt of gratitude. First and foremost, this book would not have come to fruition without the trust Ira placed in me to finish this project. I cannot thank him enough for his reassurance, insight, and confidence as this manuscript underwent its final revisions to become the book before you now. It is always a kind act for a distinguished scholar to partner with a younger colleague, but to do so in such a substantial way testifies to the uncommon generosity Ira possesses. May we all learn not only from his intellect but also his example.

I must also thank my MA advisor at Baylor University, the late Martin Medhurst, who introduced me to Ira when I was still in my first year of PhD work at the University of Maryland. Marty, may you rest in peace.

There are many outstanding scholars at Maryland who contributed to this work, none more than Shawn J. Parry-Giles. Shawn's influence can be found throughout this book in the form of crisper writing, tighter argumentation, and deeper appreciation for the power of language across time. I also thank the many scholars whose encouragement was vital to the completion of this work, including Sahar Khamis, Carly Woods, and Trevor Parry-Giles as well as Skye De Saint Felix, Alyson Farzad-Phillips, Naette Lee, Victoria Ledford, and the late Misti Yang, who is greatly missed.

My gratitude extends to my former colleagues at Fresno Pacific University, who daily challenged me to become a better member of our academic community through their patience, kindness, and brilliance. Thank you for demonstrating a selflessness that is as rare as it is refreshing. I also express gratitude to my colleagues at Abilene Christian University, particularly Lynette Sharp Penya, who have blessed me with their time, care, and confidence, which makes scholarship such as this book possible. I am grateful for the many ways you have invested in me.

I would be remiss if I forgot to thank the reviewers whose insights and comments helped strengthen this project. I particularly thank Robert McMahon of Ohio State University and David Congdon at the University Press of Kansas for their extensive feedback on earlier drafts of this book. The final product is much stronger for your input.

As will ever be, my deepest gratitude belongs to my wife, Sarah Grace, whose love and care sustain me even through the most trying of difficulties. Thank you for your constant encouragement, companionship, and tenderness. You are undoubtedly one of a kind.

Abbreviations

FDRFA	Roosevelt, Franklin D. *Franklin D. Roosevelt and Foreign Affairs.* Edited by Edgar B. Nixon. Cambridge, MA: Belknap Press, 1969–1983.
FDR: His Personal Letters	Roosevelt, Franklin D. *FDR: His Personal Letters.* Edited by Elliott Roosevelt. New York: Duell, Sloan & Pearce, 1947–1950.
FDR *PPA*	Roosevelt, Franklin D. *Public Papers and Addresses of Franklin Delano Roosevelt.* Compiled by Samuel I. Rosenman. New York: Macmillan, 1938–1950.
FDRL	Franklin D. Roosevelt Presidential Library & Museum
FRUS	Foreign Relations of the United States, Department of State. Washington, DC: US Government Printing Office.
Fireside Chats	Buhite, Russel D., and David W. Levy, eds. *FDR's Fireside Chats.* Norman, OK: University of Oklahoma Press, 1992.

Introduction
None Who Can Make Us Afraid

We imagine most things before we experience them.
—Walter Lippmann, 1922[1]

Our danger cannot be fixed or confined to one specific instant. We live in an age of peril.
—Dwight D. Eisenhower, 1953[2]

The United States has traveled a vast distance since 1776. In the beginning the nation saw itself as a beacon of hope, an outlook encapsulated in the revolutionary writings of Thomas Paine. Like many elites from that era, Paine described the American founding as an "Event," one that affected "all Lovers of mankind."[3] The Founding Fathers reflected this sentiment. Thomas Jefferson dreamt of an "empire of liberty" stretching across the Western hemisphere.[4] Jefferson's Federalist rival Alexander Hamilton likewise envisioned an American "empire" that would be "in many respects the most interesting in the world."[5] Writing an early draft of his farewell address, President George Washington recorded his yearnings for the young nation he led: "That our Union may be as lasting as time; for while we are encircled in one band, we shall possess the strength of a Giant and there will be none who can make us afraid."[6]

None who can make us afraid. Centuries later, Americans are still in search of the vision laid down by Washington. Far from reaching the harmonious state outlined by our nation's first president, public discourse today is filled with alarm, anxiety, vitriol, and danger. Regardless of one's political faction, a litany of fear appeals stands at the ready to scare others into support of one's preferred policies. From climate change and China to the alt-right and Antifa, innumerable symbols of insecurity from competing debate arsenals are daily aimed at Americans. Recent data testify to their effectiveness. Nine in ten Americans believe the country is undergoing a "mental health crisis," and another study found the highest levels of depression and anxiety on record.[7] Judged by these metrics, it would seem that we are very afraid.

Nowhere is this clearer than in foreign policy, where the specters of terrorism, cyberwar, weapons of mass destruction, revanchist powers, pandemics, and other global dangers loom over US debates. Political commentators commonly portray everything from Russian hackers to ISIS terrorists as not just damaging to national security but as "existential threats" to the United States and its democracy. In the fear-saturated airwaves of modern America, it is not hard to see the ease with which this trend has led to an explosion of perceived threats to the nation and its citizens, a product of analysts' interpretations as much as the tides of geopolitics. The recent additions of COVID-19 and climate change to the pantheon of dangers being addressed by US intelligence and military agencies—the "national security architecture"—speaks to the fungibility of this construction.[8]

Obviously not all Americans agree on the list of dangers facing their nation. From the atomic anxieties of the 1950s to environmental fears today, there are many who dissent from the threat assessments made in Washington. All the same, the above examples illustrate a central claim of this book: *the process of identifying threats to the nation is a fundamentally rhetorical enterprise.* It involves labeling situations, constructing quasilogical arguments, convincing policy-makers, deliberating over future courses of action, and assessing risk in a contingent world.[9] Just as "facts do not speak; they must be spoken for," the elements of national security are not self-evident—they must be interpreted. Threats, like test scores or home values, are assessed by human actors.[10]

Accordingly, one school of thought defines securitization as "a discursive process through which an intersubjective understanding is constructed within a political community to treat something as an existential threat to a valued referent object, and to enable a call for urgent and exceptional measures to deal with the threat."[11] Cold War scholars Hinds and Windt Jr. similarly note that "we argue about what events signify, which actions were important, and what understanding of each is more prudent and reasonable. When we begin to argue about meaning, we are engaged in constructing reality. Insofar as people believe these meanings, a reality is created upon which people act. It is in this sense that we believe political rhetoric creates political reality, structures belief systems, and provides the fundamental bases for decisions."[12] These scholars point to how notions of security exist in an embedded network of discursive relationships circulating within a political community. Consequently, the processes by which contested definitions of security achieve primacy and threats to the nation become identified can be traced through discourse. Security, like equality, is a term with a history.[13]

The project of this book is to examine one small slice of that history by exploring the rhetoric of Franklin Delano Roosevelt and the "Great Debate" over America's role in the world that occurred during his presidency.[14] Specifically, we argue that Roosevelt's unique rhetorical constellation of symbols of security and insecurity, intricately woven together over his career, supplied the discursive resources that his successors would use to mediate the transition from World War II to the Cold War. Critically, FDR generated those resources through a complex dialectic between symbols of insecurity and symbols of security hearkening back all the way to the beginning of his career, such that to restrict our study to his wartime appeals or presidential rhetoric alone would be to miss the vital contributions made by his political rhetoric prior to the presidency. Like an iceberg, the foundations of Roosevelt's thinking on security lie submerged, hidden under the shimmering renown of his transformative presidency. From that vantage, this study is in many respects an excavation as we explore the roots of his powerful rhetoric.

In short, the argument we seek to advance is this: FDR's rhetoric of security laid the discursive foundations for talking about the Cold War that would come after him. The themes of fear, security, and insecurity are apparent early in his political career, during which time he traded in the prevailing discourses of progressivism, romanticism, economic liberalism, and Mahanianism.[15] Prepresident Roosevelt subscribed to a viewpoint that abhorred radicalism, seeing the political landscape as a set of problems to be solved by collective action so as to prevent violence, desperation, and revolution. He defined the nation's challenges in these terms upon entering the Oval Office, articulating New Deal policies in a militant register on the domestic front while drawing on the tenets of liberal internationalism to depict the increasingly militarized globe as a community of good neighbors linked by trade and rule of law. With the German conquest of France in May 1940 and the collapse of the order it signified, Americans were forced to find a new way to articulate their relationship to a war-filled world. In the debate over intervention that followed, one could see competing definitions over the United States' new global role. Roosevelt fought the anti-interventionists, first arguing that he could be trusted with guiding America through the global conflict (in the midst of running for a third term) and then making a positive case for intervention, borrowing from the same rhetorical tactics that worked to pass New Deal legislation. Once conflict came, FDR worked in tandem with American allies to communicate war aims that hinted toward a world organized around trade, disarmament, civilization, and (most of all) security. Under his leadership, the US government organized an all-out domestic propaganda campaign to persuade ordinary Americans of these administration goals. By Roosevelt's passing, the domain of "security" had been expanded to heretofore unaffected arenas of American life and became the dominant idiom of foreign policy discourse.[16] He instantiated a way of talking about US international affairs that would prove fertile and resilient, swiftly giving rise to the rhetoric of Cold War and lasting in many respects until today.

In making this argument, we situate our study at the intersection of three scholarly conversations. First, this book expands upon suggestions made by those involved in the historical study of FDR that fear and security were perhaps the central themes of his presidency. Several scholars have pointed out the importance of these terms for Roosevelt. For example, in *Freedom from Fear*, David M. Kennedy writes, "Security was the touchstone, the single word that summed up more of what Roosevelt aimed at than any other."[17] Matthew Dallek likewise recounts that "FDR sought to stamp out fear. . . . This theme—conquering fear—has often defined his presidency, leadership, and legacy."[18] Ira Katznelson's *Fear Itself* highlights the role FDR's discourse of security played in his management of public fear during the first years of his presidency. He remarks on how "the reality of deep uncertainty progressively extended the sense that the United States confronted unparalleled dangers" in the New Deal period, leading to "an unremitting sense of fragility." As he continues, "The New Deal proceeded in an anguish-filled environment. In such a world, most constant features of American political life continually threatened to become unstable, if not unhinged. . . . It must be underscored that fear was not banished after just four years of the New Deal. To the contrary, it only deepened."[19] To understand Roosevelt, he concludes, "requires identifying the era's objects of fear."[20] To this brief sampling could be added others who have recorded the meta theme of security in FDR's wartime rhetoric, noting how he sought to project confidence and raise American morale.[21] By taking as our focus Roosevelt's discourse of security, we expand on these observations and offer an account that explains the deep interconnections between FDR's New Deal and war rhetoric.

Second, this book adds to the work being done concerning the Roosevelt presidency in the field of rhetorical studies. Rhetoricians have long been fascinated with the nation's thirty-second president. Studies analyzing FDR's utterances have been written from a number of perspectives, including his rhetoric of disability, economic discourse, use of radio technology, relationship with the media, crisis rhetoric, campaign discourse, speechwriting practices, sonic persuasion, views on national identity, interactions with the Black press, fireside chats, rhetorical timing, rhythm, language of rescue, war rhetoric, and how his Scottish terrier Fala contributed to his public image.[22] Contributing to this impressive array, this study specifically examines the twin themes of security and insecurity in FDR's rhetoric. In doing so, it more fully takes up the paths suggested by others in the field. Specifically, this book expands upon the work of Thomas B. Farrell, who examines Roosevelt's "doubling up and reversing our relationship to fear" in his first inaugural address, Frank Costigliola, who argues that "Roosevelt as president underscored dangers, indeed exaggerating them, in order to drive Americans to combat the Depression and the dictators," and James J. Kimble, who states that Roosevelt's Four Freedoms address "represented an international extension of FDR's aims for the New Deal."[23] We seek to build on these essay-length analyses (and the rhetorical literature on FDR writ large) by fleshing out their implications more fully in our study of Roosevelt's security discourse over the course of his political career. We thereby add to this field's understanding of FDR as a rhetorical figure.

Third, this book complements the work of international relations scholars attuned to the role of rhetoric in the making of US national security policy. Ronald R. Krebs calls for just such a sensibility in *Narrative and the Making of US National Security*, arguing that "the largest questions of national security require leaders to engage public audiences" in order to legitimate their policy choices, and thus "students of security affairs should devote attention to how debate is structured, to how the bases and boundaries of legitimation are set and reworked, and to the impact on the policies states pursue."[24] Francis A. Beer and Robert Hariman echo this theme: "Rhetoric, arguably the first political science, offers an analytical program that works well with the common sense and enduring concerns of foreign affairs. The rhetorical tradition includes appreciation of the dynamics of power, valorization of both argument and style, a focus on negotiation, involvement in the dialectic of elites and their publics, [and] a strategic sensibility . . . particularly in respect to political decision making."[25] Discourses of national security establish the common-sense boundaries of debate, working to delimit the politically permissible actions of policy-makers in a liberal democratic state. Therefore, those who study politics should pay particular attention to how those discourses emerge.[26] This book contributes to that end by showing how Roosevelt worked to concretize one particular conception of national security during a period in which the United States' military and economic power came to dwarf that of its historic rivals.

We study FDR from the perspective of the rhetorical historian, viewing history as a series of rhetorical problems that call for public persuasion on the part of human actors dealing with the imperfect world of politics.[27] Rhetoric, from this perspective,

> is not bombast and ornamentation, nor a noun to be preceded with adjectives *empty* and *mere*. It does not stand in opposition to reality because it, too, is real. Rather, it represents the old and useful art of discovering in a particular situation the means available to influence others to perceive, believe, or act differently than they otherwise would. It is called into being by an exigence, a problem for which persuasion can provide the solution. Thus, it constitutes the means by which the president, as "leader of the American people," can "shape and mobilize public opinion."[28]

Indeed, Roosevelt's words comprised a major portion of the "undelayed action" he promised to take against the crises facing the United States of his time; much of his action, as Vanessa Beasley and Deborah Smith-Howell observe, "was rhetorical," as FDR "clearly shaped his times through his words."[29] He understood that "rhetoric is a way of doing something in the real world," using persuasion, framing, metaphor, narrative, and argumentation to convince Americans to embrace not only his policy prescriptions but also his point of view.[30] In the words of Mary E. Stuckey, he served as an "interpreter-in-chief" for the country, disseminating his messages across the land through his innovative use of technology and the nascent field of public-opinion polling.[31]

FDR also knew the limits of his rhetorical leadership. An astute political actor, he rarely overstepped the bounds of public opinion, displaying a sensitivity for what classical rhetoricians labeled *kairos* (rhetorical timing) and *phronesis* (prudence).[32] Better than most, he displayed rhetorical skills such as the "ability to think clearly, reason effectively, invent arguments adapted to situations and specific audiences, speak eloquently, and move his listeners to action."[33] While many of us remember FDR for his consummate oratory, we should also remember that his rhetorical abilities included far more than just a penchant for articulacy. Precisely because of his suasory prowess, we are interested in how Roosevelt interpreted national and global events to the American public. By examining FDR's rhetoric of security, we hope to shed light on how his words mediated the United States' transition to superpower status, in the process generating a discursive field from which future presidents would draw to (re)define the nation's duties in the world. If, as Damir Marusic holds, "fear of the enemy drove U.S. Cold War logic," then the question remains as to how that fear and the rhetorical resources for creating it came to be.[34] This book is an attempt to offer a partial answer to that question via the analytical lens of presidential rhetoric.

Because of our previous work, we are both sensitive to the effect foreign-policy discourse can have on political outcomes.[35] As Karlyn Kohrs and Kathleen Hall Jamieson note, "Presidents invite us to see them, the presidency, the country, and the country's role in specific ways."[36] This topic is worthy of attention, because perceptions emanating from the Oval Office can lead to policy decisions that irrevocably impact lives and livelihoods around the world. While a social scientist or economist might argue that the United States was going to emerge as the world's greatest military power after World War II anyway, or that the Cold War was rooted in the harsh realities of economic, cultural, or geographic difference regardless of what anyone—including the president—said, we still insist that the "how" of that process matters. As Julian E. Zelizer writes, "While Americans were willing to fight when necessary in the nineteenth century and more than comfortable expanding national power through military force, most politicians and citizens were unwilling to commit to a permanent national security state. They would fight a war, then when it was done, they put away their arms and set their minds to other things."[37] This pattern was only broken following the Roosevelt presidency in the aftermath of World War II, which suggests that the pivotal importance of this time period stems perhaps less from the events themselves and more from the way the era's inhabitants made sense of the events they lived through.

How Americans came to understand themselves as occupying one pole of an atomic Cold War cannot be answered without addressing how they came to terms with their existence in the threatening world of the late 1930s and 1940s, which cannot itself be understood without contextualizing that world in the New Deal debates and presidency from which it arose. The symbols and arguments that migrate across these moments are connected like sinews. As Arnold A. Offner observes, even before Pearl Harbor, "Roosevelt had already forged the ideology and basic systems for the national security state."[38] It is with this understanding that we examine FDR's discourse of security and insecurity, in pursuit of an appreciation for how he rhetorically constructed—and continues to structure—Americans' experience of the bewildering world in which they find themselves.

In pursuing this line of inquiry, we build on the research of Mary Stuckey—notably her chapter on "The Great Debate" in volume 7 of *A Rhetorical History of the United States* and her books *Political Vocabularies* and *The Good Neighbor*—in three specific ways. First, we trace the elements of Roosevelt's rhetoric of security from their origins early in his prepresidential career to the end of his life. As she explains in the aforementioned chapter, Roosevelt steadfastly labored to convert citizens to his internationalist stance prior to the attack on Pearl Harbor, acting "on the principle that a successful foreign policy depended on domestic consensus." She likewise underscores the fluidity of FDR's threat construction; the danger from Germany and Japan was "ideological, then military, and now was also understood as economic." In the debate over intervention, she observes how he cagily appropriated anti-interventionist rationales "to advocate [for] other, more assertive policies" as he steadfastly aimed to define the purpose of the conflict in line with his viewpoint. Lastly, she also suggests that Roosevelt linked his rhetorical defense of the postwar "extension of US power abroad" to the New Deal promises he made "to the impoverished at home."[39] We do not deviate substantially from these interpretive claims. However, this project enriches the foregoing analysis by locating the origins of FDR's arguments earlier in his political career, highlighting the interposable nature of his preferred symbols of security, and illuminating the links between each stage of his political rhetoric in more detail.

Second, we expand the heuristic scope of her concept of "political vocabularies" by using this framework to understand Roosevelt's debate with the anti-interventionists. As she writes, political vocabularies comprise the linguistic components of political debate. They serve as "the indexical markers of our political imaginaries." Less broadly accepted than national imaginaries, political vocabularies come into view when there are clashes over the nature of political authority and the power arrangements and policies that flow from new configurations of governmental privilege. By analyzing them, we are granted "access into one moment of political change and the emerging set of political vocabularies that sought to capture and describe it." While Stuckey employs this framework to understand how American clergy interpreted the New Deal, we show how this analytical lens is also useful in making sense of the debate over intervention.[40]

Lastly, Stuckey contends that "the Roosevelt administration, in its entirety, can best be understood through the metaphor of the 'good neighbor,' which, while usually treated as relevant only to Roosevelt's foreign policy, actually runs throughout his domestic policy as well."[41] We agree, and indeed we demonstrate the linkages, including the good neighbor metaphor, between Roosevelt's New Deal and wartime rhetoric in detail. But we would also note that this metaphor introduced a set of associations—home, familiarity, predictability, continuity—closely linked to FDR's images of security writ large. Insofar as the good neighbor metaphor can be read as a rhetorical template for Roosevelt's career, it also displays the centrality of the rhetoric of security in his public utterances. The good neighbor metaphor—which we trace all the way back to his 1920 campaign for vice president—interacted with his other metaphors organized around insecurity (gangsters, fire, illness) in such a way as to amplify their danger in accordance with his progressive mindset. Just as a fire (or crime spree or pandemic) is more threatening in a densely packed neighborhood than at a distance, so did FDR's metaphorical imagery position dangers to the American homeland at an uncomfortable proximity.[42] Roosevelt's good neighbor metaphor, like other elements of his powerful rhetoric, ultimately provided fuel for fear.

Fear, of course, is an inexact term. Because it is experienced subjectively, it remains inscrutable to empirical analysis. Unlike levels of endorphins, sweating, or other physiological metrics, which can be measured, "fear" is a concept with a meaning classified differently by different people. Frank Furedi's definition reflects this relativity: "Fear attempts to offer a system of meaning . . . that guide[s] people in the way they go about making sense of, and responding to, threats."[43] Because "fear" is a label humans apply to an experience or state, it emerges in relation to one's social, political, economic, or religious location. Fear can therefore be understood as a culturally conditioned phenomenon that is transmitted through discourse.[44] Fears are expressed in a cultural matrix. That matrix, which is constructed through symbols of security and insecurity, provides the background context to render the articulation of fear or anxiety meaningful. Consequently, varying interpretations of what threats confront the nation represent "a clash of competing systems of meaning" as much as a clash of interests or armies.[45] One's sense of safety and fear, as David Campbell writes, is "an effect of interpretation," not "an objective condition."[46] It is shaped by the web of symbols that our culture embeds in our lives.[47] Thus, by analyzing symbols of (in)security, one gains insight into the fear a society experiences.

Fear and anxiety have long served as undercurrents in American public discourse. This point may seem odd, since Americans are commonly described as an especially confident people who generally look on the bright side, promote change, and work for a better future. Yet anxiety and optimism have persistently gone together in the American experience. From John Winthrop to Martin Luther King Jr., American orators have long offered hopeful visions alongside warnings of what may come should their hearers choose the wrong path.[48] As G. K. Chesterton remarked, "America is the only nation in the world that is founded on a creed," because it is "a nation with the soul of a church."[49] But if American identity is grounded in a sort of faith in American ideals, then there also exists the perennial threat to any such system: heresy. The very aspirational quality that typifies much of American culture also serves as its fuel for fear, since deviation from these ideals entails not only contravening cultural norms but threatening the advance toward future progress—however defined—as well.[50]

One of the most vitriolic clashes in American history over symbols of security occurred in the aftermath of the First World War, when President Woodrow Wilson attempted to redefine the nation's global role via the language of insecurity. In the buildup to American entry on the side of the Allies, Wilson had engaged in an aggressive rhetorical restructuring of the United States' relations with the belligerents. Jason C. Flanagan records how Wilson's rhetoric shifted from depicting America as the impartial friend to all the combatants to a picture of America as "the global champion of the rights of mankind," discursive moves that were "part of a larger and more fundamental reinterpretation by Wilson of the image of America and its role in the world."[51] The United States, according to Wilson, had "no self-respecting choice but to take up arms" against imperial Germany since "neutrality [was] no longer feasible or desirable where the peace of the world [was] involved and the freedom of its peoples."[52] Because Berlin prosecuted "a war against all nations" through its submarine warfare, Wilson declared, it became incumbent for the United States to enter the war: "The world must be made safe for democracy."[53] Wilson's language of insecurity therefore functioned to (1) villainize Germany as an irrational, autocratic aggressor; (2) warn that the entire world was under threat of domination; and (3) argue that the United States—as the global champion of freedom—must defeat Germany.

Although presidents before Wilson used the language of enemyship to marshal the nation to war, none had before done so to support an overseas military expedition to mainland Europe.[54] Even more, Wilson sought to extend his redefinition of America's global role to peacetime by pushing for US entry into the League of Nations. He embarked on a sweeping national tour to gain approval for the treaty. As the campaign wore on, Wilson slipped further into demagoguery. In Dorsey's evaluation, he offered "tedious rhetoric" that unrelentingly villainized his opponents.[55] The president "declared war" on the reservationists in the Senate and compared their misgivings to "pro-German propaganda."[56] If the United States rejected the treaty, he insisted, then it rejected the sacrifice of fallen American soldiers, who died to "[save] the liberty of the world." Indeed, he argued that the protection of freedom across the globe was now America's responsibility: "For nothing less depends upon us, nothing less than the liberation and salvation of the world."[57]

Wilson lost. J. Michael Hogan notes how his defiant tone worked against him, costing him support from "mild reservationists" who might otherwise have been persuaded to approve the treaty.[58] More broadly, Wilson's failure illustrated the political risk of arguing for an internationalist view of the United States' relationship to the world on a permanent basis. His inability to successfully translate his wartime rhetoric of defending democracy—itself a conglomeration of liberal internationalist, progressive, and American exceptionalist discourses—to a peacetime settlement speaks to the skepticism with which citizens viewed overseas commitments in the early twentieth century. Wilson's failure to establish an internationalist postwar order spawned a political backlash. His view gave way to a new foreign policy consensus, what historian George C. Herring calls "involvement without commitment," more popularly labeled "isolationism."[59] It would not be until the late 1930s that global events would again raise the question of the United States' role in the world, to very different effect.

Franklin Roosevelt was an active participant in these debates. As Wilson's assistant secretary of the navy, he held a strongly vested interest in maintaining US naval power. A progressive reformer, he cared intensely about questions of economics, work, and labor conditions. As a presidential namesake—he was a fifth cousin of Theodore Roosevelt—and a political animal in his own right, FDR learned much from the battle over the League of Nations treaty. When world affairs once more forced a debate over American involvement in a European war, he was ready. Roosevelt drew on the rhetorical resources he had developed throughout his presidency to argue for an expanded vision of the United States' global commitment, applying his political acumen to ensure its acceptance. FDR articulated an internationalist understanding of America's role in the world that would, unlike Wilson's, endure. He brilliantly adapted his touchstones of security and insecurity to describe the United States' worldwide responsibility in a politically winsome way. In typical Rooseveltian fashion, he reconciled the past toward a new course of action, adding an internationalist—and distinctively security-conscious—component to the way leaders had spoken about America's mission since the days of John Winthrop.

To be sure, there were other forces pushing nation in the same direction. By the late 1930s, as Andrew Johnstone has shown, several major organizations were working "to influence both the American government and the wider public about the need to stem the growing tide of fascist aggression." They rejected anti-interventionism, calling for "steps that moved the United States . . . closer and closer to conflict." These groups were politically powerful and had major influence. They "defined what internationalism was to the American people," as Johnstone writes. And their definition, which Roosevelt came to adopt, centered on the need to fend off enemies.[60] But it was FDR, with his awesome array of political skills and rhetorical prowess, that played the crucial role in the triumph of this internationalist view, in the process fixing the issue of national (in)security, set in a global context, to the center of American politics.

A complex figure, Roosevelt defies any simple explanation. If Americans are a people of paradox, FDR was the quintessential American; he was complex, vague, and contradictory, and he kept himself, in his own words, "a self-made riddle."[61] Following John Murphy, we observe that two broad positions have emerged within most modern historiographic analyses of FDR's choices during the second World War. Scholars such as Robert Divine and James MacGregor Burns portray Roosevelt as a powerful leader "frozen in the headlights of public opinion," who was more or less driven by events.[62] By contrast, the accounts of David Reynolds, Robert Dallek, Doris Kearns Goodwin, George Herring, and "court" historian Robert Sherwood, among others, paint Roosevelt as an internationalist who reluctantly conformed "to the nationalist and isolationist mood of the 1930s" while slowly, steadily, persuading the nation to his own stance.[63] Like Murphy, our sympathies lie with the latter camp. As Reynolds notes, "Roosevelt's carefully crafted speeches joined up the dots of disparate events into an interconnected pattern [that] . . . moved his country from 'neutrality' to 'world war.'"[64] Yet we try to borrow from these many perspectives to put forth our own thesis: that FDR's political rhetoric, which emerged out of an intricate symbolic interplay over the course of his career, steadfastly elevated his unique framing of security as a totalizing, collective national endeavor to the forefront of US public discourse.

By focusing wholly on Roosevelt's rhetoric of security and insecurity, this book contributes to building a multifaceted portrait of our nation's thirty-second president. As Edwin Black observed years ago, rhetorical criticism is a subjective art, and the perspective offered here seeks to complement—not replace—other narratives of FDR's political career in order to gain a fuller picture of how the man and his words impacted the nation.[65] Our account is thus revisionist to the extent it offers a competing account of Roosevelt's career and rhetoric. As the person who did more than perhaps any other to transform the presidency into an institution that wields rhetorical influence over the average American's life, Roosevelt's use of language is especially deserving of close study. Our aim as critics is not to deduce his intent, which we do not have access to, nor to render a moral judgment of his decision-making, which we leave to the reader, but to evaluate FDR's complex rhetoric of (in)security over the course of his career.[66]

To that end, the book is divided into four sections. Part 1 looks at FDR before the presidency. It is divided into two chapters that survey Roosevelt's participation in debates over domestic and foreign policy, exploring how these interactions laid the conceptual foundation for his public views of the nation and its security. Part 2, consisting of chapters three and four, takes as its focus the New Deal years of the Roosevelt presidency. Here we explore how FDR's rhetoric tied security, fear, and economic well-being together in an attempt to head off more radical approaches to the nation's domestic problems and how Roosevelt's liberal internationalist discourse depicted a neighborhood of lawful, god-fearing realists working for the prosperity of all. Part 3, comprising three chapters, surveys the debate over American intervention in World War II. Here we examine the contested definitions of threat and security put forth by FDR and the anti-interventionists, showing how Roosevelt effectively won the debate prior to US entry into the conflict through his deployment of threat appeals, narrative argumentation, and ability to blend multiple rhetorical traditions into a positive case for intervention. Chapters eight and nine encompass part 4, which explores the American debate over war aims once conflict began. Here we show how the Roosevelt administration worked to convince the American public of its war objectives and plan for the postwar world. To win assent to his vision and avoid the fate of Wilson, FDR propounded a winning wartime synthesis of the appeals he had made throughout his presidency. In the conclusion, we summarize these findings, pointing to how Roosevelt's rhetoric generated an internationalist orientation and inventional resources that his successors would draw from to describe America's role in the postwar, Cold War world.

George Washington's hope that the United States might someday inhabit a world in which it would not be afraid was given new life in the immortal words of a very different president from a very different time. "Freedom from Fear," Roosevelt's memorable phrase, hearkens back to a period when the United States rose to crush the twin challenges of the Great Depression and Nazism. We are today awash with references to Roosevelt's era. From blockbuster movies to political analogies, video games to Internet chatrooms, the memory of FDR's day is now everywhere to be found. The contemporary proliferation of references to events that occurred in Roosevelt's presidency, from calls for a "green" New Deal to Munich analogies to proposals to "pack" the Supreme Court, invites a reappraisal of the rhetoric of our nation's thirty-second president.[67] This book is a study of the symbolic language and policies deployed by FDR and his administration that provoked, represented, legitimated, interpreted, and reinforced their views of national security. By freshly appreciating Roosevelt's rhetoric, we can better understand the forces that shaped his choices, his words, and his world, as well as perhaps our own.

PART I

1 | Domestic Policy, 1912–1932

In 1912, an audience gathered in Troy, New York, to hear a speech by a young state legislator famous only for his name: Roosevelt. He spoke with the air of a scholar: "If we go back through history, or rather through the history of the past thousand years we are struck by the fact that as a general proposition the Aryan races have been struggling to obtain individual freedom." This ongoing quest for "individual liberty," a young Franklin D. Roosevelt continued, was the root issue lurking behind movements as disparate as the Reformation, the Renaissance, the American and French Revolutions, and the 1848 European uprisings. But at long last, he explained, this struggle had found its solution— representative government—and thus "in Europe and America, the liberty of the individual has been accomplished."[1] The boyish politician spun a tale that could warm the heart of any proud American.

Like any good storyteller, he then introduced conflict: changing conditions threatened America's historic accomplishment. "During the past century we have acquired a new set of conditions which we must seek to solve," Roosevelt professed, and a "new theory" was required: "the struggle for liberty of the community rather than liberty of the individual." Splitting the difference between socialism, which was naively idealistic, and cutthroat capitalism, which was "useful up to a certain point," he outlined a vision of "co-operation." Adherence to this political principle would eliminate the "evil" of monopolies, trusts, anti-conservationists, and others who "do not care what happens after they are gone and even do not care what happens to their neighbors." As part of this vision, FDR insisted that individual economic freedom should be regulated "for the benefit of the freedom of the whole people." By embracing "cooperation," he told his listeners, they could obtain the ever-elusive dream of individual liberty in the present age like their forefathers had in the past. Yet this dream "will not be obtained at once," he concluded. It must be done gradually, always "keep[ing] in view the other essential point: Law and order."[2] Liberty, for FDR, operated in concert with governmental control, oversight, and power.

This speech, like many others by Roosevelt in this period, was not very original. It repeated the same platitudes that he, his fifth cousin Theodore, and hundreds of other politicians uttered in the years leading up to World War I. But this address also distills the quintessentially progressive thinking that permeated FDR's discourse from beginning to end. As a 1931 account remarked, his was a career in "progressive democracy."[3] Though he later embraced the term *liberal* rather than *progressive*, Roosevelt's rhetoric reflected the guiding principles of the progressive movement. He read history as a series of events advancing toward a brighter future. He saw "liberty" as the chief end of politics, an end better realized in Europe and America than the rest of the world. He acknowledged the unequal social order but preferred cooperation and gradual amelioration within nationally prescribed boundaries to address these issues instead of socialism's internationalist, class-based calls for revolution. Most importantly, he articulated an expansive role for government as the guarantor of the law and order that made "cooperation" possible on a continental scale. Taken together, all these ingredients combined to echo the basic tenets of a "centrist" early twentieth century progressivism that, in the words of Belinda Stillion Southard, sought to "cultivate a national community in which all could participate as citizens and learn what it meant to be 'American.'"[4] It would also be out of these progressive political leanings that the themes of (in)security would emerge in young Franklin D. Roosevelt's rhetoric.

This chapter surveys Roosevelt's progressive discourse over matters of domestic policy from the years 1912–1932. While a comprehensive assessment of all the things FDR said in this period is not possible in the space of a single chapter, we demonstrate how nascent notions of insecurity were extant in Roosevelt's rhetoric from the earliest moments of his political career. We do so by first contextualizing the young statesman within the progressivism espoused by his political heroes, Theodore Roosevelt and Woodrow Wilson, before considering the broad contours of FDR's domestic rhetoric before the presidency. In what would become his distinctive style, Roosevelt's progressive discourse was marked by an enigmatic blending of new and old, elite and common, change and nostalgia. While politically effective, this penchant for paradox implied that calamity may ensue should the aspirational dimensions of FDR's progressivism go unrealized. These utterances thereby also laid the rhetorical foundations for Roosevelt's explicit invocations of threat later in his career.

Progressive Politics, Progressive Era

Roosevelt entered political life during a period of significant change. The technological, industrial, and transportation revolutions of the Gilded Age, replete with monopolies and robber barons, were giving way to the Progressive Era. "Progressivism" in this sense did not refer specifically to Theodore Roosevelt's Progressive "Bull Moose" Party of 1912 but rather denoted, as Richard Hofstadter notes in *The Age of Reform*, "that broader impulse toward criticism and change that was everywhere so conspicuous after 1900, when the already forceful stream of agrarian discontent was enlarged and redirected by the growing enthusiasm of middle-class people for social and economic reform."[5] This reformist impulse was a direct result of the economic transformations wrought the half century before, as the labor conditions of an industrialized economy sharply displayed the yawning gap between rich and poor. Factory work, moreover, spurred population shifts to cities and led to cultural dislocation, putting workers from around the country and world into close contact with one another. Urban migration raised the profile of problems traditionally associated with cities such as drunkenness, prostitution, disease, and extreme poverty. Ethnic rivalry amplified conflicts over working conditions, hours, pay, safety, labor rights, and worker age restrictions, leading labor activists like Eugene Debs and Mother Jones to implore workers to "march, march, march on from milestone to milestone" until they had ended the "rotten" machinery of capitalism.[6] In short, the political practices that had guided the country for over a century seemed woefully inadequate to the challenges of taming the violent social, racial, ideological, and economic divides that threatened the country.

The outworking of these clashes could be seen everywhere. Preachers such as Russell Conwell and Washington Gladden interpreted the changes taking place through the lens of Christianity, respectively advocating for the "gospel of wealth" or the "social gospel" as the answer to society's ills; Walter Rauschenbusch likewise called for a "social religion" that demanded repentance for "social sins."[7] The 1896 presidential election witnessed William Jennings Bryan accusing William McKinley's Republicans of attempting to "crucify mankind upon a cross of gold."[8] Still others turned to ideologies with overseas origins such as socialism, communism, or anarchism. Tony Michels notes that Eastern European Jewish immigrants in turn-of-the-century New York "took to radical ideas with alacrity."[9] Although responses varied, many commentators at the time agreed on two main points. First, some sort of change—whether behavioral, political, ideological, economic, or ethical—was needed. Second, the changes needed required more than personal effort. If an individual's quality of life depended more on the social or economic environment than on his or her virtue, then a retreat into private life could hardly protect one from the sources of change and disorder. Thus, the solution to issues that impacted the whole community had to occur on the societal level. By 1907, Jane Addams observed, "a large body of people" had concluded that the "industrial system [was] in a state of profound disorder" and it was unlikely that "the pursuit of individual ethics [alone] will ever right it."[10] Societal progress, the thinking went, required collective action.

Of course, "progress," as Ronald F. Reid and James F. Klumpp record, "has always been a rhetorically appealing term in American discourse" because it captures the "heritage of millenarianism and social perfectibility, rapid population increase, new technologies and astounding economic growth" characteristic of much of US history.[11] Understood broadly, progressivism comprised an aesthetic that saw these conditions of "profound disorder" as social problems capable of being overcome through collective action. Progressives' attitudes could be summarized in a statement first coined by Albert Beveridge and adopted by Theodore Roosevelt: "The Constitution was made for the people, not the people for the Constitution."[12] New means would be necessary to accomplish the same level of national welfare that the founders achieved. Progressives thus accused their opponents of contributing to "un-American imbalances in their society" even as those opponents played within the rules established by the inherited political order.[13] Theodore Roosevelt, for instance, broke with the norms of nineteenth-century presidential decorum by embracing the "bully pulpit" to publicly campaign for progressive legislation, yet he did so "in a way that retained nineteenth century objectives" of national harmony.[14] He employed innovative means to secure traditional ends. As Leroy G. Dorsey records, Theodore Roosevelt's progressive leanings inclined him to use the power of the presidency as a "license" to "punish wrongdoers . . . to curb the destruction of natural resources and to try and make the lives of all citizens that much better."[15]

But while progressive politicians such as Roosevelt and Wilson eventually exited the stage, progressive ideas persisted well into FDR's era.

Progressive thought, Ronald J. Pestritto and William J. Atto note, boiled down to an argument to move beyond the founders' vision, "an argument to enlarge vastly the scope of national government for the purpose of responding to a set of economic and social conditions which, progressives contend, could not have been envisioned at the founding."[16] In the nineteenth century, optimistic discourse had focused mainly on personal morality, opportunity, and development, assuming that good individuals would make a good community. Progressives saw it the other way around. They recognized that large-scale institutions—corporations, banking, unions, mass transit, mass media, and the like—were coming to dominate the fabric of everyday life. Since public institutions now so pervasively shaped private experience, they argued, the individual could prosper only in a flourishing social environment. Progressives' goal was thus the transformation of the entire social fabric, since the well-being of those at the top or in the middle of the socioeconomic ladder could not be separated from the well-being of those on the lower rungs—what happened to one happened to all. To lead civilization upward, they intended to build a dynamic, expansive society whose progress was based on, and measured by, the irrepressible dynamism of capitalism and democracy. If everyone made sacrifices "for the benefit of the freedom of the whole people," as the young FDR put it, the new century would bring a far better and more secure society for all.

· However, progressivism's emphasis on collectivity also opened the way to an abiding source of insecurity. If the fate of everyone was now tied together, a threat to one was a threat to all. Depending on one's vantage, the changes taking place might constitute a threat to the social order. The societal discord brought about by industrialization might easily get out of hand, some progressives feared, plunging America into chaos that could open the door to a socialist revolution. As progressive writer Vida Scudder reported, "A sense of conflict, ominous if not clearly defined, moved everywhere below the surface."[17]

The fear of disorganized, uncontrolled, or even revolutionary change brought about a corresponding shift in the symbols of insecurity circulating in progressive discourse. Whereas in the nineteenth century social reformers focused on redeeming the wayward individual, whose sin might spread like a wildfire throughout the community, by the early twentieth century it was becoming more and more difficult to trace societal ills to specific instances of individual behavior. With private homes, working environments, and public institutions growing more enmeshed, the danger compounded correspondingly—an errant institution, exercising influence through impersonal systems, might corrupt an entire society. Hence, Theodore Roosevelt worked to pass legislation such as the Hepburn Act and the Square Deal, which sought to position government as a democratic counterweight to the power of trusts, monopolies, banking, and industry so as to safeguard a social order that enabled the nation as a whole to prosper.[18]

Progressives thereby coupled their calls for institutional reform with "the other essential point" that the young FDR stressed: "law and order." Robert Wiebe summed up this aspect of progressivism when he titled his landmark study of this political movement *The Search for Order.*[19] Just as the sources generating inequity needed to be fought within corrupt institutions, so progressives also called on their fellow citizens to combat the disorder generated by anti-Americanism and radicalism generally. President Woodrow Wilson gave voice to this side of progressivism in his 1919 "Pueblo Speech," stating, "Any man who carries a hyphen about with him carries a dagger that he is ready to plunge into the vitals of this Republic whenever he gets ready."[20] Too much ethnic particularity, too much change, or too much collectivism threatened the United States. The answer to these challenges was an embrace of order, often realized through strict hierarchies.[21]

To achieve and maintain order, progressives wanted change to be rationally controlled by experts who would analyze society's institutions and adapt them to new conditions. John Dewey argued in this vein, writing, "We have inherited, in short, local town-meeting practices and ideas. But we live and act and have our being in a continental national state. We are held together by non-political bonds, and the political forms are stretched and legal institutions patched in an *ad hoc* and improvised manner to do the work they have to do." His solution, without which "the public will remain showy and formless," was education and communication on a grand scale.[22] In this sense, Dewey's *The Public and Its Problems* represents the trend of progressive discourse as a whole. It conceptualized the problems facing society as an outgrowth of new technological conditions, it argued that traditional political forms were outmoded, and it called for increased expertise to help rationalize the chaos of governing a "continental national state."

Progressives could thus be optimistic about creating a better future because they were confident that they could go on confronting social ills and transforming society for the better. They would bust the trusts, they would find cures for dreaded diseases, they would eliminate the slums, they would end illiteracy and ignorance, they would put an end to the scourge of war, and so much more. Yet the flip side of the progressive litany of hopes for the future, as Dewey's writings illustrate, was the danger of an unreformed society in the present. If progressivism cultivated a particular interpretive paradigm that saw the changing world as a series of collective problems to be solved, then it also raised the specter of peril should those problems remain unsolved. By shining the spotlight of public attention upon the nation's problems, progressives cast themselves as champions of the public good pitted against an endless array of social evils.[23] Indeed, highlighting such problems and symbols of insecurity was their trademark. And so this way of framing the world—as a panoply of sources of disorder in need of collective resolution—also introduced a formula by which virtually any phenomena could be characterized as a threat to the community meriting energetic response. And FDR, as a participant in progressive discourse, embraced its double-edged character. By relying on its language, offering shimmering visions of hope tempered by shadows of fear, Roosevelt subtly adopted the tacit themes of security and insecurity operating in early twentieth-century progressive rhetoric, which planted the early seeds of the symbolic framework that would grow into the sweeping rhetoric of the New Deal.

Roosevelt's Rhetoric of Progressivism

Roosevelt employed the language of progressivism from the outset of his public career. During his 1910 campaign for a New York state senate seat, he zoomed around the mostly rural district in his bright red Maxwell automobile shaking hands, meeting residents, and giving speeches. He emphasized his beliefs as a point of identification, telling one audience, "This country has progressed since its beginnings more than any other probably in the history of the world."[24] It worked. He won election to the New York State legislature, where he modeled his career after America's first progressive president, his "Cousin Teddy." According to biographer Geoffrey C. Ward, "FDR did everything he could think of to make himself seem like TR, in Albany. He really was a sort of caricature of a caricature of TR for quite a while."[25] Like TR, FDR took on the machine bosses, led insurgencies within his party, and voted as an unabashed progressive. Soon he followed "Cousin Teddy's" footsteps to the office of assistant secretary of the navy, serving in the administration of his other political hero, Woodrow Wilson.

Though the word *progressive* was no longer fashionable by the 1920s, FDR paved his way to the White House by relying on its language. Accepting the Democratic nomination for vice president in 1920, he called for "organized progress," urging all Americans to "subordinate individual ambition and the party advantage to the national good." But he cautioned that the world was an uncertain place, and the only alternative to renewed progressivism was disaster: "We cannot anchor our ship of state in this world tempest, nor can we return to the placid harbor of long years ago. We must go forward or founder." His vague "plan of hope" was largely a litany of dangers that he stood against and promised to avert: "We oppose the private control of national finances, we oppose the treating of human beings as commodities, we oppose the saloon-bossed city, we oppose starvation wages." He concluded that "America will choose the path of progress and set aside the doctrines of despair," implying that despair was a lurking reality, just waiting to seize the nation if the Democrats lost the election. Yet he offered no specific positive policies to right the nation's wrongs beyond voting for Democrats.[26] Like his constituents, many of whom embraced a hazily defined "commitment to social justice," FDR's brand of liberal progressivism emphasized reformist aspirations that sometimes lacked on policy specifics.[27] Still, the Democratic ticket lost the 1920 presidential election in a major setback for Roosevelt's career.

In August 1921, Roosevelt was dealt a severe personal blow in the form of polio. For the next several years, his primary goal in life was to learn to walk again. As he worked vainly toward that new goal, he also continued to pursue his old familiar one: helping Democrats get enough votes to defeat Republicans—and, in the process, helping himself to rise in the ranks of Democratic leadership. The party "must have something to sell to the American public," he told a leading Democrat.[28] The product he urged his party to sell was a new packaging of the old progressive narrative of good against evil: Democrats, advocating "liberalism, commonsense idealism, constructiveness, progress," would fight against the Republican bastions of "conservatism, special privilege, partisanship, destruction."[29] Roosevelt, the consummate politician, was always looking for the right words to market that message and win elections.

But in the first years after polio struck, he had to endure long days of enforced idleness. To pass the time, he started various writing projects, including a *History of the United States*.[30] The project was soon abandoned. But the few paragraphs he wrote privately, with little apparent political motive, revealed his personal commitment to the staples of the progressive narrative. The Crusades "accomplished more for civilization and democracy than any previous event," he claimed, because nobles began "to work with other individuals to a common end." As a result of their cooperation, trade, and commerce, cities grew, which were now filled with merchants, skilled artisans, and bankers: "Thus a middle class grew up . . . and with their acquisition of money and property came the demand for certain rights of government." The new middle class, in Roosevelt's telling, created political landmarks like the Magna Carta, which began to give ordinary people a voice in government and a way to resist the arbitrary power of monarchs.[31]

This "history" sounded standard progressive notes: political rights are linked to the rights of private property, democracy and capitalism are the twin pivots of civilization, and free-market capitalism is the engine driving the growth of both civilization and democracy. Self-centered rulers, in this formulation, endangered that process by using their power to dominate others—a lesson likely to elicit allusions to Mussolini's 1922 March on Rome for FDR's would-be readers. To promote freedom, therefore, civilized people must constantly resist the enemies of progress. And "right from the first," the structure of his project implied, the United States had been in the vanguard of civilization's march against its enemies. As with the rough story line sketched in his 1912 speech, FDR's work told history through the lens of his political values.

As he gradually became more mobile, Roosevelt again geared all his words to concrete advantage for the Democrats, sounding progressive themes as he did. The pieces of his discourse fit together to form an emerging, implicit narrative. His basic story was the inevitable advance of civilization, built on the principles of a free-market economy that promoted the good of all by simultaneously expanding and limiting freedoms. These elements emerged piecemeal, not as a coherent or systematic ideological whole. "He did not enjoy the intellectual process for its own sake," his future secretary of labor, Frances Perkins, politely commented: "He did not enjoy debate and argument based on principles of logic."[32] "He wanted the story in it. . . . [He wanted] to know what are the human values in this and who are the people" in any public issue more than the empirical facts involved."[33] FDR routinely expressed those values in vivid diction. In one 1924 speech, he declared that "the true progressive" should always work "in the vital service of humanity," a principle that "will make the dry bones rattle in Washington."[34]

Whether he realized it or not, Roosevelt was laying the foundational components of the progressive narrative that would aid his path to the White House. His emphasis on the "story in it" converted millions to his cause. FDR's rhetoric operated on this principle, that if all persuasive discourse is ultimately a story, then it might as well be a good one. He used stories, as Dorsey writes, "not only to promote policy but also to influence the conscience of the community."[35]

Roosevelt's utterances reflected the realization that the narrative form, colored by metaphor, served as a more effective vehicle for the propagation of progressive values than the didactic, professorial style of Woodrow Wilson. Roosevelt understood what Walter Fisher has labeled "narrative rationality"—the belief that no matter how one argues a case, "it will always be a story." As Fisher states, "It is not the individual form of argument that is ultimately persuasive in discourse. That is important, of course, but *values* are more persuasive and they may be expressed in a variety of modes. . . . especially metaphor."[36] Roosevelt's message of endless opportunity, combined with his air of absolute confidence (the beaming smile, the up-thrust chin, the ever-ready cheerful quip), projected just such a persuasive narrative form. As one journalist wrote: "He always gives the impression that to him nothing is impossible, that everything will turn out all right."[37] His words would easily have suggested to his audiences that they could feel the same way about themselves and their society—as long as they voted for Democrats.

FDR expressed the broad contours of his progressive narrative through an emphasis on three general themes: change, continuity, and Christianity. It is to an overview of these thematic elements of FDR's rhetoric before the presidency, each of which introduced different implicit assemblages of security and insecurity, that we now turn. These early utterances were far from extraneous to Roosevelt's later rhetoric; rather, they laid the symbolic foundation upon which his future rhetorical appeals, most notably his New Deal and wartime rhetoric, were built. Without an appreciation for the way FDR imbibed, articulated, and adapted this progressive narrative, one cannot fully appreciate the lines of rhetorical continuity that characterize his career or understand how lurking images of insecurity permeated his political rhetoric from the beginning.

Change and Civilization

FDR articulated his rhetoric of change in the idiom of civilizational advancement, tracing the deepest roots of civilization to the institution of the family. Parents have always made sacrifices, he told one audience, because they felt "a sense of responsibility for coming generations," and civilization began when that sense of responsibility was extended to a larger community.[38] Ideationally, for FDR the terms *community* and *civilization* were intertwined concepts, each invoking the other. Roosevelt's goal was to expand the size of that community so that different voting constituencies would see themselves as part of it (and vote Democrat). He explicitly laid out this strategy in one address, stating, "The term 'My neighbor' is made to apply far more to fellow men and women, rich and poor, Jew and Gentile, than it did in the days gone by when 'My Neighbor' meant one's personal friends and associates and the membership of one's own sect." What families and sects once did for themselves, he declared, a neighborly civilization would now do for all. Every citizen should "help direct the course" of civilization toward a higher level by being a "good neighbor," because "more and more we become interdependent."[39] By looking out for one's fellow citizen in the same fashion as one's family members, according to Roosevelt, Americans would reap the many benefits of civilizational advancement. Signs of "organized progress" to improve the well-being of everyone would be, at the same time, signs of an enduring civilized order—and vice versa.

This interdependency could, however, open the community to vulnerability. In contrast to the family and the community, which served as the bedrocks of civilization, FDR warned against those who might predate upon these social institutions. There were always selfish people trying to grab all they could get, heedless of their impact on others. Thus, although "everyone" wanted less government, he acknowledged, the "complexities of modern civilization" made a larger government necessary "to prevent abuses or extortion."[40] The state had to grow more powerful to protect the common people from the predatory few. Corporate tycoons and political bosses, nouveau riche and illiterate masses, the excessively strong and the excessively weak—all might threaten the community through their inability or unwillingness to participate in a shared national life of mutual dependency. In his words, government "must not add to the handicaps of the weak and inefficient by giving special favors and privileges to the strong," yet it also had to avoid bringing hard-working citizens down to the level of the weak and inefficient: "The progress of our civilization will be retarded," he said, "if any large body of citizens falls behind."[41]

In Roosevelt's schema, then, civilization—and by extension the national community—existed in a state of peril from those who may undermine its advancement or cohesion. That destabilization could come from many possible directions. He prophesied that an ever-growing urban population paired with a stagnant rural population would "eventually bring disaster to the United States." If "new problems caused by immense increase of population and by the astounding strides of modern science" were not solved, he told fellow Democrats, the country would be "headed for decline and ultimate death from inaction."[42] In addition to overpopulation and overurbanization, FDR identified the complexity of modern society as a potential hazard for the nation: "The strain of our daily doings may so weaken our mental and physical fiber that less civilized races may replace the present dominant nations."[43] As this quote indicates, FDR also conceptualized "civilization" in explicitly racial terms, his rhetoric working to extend the national "neighborhood" while keeping its minority members at arm's length. Such comments complicate his rhetoric of expanding the community, especially given the Democratic Party's reliance on the Jim Crow South's support. This would be a pattern of FDR's progressivism. According to Mary E. Stuckey, Roosevelt "expanded both the meaning of those principles [American, citizen] and the number of groups that were legitimated by them, although he did little to alter the stratification of the national hierarchies."[44] Roosevelt's concern that "less civilized races" may catch or surpass the United States framed progress as a hierarchical, competitive process.

In sum, FDR's rhetoric was trapped in the paradox of progressivism. On one hand, he emphasized the need for change via the language of civilizational advancement. Americans should continue extending their shared sense of national community to new peoples and new neighbors, thereby advancing the cause of civilization. Increasing interdependency served as a sign of social progress. On the other hand, that very interdependency heightened the collective's vulnerability to an individual threat, demanding the adaptive intervention of a strong federal government. Or, as Roosevelt said in a 1928 campaign speech, "We believe that conditions today are constantly changing. We believe that the government must change from year to year in its policies, and its programs to meet the changing conditions."[45] Consequently, every word praising the progress of civilization could also be read as an admonition to be on the alert for, and ready to fight against, the enemies of progress all around—particularly the Republican Party and its "broken promises to this nation."[46]

Continuity and Nostalgia

In addition to the rhetoric of civilizational advancement, FDR regularly connected with audiences by voicing not their hopes for the future but their fears of change and their nostalgic memories (or illusions) of a simpler and safer past. He voiced the common fear that change was eroding traditional values and "the accepted social structure was becoming demoralized."[47] He recognized that many yearned to slow down the rate of change or even stop it altogether, to go back to a halcyon era before industrialization, urbanization, and mass electrification, a time when there were no massive factories and speeding automobiles, no huge cities run by corrupt Catholic politicians, no machine guns or prospects of aerial bombardment. He conjured up images of the "Victorian atmosphere" of nineteenth-century life, when a person "lived essentially as his fathers before him," and "the home, the children, the cousins, the neighbors, made the all-important nucleus around which life was built and maintained."[48] In his telling, the very fact of technological, social, and cultural transformation could serve as a symbol of insecurity by contrasting the instability of the present with the "romantic" allure of "a past we cannot recover."[49]

Adopting a romantic style, FDR peppered his speeches with appealing images of the past. He could address the public's nostalgia convincingly because he understood it personally. He was "much in the nineteenth century," as his wife once put it.[50] Speechwriter Robert Sherwood, who worked closely with Roosevelt, saw him as "a profoundly old-fashioned person with an incurable nostalgia for the very 'horse and buggy era' on which he publicly heaped so much scorn."[51] In an autobiographical fragment, FDR wrote: "In thinking back to my earliest days I am impressed by the peacefulness and regularity of things both in respect to places and people."[52]

FDR's home at Hyde Park not only represented a safe refuge in an increasingly confusing world but also served as an inventional and imaginative resource for the future president as he crafted political appeals.[53] On the campaign trail in 1933, he told a crowd near Hyde Park, "I come back to the county on every possible occasion with a true feeling that it is home and that I am once more among my neighbors."[54] As James MacGregor Burns concludes, FDR's effort to share images of the comfort he remembered from childhood amounted to an attempt to help the nation hold on to its traditional values and the sense of order those values seemed to guarantee.[55]

Roosevelt used nostalgic reminiscence to domesticate the uncompromising edges of progressivism and chart a middle way. Just as insecurity arose from insufficient change, so it might also arise from excessive tampering with the social fabric; he often placed his message of progressive change within this essentially conservative frame. He called on Americans "to hold the gains which have been made, but to go back and reestablish the fundamentals," "the old-fashioned standards of rectitude . . . the simple rules of human conduct to which we always go back."[56] Eschewing radicalism, he reaffirmed the moral values of the past. He urged Democrats to promise a return to "the well tried principles of the Republic's founders," "the old American fundamental thought of honest government for the benefit of the many," "special favors to none," and "the keeping of the sovereignty of the individual states unimpaired."[57] In his speech at the 1924 Democratic Convention, he nominated Al Smith as the presidential candidate who would "return America to the fold of Decency and Ideals from which she has strayed." And he reminded his audience of all the ways that America had strayed: the "abuses," "extortion," and "special favors and privileges" so widely practiced by the "self-appointed aristocracy of wealth and of social and economic power."[58]

Indeed, through most of the 1920s, with the Republicans in power, FDR spoke as if all the enemies of democracy had massed under the Republican banner. But at the outset of the decade, when it still seemed possible for the socialists to regain electoral strength, he painted them, too, as dangerous enemies threatening to introduce foreign systems of thought to the country. He called "the patriotic people of our great nation to the task of ridding the land of the alien anarchist, the criminal syndicalist and all similar anti-Americans."[59] Roosevelt voiced his fear of radicalism in private as well as in public. The worst thing about the Democrats' defeat in 1920, he told a friend, was the danger "that the old reactionary bunch will so control things that many Liberals will turn

to Radicals."[60] In a letter, he asserted that "there will be a gain throughout our country of communistic thought unless we can keep democracy
up to its old ideals and its original purposes," adding: "We face in this
country not only the danger of communism but the equal danger of the
concentration of all power, economic and political, in the hands of what
the ancient Greeks would have called an Oligarchy."[61] After winning the
1932 election, FDR told the "brains trust" he assembled that he was determined to preserve the capitalist system, to protect against the kind of
violent revolution that he saw as a very real possibility.[62] The implication
was clear. In order to protect civilization, it was necessary to protect the
existing political and economic structure, even as he sought to adapt
them to changing conditions.

For FDR, progress was marked by rational predictability and political stability. Civilized people must respond creatively to new conditions,
but not by creating fundamentally new values or structures. Rather,
they should adapt the traditional ones to new situations—since social
unrest is "caused as much by those who fear change as by those who
seek revolution"[63]—but contain change within fixed structures and permanent boundaries to avert violent revolt. Like his cousin, FDR could
thus simultaneously portray himself as a champion of both progress and
continuity, seeking both to expand freedom and well-being to more
and more people while also protecting civilization against the harmful
effects of excessive change initiated by the selfish (usually nouveau) rich
and the innovators of every kind (particularly the radical, leftist kind).[64]

Christianity and Transcendence

FDR was not a religious man. According to Henry Wallace, Roosevelt's
vice president from 1940 to 1944, "His fight for justice to the 'forgotten man' was not hooked up directly to his church going or outward
religious beliefs. His real inner belief was something quite else and I do
not think anyone is qualified to talk about it."[65] Nevertheless, from his
earliest days of political campaigning, Roosevelt sought the support of
Christian leaders and adopted the language of Christianity to win supporters to his cause. Weeks before being sworn in as assistant secretary
of the navy, he made sure that the clergymen in his district knew of his
support for the One Day Rest in Seven bill that guaranteed a day off
on Sunday, and he later concocted a story placing himself at the cen-

ter of its passage in Albany.[66] Progress, as Roosevelt portrayed it, went beyond the political arena into the transcendent realm of the spirit. "A righteous life calls of necessity not only for goodness within our individual selves, but also for goodness in relations to our neighbors," he preached, sacralizing the Democratic policies he promoted as the route to a better future. "Through the centuries the divine spirit which is in man has spurred him forward."[67]

Despite his personal lack of piety, Roosevelt adeptly deployed Christian symbols in his political dealings. As president, for example, Roosevelt would help plan out a church service on his first inauguration day and every year thereafter on the anniversary of that day.[68] Robert H. Jackson, who first met Roosevelt in 1910 and later served as his attorney general, confirmed that in private conversation "he frequently went back to quotations from the Scriptures." FDR wrote to his mother, "I have read Jefferson's Bible many times."[69] Ever the ecclesial iconoclast, Roosevelt even took Winston Churchill to a Methodist service during a transatlantic visit. No matter his internal beliefs, his external observances extolled a broad (popular) Protestantism.

A consummate politician, Roosevelt strongly affirmed religious truths publicly. He offered his ideological platform as the strongest link to the eternal truths of the Judeo-Christian past and the surest protection against the dangers of the present: "[Progressivism] conforms more truly to the teachings of religion than any objective of previous centuries. . . . The simple moralities, true in the day of Moses, true in the day of Christ, are true today." It amounted to "Christ's greatest teaching," he professed, speaking of "civilization and Christianity" as if the two were virtually identical. He found the eternal principles of civilization fulfilled in "the American system of economics and Government [which] is everlasting." In that system "the rights of the average citizen are given a higher spiritual value. . . . Let us restore and at the same time remodel."[70] By framing his political and social principles as spiritual values, FDR could better blend the future and the past as well as the secular and the sacred in his public rhetoric. If a failure to adequately blur these lines was a root cause of Wilson's rhetorical failure in the League of Nations campaign, as Leroy G. Dorsey argues, then Roosevelt was seemingly determined to avoid this misstep and consistently labored to "imbue the mundane with the Divine."[71]

FDR also encouraged Democrats to advertise themselves as being dedicated to "things other than materialistic."[72] He urged fellow party members to call for "practical idealism" while labeling their opponents the advocates of "gross materialism."[73] In an address at the 1928 Democratic National Convention in Houston, he declared that only the Democrats could lead the nation along "the high road that will avoid the bottomless morass of crass materialism," because they were "interested in whether that national destination be heaven or hell" while Republicans cared only about "a full bank account and a soft bed."[74] For Roosevelt, Christianity provided a language of judgment as well as uplift. Roosevelt had good precedent for such religiously laden language in his two progressive heroes. He surely recalled the tremendous impact his "Cousin Teddy" made when he told the Progressive Party: "In the endless crusade against wrong . . . We stand at Armageddon, and we battle for the Lord." FDR likewise invoked the authority of Woodrow Wilson, echoing his appeals by promoting the idea that conservatives care only about material things while progressives promote spiritual values.[75]

Taken as a whole, the language of Christianity served as more than just a way for FDR to attack political opponents. Roosevelt's rhetoric fused together the eternality of religion, the force of moral truth, the economic and political structures of the United States, and the ideal neighborhood that many Americans wanted to believe they had once lived in. He wrapped them all into a single package—a package essentially the same as the fundamentals of his own political views—and labeled it the "Democratic Party." By bundling his political views in this complex package, and equating it all with true religion, Roosevelt could put those views beyond the reach of criticism and doubt. He simply stated his principles and policies and then christened them "religion" or "the spiritual." As part of FDR's progressive narrative, these sacralized political principles presented themselves as self-evident articles of faith that had unquestioned authority, to be accepted not so much by the head as by the heart. If there is a deep kind of security that comes from believing in eternal, unquestionable, authoritative truths—the kind of truths offered in myth—FDR's words could offer that kind of assurance. As James MacGregor Burns concludes of Roosevelt, "Probably no American politician has given so many speeches that were essentially sermons rather than statements of policy."[76]

Yet the same language that positioned his own party on the side of divine righteousness also worked to escalate the political conflicts of the 1920s to a cosmic scale. Just as religious terminology bestowed the certainty of God's justice on FDR's progressive platform, so it also unveiled the existence of perils that threatened the progressive movement. If the social good espoused by FDR's Democrats embodied the teachings of God, Moses, and Jesus Christ, then all that threatened the good could easily be understood as the work of the devil and his minions. Progressive language had always made room for this implied apocalyptic dualism. When Theodore Roosevelt portrayed the movement, and the nation, as "standing at Armageddon," he cast the progressives' opponents as agents of the devil, implying that the end of the world might soon be at hand. FDR never went so far as to say this. But his hearers, many of them steeped in biblical religion (whether Evangelical, Catholic, Judaism, the Gospel of Wealth, or the Social Gospel) could easily draw out the logical consequence that the speaker left unspoken. FDR, by sacralizing his progressive platform with the language of Christianity, implicitly invoked the eschatological dimensions of divine conflict, thereby offering the ultimate proof—and ultimate warning—in favor of his political program.

Conclusion

By 1930, it was hard to deny that America did face an objective threat of unprecedented gravity: the ever-deepening economic depression. The Great Depression gave Roosevelt a fresh opportunity to do what he did best: preach a vision of a more neighborly society and project confidence that his vision would be realized. Against growing economic insecurity, his trademark display of beaming confidence could stand out even more clearly as he became one of the most powerful spokespersons for the progressive hope of realizing a better society through collective action against the nation's social, political, spiritual, and economic threats.

However, the new situation led him to articulate his vision in new terms, making security for the first time the overt focal point of his rhetoric. "Wealth and security are wholly different," he wrote. Government was not obligated to help everyone become wealthy.[77] But the state was obligated to guarantee security—"to prevent the starvation or the dire want of any of its fellow men and women who try to maintain themselves but cannot . . . not as a matter of charity, but as a matter of social duty," even if their dire want arises not from "illness or accident or old age but temporary economic conditions." Security, FDR's formulation suggested, now meant protecting everyone from economic as well as physical harm. Government would safeguard civilization by protecting, in his words, "the forgotten man at the bottom of the economic pyramid."[78] And, just as in his rhetoric of change, continuity, and Christianity carried implicit notions of danger, so Roosevelt's now explicit embrace of security led him to emphasize symbols of insecurity: "It is no longer sufficient to protect [citizens] from invasion, from lawless and criminal acts, from injustices and persecution, but the State must protect them, so far as lies in its power, from disease, from ignorance, from physical injury, and from old-age want."[79]

This promise of security was a natural outgrowth of the progressive politics FDR had been promoting for decades. In *To Become an American*, Leslie Hahner shows how "Progressive public discourses" of the 1920s were caught in a double bind regarding the immigrant's "patriotic performance as proof of his drive toward assimilation."[80] As she notes, newly arrived citizens' performance of patriotic acts such as singing, marching, or scouting worked to continually resignify them as outsiders, even as they participated in overtly patriotic visual pedagogies. Roosevelt's rhetoric of progressivism was caught in a similar sort of paradox. In his attempts to pioneer new advances of American civilization by voicing a progressive vision for society, he also raised the profile of potential threats to those various signs of progress. Thus, selfish millionaires or urbanization might undermine the social change that needed to occur, just as radical socialists or the proponents of "crass materialism" endangered the traditional values that sustained American life. Roosevelt's attempts to advance the progressive agenda required the discursive construction of threats to that agenda so as to generate political support. Viewed from this vantage, FDR's call for a new kind of security that would protect the public—not only against institutions designed to serve the evil interests of the rich and powerful but also against ills that were no one's fault such as sickness, injury, and old age—can be seen as the logical outworking of the progressive mythology that Roosevelt would carry into the White House.

These tensions were far from confined to the young Roosevelt's discussions of domestic issues but extended also to his rhetoric concerning foreign affairs. As he had provided glimpses of a new kind of bond between Americans and their government, so he was also busy outlining a new vision for the nation's relationship to the world. It is to the elements of that internationalist vision, which, alongside FDR's domestic rhetoric, laid the discursive groundwork for his transformative presidency, that we turn next.

2 | Foreign Policy, 1912–1932

Like all early-twentieth-century progressives, the young Franklin Roosevelt spent most of his time addressing domestic issues. His primary attention was absorbed by local, state, and national reforms in his quest to find a role for government in establishing a more equitable social equilibrium. The various offices he inhabited in New York State government, offices that comprised the majority of his political experience, hardly lent themselves to frequent grandstanding on issues of international affairs.

But when he did address the role of the United States abroad, he did so in a way that maintained continuity with his overarching narrative of progress. Upon reflection, this is easy to understand. The same progressive discourse that dominated Roosevelt's speech surrounding domestic issues also posited that the United States had a leading role to play in guiding the world into a better future. As Rogers Smith notes of FDR's brand of progressive, "They held that the U.S. should be a modern democratically and scientifically guided nation that was also culturally ordered, unified, and civilized due to the predominance of northern European elements in its populace and customs. Thus structured and guided, centrist progressives promised, Americans could do more than cope with a rapidly changing world: they would lead it."[1] Progressives like FDR promised that they could create a better society than had been seen, not only in the United States but in the history of the world, overthrowing, in his words, the wealthy "Oligarchs" with the "weapon" of democratic activism.[2]

Roosevelt, a good Democrat, voiced this general progressive view throughout his early political career. He did so during a somewhat serpentine path to the nation's top executive office, going from state senator to assistant secretary of the navy to vice presidential candidate to homebound, stricken with polio, and then back to the top of New York politics. Consequently, by the time Roosevelt reached the White House he would bring with him a complex history of well-developed arguments about foreign affairs, a history that swung from stern militarism to idealistic disarmament and included a host of positions in between. That history is worth close study, because all of its elements would reappear when foreign affairs became the center of his, and the nation's, concern during his second term as president. He would combine them in ever-changing constellations and permutations to meet the immediate needs of the day.

During this time frame, Roosevelt's embryonic views of foreign policy combined various elements of realism, commercialism, and the teachings of naval theorist Alfred Thayer Mahan. He frequently paired his private views with public idealism, articulating his progressivism in foreign affairs through a collection of metaphors, references to civilization, and various generalizations. As he charted his political path to the presidency, FDR endorsed a variety of policy stances as the nation's mood oscillated from war fever to isolationism. In every case, though, he foregrounded the unparalleled importance of security even as his rhetoric introduced the prospect of new threats to the United States.

Before the Great War: Mahan, Theodore Roosevelt, and the Early FDR

Much of FDR's earliest thinking about foreign policy and national security came from reading the works of Alfred Thayer Mahan. In an age of rapidly expanding global commerce, Mahan argued, all sorts of dangers awaited the nation if its ships could not move freely across the high seas. Appointed head of the US Naval War College in 1886, Mahan developed a series of lectures and books on the effect of naval power in European history. In his *The Influence of Sea Power Upon the French Revolution and Empire*, he focused particularly on the contrasting experiences of Britain and France during the Napoleonic Wars. The British Empire's ascent, he claimed, was achieved "not by attempting great military operations on land, but by controlling the sea, and through the sea the world outside Europe."[3] By controlling the sea, Britain was able to "sustain her own strength" and "cut France off from the same sources of strength and life."[4] Rather than dwell on specific naval maneuvers or tactics, Mahan's prolific writings drew attention to "the relationship between naval and economic power."[5] Like Britain, Mahan argued, the United States should abandon a defensive, "continentalist" strategy and instead embrace a more outward-looking approach that entailed building a modern fleet, expanding its access to foreign markets, and establishing colonies with naval bases and refueling stations.[6] This thinking exercised a formative influence on FDR; Franklin's mother recalled that as a youth he "used to pore over Admiral Mayan's *History of Sea Power* until he had practically memorized the whole book."[7]

A more immediately influential convert to Mahan's thesis was Theodore Roosevelt, who in the aftermath of the Spanish–American War applied the naval theorist's teachings to promote a more aggressive US foreign policy.[8] In a 1901 speech as vice president, TR declared, "We may be certain of one thing: whether we wish it or not, we cannot avoid hereafter having duties to do in the face of other nations. All that we can do is to settle whether we shall perform these duties well or ill. . . . Speak softly and carry a big stick—you will go far."[9] These "duties" were frequently conceptualized as a particular calling for the Anglo-Saxon race to uplift other peoples, such as when the United States assumed the "White Man's Burden" of imperial control of the Philippines.[10] As president, TR dispatched the US Navy on a worldwide tour to underscore the nation's commitment to "play a great part" in world affairs.[11] He also employed the language of burden and duty to speak of America's role in Asia: "This, the greatest of all the oceans, is one which more and more during the century opening must pass under American influence; and as inevitably happens, when a great effort comes, it means that a great burden of responsibility accompanies the effort. A nation cannot be great without paying the price of greatness, and only a craven nation will object to paying that price."[12] He did the same regarding Latin America, voicing the "Roosevelt Corollary" to the Monroe Doctrine, the idea that the United States possessed the exclusive right to act as "an international police power" in the affairs of its southern neighbors should their conduct result in "a general loosening of the ties of civilized society."[13] As Serge Ricard notes, TR's utterances translated the progressive imperative for Anglo-Saxons to advance civilization into the realm of US foreign policy, the "Americanized version" of the white race's "civilizing duty."[14]

While the familial legacy of Theodore Roosevelt's civilizing impulse would be most faithfully realized by his eldest son, who later served as the governor of Puerto Rico and governor-general of the Philippines, Franklin did not dissent from these views of Anglo-Saxon superiority. He assumed that some groups were more civilized than others, and the less civilized a nation, the more uncontrollable—and potentially dangerous—it was. While FDR highly admired British civilization, for example, he blamed German ideas of "terrorism" for evils stretching back to the horrors of the Dark Ages.[15] In domestic politics, his approach to race remained "janus-faced," in the words of historian William Leuchtenburg, as he spoke against the horrors of lynching and found the poll tax repugnant even as he declined to back legislation to change these realities.[16] While it often went unarticulated, a similar hierarchical view of civilization and race always operated in the background of FDR's approach to foreign affairs.

FDR was also busy following the footsteps of his "Cousin Teddy" in a different way. In 1913, he became Woodrow Wilson's assistant secretary of the navy, and like TR he too advocated for a strong navy, applying the opinions developed through his early study of Mahan to his new role in the Wilson administration.[17] Roosevelt held a keen appreciation for the limits of moral crusades that aimed to improve individual conduct, hence the need for military power. Human fallibility precluded a world free of conflict, whether personal or political.

In terms of foreign policy, FDR advocated a policy thoroughly in line with Mahan's style of thinking: "The answer is . . . 'build the ships.'" As he wrote to Eleanor, "It is my duty to keep the Navy in a position where no chances, even the most remote, are taken."[18] In a world where decent individuals may fall into sin and civilized nations may still exploit others' weaknesses, the only rational strategy was to build one's own strength. He likened assembling a powerful navy in a December 1914 speech to Swiss or Australian efforts to teach young boys "how to put a cartridge into a gun" in peacetime: "This I do not call militarism. It is just plain common sense."[19] This was a perspective he had taken since his days as a New York State senator. As he had said then, "Conflict, like everything else in modern civilisation [sic], is so complicated that preparation is essential."[20] For Roosevelt, military preparation seemed like the natural response to conducting foreign policy in a complex world. His advocacy for military preparedness in the absence of an immediate threat took on the ethos of what Brian J. Auten labels offensive realism: "Without an ultimate authority, survival is best ensured by being the strongest state around."[21] In this regard FDR was a pioneer, for such thinking did not become accepted wisdom in American foreign policy circles until World War II. Even prior to the start of World War I, Roosevelt's Mahanian views led him to support the expansion of US military power on the basis of potential threats that *may* materialize. As he wrote in one 1915 article, the United States Navy was "far behind other nations," especially with technologies such as updated scout vessels and aircraft.[22]

He also pointed in possible directions from which such dangers might come. In his correspondence as assistant secretary, Roosevelt argued that ships, and military strength in general, were necessary because there were many different sources of insecurity threatening American interests on every side. Mexico was so unstable that the United States might be forced to invade it: "I do not want war, but I do not see how we can avoid it. Sooner or later, it seems, the United States must go down there and clean up the Mexican political mess." Japan or Germany might also someday threaten American interests, as could events elsewhere in Latin America, Africa, or East Asia. After all, "Cousin Teddy" had intervened diplomatically to resolve both the Russo–Japanese War and the prospect of a Franco–German war over Morocco, both times operating on the assumption that an ongoing major conflict could harm US interests.[23]

In public, however, FDR sketched dangers in more abstract and ahistorical terms. In a magazine article, he analogized international relations to a schoolyard brawl: "Every boy who goes to school is bound sooner or later, no matter how peaceful his nature, to come to blows with some schoolmate." Now that the United States had "gone to school. . . . Almost inevitably, under modern conditions of international relations, the clash of interest, or the magnified insult, or the bully, or the 'only thing left to do,' will bring on the crisis." And everyone should know "how to use his fists in such a crisis."[24] He cautioned another audience, "The national life can never be called free from danger even in the most unruffled periods of peace. The fight is constant and will be never ending so long as the nation endures." If the United States built up no military defense, "anybody that wishes [would] come right along and take from us whatever they choose," including the foreign trade routes that Mahan had stressed. "If you cut off the United States from all trade and intercourse with the rest of the world you would have economic death in this country before long."[25] Rather than focus on a specific country or region that may present a threat to the United States, FDR's rhetoric—by stressing the commercial rationale driving his proposed buildup of the navy—emphasized the nation's need to be able to respond to unforeseen dangers wherever they may pop up.

As American entry into World War I drew closer, FDR's utterances pulled more and more from Mahan's thinking to outline a doctrine of

American military strategy premised on the ability to project defensive naval power.[26] He summarized his view in a set of 1915 articles. In the first, he wrote:

> Strictly speaking, if the national defense applies solely to the prevention of an armed landing on our Atlantic or Pacific coasts, no navy at all is necessary. . . . But if defense means also the protection of the vast interests of the United States as a world nation, its commerce, its increasing population and resources in Alaska and other territory cut off from the United States except by sea, its "mankind benefitting" enterprises like the Panama Canal, then and then only does a navy become necessary. And if a navy is necessary the success of that navy against any other naval power demands that it be able to receive and repel an attack in force anywhere on the high seas within that sphere in which American interests lie.[27]

Roosevelt argued along similar lines in an essay appearing alongside other administration officials' statements regarding military preparedness in the December 1915 edition of the *Nation's Business*, a publication of the Chamber of Commerce of the United States of America:

> Preparedness is of necessity a relative term. American preparedness has never sought to develop military power to be used for aggressive purposes. What its military power for purely defensive purposes shall be must depend upon the military power which could probably be brought aggressively against it . . . naval defense does not mean merely the protection of certain harbor mouths along our Atlantic and Pacific coasts. Naval warfare from its earliest days has meant the control for defensive purposes of those portions of the ocean in which a country is immediately interested. I assume that in case of war the American people would wish to be able to continue to their trade relations, export and import, with other nations of the world. I assume, furthermore, that they wish also the safety of the Panama Canal, of Hawaii, and of the great territory of Alaska. But if these objects are to be accomplished, an adequate navy must emphatically be an adequate sea-going navy . . . a real beginning has for the first time been made in defining the true requirements of national safety.[28]

Both these essays followed the same lines of reasoning. FDR contended that whatever military capabilities the United States developed would be purely defensive, not meant for aggressive action against other countries. At the same time, he insisted that the adequacy of American defensive preparations depended proportionally on the capabilities of other, potentially hostile countries. Thus, military advances in Japan, Germany, or other nations demanded a reciprocal American defensive response to ward off the possibility of conflict. And because FDR defined "defensive" not only to mean the ability to repel a coastal invasion but also to include the security of the Panama Canal, the integrity of Alaska and Hawaii, and unrestricted access to commercial sea lanes, the United States should develop a powerful "sea-going navy."

Roosevelt's security doctrine thus interwove economic and imperial rationales to argue that "the true requirements of national safety" demanded the ability to project significant naval force anywhere on earth. To do less would be to court catastrophe; the United States must therefore "build the ships." Hence, on the eve of American entry into World War I Franklin Roosevelt positioned himself as a staunch advocate of military rearmament for the purposes of preparedness, drawing on Mahan's theories to argue in public and private for an expansion of US naval power. As he bluntly put it in a speech that same year, "The time has come when the people of the United States are going to be called upon to declare in no uncertain terms whether they believe in passive resistance or whether they believe in the security of the nation."[29] To disagree with his stance, Roosevelt asserted, was to disbelieve that the nation should be secure.

World War I

FDR emerged as one of the early advocates for American entry into the war within the Wilson administration, his "big navy" approach putting him at odds with other members of the executive branch who held to a stricter view of American neutrality.[30] While his boss, secretary of the navy Josephus Daniels, urged Wilson to find a path to peace, FDR was eager to see the United States enter the war. "I feel hurt because the Emperor William has left the U.S. out," he told his wife, deriding Daniels for having "faith in human nature and civilization and similar idealistic nonsense." Once the United States was in the war, he told Daniels that "a drastic lesson against the Germans themselves on German soil will be necessary before any understanding can be hammered into the German mind."[31] He likewise described an encounter with a U-boat during an Atlantic crossing as an encounter with "the hand of the Huns' False God," which confirmed his belief that the Germans must be "utterly cut down and purged" for there to be peace. Security demanded the total defeat of the enemy; otherwise, Germany might "enslave the United States" or cut the US economy off from Latin America and "choke us" like a tightly drawn "noose."[32]

With the United States' declaration of war, Roosevelt worried about Germany's ability to strike America. He asked his director of naval intelligence to investigate people living near the Portsmouth Navy Yard who "spoke, looked, or allegedly acted like Germans," because "these foreign born people might purchase an aeroplane, fly over the naval yard and bomb it." So troubled was he about the prospect of a German attack on the Eastern Seaboard that he warned his wife that a German submarine might strike at Campobello, where the family summered. If a sub appeared offshore, he said, "I want you to grab the children and beat it into the woods. Don't stay to see what is going on. I am not joking about this."[33] His unwillingness to forsake any precaution extended to his own family, reflecting the genuine fears he presumably felt about the war.

For his part, President Wilson was free to advocate entry into the war following the Russian Revolution of February 1917, which removed the tsar's government from the conflict and with it progressives' main ideological objection to fighting (that it would support the tsar's autocracy). Advocating for war to support a "democratic Russia" as well as Britain and France, Wilson faced a public skeptical about sending its young men to the trenches of Europe.[34] Wilson drew on different sides of the progressive narrative to frame the decision in idealistic terms. At first, Wilson only depicted his action as necessary to keep faith with American values: "We seek merely to stand true alike in thought and inaction to the immemorial principles of our people."[35] His language quickly progressed from idealistic to apocalyptic, however. Asking Congress for a declaration of war, he charged Berlin with "the wanton and wholesale destruction of the lives of noncombatants, men, women, children . . . [beyond] the darkest periods of modern history." Germany's "submarine warfare" constituted "a warfare against mankind. It is a war against all nations. . . . The challenge is to all mankind." This state of affairs, according to Wilson, left the United States without options other than war: "There is one choice we cannot make, we are incapable of making: we will not choose the path of submission. . . . The wrongs against which we now array ourselves are no common wrongs; they cut to the very roots of human life."[36] War in his telling was necessary both for reasons of American values and due to the existential threat Germany posed to the United States, democracy, and the world.

By depicting the decision to go to war in such universalist language, asserting that Germany threatened not only the Entente Powers but indeed "the peace of the world," Wilson's language reflected the progressive tendency toward dualism. Americans fought not only for themselves, but "all mankind." Like FDR, TR, and other progressives, whose rhetoric portrayed progressive causes as marshalling the forces of justice to combat immoral enemies, Wilson's war message made no room for neutrality in a world besieged by evil. The choice was urgent and clear: fight for universal peace and justice or allow the destruction of everything that Americans held dear. By applying the binary, universalist inclinations of progressive discourse to foreign affairs, Wilson's war rhetoric starkly raised the specter of insecurity to the American public. Indeed, the president proclaimed that "liberalism [the newly emerging term for American-style progressivism] is the only thing that can save civilization from chaos."[37] In short, he combined his progressivism with a rhetorical tradition of American exceptionalism that emphasized the United States' obligation to spread its values across the globe, interpreting this tradition in a manner that justified war. As James Andrews observes, Wilson's rhetoric "transformed the long-held vision of America as a shining example of liberty for the world to emulate to its embodiment as the self-sacrificing defender of liberty. Democracy . . . was now constructed as a moving force in history, and America was its agent in the world."[38]

The assistant secretary of the navy echoed this positive, millenarian side of Wilson's message in his own public statements despite his private cynicism over the idealistic dimensions of the president's rhetoric. For example, he told one group of bankers who had contributed to war loans, "We feel that you, even to a greater degree than our boys who have left their homes for the front . . . have met the sneers and taunts of our adversaries that we are mere nation of money-makers interested only in profits." Indeed, he declared, "We have given the World a new conception of Democracy; a Democracy that is real and virile and sincere and not a mere hypocritical camp of politicians and diplomats, but a Democracy that *believes* in Democracy."[39] FDR literally underlined the importance of belief in capital *D* "Democracy" to America's war effort. He adapted his discourse to the idealistic tone of the Wilson administration despite his skeptical view of the limited gains to be hoped for from international relations. After all, FDR was the same man who wrote to his wife months after the conflict started, scoffing at "the soft mush about everlasting peace which so many statesmen are handing out to a gullible public."[40]

While he may not have been a true believer, Wilson's example was instructive to FDR. As Jon Meacham notes, "We forget sometimes how important Woodrow Wilson and the legacy of Wilson was to Roosevelt's generation. He spent 7 years next door to Wilson's White House. Wilson was hugely important to him and he learned from Wilson's mistakes but also in serving that administration he came to understand politics in a very practical level."[41] A very practical lesson he learned was to not voice his private concerns over Wilson's idealistic words too loudly.

As the war neared its end, FDR resumed warning the nation about the dangers that lurked abroad. In a 1918 article titled "More Wars Are Still to Come," one journalist paraphrased a speech FDR gave in Annapolis, Maryland: "The present world conflict is not going to be the last war America will have to fight, and because of [this] . . . there is no falling back into the old ways of unpreparedness."[42] Likewise, in a 1919 article titled "The National Emergency of Peace Times," he argued that war was caused by "antagonism[s] which are ever present—even in days of peace. . . . The nation is constantly going through national emergencies, in the midst of piping times of peace . . . and today we face as many as ever."[43] Potential sources of insecurity could come from any number of directions. For that reason, Roosevelt naturally supported Wilson's proposal for the United States to enter the League of Nations, so as to prevent the country from backsliding into "unpreparedness" and becoming vulnerable to a sudden, foreign threat.

Opposing Wilson's League of Nations campaign stood Republican senators such as Henry Cabot Lodge. Like Wilson, Lodge also laid claim to the traditional values of American democracy but argued that Wilson's proposed League of Nations Treaty would surrender American control over its own foreign affairs. He stated in one speech, "I am as anxious as any human being can be to have the United States render every possible service to the civilization and peace of mankind, but I am certain we can do it best by not putting ourselves in leading strings or subjecting our policies and our sovereignty to other nations."[44] For Lodge, the League of Nations Treaty risked giving up inordinate control over the nation's decision-making to an international body. As he continued, he linked his objection to the League to the principle of

American exceptionalism. If the United States gave up its sovereignty in foreign policy, then it would "fetter" the nation's ability to serve as "the world's best hope" going forward:

> You may call me selfish if you will, conservative or reactionary, or use any other harsh adjective you see fit to apply, but an American I was born, an American I have remained all my life. I can never be anything else but an American, and I must think of the United States first, and when I think of the United States first in an arrangement like this I am thinking of what is best for the world, for if the United States fails the best hopes of mankind fail with it. . . . Internationalism, illustrated by the Bolshevik and by the men to whom all countries are alike provided they can make money out of them, is to me repulsive. National I must remain, and in that way I like all other Americans can render the amplest service to the world. The United States is the world's best hope, but if you fetter her in the interests and quarrels of other nations, if you tangle her in the intrigues of Europe, you will destroy her power for good and endanger her very existence.[45]

Lodge, arrayed against Wilson, disclaimed the League of Nations Treaty. He did so in words redolent of Washington's Farewell Address ("tangle her in the intrigues of Europe") and Lincoln's Second Inaugural ("last best hope"), situating himself as an adherent of the way Americans had long conceptualized their place in the world—as a nation apart, setting a democratic example for others.[46] Lodge and his allies rejected the arguments of the Wilson administration. And because Wilson failed to secure American entry into the League, it was the perspective of Lodge and the Republicans that set the parameters of US foreign policy for the next twelve years, presaging the foreign policy debates that would occur in FDR's presidency.

Roosevelt as Candidate: The Election of 1920

By the election of 1920 the language of war and fear was no longer popular with a nation bloodied by conflict. Roosevelt thus tended to avoid any talk of danger from abroad, although he told the country in no uncertain terms that what happened overseas impacted American lives at home: "If the World War showed [anything], it showed the American people the futility of imagining that they could live in smug content their lives in their own way while the rest of the world burned in the conflagration of war across the ocean."[47] While this "fire" meta-phor gave a stark image of peril—and one that he would return to in the lend-lease debate—FDR more commonly communicated his inter-nationalism through metaphors that implied open, congenial relations with other nations. In his nomination acceptance address, for example, FDR urged the United States not to live as in isolation as "a hermit na-tion" but to join the League of Nations and mobilize "the opinion of civilization" against "the warmakers." Warning that in the "world tem-pest . . . we must go forward or founder," he concluded this address on an ominous note: "In a thousand ways this is our hour of test."[48] By employing metaphorical language such as "tempest" or "hermit nation," FDR did his best to shift the argumentative terrain of the foreign policy debate away from Republicans' preferred themes of sovereignty, peril, and exceptionalism.

While it may be tempting to dismiss Roosevelt's flourishes as mere ornamentation, Michael Osborn reminds us of the vital role metaphors play in constructing public understanding. As he affirms, metaphors "discipline the imaginative" by constantly refreshing a certain way of thinking about an issue.[49] Londa Schieberger likewise writes, "Meta-phors are not innocent literary devices used to spice up texts . . . [they] function to construct as well as describe—they have both a hypothesis-creating and proof-making function."[50] Stated otherwise, metaphors provide warrants for policy. They stimulate reasoning chains, transmit tacit appeals to authority, and spur emotional identification in a com-plex symbolic and cognitive interplay that works to "construct political meaning and orient political action."[51] Roosevelt, a master of metaphor, skillfully deployed this device to shape Americans' perception of poli-tics—often decisively.

It was during this campaign that FDR began to rely on what would become his favorite metaphor: the good neighbor. This metaphor, Mary E. Stuckey argues, encapsulated FDR's entire political philosophy; it en-abled him to separate "the nation's material and moral essences, and then [associate] the nation's strength with the latter than the former." The metaphor operated on two levels, depicting both the nation and the globe as a fundamentally decent "community of people who did not have to be equals materially, but who did have to have a reason-ably equal commitment to the values animating that community."[52] In foreign affairs, the brilliance of the metaphor was its adaptability to the ever-changing world of international politics, allowing FDR to portray the United States as a goodwilled, self-governing household seeking friendly relations with the various residents of neighborhood that, like any community, required order to flourish. A war or revolution is like a fire breaking out, FDR said, and when people realize "that the fire in their neighbor's house was apt to spread to their own houses," they create a fire department for collective self-protection. Since an international "fire" might still break out at any time, "what the League of Nations needs today is a chief—a man who knows how to keep fire from spreading—and that man is the United States."[53] Roosevelt depicted his stance on foreign affairs with this (masculine) imagery throughout the 1920 campaign. Rather than emphasize the realpolitik need for battleships or highlight the risks that may come from any corner of the globe, as he had intermittently done for the past seven years, he argued for American entry to the League of Nations on the basis that the world needed the United Sates for moral leadership.

Although Woodrow Wilson had hoped to turn the 1920 presidential election into "a great and solemn referendum" on the League of Nations vote, Americans failed to rally to the League, and both major candidates ultimately hedged on the issue.[54] Roosevelt and the Democrats, campaigning on a modified pro-League platform, went down to terrible defeat; Senator Lodge gloated, "We have torn up Wilsonism by the roots."[55] Through the rest of the 1920s, FDR seemed to back away not only from the League but also from the overt themes of insecurity and fear that had marked his prewar and wartime discourse. Now he adopted a discourse of vague, optimistic nonaggression that matched the nation's foreign policy mood. His utterances in this period coalesced around three main topics: disarmament, race, and economics.

Interwar Roosevelt: Disarmament, Race, and Economics

During the 1920 campaign, President Warren G. Harding had declared his intent to return the country to the prewar status quo: "America's present need is not heroics, but healing; not nostrums but normalcy . . . not submergence in internationality, but sustainment in triumphant nationality."[56] The "normalcy" of Harding and his GOP successors was marked by attempts to influence world affairs without fully investing the nation in any firm political structures such as the League of Nations. To that end, the United States led the way on global arms reduction—the

Washington Naval Conference, Nine-Power Treaty, and Kellogg–Briand Pact outlawing war—and traded with Europe to an unprecedented degree.[57] Harding and Secretary of State Charles Evans Hughes liquidated the US quasiprotectorates in Latin America, with Hughes even going so far as to repudiate the Roosevelt Corollary in a 1923 speech in Brazil: "I utterly disclaim as unwarranted . . . a claim on our part to supervise the affairs of our sister republics."[58] In short, the successive Republican administrations of the 1920s followed the public's desire to withdraw from global affairs, downscaling American commitments abroad and shrinking the US military.

As he charted a political comeback from his diagnosis of polio, Roosevelt reentered debates over foreign policy, reinventing himself as an advocate for disarmament. He pledged that Democrats would reduce "the terrible burden of armaments from which all nations are suffering" and "relieve the common ills of mankind." He composed "a Plan to Preserve World Peace," complaining that the world had failed "to restore order in the economic and social processes of civilization." But "the world patient cannot be cured over night [sic]," he cautioned, adopting a medical metaphor, because it was on its deathbed: "A systematic course of treatment extending through the years will prove the only means of saving his life."[59] By 1928 he was privately urging congressional Democrats to oppose appropriations for more ships. Rather than "merely handing a cudgel to the State Department to use over the heads of other nations," the United States, à la FDR, should negotiate new treaties limiting the size of navies. The former champion of a big fleet now publicly declared that US naval forces should be cut because there was "no real need for much more than a police force on the seas of the civilized world today."[60] The image of a "police force" fit well within the logic of the good neighbor metaphor, which now assumed primacy in Roosevelt's rhetoric to fit with the prevailing public appetite for neutrality.

Whenever Roosevelt talked about foreign affairs, he showed how well he could adapt to changing events and changing public opinion in pursuit of his one constant goal: winning votes for Democrats. He well knew that there was political hay to be made by promoting the popular issue of naval disarmament, and he displayed sharp enough instincts to avoid branding himself or his party as warmongers. His most important foreign policy statement of the 1920s was an election-year article in *Foreign Affairs*, where he promised that Democrats would "relieve the common ills of mankind" not by war but by "sitting around a table" in "friendly conference." The article was, in his own words, "exceptionally a practical political one," meant to boost his party's chances in the 1928 election.[61] He brilliantly appropriated the exact positions he had privately disparaged and publicly battled during his tenure as assistant secretary, all under the rhetorical guise of neighborliness, medicinal treatment, or some other metaphor.

One reason disarmament was so politically popular is that the 1920s saw vigorous debate over the new weapons that had been deployed during World War I. In 1921 Thomas Edison made headlines by declaring that an air fleet dropping poison gas could destroy an entire city and kill every creature in it in five minutes. In 1929 Stuart Chase wrote in the *New Republic* that two hundred planes could destroy "every living thing in the London area."[62] FDR himself offered an opinion on air power in 1925, warning that "airplanes can reach portions of an enemy's country hitherto safely 'behind the lines.' . . . If in the next war nations feel themselves at liberty to destroy and injure the enemy civilian populations outside of the actual fighting zone, we shall go back to the unlimited and horrible conditions of warfare in the Dark and Middle Ages."[63]

Because the Great War had taught the terrible lesson that entire societies now went to war, not just armies, strategists increasingly thought about how to break the will of civilian populaces as a shortcut to victory should another conflict arise. Military thinkers theorized intensely about the "civilian will to fight," believing that the Allied victory in World War I was a result of breaking the German home front's ability to endure the strains of war (an interpretation not entirely dissimilar from Hitler's stab-in-the-back conspiracy).[64] These discourses lent themselves to racially essentialist logics. In the arena of air power, such logic was aptly on display in the wanton British raids against Arab tribesmen living in the newly colonized territories of Iraq and Transjordan. One RAF report stated that air control would discipline "stubborn races" to "moral effect" by making "it practicable to keep a whole country under more or less constant surveillance."[65]

Similar issues of disarmament and race intersected in FDR's treatment of Japan. As early as 1922 he told friends that the United States and Japan should negotiate naval limitations treaties and "accept the assurances of good faith on both sides." There was, in his telling, "no fundamental reason why our relations with Japan should not be on a permanent and cordial basis." He wrote an article and a letter to the editor urging "the establishment of a rule of reason in the Pacific. We believe that present day Japan is meeting us a full half way."[66] Friendly relations with Japan intersected with progressive causes such as pacifism, disarmament, and race-based colonialism; in fact, labor activists such as Hellen Keller argued against American entry into World War I precisely on the fear of picking up "some islands in the Pacific Ocean which may some day be the cause of a quarrel between ourselves and Japan."[67] Ironically, the area where Roosevelt most voiced optimism in the power of verbal agreements between nations was the region the United States would fight most viciously over during his presidency.

At the same time, another reason Roosevelt gave for why Japan posed little threat to American interests in the Philippines and Pacific Rim had to do with race. Like other politicians of his day, FDR expressed racist stereotypes when it came to the Japanese: "The people of Japan are not a tropical race—they do not thrive near the equator." The same racism led him to see a real threat in Japanese immigration to the United States. They "are not capable of assimilation into the American population," he wrote in a newspaper column: "The mingling of Asiatic blood with European or American blood produces, in nine cases out of ten, the most unfortunate results." In another column, again riding the tides of popular opinion, he called for a temporary total ban on immigration: "For fifty years the United States ate a meal altogether too large—much of the food was digestible, but some of it was almost poisonous. The United States must, for a short time at least, stop eating, and when it resumes should confine itself to the most readily assimilable foodstuffs. . . . A little new European blood of the right sort does a lot of good in any community."[68] FDR called for peaceful relations but restricted migration when it came to Japan, his rhetoric reflecting popular discourses of disarmament and racial prejudice.

Roosevelt interpreted international politics through the prism of race elsewhere as well, which, in his telling, carried the possibility of threat. He cautioned that relations with some of the nation's neighbors to the south might be especially difficult to manage, expressing his prejudice against Latin Americans most fully in a report on the 1915 US occupation of Haiti (which would continue until 1934). According to FDR's report, the United States had no selfish commercial motives in moving to restore law and order following the assassination of president Jean Vilbrun Guillaume Sam.[69] Roosevelt cast the occupation as a mission to civilize the natives, who were "little more than primitive savages.

. . . Conditions approaching anarchy prevailed . . . almost unbelievable butchery and barbarism." Their form of Christianity was "the recrudescence of the primitive religions of Africa, which, it is well established, included in many cases the well-known forms of human sacrifices of the Congo region." Reflecting the typical racist language of his day, Roosevelt warned that such barbarism could easily spread dirt, disease, and disorder to other Caribbean islands and to the United States itself. American troops therefore went to Haiti, in FDR's words, only to bring order and teach the natives "the elementary rules of civilization and self-government."[70]

In Mexico, he similarly warned in another column, "disorder and bad government may require that a helping hand be given her citizens as a matter of temporary necessity to bring back order and stability." In that event, it was "the duty of the United States" to restore order by force because the American form of government was "a pattern for other peoples." In fact, the United States was itself "the idea and inspiration of all those who dream of a kinder, happier civilization in the days to come." Roosevelt did add the caveat that, should the United States be reluctantly forced to impose order, it should at least "associate itself with other American Republics" as it did so.[71] While he had the good sense not to draw attention to the Wilson administration's sporadic interventions into the ongoing Mexican Revolution, FDR was presumably among those in the administration who saw Mexican violence against Anglo expatriates as a "serious affair."[72]

FDR's rhetoric, not much different than that of fellow progressives like Woodrow Wilson on matters of race at this juncture, depicted international politics as an untamed habitat in need of domestication. When it came to Latin America, race and foreign affairs came together in such a way as to impose a civilizing responsibility on the United States to maintain order. While these columns had no clear-cut political motive, it is perhaps worth pointing out that the Democratic bosses garrisoned inside New York's Tammany Hall—the same bosses Roosevelt fought so stridently against during his time as state senator—drew much of their strength from immigrant communities. FDR's anti-immigrant animus therefore betrayed political as well as class and racial sensibilities. Progressive beliefs, David W. Southern argues, proved no barrier to racism for politicians like Roosevelt. As he notes, "All but a tiny handful of white progressive thinkers subscribed to either biological or cultural racism. . . . The question then, is not whether a white progressive thinker was racist, but what kind of racist was he: mild, strong, or even vicious?"[73] One can debate whether "vicious" describes Roosevelt's attitudes, but he certainly reflected the hierarchical views of his time, and it showed in his foreign policy discourse.

While the 1920s offered Roosevelt the opportunity to tout his progressive ideals in foreign affairs and reinvent himself as an arms reductionist, he also developed a more complex view of the practical links between diplomacy and economics during this period. He began tying his conception of security more closely to prosperity, and the symbols of insecurity in his rhetoric clustered more closely around fears of economic distress both abroad and at home. For instance, he told his former running mate James Cox that isolationism would be dangerous because it would "bring hard times, cut off exports, etc.," thus equating "danger" with economic distress. He associated other nations' economic vitality with America's security in another letter in which he urged "helping the other nations of the world to get on their feet without [the United States] entering into entangling alliances in order that we will have added prosperity through world markets." He argued explicitly for this kind of approach to US relations with Japan, stating, "There is a real necessity to Japan of the markets and the raw product of that part of the Chinese mainland contiguous to her island shores," and he called for increased trade between China and Japan as the solution to Tokyo's economic problems (Japan would instead invade Manchuria with the intent of establishing an economic colony on September 18, 1931).[74]

FDR expressed the view, common in the 1920s, that economic tensions were a key (though not exclusive) cause of war.[75] In a memorandum on global leadership, he reflected on the larger historical factors shaping international politics and the United States' role: "We have today side by side an old political order fashioned by a pastoral civilization and a new social order fashioned by a technical civilization. The two are maladjusted. Their creative inter-relation is one of the big tasks ahead of American leadership." For that task, he argued, the United States could hardly hope to succeed without electing the best possible men to lead. He continued, "The hope of democracy seems to lie in our selecting leaders who are superior to the rank and file of us," evincing his own patrician preferences (the document was written in mid-1928, when he still purportedly had no explicit plan to run for governor of New York).[76] As he did elsewhere, FDR seemed to argue for an aristocratic appreciation of the old that was blended with a progressive embrace of the new as the guiding formula for US foreign policy.

In any case, as Roosevelt said in one speech, the concomitance of economics, politics, and technological growth offered an irreplaceable opportunity for "the greater unification of mankind." In his public utterances on capitalism, technology, and politics Roosevelt often adopted an optimistic register to describe the changes taking place: "Factories everywhere are seeking location at the source of their raw materials. Backward peoples are made wards of those more advanced. Power is exported. Capital is international."[77] Rather than emphasize the increasing vulnerability generated by an increasingly complex global political economy, as he had done before, now FDR cheerily noted that civilization, capital, and progress all went hand in hand. From a progressive point of view, the diplomatic agreements into which the country had now entered, the growth of new commercial supply lines, and the expansion European colonial influence to even more regions—all features of the world scene of the 1920s—provided clear evidence that civilization was trending upward: "First, the self-sufficient small community, then the grouping of several communities, then the small state, then the nation, then alliances between nations, and now a permanent congress of nations." The "laws of the history of progress," FDR told his audiences, would inevitably bring a time when class consciousness would disappear and "all the world recognizes all the rest of the world as one big family." He exhorted the American people to support globalization and thereby "play the part of a man and lead in the advancement of civilization as a whole." This approach to foreign affairs, he explained via reference to the good neighbor metaphor, was "only an extension to the larger field of what right-minded people are trying to do with their own lives in their own communities."[78]

To be fair, FDR's rhetoric mostly veered away from naïve idealism, especially when it came to the economic gains of globalization. He argued that all American policies should pass the test of both "the argument of financial gain" and "the sounder reasoning of the Golden Rule." By implying that these two rules were compatible, FDR articulated a commercial internationalist understanding of foreign affairs. Within this schema, America should play a "magnanimous part" in global politics, "whether it be from a purely selfish desire for additional prosperity, or whether it rise from the deep belief that we owe a little something to mankind as a whole." He expressed the same view privately, writing to his half-brother Hall that a Democratic candidate should be "economically sound and at the same time somewhat idealistic in his view of foreign affairs."[79] Economic gain and friendly collaboration with other nations went together, according to FDR.

Roosevelt developed a new metaphor in 1926 speeches that captured his view of the interconnections between American ideals and economic power: the wise banker. Personifying the nation, he stated, "We have become the Bankers of the World, but there are two kinds of bankers." Under the Republicans, the nation had become an "an immoral banker . . . tight-lipped, steely-eyed, tight-fisted," caring only about short-term profit. This fact discouraged other countries from trading with the United States and from taking out more loans to (re)build their national economies. However, he promised, under the Democrats the United States would act like a wise banker who is "kindly, understanding, sympathetic" to even the lowliest customer, treating all with dignity. A "banker" of this sort, he detailed, "saves many a shaky loan for his bank and is blessed and honored in the community . . . regarded as a sort of father confessor and disinterested and wise counselor for all the neighborhood." Again, returning to the imagery of a neighborhood, he said that if the United States showed "a clear-cut desire to aid the other nations," it would be seen by other countries as "their friend in need" and reap the reward in increased trade. After all, he observed, the US economy would soon need more foreign markets, and "nations even as human beings prefer to trade with their friends." Moreover, as the logic of the "wise banker" metaphor went, the wise banker's idealism boosts the morale of his customers, encouraging them to build more, which increases the bank's business in the long run.[80]

FDR explained the benefit of a "wise banker" policy again in a 1928 newspaper column. Under Republican policies, "this country is not liked by its neighbors. . . . Our commercial trade backwards and forwards is necessarily injured." The policies of Al Smith, FDR's political ally and the Democratic presidential nominee, would aid peace and prosperity by "making people understand that we are not working for purely selfish ends." FDR continued to make the same point in a private letter to a cousin. Republican foreign policy was all "from the dollars and cents point of view," while Democrats would show the world "that we are once more approachable in the interest of humanity," thus reaping more profit in the long run.[81] In the logic of Roosevelt's discourse, transforming the United States into "the Bankers of the World" would not be a form of imperialism or American self-aggrandizement, since if the nation did end up reaping some advantage that was only the natural reward that falls to every businessman or banker who is "kindly, understanding, sympathetic."[82] Throughout Roosevelt's rhetoric in the interwar period, American idealism and American economic self-interest were utterly inseparable.

Although the Great Depression drastically cut international trade, the subject remained a staple of Roosevelt's public speeches. By 1932, he was looking ahead to a day when US factories would again produce more than could be consumed at home. The nation would have to sell some of its goods abroad to again prosper. But other nations could not buy them unless they could sell their own goods here, and "this foolish tariff of ours makes that impossible," he complained in a speech. Under the prevailing system, "each nation attempts to exploit the market of every other, giving nothing in return."[83] FDR's rhetoric depicted the Republicans' tariff policy as the exact opposite spirit as that possessed by his good neighbor. The answer was to provide a "reciprocal exchange of goods," with each nation producing what it could make best and what others needed most; trade was natural in the good neighborhood. As he explained, trade was simply "the same old-fashioned horse sense that you and I would use in dealing in our own business with our own neighbor." Yet it would "do more for the peace of the world and contribute more to supplement the eventual reduction of armament burdens, than any other policy which could be devised."[84]

He issued the same message in his campaign correspondence during the 1932 election. Roosevelt assured that "the welfare of your home is the first concern of government" to one supporter. He continued, linking trade with familial well-being: "I will endeavor to open world trade channels not only for reviving prosperity, but as a practical step toward renewing world friendship and removing the threat of future wars from your children."[85] By answering how he would protect American homes through international trade policy, FDR's letter reveals the extent to which the foreign and domestic realms of US politics merged in his understanding.

FDR's rhetorical fusion of domestic and foreign policy had far-reaching implications. Even at his most optimistic and idealist, as he gave voice to hopes for globalized economic progress, his rhetoric carried the seeds of inversion endemic to progressive discourse—the very collective organization that held potential for such prosperity also exposed individual members of the global community to new sources of insecurity. Extending the premises of his good neighbor metaphor and discourse of civilization might reveal an unsettling chain of reasoning: if civilized cooperation should be practiced on a global scale, and if civilization entailed protecting people from suffering beyond a certain limit (as his domestic discourse suggested), then civilized people (like Americans) carried an obligation to protect others to an impossibly worldwide magnitude. Even circumscribing the implications of FDR's rhetoric to purely US concerns reveals fecund potential for insecurity latently lurking in his discourse. If the United States, as the world's banker, was obliged to be a "friend in need," and if Americans needed foreign markets to again prosper, then the nation in fact had much to fear—it was painfully clear by 1932 that a collapse anywhere in the global economy would be felt by American workers.

FDR's blend of economic and foreign policy rhetoric opened the way for the American people to conceptualize new dangers to themselves and their country, even as he tried to promote policies and thinking that opposed such a perspective. Indeed, if Roosevelt truly believed civilization, capitalism, and democracy were intertwined, then one leg of the stool collapsing—capitalism—might very well, in his thought, threaten the other two. As the Depression deepened, that worry is exactly what he expressed in a private letter: "We are in a period of real danger to our type of civilization and because of the confusion the time will soon be ripe for some formal definite leadership not only here but in every European country." Economic collapse endangered civilization, which in turn imperiled democracy by creating a desire for "formal definite leadership." In public, FDR articulated these misgivings in language reminiscent of Wilson's campaign for the League of Nations: "Our civilization cannot endure unless we, as individuals, realize our responsibility to and dependence on the rest of the world."[86] Roosevelt periodically alluded to these kinds of concerns—the kind of concerns that occupied his attention and rhetoric during his years as state senator, assistant secretary, and vice presidential candidate—even if the bulk of his foreign policy discourse in the 1920s was decidedly optimistic and idealistic in tone.

To sum up, in all this shifting wartime and postwar discourse, a relatively consistent and essentially moralizing narrative can be discerned: civilized people are, in effect, progressives. They want organized progress, global cooperation, and open trade. They will therefore be good neighbors, cooperating through mutually beneficial trade, disarmament agreements, and reasonable conciliation of differences. They will maintain orderly democratic capitalist systems—the system perfected in progressive America—to secure peace and promote the advance of civilization. For the foreseeable future, though, there would continue to be uncivilized peoples needing guidance to learn these values. And there would always be bad people (like "the warmakers" or "bad governments") risking the security of civilization through misgovernment or war. Civilized people would always face the possibility of attack from bad people or the problems generated by uncivilized people, but technological advancements made these issues more pressing now than ever. So, the civilized must always be prepared to subdue the bad and control the uncivilized everywhere, by readiness for war (1910s FDR) or via cooperative means like the League of Nations, naval treaties, or expanded trade (1920s FDR).

Conclusion

When Franklin Roosevelt declared he was running for president of the United States in 1932 he was first dismissed by others as an unserious candidate. Supreme Court Justice Oliver Wendell Holmes said he had a "second-class intellect but a first-class temperament."[87] He was characterized as a superficial "grown-up Boy Scout" in the *New Yorker* and derided by Walter Lippmann as "a pleasant man who, without any important qualifications for the office, would very much like to be president."[88] Journalist Elmer Davis of the Baltimore *Evening Sun* wrote that Roosevelt was "the man who would probably make the weakest President of the dozen aspirants" for the Democratic Party's nomination.[89] Yet Roosevelt proved formidable. Weaving together the various threads of his decades-long career in public life, he positioned himself as a compelling candidate for the nomination as he mercilessly assailed the Hoover administration. Like Napoleon, who "lost the Battle of Waterloo because he forgot his infantry," explained FDR in a martial metaphor, so "the present Administration in Washington provides a close parallel. It has either forgotten or it does not want to remember the infantry of our economic army."[90] In the end, FDR overcame a strong Democratic field to claim the nomination after four ballots. He won, in part, because the convention delegates trusted the man with a reputation as a courageous innovator to keep his innovations within the bounds of conventional Democratic wisdom.

Breaking with precedent, Roosevelt flew to Chicago to become the first major party presidential candidate to give an acceptance address at a nominating convention. "The appearance before a National Convention of its nominee for President to be formally notified of his selection is unprecedented and unusual," he said, "but these are unprecedented and unusual times." Deploying polysyndeton, a favorite rhetorical device of his "Cousin Teddy," FDR drew on standard progressive themes to frame the problems facing the nation: "Let us now here highly resolve to resume the country's interrupted march along the path of real progress and of real justice and of real equality for all our citizens, great or small." He praised the "indomitable leader" who began the Democratic leg of that march, "the great indomitable, unquenchable, progressive soul of Woodrow Wilson." In typical partisan fashion, he declared that "at last the American people are ready to acknowledge that Republican leadership was wrong and that . . . Democracy is right." And he gave a name to his "march" that would soon come to define his first term as president: "I pledge you, I pledge myself to a new deal for the American people. . . . This is more than a political campaign. It is a call to arms."[91]

His pledge fell upon the ears of a distressed people. From November to March 4, Hoover's last day in office, the country listened as the economic depression showed no signs of abating. "Farmers Besiege the Legislatures" read one *New York Times* article chronicling the "desperate determination" of agrarian workers from twenty-one rural states.[92] Employment dropped 3.9 percent in January alone.[93] The *Nation's Business* editor lamented rhapsodically: "Now is the winter of our discontent the chilliest. . . . Fear bordering on panic, loss of faith in everything, our fellowman, our institutions, private and government. Worst of all, no faith in ourselves, or the future. Almost everyone ready to scuttle the ship, and not even women and children first."[94] As they awaited the dawn of the Roosevelt presidency, the American people knew nothing if not biting insecurity. Perhaps for this reason, yet another periodical found inspiration in the words of William Shakespeare to give form to Americans' deep anxiety: "I find the people strangely fantasied: / Possess'd with rumours, full of idle dreams; / Not knowing what they fear, but full of fear."[95]

PART II

3 | Economic Policy
The New Deal

On March 4, 1933, Franklin D. Roosevelt stood on the east portico of the US Capitol Building and was sworn in as the thirty-second president of the United States of America. In his initial moments as president, before he addressed the Depression or economic policy or anything else, Roosevelt declared his intent to speak "the truth, the whole truth, frankly and boldly." And the first topic he spoke the "truth" about was fear: "The only thing we have to fear is fear itself—nameless, unreasoning, unjustified terror which paralyzes needed efforts to convert retreat into advance."[1] That phrase, which soon became synonymous with FDR's inaugural address as a whole, earned the laudation of media nationwide.[2] Even the *Chicago Tribune*, the leading conservative newspaper of the day, applauded: "President Roosevelt's inaugural strikes the dominant note of courageous confidence."[3]

Roosevelt's speech did not stop there. He castigated the "money changers" in the language of an indignant prophet, denouncing them as "self-seekers" with "no vision, and when there is no vision the people perish." Like Christ himself, who cleansed the temple in Jerusalem by driving out "the moneychangers who would turn a house of prayer into a den of thieves," FDR promised to restore "the temple of our civilization" to "the ancient truths," and in a turn of phrase that chilled the First Lady herself he announced his intent to claim "broad Executive power to wage a war against the emergency, as great as the power that would be given to me if we were in fact invaded by a foreign foe."[4] Those words got more applause than any other line in the speech.[5] Extending the martial metaphor, he declared that he would assume "unhesitatingly the leadership of this great army of our people dedicated to a disciplined attack upon our common problems." His address touched the hearts of millions of his fellow citizens. Americans such as Clifford Maxwell of Waco, Texas, wrote letters to him, saying, "Tears came to my eyes while you delivered your inaugural address. It was wonderful, breathing confidence and the dawning of a new day!"[6] Nearly half a million others did the same, sending messages of support and congratulations to the president, his words falling on newly inspired ears.[7]

Just as the rhetorical tour de force that was FDR's first inaugural address invigorated the public then, so it has attracted the attention of rhetorical scholars in more recent times. Halford Ross Ryan writes that Roosevelt's "coup" in the speech was to blame the "moneychangers" for the Great Depression, thus deploying a scapegoat mechanism alongside military metaphors "to persuade the citizens of the nation to support his quasi-military leadership in his war on the Depression."[8] Thomas B. Farrell sees in the address the forging of a new civic culture reflecting progressives' faith in powerful centralized authority. The president had created "a reciprocal bond with the public" in which he acted as a trusted commander who could equally rely on his troops. According to Farrell, Roosevelt successfully invited "the people to enter his own regime of discourse, wherein submission and sacrifice and yes, discipline are transformed into instruments of power. In return for this sacrifice . . . is the pledge of a larger vision that will bind this newly empowered people together in a sacred trust, like an army."[9] Similarly, in their study of the speech's composition and reception, Davis W. Houck and Mihaela Nocasian discover in FDR's inaugural a text "in which the Judeo-Christian civic religion" and "the vernacular of the Bible" are linked with "Roosevelt's direct reference to extra-constitutional powers," all these elements coming together in a consummate rhetorical performance that elicited widespread public approbation.[10]

We agree with these analyses. Roosevelt's first inaugural represents a singular moment in the history of American politics and public address. This speech communicated his progressive vision in compelling terms, adopting the language of war and biblical allusion to win public assent for him to wield authority in unprecedented ways. He foregrounded the role of fear, casting a spotlight on and underscoring the theme of insecurity. He defined this fear ambiguously while asserting the need for the nation to fight it unambiguously, which his audience could only do by fully supporting his decisions. He promised to protect "essential democracy," noting that in claiming unmatched authority he was merely acting in accord with the people's desires: "They have made me the present instrument of their wishes. In the spirit of the gift I take it."[11] The president thereby concluded his speech, a speech in which he asserted that he would fulfill his "clear course of duty" to prosecute war against a domestic crisis with or without congressional support, by portraying himself the humble servant of the people.

We would also draw attention to how this speech repackaged Roosevelt's prior political rhetoric. By drawing on religious symbols and allusions to portray himself as a Christ figure who was fighting, in Ronald Isetti's words, "the evil capitalists who had betrayed the country's ethical and religious values," FDR deployed the same dialectic he had used his entire political career, highlighting the causes of insecurity in order to proclaim the good news of security.[12] Although numerous commentators have pointed out how this speech foreshadowed Roosevelt's continuing fight with Republicans, Wall Street, and other domestic rivals, fewer have noted the critical links this speech displays with his prior rhetoric, especially his previous utterances regarding security.

Yet FDR's rhetorical influence went beyond this one speech, however forceful it was. In this chapter we therefore view his first inaugural address as the germinal moment of a greater rhetorical shift that occurred in the opening years of Franklin Roosevelt's presidency. Our goal is to show that FDR adopted the same rhetorical framework during his first years in office for addressing the nation's economic and other domestic problems as he did in this speech; that is, his rhetoric framed his domestic policies meant to address the "national emergency" in the language of security (manifested in metaphors of home, military language, and moral appeals) not only in this address but over the course of the New Deal years. In doing so, FDR altered the stylistic registers of political debate in American public discourse by infusing it with references to security, fear, danger, and insecurity. In short, his presidential rhetoric assumed the ethos of his inaugural, interpreting the challenges facing America through the prism of national security.

Indeed, evidence for our claim can be found in the inaugural address itself. As Houck notes in his detailed account of the inaugural's composition, *FDR and Fear Itself,* Roosevelt intentionally kept his reference to "fear" found in the speech's first paragraph vague and abstract. The line was initially penned to only serve as a reference to economic despair. The original author of the sentence, Roosevelt's close advisor Louis Howe, had written the line as "terror which paralyzes the needed effort to bring about prosperity once again," putting the focus solely on fear of economic breakdown. Roosevelt rejected that version in favor of his own, much more ambiguous wording, a wording that opened up the possibility that immobilizing sources of terror might exist beyond economic collapse.[13] More precisely, the new wording implied more urgently that the president needed the public's "understanding and support" on matters besides those of purely economic concern. By phrasing his "fear itself" line as he did, FDR created for himself the rhetorical flexibility to portray any policy, not just ones immediately concerned with the Depression, as issues of "retreat and advance." We contend that this sentence represents just one instance of a repeated pattern of FDR's discourse, whereby he articulated his administration's agenda in the strident discourse of security so as to gain the broadest possible assent—in the process saturating the airwaves with the rhetorical ingredients for public fear.

The New Deal: An Exercise in Security

Once the inaugural festivities were done, it was time to get to work. Some of the New Dealers wanted to transform America into a utopia. Roosevelt aide Donald Richberg called the New Deal "a revolutionary program of cooperation."[14] Another one of them, Rexford Tugwell, called it "a vision of villages and clean small factories."[15] Historian William Leuchtenberg later described it as the New Deal's "Heavenly City: the greenbelt town, clean, green, and white, with children playing in light, airy, spacious schools."[16]

But the president, who was firmly in charge, was no utopian. As his twenty-year record revealed, he was intensely practical. He once told an audience at Oglethorpe University that "true leadership" was to unite thought behind a chosen method, and "it is common sense to take a method and try it: if it fails, admit it frankly and try another. But above all try something."[17] As H. W. Brands writes, "Roosevelt was more the pragmatist than the idealist, more the tinkerer than the true believer."[18] The New Deal reflected the "improvisatory character" of this pragmatism.[19] Always a shrewd political operator, Roosevelt maintained public trust not by setting out to initiate great long-term transformations but by merely portraying his actions as necessary to stave off immediate disaster.[20] The first New Deal—the Agricultural Adjustment Act, Tennessee Valley Authority Act, National Industrial Recovery Act, Glass-Steagall Act, Home Owners' Loan Act, and other laws—fulfilled that promise by raising prices and wages while cutting working hours and putting more people to work. With more money in circulation, buying power was soon on the rise. By the end of 1934, if it was too soon to say that things were surely getting better, at least there was widespread agreement that things were no longer getting worse.

The commonplace descriptor of FDR as "Dr. New Deal" reveals the critical symbolic function the president played in the drama of the Great Depression. As Suzanne M. Daughton records, the economic calamity's devastation was as much psychological as material; for a people who venerated "the prevailing doctrine of rugged individualism," the collapse of one's livelihood represented an incomprehensible nightmare. In the face of this spiritual and emotional tragedy stood Roosevelt, who embraced his role as "doctor" to the nation. Per Daughton, this metaphorical role "was well suited to the crisis of the Depression because Americans in the 1930s relied on doctors for practical advice and actions as well as for comfort, confidence, and hope."[21] That this persona was deeply consoling for millions of Americans equally highlights another key aspect of Roosevelt's New Deal rhetoric. Namely, that this formulation—FDR as doctor and nation as patient—reinforced the president's rhetorical emphasis on security. Nobody goes to the doctor to say hello, after all; the doctor is only called in moments of distress.

Thus, in addition to revealing Roosevelt's deep-seated pragmatism, the New Deal also reflected the president's emphasis on security.[22] To generate support for his policies, he invoked the specter of insecurity, reminding the nation over and over that "the nation-wide frontier of insecurity, of human want and fear," was never far away. The New Deal was framed as an exercise in security at its most basic level. One of his aides called the New Deal "a real people's movement getting at the heart of the great modern problem, insecurity—insecurity in jobs and insecurity in feelings."[23] Insecurity was no longer a secondary effect, the result of unsolved social problems. It was now the center of political life, the principal problem to be attacked. In Leuchtenberg's words, "The conviction that the [federal] government both should and could act to forestall future breakdowns gained general acceptance."[24] New Deal policies implemented by the Roosevelt administration enacted this vision of the federal government as the preeminent crisis manager, the doctor, the guardian of first resort against citizens' insecurity. As in the inaugural address, that insecurity would continue to be defined elastically but infused with the moral energy bestowed by Roosevelt's arrogation of prophetic authority.

Consequently, the word the New Dealers used to describe their goal was *security*. Roosevelt said so bluntly and publicly: "Security is our greatest need. I am determined to do all in my power to help you attain that security." Again: "I place the security of the men, women, and children of the Nation first."[25] FDR's most trusted advisor, Harry Hopkins, urged his staff to develop "a complete ticket to provide security for all the folks if this country up and down and across the board."[26] Washington had always been responsible for protecting Americans against dangers that might threaten from foreign lands, while the people typically relied on family and local community to safeguard them against the more quotidian threats to life and livelihood at home. But that was no longer possible, FDR told Congress: "We are compelled to employ the active interest of the Nation as a whole through government in order to encourage a greater security for each individual who composes it." In 1940 he retrospectively interpreted the New Deal as an exercise in security-building while sketching out ideas for the Democratic platform, writing, "Human security based on human values has come to the front as a supreme objective," adding that the motive for all of the New Deal policies was "to protect people" without sacrificing basic freedoms.[27] According to Charles Alexander, even New Dealers who advocated strong centralized planning wanted "a democratic collectivism founded on individual security from catastrophic swings of the economic pendulum."[28] In collapsing the distinctions between problems that might afflict any individual home with structural institutional problems that beset society as a whole (or even foreign threats), the Roosevelt administration's rhetoric portrayed all the nation's challenges as merely different forms of insecurity, thus mandating federal action.

Moreover, the list of misfortunes that could make anyone insecure now included troubles that had once been considered part of the normal course of events. Some were tragedies that might strike anyone at any time—accident, illness, unemployment. Others were difficulties sure to strike everyone sooner or later, such as old age and death. Democracy "has the innate capacity to protect its people against disasters once considered inevitable," FDR confidently proclaimed in his second inaugural address.[29] At the same time that he promised that the government would now protect its citizens against the inexorable troubles of life, however, he also acknowledged the state's limited ability to protect against such threats: "No one can guarantee this country against the dangers of future depressions," the president told Congress when he proposed his Social Security plan, "but we can reduce those dangers . . . and we can provide the means of mitigating their results." He promised only "a margin of security against the inevitable vicissitudes of life." That margin of security, Roosevelt's highest goal, was essentially a defensive goal: "to protect us against catastrophe."[30] As his secretary Grace Tulley recalled, he often declared himself ready to "cross a bridge with the devil" if he thought it would serve the interests of the people.[31]

In contrast to the utopian visions of other progressives, FDR framed the New Deal as an exercise in provisioning security while simultaneously downplaying the government's actual ability to ward off against anything except the worst crises. Like the pessimistic foreign policy realism he advocated as assistant secretary, promoting strength as the only guarantee of security in a world where threats might materialize anywhere, so now he asserted that every American should have at least minimal resources to fight the inevitable trials of life—and it was the job of the federal government to furnish those resources. "Security," in an archetypical instance of definitional drift, now included life itself.

At root, FDR's New Deal rhetoric cast a negative vision. It offered not a substantive ideal of a richer, fuller life that everyone could work toward and share in together but rather a commitment to managing insecurity to prevent the worst for everyone. The prophetic persona Roosevelt assumed in his first inaugural complemented this vision. His role was to attack the "moneychangers" and opponents of the people, and he continued to demonize "the forces of selfishness and of lust for power" throughout the New Deal years.[32] Whatever and whoever was on his side was good; whatever and whoever was against his administration was bad. This is why historian Charles Beard lamented Roosevelt's having adopted "the relativism which will ruin liberalism yet" against a fixed, positive conception of the good.[33] His role was to lead the people to the "promised land" of security, which required rhetorical flexibility because the sources that might endanger such a vaguely defined security were ever changing.[34]

This view emerged directly out of the progressivism of Roosevelt's early career, which looked for governmental solutions to problems a past generation would have attributed to sin or personal failures. As Tugwell put it: "The New Deal is attempting to do nothing to people, and does not seek at all to alter their way of life, their wants and desires." As Eric Goldman states, Tugwell's colleague Raymond Moley "sought solutions of the nation's ills that assumed the necessity of a battle against 'ignorance' rather than against 'sin.'" Leuchtenberg later made the same point more colorfully: "While the progressive grieved over the fate of the prostitute, the New Dealer would have placed Mrs. Warren's profession under a code authority."[35]

In the story told by Roosevelt, American society had to protect its weakest members, and his rhetoric reflected the tensions of his earlier progressive rhetoric between interdependency and vulnerability. He had run for president on the platform of building up "the forgotten man at the bottom of the economic pyramid," and he similarly advanced the New Deal on the basis of lifting up those at the bottom (not by overtly embracing the value of equality).[36] Critically, FDR argued that his New Deal policies—policies designed most of all to help the destitute, jobless, and hopeless—were necessary on the basis of national security. Supporting those suffering the most was a matter of national security according to the logic of Roosevelt's progressive framework, since whenever one person suffered from insecurity all persons became less secure. There could be no security for the rich without security for the poor, in his words, because "national security is not a half and half matter; it is all or none." Indeed, he said, "We all go up, or else we all go down, as one people."[37] This formulation foregrounded the proximity of danger to everyone, implying that as long as there were unemployed or otherwise insecure Americans that every citizen was under tacit threat.

This analysis need not imply any criticism of the New Deal. Indeed, FDR and his administration deserve praise for caring so much about the worst that might happen to anyone. New Deal programs certainly eased the suffering of many millions, and the nation rewarded the president with an overwhelming reelection victory in 1936. Yet what brought millions of new voters into the Democratic camp was not so much the reality of prosperity, as nearly 20 percent of Americans remained unemployed at that time, but the constant promise that prosperity would come.[38] The public could take some solace in the gradually improving economy, but not much. On Inauguration Day, 1937, the president acknowledged that fully "one-third of a nation" was still "ill-housed, ill-clad, ill-nourished."[39] Indeed the economy was so weak, and resistance to further New Deal reforms was growing so strong, that the economy would collapse again in 1937. The only stable and continuing source of reassurance was in the president's overarching narrative, a story of a unified nation locked in mortal combat with an economic challenge as treacherous as any invading army.

He communicated this narrative through his public discourse, drawing on his past rhetoric to persuade a wounded country to embrace his view of the crisis. Over the course of his first two terms in office FDR would use a variety of rhetorical strategies to win support for the New Deal, adapting elements of his prior utterances to winsomely organize the defense of his administration's policies. The central component of this discourse was Roosevelt's repeated appeals to security. To demonstrate this claim, we highlight three patterns of FDR's rhetoric that framed the New Deal as an exercise in building national security: metaphors of home, military language, and appeals to abstracted religious values. These strategies correspondingly worked to portray his policies as continuous with the past, urgently needed, and morally above reproach, each rhetorical vehicle exhibiting FDR's trademark dialectic between security and insecurity.

Metaphors of Home

FDR reinforced the importance of "home" through his famous "fireside chats," designed to create the feeling that he was just a neighbor who had dropped by for a friendly visit. These radio messages were, in the words of John Sharon, "the greatest weapon of the New Deal."[40] Multiplied dozens of times, these chats and the metaphor of home they conveyed created the image of the entire nation as a single secure neighborhood. FDR, in turn, conjured up that image to legitimate New Deal policies: "Our well-being depends, in the long run, on the well-being of our neighbors. The good-neighbor idea—as we are trying to practice it in our international relationships—needs to be put into practice in our community relationships."[41] Davis Houck's observation of FDR's first inaugural could be extended to cover much of the president's rhetoric over the New Deal period: "At a time when domesticity was threatened by uncertainty, unemployment, and the specter of hunger, it was only natural for Roosevelt to return to that idealized image of the home."[42]

He described the entire nation as a shared home in that neighborhood. "We have the opportunity of improving conditions and making our country a better home, materially and spiritually, for more than 120,000,000 people," he told one audience. "To do this will require the concerted aid and continued efforts of many forces."[43] The New Deal's "first principle," he declared in a 1934 fireside chat, would be to offer security by "providing homes for the people of the Nation."[44] In the overall context of his discourse, the words *home* and *neighbor* became powerful symbols of security, and according to the metaphor's logic, anything that seemed to threaten home, neighborhood, or the American way of doing things could be invoked as sufficient reason to support the government's program for security.

Roosevelt's warnings about dictatorship reflected the broader link he drew between economic security and freedom. He treated these terms as virtual synonyms in a 1934 fireside chat, when he endorsed "that broader definition of liberty under which we are moving forward to greater freedom, to greater security for the average man than he has ever known before."[45] Clearly, the security he meant was freedom from economic poverty. In 1937 he wrote to Felix Frankfurter, telling him that his goal boiled down to trying "to save our system, the capitalist system, from crackpot ideas."[46] As these statements attest, FDR saw himself and his policies as an attempt to preserve capitalism, freedom, and the American way of life—in short, home.

Roosevelt justified his policies as necessary steps to preserve the valued things from the (white) America of the past. He labored to show that the New Deal was, in a race-inflected turn of phrase, "in complete accord with the underlying principles of orderly popular government which Americans have demanded since the white man first came to these shores."[47] To demonstrate the historical continuity between the principles of the American founders and the New Deal, he depicted the "economic royalists" he so vehemently decried as the heirs of the British royalty defeated in the American Revolution. This analogy not only underscored the equation New Deal = freedom = Americanism, but also worked to erase the distance between the eighteenth and the twentieth centuries, suggesting that no fundamental change had occurred since the country's birth. In echoes of his prepresidential progressive discourse, FDR's rhetoric attempted to show how the New Deal embodied cherished American values even as it introduced changes that dramatically reshaped American society.

Examples of Roosevelt making arguments to this effect abound. "The task of reconstruction does not require the creation of new and strange values," he told Congress. "It is rather the finding of the way once more to known, but to some degree forgotten, ideals and values." In a fireside chat he linked that message to his favored theme, security: "We are seeking to find the way once more to well-known, long-established but to some degree forgotten ideals and values. We seek the security of the men, women, and children of the nation. . . . What we are doing today is a necessary fulfillment of what Americans have always been doing—a fulfillment of old and tested American ideals."[48] In his second fireside chat, which introduced the New Deal, he told hearers that his administration was only acting in ways that were "constitutional and in keeping with the past American tradition."[49] FDR's rhetoric venerated an understanding of American history that served as a symbol of security for many citizens, and he praised continuity with the past while portraying the New Deal as the key to an enduring, stable social order. He played the notes of both present and past like a skilled jazz musician plays an instrument, improvising in ways that were creatively new yet comfortingly familiar.

Indeed, there was always a tension in Roosevelt's public discourse between promoting and preventing change, between hoping for something better and fearing something worse. His speechwriter Robert Sherwood once remarked: "No one is as good as the President in fixing the line between keeping up morale and confidence on the one hand and being too optimistic on the other." FDR relied on his famed air of confidence to smooth over whatever anxieties his rhetoric raised: "We are all bound together by hope of a common future rather than by reverence for a common past. . . . A better civilization than any we have known is in store for America and by our example, perhaps, for the world."[50] FDR's confident delivery—a political imperative given his disability—worked to assuage the paradoxes and tensions of his discourse, especially when it came to the mixing of new and old.

In addition to continuity, home served as a powerful symbol of a related New Deal goal: stability. For FDR, stability and security were virtually transposable terms. As David Kennedy writes, stability encapsulated the basic objective of the New Deal, which was "to sustain balance and equity and orderliness throughout American society. Roosevelt's dream was the old progressive dream of wringing order out of chaos, imparting to ordinary Americans at least some measure of the kind of predictability to their lives that was the birthright of the Roosevelts and the class of patrician squires to which they belonged." Hence, Kennedy states that the New Deal's aim "can be summarized in a single word: security." In his analysis, as in the president's rhetoric, the terms *stability* and *security* were interchangeable. FDR wanted millions to have "a measure of the security that the patrician Roosevelts enjoyed as their birthright."[51]

Roosevelt made these connections in his public rhetoric explicitly, especially when it came to jobs. For example, he argued in April 1933 that Congress should pass his policy to prevent foreclosures because "special safeguards should be thrown around home ownership as a guarantee of social and economic stability, and that to protect home owners . . . in a time of general distress is a proper concern of the Government."[52] Later that year he told the president of the American Farm Bureau in a letter that the goal of his administration's agricultural policy was to create "a stable future" for farmers, looking "not alone to immediate relief, but to a sustained prosperity based on sane principles."[53] His administration worked "toward greater stability of automobile employment" and for "the stability of employment" for all the nation's workers.[54] As he had done previously, Roosevelt used "home" to communicate solidity, grounding his transformative proposals in a way that underscored their deeper consistency with popular values.

In that sense, the New Deal brought to the surface the link between security and stability that lay hidden within progressive mythology. Its policies were designed to help citizens realize the central tenet of progressivism—the uniquely American belief in endless advancement—not by promising individuals endless economic improvement, which was relegated to a private concern, but rather by guaranteeing Americans a baseline of financial well-being. This well-being was articulated as the achievement of security. As historian Eric Goldman writes, "Millions of Americans were supplementing the credo of opportunity with a demand for laws that would guarantee them greater economic security"—the minimum level of economic security that would, the president promised, keep the nation safe. The government, the agent of the public good, would worry only about "that minimum necessary [for the individual] to keep a foothold," as FDR put it, because "that is the kind of protection Americans want."[55] He thus depicted the federal government as providing the safety and stability of home, working to ensure that citizens would have their bare necessities provided for in an environment of support.

Roosevelt, of course, realized that some might find more appealing alternatives to his proposals in various forms of Marxist, fascist, or other radical narratives. He reportedly replied to an onlooker who told him he would become America's greatest president if he "licked" the Great Depression, "If I fail, I shall be the last one."[56] He therefore sought to address the concerns of workers and others who might prove susceptible to radicalism. "Everywhere the object was the same," David Kennedy explains of the Roosevelt administration, "to create a uniquely American system of relatively riskless capitalism. . . . Its cardinal aim was not to destroy capitalism but to devolatilize it, and at the same time to distribute its benefits more evenly."[57] To wit, FDR once said that his greatest accomplishment as president was "saving American capitalism."[58]

To ward off any rising tide on the left, Roosevelt intensified his critique of so-called "economic royalists," wealthy capitalists whom he castigated for taking more than their fair share.[59] Workers needed "a margin of security against the inevitable vicissitudes of life," he told the nation, "if we are to avoid the growth of a class-conscious society." At the same time, with indirect turns of phrase such as "class-conscious society" or the threat of "industrial and labor chaos," FDR obliquely but firmly highlighted communism as a greater peril to capitalism than anything contained in the New Deal.[60] Perhaps Roosevelt had read the open letter addressed to him by the British economist John Maynard Keynes, urging him to lead in "reasoned experiment within the framework of the existing social system." If he failed, "rational change will be gravely prejudiced throughout the world, leaving [conservative] orthodoxy and revolution to fight it out."[61] In line with this advice, Roosevelt promoted the New Deal by focusing public attention on the threat of violent change brought about by socialism or communism. By comparison to revolutionary ideologies, his administration's policies seemed relatively tame. FDR's rhetoric concerning "economic royalists" or the plight of laborers thereby worked in concert with his other appeals to portray the New Deal as a middle-ground, practical American alternative to the street violence and political tumult taking place in Europe during his first years in office.

To drive home this argument, FDR frequently defined the meaning of security through antithesis, via recourse to symbols of insecurity, such as when he explained that the way to avoid collapse was "to give balance and stability to our economic system, to make it bomb-proof."[62] Every invocation of such symbols of insecurity admitted the existence of a lurking fear that the American way might soon explode (or implode, or burn up, or otherwise perish depending on the metaphor). By taking on the role of providing a minimum level of predictability in each person's life, the federal government under FDR effectively took aim at unpredictability itself, rendering anything that seemed too chaotic, too unpredictable, or too radical a potential signal of insecurity or disorder; against these forces stood a New Deal he exulted as a force for continuity.

One tactic Roosevelt used to reinforce this message was to equate the New Deal with prosperity and democracy. He made this case many times in his public rhetoric; for example, he told one audience that democracy could only be saved by showing that "democratic government is equal to the task of protecting the security of the people." If democratic government could not provide economic relief, he admitted, the people would turn to a dictator to do the job.[63] As he entered office Roosevelt offered private confirmation of these fears to his close aide, Rexford Tugwell, remarking, "There had never been a time, the Civil War alone excepted, when our institutions had been in such jeopardy."[64] FDR framed economic well-being as the chief aim of democracy, linking representative government with free enterprise as two sides of the same protective coin: "The deeper purpose of democracy is to pursue the happiness which comes from security."[65] If, for Roosevelt, the Great Depression threatened democracy itself, then by the same token, the New Deal represented a stalwart attempt to rally the nation to democracy's defense.

The president framed his defense of capitalism and democracy as a simple matter of patriotism. America, he decreed in his speech accepting the Democratic Party's renomination for the presidency in 1936, had "a rendezvous with destiny." Freedom served as the foundation for this bright future. As FDR said in his speech accepting renomination for president in 1936, "The people of America are in agreement in defending their liberties at any cost."[66] He tied freedom and security together with these metaphors of home. As historian Eric Foner notes, owning a home was conceptualized not merely as "a form of economic security" but also as "an economic measure of freedom."[67] John Dewey noted at the time how the meaning of freedom had changed: "[freedom] today signifies liberation from material insecurity" rather than the traditional concept of liberty as the unfettered freedom to try to get rich, with all the risks that entailed.[68] Roosevelt embraced this redefinition of freedom and promulgated it in his public rhetoric. As a result, FDR was able to depict anything that created economic insecurity as a threat to freedom and to portray his policies as an appropriate answer to these threats. Roosevelt extended the metaphor of home to cover a dizzying number of phenomena, marketing the New Deal as an attempt to create a sort of collective national home for all Americans. Government's responsibility in this schema was redefined as that of an honest broker, working to guarantee that each American received a fair deal while also "preserving the balance between all groups," as Roosevelt put it.[69] To maintain that balance while also preserving a sense of national unity required a complementary rhetorical strategy: the use of military language.

Military Language

The New Deal legislative consensus quickly broke down after FDR's first hundred days in office, bitterly dividing the Democratic Party and leaving some Americans even unwilling to say the president's name aloud.[70] Moreover, the New Deal's progressive logic entailed a belief in collective action, a belief that was often difficult to cultivate in a nation as large and disparate as the United States. Precisely because of these challenges, it made sense for Roosevelt to rely on military language—martial metaphors, the labeling of enemies, and war discourse—to maintain the national consensus necessary for the New Deal's political momentum. This overarching metaphor of war was perhaps the only one that could provide all the various segments of American society a sense of participation in a homogenous, unified country. FDR employed military language in a variety of ways, each utterance working to portray the nation as a united body with him at its head, confronted by a terrible foe.

The most overt use of military language by FDR was his depiction of the American body politic as an army. He oratorically conscripted his fellow Americans, his rhetoric instilling a sense of national unity by depicting the disparate citizens of the United States this way. Roosevelt debuted this aspect of his presidential rhetoric in his first inaugural. In that speech he called upon the people as though they were a vast military host, claiming leadership of "this great army of our people dedicated to a disciplined attack on our common problems."[71] He used military language again in a fireside chat: "The first line of [national] defense lies in the protection of economic security."[72] Indeed the president repeated the point even into 1939: "Our nation's program of social and economic reform is a part of defense as basic as armaments themselves."[73] FDR's head of the National Recovery Administration (NRA), General Hugh Johnson, likewise adopted a militant tone, combining martial rhetoric with biblical allusion: "Those who are not with us are against us," he said, "and the way to show that you are a part of this great army of the New Deal is to insist on this symbol of solidarity."[74] Roosevelt himself compared the NRA badge to the badge that soldiers wear "*in war, in the gloom of night attack.*"[75] He forcefully conveyed the image of the American people as an army, wielding the reforms of the New Deal as weapons (and literally underlining this idea in his manuscripts).

FDR's choice analogy was to compare the Great Depression to the German enemy of World War I. When he first spoke in praise of "the forgotten man at the bottom of the economic pyramid," it was to enlist him in "the infantry of our economic army. . . . These unhappy times call for the building of plans . . . like those of 1917." "National defense and the future of America were also involved in 1933," just as in 1917, the president recalled. "Don't you believe that the saving of America has been cheap at that price?"[76] War rhetoric such as this implied that "nothing less than the nation's survival and honor were at stake," Michael S. Sherry observes. Roosevelt went so far as to extend the "conflict's" horizon beyond the nation's shores by treating America and its institutions as the epitome of civilization itself. Invoking the language of World War I (and echoing Lincoln's Gettysburg Address), he cast the New Deal as "a war for the survival of democracy. . . . We are fighting to save a great and precious form of government for ourselves and for the world."[77] Naturally, this grand statement implied the obverse—that democracy and civilization itself could disappear from the world—reminding the nation of the unparalleled level of alarm that Woodrow Wilson had raised. Hence, FDR's military language communicated urgency by portraying the destruction wreaked by the Depression as equivalent to that of the Kaiser's army.

Another obvious way FDR used military language was to personify the economic challenges facing the country as a kind of national adversary. Roosevelt often compared the Great Depression, in William B. Leuchtenburg's words, to "the menace of a foreign enemy who had to be defeated in combat."[78] Starting with his inaugural, where he explicitly analogized the Depression to "a foreign foe," FDR made constant references to "the emergency" or "the crisis." One of his first acts as president was to declare "the existence of a national emergency" necessitating a bank "holiday" (FDR preferred this term to Hoover's "moratorium") while the government addressed the ongoing currency crisis.[79] In 1937 he wrote to Richard Lieber, a leading conservationist, that "as the period of the emergency passes" the federal government would begin relinquishing its control over the parks system back to the states.[80] He told an audience at Vassar College, "There is a unity in this country which I have not seen and you have not seen since April, 1917." At the dedication of a memorial to Samuel Gompers, FDR remarked, "The whole of the country has a common enemy." And he intended to enforce that unity, he told the gathered labor leaders: "Just as in 1917 we are seeking to pull in harness; just as in 1917, horses that kick over the traces will have to be put in a corral."[81] If the Depression was America's great enemy, then Roosevelt, his military language seemingly implied, commanded the nation as its general.

Roosevelt did not shy away from exploiting this kind of rhetoric to extend the label of enemy to his political opponents, although he typically did so in indirect fashion. As Mary E. Stuckey notes, FDR often characterized his domestic foes as "obstructionists" or "agitators" who sought to disrupt the nation's unity, wielding invective in such a manner as to avoid being directly drawn into a debate with a specific personality.[82] Scholarly experts on FDR's fireside chats point out that

> in many of the speeches he united the audience by calling attention to some enemy, some small minority of the perverse or wrongheaded, whose pernicious ideas the rest of us had to resist at all costs. . . . The stratagem of finding and naming an enemy signaled to average Americans what attitude and actions were unpatriotic; but the device also served the larger purposes of instilling in listeners feelings of unity with the vast majority of their fellow citizens.[83]

Elvin T. Lim arrives at a similar conclusion in his study of FDR's fireside chats, noting that "FDR did not hesitate to verbally abuse and denigrate his political opponents. . . . FDR's Fireside Chats, even though they were broadcast on radio and subject to the alleged imperatives of the medium, nevertheless held on to the fiery elements of platform rhetoric."[84] Roosevelt deployed his military language to his political advantage, selectively extending the label of "enemy" to his domestic opponents when advantageous.

And, of course, FDR's military language implied a significant role for the federal government in addressing the nation's problems. The dualism of his language, occasionally bordering on an apocalyptic tone, reinforced his tendency to affirm maintaining order. As William Appleman Williams has noted: "The pattern of either-or thinking about representative government and economic welfare was reasserted and even intensified. Different solutions were dismissed because they would undercut the existing order of business and politics."[85] For FDR and his progressive principles, it was the role of the federal government to uphold the existing order against threats that might disrupt it. For example, he told an audience at the University of North Carolina: "Almost every crisis in the history of our Nation has become a crisis because of a lack on the part of leaders or on the part of the people themselves, a lack of some of those essentials."[86] In this schema, the country's leaders held the ultimate responsibility for preventing national calamity—leaders were either directly to blame for crises that befell the United States or, should they fail to properly lead the people, indirectly to blame. There existed only one path to national salvation, according to the logic of New Deal discourse. The federal government must do what it had done during the Great War: coordinate the "great army of our people" to save the economic life of the nation and preserve the American constitutional system.

Unsurprisingly, Roosevelt's frequent recourse to invective and the labeling of enemies spurred resistance to his personality, policies, and party. As Stuckey notes in *Voting Deliberatively: FDR and the 1936 Presidential Campaign*, FDR faced a tremendous amount of criticism from all sides of the political spectrum. From right-wing businessmen like William Randolph Hearst who decried the "Raw Deal" to leftist political critics such as Huey Long, Francis Townsend, and Upton Sinclair, Roosevelt faced a "precipitous drop" in his and the New Deal's popularity over the course of his first term.[87] As he ran for presidential office a second time and indeed throughout his first two terms, he sought to rally the nation to the New Deal by framing it as an exercise not only in building security, establishing home, or marshalling the nation to fight an economic foe, but also as the realization of cherished traditional values.

Moral Appeals

Ultimately, Roosevelt claimed, the New Deal was an expression of traditional moral and spiritual values. He described his office as "preeminently a place of moral leadership": "I want to be a preaching President—like my cousin," he declared, and he pursued that goal with words like these: "The great struggle we are engaged in today [is] the struggle for the maintenance of the integrity of the morals of democracy."[88] FDR's platform elevated a set of values, the chief of which was self-abnegation. While the pursuit of self-interest served as the foundation of the American economic and political systems—as he acknowl-edged, "In our personal ambitions we are individualists"—too much self-interest at the expensive of others threatened the nation's demo-cratic soul.[89] Thus the opposite of self-abnegation—selfishness—also served as a main source of society's ills. As a result, Roosevelt (ever the patrician) promoted moderation as a key virtue so that individual self-ishness did not inflict others with undue suffering: "There is placed on all of us the duty of self-restraint. That is the discipline of democracy."[90]

There were clearly some who failed in this moral task. "There are, of course, men, a few of them, who might thwart this great common purpose by seeking selfish advantage," the president often cautioned in admonishing tones. And he promised that the government would use its new powers only "to protect the commerce of America from the selfish forces which ruined it."[91] He used this moral framework to justify his attack on the "economic royalists," relying on the familiar dualism of progressive discourse, "the general good" of the whole nation against "individual self-interest and group selfishness."[92] If, as Warren Kimball writes, Roosevelt's leadership style "needed a popular sense of crisis" in order to work, then it is worth noting that FDR's rhetoric extended this sense of crisis to the realm of morals, invoking national values as the basis for his administration's New Deal policies.[93]

Indeed, the president often justified his chosen policy prescriptions on the explicit basis of their spiritual or moral character. In his message to Congress on unemployment relief on March 21, 1933, Roosevelt de-clared that the government should organize what would become the Civilian Conservation Corps not only for economic, but also moral rea-sons:

> More important, however, than the material gains will be the moral and spiritual value of such work. The overwhelming majority of unemployed Americans, who are now walking the streets and receiving private or public relief, would infinitely prefer to work. We can take a vast army of these un-employed out into healthful surroundings. We can eliminate to some extent at least the threat that enforced idleness brings to spiritual and moral stabil-ity. It is not a panacea for all the unemployment but it is an essential step in this emergency. I ask its adoption.[94]

In this statement the president combined his predilection for military language with a moral appeal for his policies: because unemployment relief would offer "moral and spiritual" gains to the "vast army" of jobless

Americans, Congress should pass legislation to that effect. By employing such language, FDR could portray his policies, and democracy itself, as the political embodiment not only of security but of self-disciplined "decency," the moral foundation (for him) of all genuine religion: "The development of civilization and of human welfare is based on the acceptance by individuals of certain fundamental decencies in their relations with each other." *Decency* operated as a key term through which FDR could talk about the aspirational values of the New Deal. When he announced that "security is our greatest need," he defined security as the chance for everyone to have "enough money for our families to live on decently."[95] By associating his proposals with notions of decency, spiritual value, democracy, and civilization, in short, Roosevelt used rhetoric to advance a vision of the New Deal as not only an economic endeavor but also a moral crusade. This tactic also helped him allay fears among more religious Americans that the New Deal might "Russianize America."[96]

In the spiritual realm, as in economic matters, he linked security to stability. His proposed public works projects, in his telling, should be enacted because they would endow millions of Americans with a sense of "spiritual and moral stability."[97] In his 1934 annual message, he declared that disorder was inimical to the principles of the United States, stating, "Disorder is not an American habit. Self-help and self-control are the essence of the American tradition—not of necessity the form of that tradition, but its spirit. The program itself comes from the American people."[98] Indeed, in his discourse, protecting America often meant protecting the legacy of civilization itself, and by safeguarding the nation's values the New Deal worked to preserve the ideals of freedom, democracy, and liberty. "The country was dying by inches," FDR recalled in a fireside chat, in "conditions which came very close to destroying what we alive call modern civilization." Private enterprise needed assistance and "reasonable safeguards" to preserve "not only itself but also our processes of civilization." Roosevelt depicted the New Deal as defending the political heart of civilization, "the message of liberty which America sends to all the world."[99] According to his rhetoric, the Great Depression threatened both American jobs and the nation's very democratic moral core. Like Roosevelt, who famously told a reporter that the source of his "political philosophy" was that he was "a Christian and a Democrat," the New Deal was wrapped in the shared garments of economic and spiritual security.[100]

Roosevelt also used the language of morality to proclaim national unity, and he did so by quoting the one book most Americans still shared in common, the Bible: "We have learned to feel ourselves a nation. As never before, each section of America says to every other section, 'Thy people shall be my people.'" He tied the package together neatly in an early fireside chat, saying that the New Deal aimed to avert "a loss of spiritual values—the loss of that sense of security for the present and the future that is so necessary to the peace and contentment of the individual and of his family." Such religiously laden language had a powerful political impact because, as Barry Karl has suggested, Americans were eagerly seeking "redemption" and "salvation" from a crisis that seemed to be of universal scope.[101] By employing religious language, FDR appealed to a public imagination deeply shaped by Christianity.[102]

Roosevelt's address accepting the Democratic nomination for president in 1936 was filled with such references to biblical language. He excoriated the Republicans, telling his hearers that "divine justice weights the sins of the cold-blooded and the sins of the warm-hearted in different scales.[103] He alluded to Christ's Parable of the Talents found in Matthew 25, saying that "to some generations much is given. Of other generations much is expected." He then invoked the military metaphor, concluding his speech by declaring "that here in America we are waging a great and successful war." He continued, drawing together themes of politics, economics, and America's higher calling: "It is not alone a war against want and destitution. It is more than that; it is a war for the survival of democracy. We are fighting to save a great and precious form of government for ourselves and for the world."[104] FDR blended his biblical language with his other rhetorical strategies of defending the New Deal, which had the effect of saturating his discourse not only with references to the military but also transcendent values.

In that campaign Eleanor also used religious language to describe her husband's cause. In a column defending the president against charges of proffering a "mollycoddle philosophy" from an Oyster Bay relative still loyal to the Republican Party, Eleanor wrote that her husband exhibited strength, "physical and mental and spiritual," like Theodore Roosevelt. And, as she noted, "Theodore Roosevelt always preached the strenuous life to keep yourself fit physically, mentally and spiritually but the ultimate objective was before any other—making a home secure."[105] In turns of phrase that echoed the style of "Cousin Teddy," Eleanor attributed FDR's overcoming the limitations imposed by polio to his spiritual and mental strength, arguing that both men pursued the same overarching goal of individual security to the benefit of the home and nation.

As the president explained the New Deal, he turned economic, political, and social issues into moral and spiritual ones. By drawing on the language of Christianity, FDR was able to portray his agenda as an embodiment of transcendent spiritual values while also addressing the gritty everyday needs of individual citizens. In doing so he steered away from outright idealism. He did not urge the nation to strive for a utopian, totally transformed society in which economic woes and evil would be eradicated. The New Deal vision rested on the premise that "inevitable vicissitudes" would always threaten security and stability. But "the American way of life" would be considered victorious as long as the nation created a permanent stable structure to manage class discontent, to prevent civilization from being destroyed, and to prevent the worst from coming to pass.[106] Hence, by baptizing his proposals in the language of morality, Roosevelt pooled his economic, political, and spiritual appeals into one compelling package: the New Deal. The moral dimension of his rhetoric worked to transfigure the New Deal, elevating it, in all its legal, economic, and political complexities, to a simple proposition of helping others according to the dictates of Christian morality, American decency, and liberal sentiment—as interpreted by the president.

Conclusion

Under the New Deal, the goals and legitimations of government policy embraced all the main elements of the progressivism Roosevelt had promoted before he became president. These included a wide array of symbols of insecurity, a primary focus on protection against insecurity, and a clear vision of the sources of protection: democratic capitalism, a fair marketplace, home and neighborhood, decent middle-class self-restraint, individual freedom and shared responsibility, the preservation of traditional moral and spiritual values, and an ever-vigilant government as the bulwark needed to maintain every other source of protection. He often deployed three prominent rhetorical maneuvers to communicate this program: the metaphor of home, military language, and moral appeals. The metaphor of home allowed Roosevelt to link his proposals to massively expand the federal government with notions of freedom, stability, and security. FDR's military language abstracted the nation's economic struggles into a total war, smoothing over numerous intranational and intracoalitional conflicts to frame his political enemies as unpatriotic, potentially disloyal foes. The president's use of moral appeals, sprinkled with allusions to the Bible and Christian spirituality, elevated the New Deal into a political manifestation of transcendent religious values.

FDR's repeated use of figurative language amounted to a continuation of the militant language he employed at his first inaugural address. His rhetoric over the course of his first two terms, like that speech, highlighted potential security threats to the nation while asserting an unwavering need to defeat those sources of insecurity, thus foregrounding the role of fear even as he sought to rally Americans to fight. He endowed his domestic agenda with the "considerable rhetorical force" that stems from widely accepted political abstractions. Like Lyndon Johnson's "Great Society" or George W. Bush's Global War on Terrorism, the New Deal grouped a myriad of policies into a coherent and politically compelling whole.[107] In linking all these appeals together under the umbrella of the New Deal, FDR gave coalescent rhetorical form to the many threads of his progressive political ideology.

All the threads in that package—security, stability, freedom, democracy, capitalism, prosperity, government, America, civilization, and the human spirit—were woven together in a single fabric, creating a new mythology for the nation. At his rhetorical best, he would offer both arguments as parts of a single package of discourse. Words like *decent* and *civilized* were as vaguely defined as *America* and all the virtues it stood for. Each of those key words operated as metonyms; each could represent the whole discursive chain and amorphous complex of values that Roosevelt promoted as his antidote to economic insecurity. Roosevelt additionally cultivated a counter-fabric of symbols that represented all that was uncivilized, un-American, and unsafe. It was easy enough to imagine chaos, totalitarianism, communism, materialism, poverty, and "economic royalism" as abstract enemies of the nation. Each of these terms could be used to evoke notions of insecurity, opponents of civilization, or threats to the American way of life.

Here, then, was the fundamental argument of the New Deal: government had to coordinate all economic activities to protect the American home, moral decency, and civilization itself from being destroyed by the great new enemy, insecurity (in all its guises). Every time he made that argument, FDR accentuated and linked together the symbols of the insecurity he was trying to dispel. By blending all these sources of insecurity into his rhetoric, he could mount a more powerful case that government could now indeed allay all of them simultaneously. It is not surprising, then, that the New Deal was often interpreted as a source of insecurity, even as it fostered economic revival. As Eric Goldman observes, "By the late Thirties students of American society were also writing of 'the specter of insecurity' raised by the steadily mounting percentage of the population who depended on someone else for a job, the growing proportion of women supporting themselves or contributing a vital portion to the family income, the ineluctable decline in independent farming."[108] Anthropologist Margaret Mead, looking back at the end of the New Deal era, likewise saw a broader sense of insecurity: "The most striking change since 1929 is the alteration of the average man's expectations from his life, from an attitude of robust, overconfident optimism . . . to an attitude of equally disproportionate pessimism, in which every individual's chances to succeed are felt to be narrow, constricted, and unrewarding."[109] So even as FDR worked to instill a sense of public confidence through his words, his rhetoric, by relying on symbols of insecurity, also drew attention to the myriad threats that faced the nation—and, by extension of his progressive logic, everyday Americans.

Of course, Roosevelt's attempts to persuade the public to support his agenda through these strategies did not always find success. During the court-packing controversy of 1937, FDR declared to the nation, "We cannot yield our constitutional destiny to the personal judgment of a few men who, being fearful of the future, would envy us the necessary means of dealing with the present."[110] This statement combined the various elements of FDR's New Deal rhetoric. He uttered these words in a fireside chat, he invoked the idea that the United States had a bright future founded on its democratic values, and he decried judges who acted on personal motives instead of the good of the whole nation. Yet, as Marian McKenna notes, "In this case the result was different."[111] FDR's attempt to force the retirement of federal judges did not succeed. His proposed legislation, the Judicial Procedures Reform Act, failed to gain congressional approval (although Roosevelt would eventually appoint eight Supreme Court justices). In the estimation of Trevor Parry-Giles and Marouf Hasian Jr., Roosevelt's failures partly stemmed from "powerful rhetorics of 'liberty'" that were marshalled in response to his efforts and framed the debate as a clash between freedom and tyranny.[112] Viewed as a short-term strategy meant to secure instrumental gains, then, FDR's New Deal rhetoric carried a mixed record.

Seen more broadly, however, FDR's New Deal rhetoric proved nothing short of transformative. His way of making sense of the Great Depression created a unified pattern of discourse premised upon the symbolic interplay between figures of security and insecurity. By interpreting the economic struggle afflicting Americans through the lens of security, Roosevelt's words imposed a seemingly stable, well-ordered structure that made sense out of the apparently senseless suffering of the Depression. In the process, his rhetoric saturated US public discourse with referents to fear, insecurity, enemies, and their opposites. From this vantage, Roosevelt's New Deal rhetoric is notable not for its instrumental or strategic utility but for its wholesale transformation of the language used to talk about American politics. FDR altered the stylistic registers of debate, framing economic challenges and other problems as issues of security.[113]

This discursive structure would show its overwhelming power and influence even more clearly when the nation turned its focus from domestic to foreign affairs. In the battle over how to interpret America's relationship to a rapidly changing world, a modified version of FDR's New Deal rhetorical structure would ultimately win out. Once the primary sources of insecurity were seen as coming from abroad, the interpretive framework introduced by the New Deal—portraying a problem for one a problem for all, seeing challenges facing the nation primarily in terms of economic security, and highlighting perils threatening the American way of life—would point the way toward a new understanding of the United States' role in world politics.

4 | Prewar Foreign Policy, 1933–1939

The lines between economic and foreign policy have often been blurry in the American experience. In the early days of the republic, President Thomas Jefferson declared that "peace, commerce, and honest friendship with all nations, entangling alliances with none" would be the guiding principle of his foreign policy, and after a brief experiment in autarkic diplomacy his administration practiced a "relentless pursuit of foreign trade."[1] During the 1880s a "Pork War" raged between the United States and Western Europe over the importation of US meat products, leading the *New York Herald* to rally Americans to the cause of "avenging the American hog."[2] In more recent times, President Donald Trump's "trade war" agenda reoriented US foreign policy debates around commercial issues; Chinese telecom giant Huawei's plan to create 5G cellular networks in Europe, for example, sparked diplomatic disputes between the Trump administration and America's NATO allies.[3] For much of US history, the nation's economic policies and international agenda have largely overlapped.

The New Deal era was one such time. Given the centrality of economic reform to Franklin Roosevelt's first two presidential administrations, it is unsurprising that commercial concerns greatly impacted his approach to foreign policy. Just as FDR used the language of international conflict to frame his economic program, he often articulated his foreign policy agenda in terms of economic interest. Consequently, even though FDR's first inaugural address had relatively little to say about foreign policy beyond the invocation of his "neighborhood" metaphor ("In the field of world policy I would dedicate this Nation to the policy of the good neighbor—the neighbor who resolutely respects himself and, because he does so, respects the rights of others"), the president's assertion that the nation's first priority was "putting our own national house in order" carried with it important implications for American foreign policy.[4] Specifically, we hold that FDR and his subordinates promoted trade, rule of law, disarmament, and cooperation in international affairs during the New Deal era and that these different foreign policy priorities coalesced into a broad platform of liberal internationalism that was portrayed as the global economic counterpart to the New Deal. A world order premised on friendly relations, uninhibited trade, stability, demilitarization, and lawfulness, Roosevelt argued, would be a scene in which Americans could realize the economic security promised in his New Deal rhetoric. He delivered this vision through a bevy of metaphors, most prominently that of the "good neighbor."

In the process, FDR generated rhetorical resources for talking about global affairs in a binary schema that placed rule-following, law-abiding, trade-promoting, and Christian-values-affirming nations on one side and situated their opposites on the other. This developed as an adaptation and extension of his New Deal rhetoric, which made frequent recourse to us-versus-them appeals and asserted a universalism endemic to progressive ideology. This framing had two effects. First, it led FDR to criticize economic models embraced by other nations that differed from his own, particularly imperialism and economic nationalism. Second, Roosevelt's economic focus and penchant for dualism also led him to label Germany, Japan, and Italy as aggressor nations that imperiled global stability well before those nations embarked on foreign policy paths that directly threatened the United States. When his efforts to promote a peaceful global order on the lines of liberal internationalism proved unsuccessful, FDR reverted to the "realism" that he had embraced in the 1910s to warn his nation and the world of the impending crisis as he understood it. Throughout this period, Roosevelt consistently interpreted global events through his matrix of dualism, internationalism, and realism, ultimately working to insert new symbols of insecurity into American foreign policy discourse. By the time conflict broke out in 1939, Roosevelt had developed a broad narrative drawing on these rhetorical strands that he would use to debate the anti-interventionists over the United States' entry into World War II.

Liberal Internationalism: Trade, Stability, and Disarmament

The New Deal was, above all, a war against an internal economic threat to the American way of life. Yet as early as his second fireside chat Roosevelt told the nation that any economic recovery would "not be permanent unless we get a return to prosperity all over the world."[5] Since the

Great Depression affected countries worldwide, Roosevelt correspondingly portrayed the task of economic recovery as a transnational, not merely American, endeavor. For the president, the path to global prosperity and stability could be realized through international cooperation, the "neighborliness" he so frequently advocated in his rhetoric. Like the progressive discourses of civilizational advancement, diplomatic conciliation of differences, and arms reduction he advanced in the 1920s, FDR's early presidential rhetoric concerning foreign affairs promoted a vision of international collaboration oriented toward mutual economic revitalization.

In terms of policy, this friendly disposition toward other countries could be achieved through the first tenet of Roosevelt's liberal internationalism: *trade*. He promoted what Warren Kimball calls "the curiously American belief (often masquerading as anticolonialism) that the way to peace and prosperity was unrestricted commercial access, what Americans historically called free trade."[6] FDR advanced a kind of mirror image of the New Deal in foreign affairs during his first two presidential terms. Just as financial prosperity assured each American's security, thus mandating the New Deal's reforms, so individual nations needed economic growth to ensure their own peaceful stability, thus necessitating the development of an organized system of reciprocally beneficial global trade. Growth, in this formula, was the path to world peace.

The prime mover of and public spokesman for this vision was secretary of state Cordell Hull, who preached the gospel of liberal internationalism with evangelical fervor. As Beate Jahn notes, liberal internationalists like Hull viewed private property and free exchange as the basis for economic productivity, leading them to advocate "liberal foreign policies" that would "spread free-market and free-trade practices throughout the international system."[7] According to Hull, only a constantly growing volume of international trade could revive and maintain worldwide prosperity, which was the key to saving capitalism and the American way of life at home. Unless world trade kept expanding, he said, the United States would face "permanent regimentation on an ever-increasing scale," because "the withdrawal by any nation from orderly trade relations with the rest of the world" would lead inevitably to "regimentation of all phases of national life [and] the suppression of human rights."[8] Like the "economic royalists" or other villains of FDR's New Deal rhetoric, who sought their individual enrichment at the expense of others, countries that shut themselves off from exchange with their neighbors threatened the fragile order that made peaceful prosperity possible for all nations.

Hull had expounded this doctrine as early as 1916: "If we could get a freer flow of trade . . . so that one country would not be deadly jealous of another and the living standards of all countries might rise, thereby eliminating the economic dissatisfaction that breeds war, we might have a reasonable chance for a lasting peace." In his analysis, peace stemmed from prosperity, which could be achieved through the global exchange of goods. His policy prescriptions in the 1930s followed the same pattern now that he was a spokesperson for the administration: "The basic approach to the problem of peace is the ordering of the world's economic life so that the masses of the people can work and live in reasonable comfort. . . . The principles underlying the trade agreements program are therefore an indispensable cornerstone for the edifice of peace."[9]

The best way to expand trade, Hull held, was to lower tariffs and, even more importantly, to assure reciprocal treatment for all trading partners—what has come to be known as "free trade." Once preferential tariffs and rules were abolished, each nation would open its markets and resources to all other nations equally, trade would flow unrestrictedly, and all humanity would grow more prosperous. FDR by and large endorsed his secretary of state's viewpoint and often let him speak for the administration overall. As he told a journalist in 1936, "We all go along with the Hull principles." Before that he had told Hull himself, "In pure theory you and I think alike," although he added that as president he could not afford to be such an ideological purist: "Every once in a while we have to modify a principle to meet a hard and disagreeable fact."[10] Roosevelt bought into the broad outlines of Hull's liberal internationalist stance.

FDR did not enter office with the consistent track record of Hull, although he had been viewing world affairs through the lens of trade, naval power, and economics since his early days of reading Mahan. International affairs took a backseat to national policy during the first months and even years of his presidency. He signaled his preoccupation with domestic issues by sending Hull to the 1933 London Economic Conference in his stead while also denying Hull the authority to make any binding agreements. More broadly, according to his undersecretary of state and close friend William Phillips, Roosevelt approved Hull's trade policy but did not possess "any great confidence in its results."[11]

By the end of his first term, however, FDR actively promoted a pro-trade agenda through his public rhetoric. As he told an audience in Buenos Aires in 1936, "Our present civilization rests on the basis of an international exchange of commodities. Every Nation of the world has felt the evil effects of recent efforts to erect trade barriers of every known kind."[12] Freer trade, he argued, would stabilize the global economy and help avoid the "evil effects" of depression.

This shift was visible throughout the administration. A 1936 State Department dispatch stated that the nation's goal was nothing less than the "economic rehabilitation of the world," to be achieved through expanded world trade and "a regime of equality of treatment in international commercial relations." Assistant secretary of state Francis Sayre described the same program bluntly as "an instrumentality for throwing the weight of American power and influence against the current disastrous movement toward economic nationalism." Averting disaster around the world was seen by Roosevelt as an extension of efforts to turn the tide of economic disaster at home. "An increase in exports," he wrote in a private letter, "means an increase in domestic payrolls, and this in turn means a gain in the volume and in the profitableness of domestic sales."[13] In short, other countries' economic vitality directly benefited the United States in its "war" against the Great Depression, and therefore US foreign policy would be organized around an attempt to bring about such a revitalization of commercial relations worldwide.

Roosevelt also signaled his move toward Hull's approach most clearly when he agreed to work for congressional passage of a reciprocal trade act, which would enshrine the principle of most favored nation (MFN) status as the basis for US trade policy. American commercial advantage was, as always, a primary consideration. Whenever reciprocal trade laws were not to US advantage, the law stipulated that the president was free to ignore its provisions. Overall, the thinking went, a world organized around nondiscriminatory, equal-access trade would benefit the largest producers, the United States most of all. As J. Pierrepoint Moffat, chief of the State Department's Division of European Affairs, wrote succinctly: "In a system based on commercial equality we can drive England out of the market every time, due to our better goods and better sales methods." Trade, and the postulated economic growth it would deliver, served as the central pillar of the Roosevelt administration's liberal internationalist approach to foreign policy during the New Deal years. In this situation, Robert Dallek's conclusion seems apt: "Whatever Roosevelt's or Hull's intentions, the reciprocal trade program chiefly served

American rather than world economic interests."[14] They were linked in FDR's public rhetoric as well. In the 1937 Annual Address he affirmed his commitment to outlawing "unfair trade practices" in the same sentence he vowed to keep building "the beginnings of security for the aged and the worker."[15]

While the actual economic benefits of the Roosevelt administration's early trade policies are a matter of debate, these agreements served a powerful symbolic function. As historian Emily Rosenberg suggests, they signaled a determination to integrate the United States into the world economy so as to jumpstart the American economy and ward off any future collapses. To ensure that "American trade and investment could flourish," she writes, "and to safeguard against the kind of breakdown experienced after 1929 . . . the United States government moved toward becoming an international regulatory state," aiming to create a "stable international system."[16] Trade, in addition to constituting an analeptic for the US economy, was also conceptualized by FDR and his subordinates as an instrument for realizing the second major aim of their liberal internationalist approach to foreign policy: *stability*.

When Roosevelt and Hull talked about the virtues of freer trade, they often highlighted the importance of a peaceful, predictable political environment for economic growth. But their rhetoric also frequently depicted stability as an end in itself or as the means to the abstract goal of preserving a rational, civilized world order. On this note, the Roosevelt administration inflated its New Deal vision of collective civilizational advancement to a global scale. FDR's domestic policy, as David Kennedy suggests, was shaped by "the old mercantilist dream that a class of informed and disinterested mandarins could orchestrate all the parts of the economy into an efficient and harmonious whole."[17] In similar fashion, the administration's international agenda depended on an even grander attempt to organize the world, according to Hull, in a way that attained "as much stability among nations as there is among persons." Hull summed up his view in a dialogue with the Japanese ambassador in Washington: via reciprocal trade agreements, all advanced nations could work together to "meet their duties to civilization and the more backward populations of the world." Hull held to these principles with religious fervor. "To me," he wrote, "these doctrines were as vital in international relations as the Ten Commandments in personal relations."[18] For him, liberal internationalist principles carried eschatological promise. As he wrote in his memoirs, "If the world followed them, the world could live at peace forever. If the world ignored them, war would be eternal."[19] Order, far from the default state of global conduct in Hull's view, must be diligently maintained to prevent chaos—thus the importance of trade agreements.

Roosevelt used similar language, in private correspondence as well as before audiences. He publicly called for "an end to economic chaos—order in place of chaos" as early as May 1933, and that same month he also wrote to the king of England that global economic reform would "establish order in place of the present chaos."[20] When his future secretary of war, Henry Stimson, wrote that only expanded exports could preserve freedom, Roosevelt agreed; he added that European liberal values were now the values of a global civilization that was unified in a single political and economic system. Like Hull, who told him that he trusted in Americans' "Anglo-Saxon ideals, conceptions, and training over many centuries," FDR's image of an orderly world was one organized around British and American values, which would allow all nations to prosper.[21] As historian David Reynolds observes: "Just as [FDR] was arguing that American security was not divisible from that of the world, so he insisted that American values could not flourish in an alien ideological environment." In Frank Ninkovich's words, he assumed that "the diamond of American cultural uniqueness could shine only within the setting of a liberal Western civilization."[22] Stability, for Roosevelt and his subordinates, was signified by the success and spread of Anglo-American liberal values across the globe. Similar to how FDR's New Deal was portrayed as an attempt to provide basic stability for individual Americans, so his international agenda emphasized the importance of each nation's internal economic solvency. In foreign affairs as in domestic ones, stability was virtually synonymous with security. As Hull proclaimed: "Without expansion of international trade, based upon fair dealing and equal treatment for all, there can be no stability and security either within or among nations."[23]

Throughout his political career, FDR expressed confident optimism that the upheavals of modernity could be managed by transforming the United States into one huge neighborhood. By 1935 he applied this imagery to the whole world. He connected this vision to the even greater solidity represented by religion, telling a Catholic group, for example, "With every passing year I become more confident that humanity is moving forward to the practical application of the teachings of Christianity," and expressing his "deep belief that God is marching on" and that a new "spirit of neighborliness" prevailed.[24] Like the national society the New

Dealers hoped to build, this congenial, trade-based world order was sup-posed to run smoothly and predictably. George Peek, once a New Deal insider and a disaffected anti-internationalist by 1936, stated that "the internationalists base their views on trade, world peace and what not on the conception of a static world. . . . When they talk about restoring international trade, they have in mind going back to some period when this or that country had a supremacy."[25] Peek could not know what was in the mind of FDR and his advisors. But he did accurately describe the logic of their discourse and the nostalgia it could easily conjure up for a (perhaps imagined) yesteryear, when the world and all its neighbor-hoods seemed stable because one great power prevented any funda-mental change.

War served as the antithesis of the Roosevelt administration's foreign policy goal of a stable international order, and for that reason the presi-dent promoted measures to avoid conflict. He outlined this vision in an October 1937 fireside chat. "America actively engages in the search for peace," he declared; just as the human welfare intrinsic to civilization depended on "certain fundamental decencies" in personal relation-ships, so "the development of peace in the world is dependent similarly on the acceptance by nations of certain fundamental decencies in their relations with each other." Decency, a god term FDR borrowed from New Deal discourse, connected the values of peaceful conduct and an open, trade-oriented international economic system:

> By a series of trade agreements, we have been attempting to recreate the trade of the world . . . but we know that if the world outside our borders falls into the chaos of war, world trade will be completely disrupted. Nor can we view with indifference the destruction of civilized values throughout the world. We seek peace . . . [and] the continuance of world civilization in order that American civilization may continue to be invigorated."[26]

If war should break out, Roosevelt warned, it would introduce "chaos" that would "completely" disrupt the system of world trade his admin-istration so painstakingly labored to advance. The United States thus had economic as well as moral reasons to work against the outbreak of war, to make certain that the peacefulness necessary for the world's economic recovery was sustained.

For the president, this crucial path to peace, global prosperity, and orderly civilization could be realized through *disarmament*, the third te-net of his liberal internationalist approach to foreign policy. "Armament is the real root of the world disease," he wrote privately, "and all other difficulties are resulting symptoms. When everybody goes a little more bankrupt there will be war or disarmament!" Rearmament stood against all the liberal internationalist values that he sought to spread. Rather than invest in tradeable goods, it created closed national economies; instead of openness to trade, weapons production diverted nations' resources inwardly. Far from exhibiting the affectations of FDR's good neighbor, rearmament signaled that a country saw those outside its borders in terms of threat. He blamed democrats as well as autocrats for this "world disease" that distracted from the real fight against the Great Depression. As he stated in one letter, "The re-armament complex in England seems to hinder any positive action."[27]

Those who pursued rearmament were, in the world of Roosevelt's rhetoric, the opposite of neighborly. Indeed, the president connected his good neighbor metaphor overtly to the policy of disarmament in a public letter to the Daughters of the American Revolution. He stated that his policy was "to press, continually, for a limitation of armaments by international agreement." This commitment was, he reminded them, an outgrowth of "the principle of the good neighbor," which served "as the standard of the conduct of our foreign policy." He forecasted that these objectives would generate "an atmosphere of unprecedented friendliness" in the Americas and worldwide.[28]

FDR uplifted trade and stability because they would reduce the incentive for armament, and he praised disarmament as a means to promote this principle of "decency." "The difficult situation of modern civilization throughout the world demands for the social and economic good of human beings a reduction in armaments and not an increase," he wrote to one of his advisors. Disarmament agreements, mandating "inclusive" supervision and inspection, were "the only answer."[29] If FDR defined security in economic terms and, as biographer Frank Freidel writes, his "constant goal was world security," then his promotion of liberalized trade agreements and disarmament can be seen as an extension of New Deal principles to the international scene.[30] Rhetorically, Roosevelt and his subordinates refashioned the nation's discussion of foreign affairs around issues of liberal internationalist concern: free trade, disarmament, reason, order, civilization, peace, and stability. All these terms operated as symbols of security, suggesting that the world could become unified, harmonious, and peaceful. It was, as historian Robert Dallek put it, "a new crusade to save the world from itself."[31]

This vision, however, faced challenges. As in his domestic rhetoric, Roosevelt's foreign policy discourse carried a flip side, creating a moral dichotomy between those who stood with the president and those who were against his cause. Just as he listed a series of proposals to be adopted such as disarmament and nondiscriminatory trade, so also did he provide a corresponding series of negative principles to be resisted: imperialism, autarky, militarism, and economic nationalism. The specific dangers the administration hoped to forestall—aggression, war, poverty, and economic depression—were grouped together in the president's rhetoric as a single danger that threatened the peaceful, civilized, decent, and cooperative neighborhood FDR wished to bring about.[32] This danger emanated from two potential sources according to Roosevelt's rhetoric: imperialism and aggressor nations.

Imperialism and Aggression

FDR freely used the language of imperialism to support the New Deal, decrying his corporate enemies as "private empires within the Nation" stifling effective government and telling Americans that "industrial efficiency does not have to mean industrial empire building."[33] As Andrew Preston observes, the continuities between Roosevelt's rhetorical treatment of empire and concentrated wealth are "striking," as he often deployed "anti-imperial demonology" to build support for the New Deal, at times decrying autocracy and Henry Ford in the same breath.[34] In like fashion, although his foreign policy rhetoric generally stayed away from offering detailed, comprehensive plans, FDR freely critiqued the values and actions of other countries, thereby promoting his dream of a cooperative neighborhood of friendly nations by distinguishing his administration's approach to world affairs with that of its peers. He criticized imperialism as an organizational logic of international relations, regularly contrasting the United States' global aims with those of colonizing powers.

In the same way he used these critiques of empire to attack domestic opponents, so too did FDR denounce imperialism in the style of the New Deal. In one 1933 radio broadcast he declared, "The United States does not seek to annex Canada or any part thereof, to annex Mexico or any part thereof, or to annex Cuba or any part thereof. . . . The great majority of the inhabitants of the world feel the same as we do about territorial expansion or getting rich or powerful at the expense of their neighbors." This impulse to territorial aggrandizement by those who "still have imperialistic desires for expansion and domination in their minds or hearts" represented, in FDR's telling, the only true threat to "world peace." A good neighbor (the United States under Roosevelt) would serve the cause of peace, not conquest. As he continued, "It is only through constant education and the stressing of the ideals of peace that those who still seek imperialism can be brought in line with the majority."[35] By portraying the United States as peace's advocate in the global arena, FDR's rhetoric reiterated the central conceit of his New Deal discourse; namely, that his administration merely sought to enact the will of the majority in its political dealings. America, in Roosevelt's schema, championed peace on the rest of the world's behalf.

He drew a hard contrast between the United States and imperialism again in a 1935 speech in San Diego, arguing that US foreign policy deviated from colonialism at a basic level:

> This country seeks no conquest. We have no imperial designs. From day to day and year to year, we are establishing a more perfect assurance of peace with our neighbors. We rejoice especially in the prosperity, the stability and the independence of all of the American Republics. We not only earnestly desire peace, but we are moved by a stern determination to avoid those perils that will endanger our peace with the world.[36]

Juxtaposing "imperial designs" with Americans' desire for cordial relations—wrapped in an allusion to the "more perfect" language of the US Constitution—FDR's rhetoric highlighted the United States' essential peacefulness. By contrasting his policy with imperialism—a force that threatened stability, prosperity, and peace by enhancing one nation's power at the expense of others—Roosevelt positioned his good neighbor approach to foreign relations as prudential and mutually advantageous. His "gospel of the good neighbor," moreover, was consistent with long-standing American traditions of foreign policy-making—or so he argued:

> Our national determination to keep free of foreign wars and foreign entanglements cannot prevent us from feeling deep concern when ideals and principles that we have cherished are challenged. . . . Our flag for a century and a half has been the symbol of the principles of liberty of conscience, of religious freedom and of equality before the law; and these concepts are

deeply ingrained in our national character. . . . I hope from the bottom of my heart that as the years go on, in every continent and in every clime, Nation will follow Nation in proving by deed as well as by word their adherence to the ideal of the Americas—I am a good neighbor.[37]

By fixing neighborliness as the guiding ideal of international politics and linking it to religious liberty, equality, and freedom of conscience, Roosevelt promoted a vision of global affairs to rival that of the imperialists. His critique of empire specifically targeted the European powers, seeing in their conquest of land and establishment of colonies the same selfishness that enriched the elite at the expense of the common people. His rhetoric thereby echoed the populist, us-versus-them style of his domestic New Deal discourse.

As David Zietsma has pointed out, the rhetoric of "good neighborism" created a discursive "world of neighbors [portrayed as] intrinsically impoverished and in need of U.S. beneficence," reflecting Roosevelt's intention to promote American economic power through international trade. It was implemented most explicitly in Latin America, where "U.S. economic policies designed to illustrate American neighborliness increasingly relegated Latin American nations to a mono-culture while U.S. goods flooded their markets."[38] Unlike the New Deal, which intended to set a solid economic floor under each individual, the good neighbor policy was principally designed to establish a firm foundation for the world system as a whole. The symbols of insecurity to be monitored abroad were not the poverty and suffering of individuals, as they were in the United States, but the autarkic and militaristic policies of foreign governments.

On a practical level, the Roosevelt administration opposed imperialism because it erected commercial barriers to trade. To that end, Hull told British diplomats that a program of free trade would eventually "restore full and stable prosperity and conditions of permanent peace." If Britain would leave its closed trading bloc "it would literally thrill . . . the forces of law, order, morality, and religion everywhere." The only alternative he could see was "further movement by all countries toward commercial anarchy."[39] In the end, "a few desperado nations . . . would be meandering up and down the earth taking by force what the necessities of their own nationals would require."[40] Hull's admonition pointed toward the second danger to Roosevelt's global neighborhood: aggressive, revanchist powers.

As it did with imperialism, the Roosevelt administration juxtaposed its foreign policy with that of "aggressor nations" such as Italy, Germany, and Japan. In the thirties, watching the rise of fascism, Hull focused more on the threat of war than the hope for peace, sounding the alarm for trade, peace, and civilization itself: "There is no more dangerous cause of war than economic distress, and no more potent factor in creating such distress than stagnation and paralysis in the field of international commerce." Again: "Fierce and unregulated struggles among nations for trade produce both economic and political disturbances. They are almost certain precursors of war." The "suicidal movements" of extreme nationalism, if not stopped, would soon "wreck our entire structure of western civilization." With FDR's approval, he sent a message to the Japanese government with a stern, dire prophecy: "International practice must envisage an orderly world based on law in which all can live; or else all peoples must resign themselves to the progressive destruction resulting from an international anarchy based on uncontrolled force."[41] Hull's intense language reflected the seriousness with which the administration regarded "uncontrolled force." If economic energies were not safely channeled into commerce, Hull and his boss asserted, then they would break out in unrestrained destruction.

FDR was willing to admit that liberalized trade might not prevent war. But he agreed that "without a more liberal international trade[,] war is a natural sequence." He praised Belgian efforts "to restore a more stable world order. . . . I feel strongly that the importance of economic equilibrium as an aid to world peace has often been underestimated."[42] For him, maintaining an even worldwide balance of power was as much a commercial goal as it was a military question. If the "aggressor" nations created closed trading blocks, Roosevelt argued, they would become immune to pressures such as economic sanctions, and fear of aggression would prevent nations from entering into new trade agreements. This, in turn, would deprive the United States of its (limited) diplomatic leverage via economics. And the aggressors were transforming the world at a much faster rate than he was. "Trade treaties are just too goddamned slow," he told Treasury Secretary Henry Morgenthau: "The world is marching too fast."[43]

Roosevelt indicated his fear of Germany and Japan from the outset of his presidency. At his very first cabinet meeting he warned that the United States might go to war with those two powers. Before he was even inaugurated, he had mused that it might be better to go to "war with

Japan now rather than later."[44] Scarcely a year later he floated the idea of a conference to impose a disarmament plan on Germany, including inspection of all weapons plants. If the Germans refused, he suggested an economic boycott, which "would quickly bring Germany to terms." Reviewing his first year in office, Ninkovich comments: "One is struck by the premonitory fears in the president's world picture at that time."[45] In 1934 he continued to discuss the possibility of an economic boycott of Germany. A year later, he told his secretary of agriculture that he was interested in shutting off Japan's supply of cotton to help China in its brewing conflict with Tokyo.[46] In private correspondence, he cast Germany and Japan as aggressors, and Mussolini's invasion of Abyssinia gave him reason to include the Italians among their number too.[47]

Publicly, the president castigated the "aggressor" nations in vivid biblical language. The 1936 State of the Union Address provides a strong case in point. He told his audience that some nations had "reverted to the old belief in the law of the sword, or to the fantastic conception that they, and they alone, are chosen to fulfill a mission and that all the others among the billion and a half human beings in the world must and shall learn from and be subject to them." In contrast to the good neighborhood of equals, these countries "seek the restoration of their selfish power." The leaders of these nations, he warned, embraced "autocracy toward labor, toward stockholders, toward consumers, toward public sentiment." Propounding the allusion with flourish, FDR drew his appeal to a close: "Their weapon is the weapon of fear. . . . Autocrats in smaller things, they seek autocracy in bigger things. 'By their fruits ye shall know them.'"[48] This language potently fused Roosevelt's previous rhetoric with contemporary fears and religious truths. As Murphy writes, "The wrath of a biblically literate president is a terrible thing to behold."[49]

As FDR's "stockholder" lines suggest, the administration defined Germany, Japan, and Italy as dangers as much for their closed economic systems as anything else. Williams notes that within the administration this talk was going on "before those countries launched military attacks into or against areas that the United States considered important to its economic system." What those countries *had* done by 1935 was to embark on a program of economic autarky, which would further limit US access and expansion in foreign markets just as Whitehall constrained Americans' commercial opportunities within the British empire. As Williams recognizes, "The American outlook defined as a danger any nation (or group) that challenged or limited such expansion. . . . American recovery and prosperity were made dependent upon the acceptance of American policies by the rest of the world."[50] Within the administration, aggressor nations were defined as aggressors as much as for their economic actions as their military adventurism (in the case of Italy and Japan) or rearmament (Germany).

The president thereby framed the challenges posed both by imperialism and by the rising fascist powers in binary terms rendered intelligible through his New Deal focus on economics and liberal internationalist emphasis on trade. His rhetoric at times blurred the distinct problems European empires and revanchist fascism presented to his good neighbor foreign policy. Indeed, Preston notes that FDR "came to portray Italy, Japan, and Germany as imperialistic powers of the most atavistic kind."[51] In short, the Roosevelt administration's foreign policy rhetoric, like its New Deal discourse, was built on the principle of moralistic dichotomy. Similarly to how trade, stability, disarmament, prosperity, and peace were all interconnected under FDR's rubric of neighborliness, so symbols of insecurity such as imperialism, aggression, rearmament, and economic isolation were rhetorical links in a single metonymic chain. All these opposites were woven together to tell a single mythic story about a pervasive, fluid, vaguely defined sense of evil threatening an equally pervasive, fluid, vaguely defined vision of civilized goodness.

Like he did in domestic politics, Roosevelt placed virtually every foreign policy issue within this frame of moral dualism, aided by his rhetorical arsenal of metaphors.[52] Evil formed "a seamless whole," and good citizens should be inclined to oppose it here and there.[53] He told Canadian prime minister MacKenzie King that reliance upon force was "armed banditry," uncivilized and irrational, leading to only two outcomes: "reliance upon force" or "reliance upon reason—Public opinion." This bifurcation extended into a clear-cut distinction between "nations which are arming with some intent, expressed or implied, to use those armaments for offensive purposes on the one side and nations which are arming with great reluctance, obviously, for defensive purposes only." Roosevelt left no doubt that the United States was in the camp of "great reluctance."[54] He publicly proclaimed this binary view of international affairs in his 1936 Chautauqua address: "We seek to dominate no other Nation. We ask no territorial expansion. We oppose imperialism. We desire reduction in world armaments. We believe in democracy; we believe in freedom; we believe in peace. We offer to every Nation of the world the handclasp of the good neighbor." Hence, even as he affirmed the nation's total commitment to peace—"We are not isolationist except insofar as we seek to isolate ourselves completely from war"—he also warned Americans that "our people should not overlook problems and issues which, though they lie beyond our borders, may, and probably will, have a vital influence on the United States of the future."[55] Though friendly, the good neighbor was mindful of others' intent.

The Roosevelt administration tended to phrase every question of ultimate importance in these simple terms, the president exuding supreme confidence, as biographer James MacGregor Burns records, "in the essential ethical rightness of his own position."[56] This moral dualism reflected the progressives' narrative of orderly civilization inexorably triumphing over chaos. Roosevelt told this story through a litany of metaphors that "[blotted] up potential policy objections by strategically framing the meaning of present events."[57] When confronted with a world that proved recalcitrant to his entreaties for disarmament and trade, however, FDR's idealistic rhetoric that echoed his foreign policy discourse of the 1920s began reverting to the more hardline stances he had espoused as assistant secretary of the navy in the 1910s. Combined with his moral dualism, this renewed appreciation for the dangers lurking around the globe led him to increasingly articulate his foreign policy priorities in the language of what was rapidly becoming known as geopolitical "realism."

FDR's Rhetorical Synthesis: Internationalism, Realism, and Dualism

At its most basic level, realism consists of the view that view nation-states, driven by an insatiable drive for power, battle each other in an anarchic, Hobbesian war of all against all in which one country can be stopped only by the force of another state or group of states. In 1932 Reinhold Niebuhr connected this idea to the doctrine of original sin in *Moral Man and Immoral Society*, writing, "The selfishness of human communities must be regarded as an inevitability. Where it is inordinate it can be checked only by competing assertions of interest; and these can be effective only if coercive methods are added to moral and rational persuasion. . . . Thus society is in a perpetual state of war."[58] To this diagnosis

he added an addendum that Mahan himself would embrace: "a technical age has made economic power the most basic power, from which
political power is derived."[59] Niebuhr's influential work helped spread
the reasoning presaged by others before him: there would always be
international actors driven by irrational forces, and therefore civilized
nations would always face dangers and should adopt what Reynolds has
called a "preemptive concept of national security"—the active development of strength by civilized nations to restrain the ability of potential
aggressors.[60]

While most liberal internationalists in the United States drew selectively on the intellectual stock of the realists, they generally accepted
the idea that nations compete, arm, and go to war because they are
motivated by greed and a lust for power (irrational and ineradicable impulses of human nature). In FDR's case, he tended to adapt Niebuhrian
thought to his more fundamental pattern of moral dualism. When he
applied this model to foreign policy, the boundary between security and
insecurity—the line along which catastrophe threatened—could now
be found everywhere. Early in 1939, Roosevelt told a group of senators
that "if the Rhine frontiers are threatened the rest of the world is too."
Although he denied reports that he had said America's frontier rested
on the banks of the Rhine, he again told the senators that there was
good reason to fear "the gradual encirclement of the United States by
the removal of first lines of defense."[61] Indeed, the Roosevelt administration more and more came to define the nation "as an embattled outpost
in a hostile world."[62] The president wrote to his ambassador in Poland
that the "continued existence of independent nations in Europe" was
"of actual moment to the ultimate defense of the U.S." Publicly, FDR
told a press conference that there were about thirty countries whose
political and economic independence "seriously affect the defense of
the United States."[63]

In the dualistic logic of the Roosevelt administration's foreign policy
discourse, resistance to the liberal international system anywhere could
threaten US interests everywhere. Hull left no doubt on that point: "A
threat of hostilities anywhere cannot but be a threat to the interests of
all nations." Again: "There can be no serious hostilities anywhere in the
world which will not one way or another affect interests or rights or obligations of this country." He later stated that this evolved into his leading
theme "for years to come."[64] The logical consequences of this thinking
were inescapably realist. In any serious hostility anywhere in the world,

US interests would in some way be threatened, meaning any attempts to alter the geopolitical status quo through warfare represented a source of insecurity for the United States.[65] To remain aloof from world conflicts (what was popularly called "isolationism") would be, in Hull's words, "a fruitful source of insecurity."[66] Consequently, the administration's viewpoint combined internationalism's focus on trade, realism's concern with the balance of power, and dualism's reductive division of the world into grand conflicts of good against evil to frame global affairs such that regardless of whether the United States itself got entangled in perilous situations abroad or not, it would face insecurity so long as a potential conflict might arise. Stated otherwise, in FDR's foreign policy rhetoric, change itself became a source of insecurity.

At the same time, the presence of revanchist, fascist powers meant that this source of insecurity was not going to disappear any time soon. FDR acknowledged that these "aggressors" were unlikely to change; once war broke out in Europe, he would remark that "there can be no reasoning with an incendiary bomb."[67] Although he had once written privately that he was "deeply impressed" by what Mussolini had accomplished in Italy, Roosevelt was less charitable to Hitler, calling him "a madman" when he first came to power, adding that some of his advisors were "even madder than he is." He told his ambassador to Germany, William Dodd, that "the German authorities are treating the Jews shamefully. Whatever we can do to moderate the general persecution by unofficial and personal influence ought to be done."[68] Speaking of the Japanese in early 1939, he told a group of journalists, "When people get into that frame of mind, you never can tell where they are going to stop."[69] Two months later he warned journalists that Hitler planned to "dominate South America without a war," admitting that "from Hitler's point of view, it is rational. And if any of us were in his place," he added, "with his methods, we would do it."[70] This was another extension of the logic of Roosevelt's New Deal rhetoric. Like FDR's economic royalists, who pursued their private good over the nation's prosperity, so aggressor nations sought their own selfish gain at the expense of all nations' welfare.

Unlike the president's domestic opponents, however, the future Axis powers could not be so easily disciplined by acts of Congress and appeals to the American people. If potential conflict anywhere on earth would harm American interests, then Germany, Japan, and Italy represented a problem for FDR, as these countries sought to reshape the global order to their advantage throughout the 1930s. Roosevelt described all three nations as threats to civilization itself. He wrote to the president of the Council on Foreign Relations that he desired to "solidify the forces of non-aggression." He expressed a similar sentiment to Ambassador Dodd at the end of 1935: "I do not know that the United States can save civilization but at least by our example we can make people think and give them the opportunity of saving themselves. The trouble is that the people of Germany, Italy and Japan are not given the privilege of thinking."[71] While his public discourse sometimes expressed a vision of universal peace and prosperity, he always tempered it with skepticism, especially in private, as he had during World War I. Writing to a journalist in 1939, FDR stated that he had no expectation of a "permanently lasting peace—that is a peace which we would visualize as enduring for a century or more." The best he dared hope for was a mere "patched up temporizing peace which would blow up in our faces in a year or two."[72]

The president used this explosion metaphor to convey his unease as early as 1934, when he agonized over the "hair trigger times" he inhabited and worried about what would happen if "the European bomb explodes." In an open letter circulated in 1938 reminding European leaders that "every civilized nation" had signed the Kellogg–Briand Treaty, he urged them to choose the rational path of negotiation to "escape the madness of a new resort to war." If they fell into that "madness," he warned them of "the consequences of the world catastrophe. . . . The economic system of every country involved is certain to be shattered," plunging all nations into "a long chaos."[73] Sounding the economic alarm, he predicted that war could "drag civilization to a level from which world-wide recovery may be all but impossible." And by 1939, he described all of Europe as a "madhouse," telling one correspondent that a time would soon have to come that either "the madhouse burns down or becomes sane."[74] Such language powerfully shaped the imaginations of its hearers, and, as Frank Ninkovich contends, Roosevelt's "articulation of this apocalyptic global strategic threat . . . set internationalism on a new course by emphasizing the catastrophic implications of modernity's downside."[75] If metaphors ultimately work to "construct political meaning and orient political action," as Francis A. Beer and Christ'l De Landtsheer contend, then these metaphors (bomb, gangster, madhouse) primed audiences to fear another world cataclysm.[76]

In response to the threat of war—and the utter upheaval of the hoped-for liberal order war would represent—the Roosevelt administration did try to act in limited ways to dent Nazism's ascent. Even as he officially told his ambassador that German politics "were not a governmental affair," FDR still ordered the State Department in 1933 to "take every step that one Government can take in a situation where another Government is dealing with a domestic problem of its own."[77] Three years later, Roosevelt warned Ambassador Dodd that a president had to be ready for war, "just like a Fire Department," thereby reviving the "war as fire" metaphor he had used years earlier to support the League of Nations. In 1938, when he heard about Kristallnacht, he said that he could "scarcely believe that such things could happen in a twentieth-century civilization." Despite his moral outrage at fascism and the threat to his liberal internationalist vision the Nazi regime symbolized, however, Roosevelt (like other world leaders) stopped short of more aggressive attempts to curb German behavior on the international stage.[78] Furthermore, FDR's sympathy for German Jews did not lead him to increase the quantity of refugee visas granted by the United States, and he publicly repeated the unverified claim that American officials had apprehended among refugee applicants "a number of definitely proven spies."[79] In sum, Roosevelt's matrix of internationalism, realism, and dualism led him to interpret the actions of aggressor nations—because they sought to disrupt global stability—as a danger to the United States, yet he was inclined to pursue less direct courses of action to address the insecurity (as he saw it) that threatened his country and the world. He did so for a reason—the staunch resistance of the American public to anything that smacked of "entanglement" in European affairs.

Roosevelt's Response and the Rhetorical Challenge

Even as he described Germany in the ardent language outlined previously, FDR studiously avoided actions or public statements that would indicate he was contemplating conflict. He had little choice. The idea of getting involved in a foreign war was unthinkable to the vast majority of Americans. In 1931, over twelve thousand clergymen announced that they would never support any war. In 1932, a vehicle procession one mile in length delivered President Hoover a peace petition. In 1933, over fifteen thousand students across sixty-five colleges publicly committed themselves to pacifism or vowed to only serve in the military in the case of invasion. In 1935, fifty thousand US veterans paraded through Washington on the eighteenth anniversary of American entry into World War I, and days later roughly one hundred and seventy-five thousand college students held a one-hour strike against war.[80] Hence, it is unsurprising that Manfred Jonas began his classic study of anti-interventionism with the words of *The Christian Century* in 1935: "Ninety-nine Americans out of a hundred would today regard as an imbecile anyone who might suggest that, in the event of another European war, the United States should again participate in it." The American Institute of Public Opinion set the exact figure at 95 percent a year later.[81] Ernest Hemingway summed up his fellow citizens' feelings with his literary flair: "Of the hell broth that is brewing in Europe we have no need to drink. . . . We were fools to be sucked in once in a European war, and we shall never be sucked in again."[82]

Indeed, so staunch was the public feeling against any sort of international involvement that the Senate voted to kill American participation in the World Court—an innocuous body with no legal jurisdiction over US citizens—following the vociferous opposition of William Randolph Hearst and Father Coughlin.[83] In the judgment of H. W. Brands, "Only the willfully obstinate, one would have thought, could oppose such a worthy goal."[84] This public mood, coupled with the immense need for domestic spending, meant that the military's budget remained far too low to be effective at checking the rapidly rearming revanchist powers.[85]

Consequently, FDR bided his time as he tried to persuade others to follow his foreign policy lead throughout the New Deal years. "At home and abroad," as William Appleman Williams writes, "peace and order were the main objectives of the New Deal. In general, therefore, the United States at first gave ground before the assertiveness of Germany, Japan, and Italy." In 1937, FDR wrote to a British diplomat friend: "I still believe in the eventual effectiveness of preaching and preaching again." He told Columbia University president Nicholas Murray Butler that, in foreign affairs, "much can be accomplished by the iteration of moralities even though the tangible results seem terrifically slow."[86] These writings indicate that FDR conceptualized the foreign policy challenges he saw in fundamentally rhetorical terms; that is, Roosevelt sought to change public opinion through his speech so that it would support a more robust response to the dangers he perceived. He would, as it were, preach and preach again his internationalist gospel of the good neighbor to the American people until it won him enough adherents to act.

In the meantime, he tried to do what he could. Three episodes illustrate his attempt to navigate the political constraints of the situation to address the insecurity he saw in the actions of Germany, Japan, and Italy. The first, his "Quarantine" speech given in the fall of 1937, illustrated the limits of his ability to guide public opinion when it came to a more interventionist foreign policy. Speaking in Chicago, he lamented that "the hopes for peace thus raised have of late given way to a haunting fear of calamity," tracing this fear's origin to the rise of newly aggressive powers: "The present reign of terror and international lawlessness began a few years ago." These countries, which remained nameless, had engaged in "unjustified interference in the internal affairs of other countries," they "are fomenting civil warfare in nations that have never done them any harm," and their actions led "vast numbers of women and children [to be] ruthlessly murdered by bombs from the air." Having detailed the aggressors' wrongdoings, FDR then asserted the central belief motivating his foreign policy: "Let no one imagine that America will escape, that America may expect mercy, that this Western Hemisphere will not be attacked and that it will continue tranquilly and peacefully to carry on the ethics and the arts of civilization." As he often did, Roosevelt then turned to a metaphor to communicate the essence of his appeal, this time comparing international aggression to a contagious disease, declaring, "It seems to be unfortunately true that the epidemic of world lawlessness is spreading."[87]

In the face of such a potentially devastating "disease," the president suggested the idea of quarantining the aggressors "to protect the health of the [world] community."[88] He apparently had considered this turn of phrase for several months; nevertheless, as rhetorical scholar Halford Ryan contends, "The quarantine metaphor was the wrong prescription."[89] Thanks to the legal restraints imposed by the Neutrality Act of 1936, there was little the president could do in terms of policy to enforce a quarantine of Japan or any other country. The epidemiological energy implied by a "quarantine" went nowhere. The day after the speech FDR retreated before a press conference, saying that his speech merely represented "an attitude, and it does not outline a program."[90] Still, he expected his moralism to strike a nerve. Several days later he wrote to his former Groton rector Endicott Peabody that he expected "a growing response to the ideal that when a few nations fail to maintain certain fundamental rules of conduct, the most practical and the most peaceful thing to do in the long run is to 'quarantine' them. I am inclined to think that this is more Christian . . . that the world should go to war with them."[91] Whether this path was "more Christian" or not, the speech failed to substantially shift public opinion or significantly alter American policy toward Japan (although, to be sure, FDR's speech created a powerful and lasting image of insecurity that would serve as an inventional resource for future presidents).

Second, Roosevelt strongly endorsed attempts of other powers to reach a negotiated agreement with aggressor nations, particularly Germany. In September 1938, his and the world's attention was fixed upon the Sudetenland crisis and British prime minister Neville Chamberlain's efforts to appease Hitler. By then, FDR was privately referring to Hitler's regime as not merely bad neighbors but "the leading gangsters." Extending this analogy, he compared Britain to the police as he told his ambassador in Ireland that he would wait to see the outcome: "If a Chief of Police makes a deal with the leading gangsters and the deal results in no more hold-ups, that Chief of Police will be called a great man—but if the gangsters do not live up to their word the Chief of Police will go to jail."[92] After Chamberlain reached agreement with Hitler at Munich, FDR cabled the British leader simply: "Good man." Reflecting on the war scare, he told his ambassador to Italy, "I am not a bit upset over the final result." The president made it known to the European powers that he was politically constrained in what actions he could take to deal with Hitler. As he told Chamberlain, "Public opinion in the United States will only support . . . measures of pacific cooperation."[93] By telling the prime minister this message, FDR made it clear that Britain and France needed to handle the European powder keg without the expectation of US assistance. Early in 1939 he wrote in a private letter, "What the British need today is a good stiff grog, inducing not only the desire to save civilization but the continued belief that they can do it."[94] If FDR could not convince the American people to act against the aggressors, at least he would try to strengthen the resolve of nations that could.

Though he expressed hopes for peace, Roosevelt concurrently expressed a fear that peace was no longer possible. When his ambassador in Germany told him, "All the representatives of democratic countries in Berlin have again and again said, 'the United States is the only nation that can save our civilization,'" the president responded: "I agree with you." America was still, he told the world, "the last best hope of earth," and it was up to "this generation" to save it.[95] While Chamberlain was meeting with Hitler, Roosevelt told Phillips that a war would inevitably break out within the next five years. When that happened, he foretold, the United States "will be in a position to pick up the pieces of European civilization. And help them save what remains of the wreck." But that was "not a cheerful prospect." A few weeks later he wrote to MacKenzie King: "Unless very soon Europe as a whole takes up important changes in two companion directions—reduction of armaments and lowering of trade barriers—a new crisis will come." "The immediate test" of Hitler's intention, he told King, was his willingness to make those two changes.[96] By confiding his pessimism in his Canadian counterpart yet again, FDR laid the diplomatic groundwork for the defense of North America even as he publicly spoke of peace and privately urged European leaders to find some way to keep it.

Of course, no lasting peace agreement materialized, leading to the third episode in which FDR tried to act in response to the threat posed by the aggressors to world peace within the constraints imposed by US public opinion. In the spring of 1939, the president sent a last-ditch letter to Hitler himself, stressing the rationality of disarmament and trade that stood against the madness of another war. The White House released the letter to the press simultaneously so as "to have it broadcast widely so that it would be received by as much of the German and Italian public as could possibly be reached."[97] The president was afraid to press his demands more forcefully, lest they be rejected, which he feared would make matters worse.[98] "This situation must end in catastrophe unless a more rational way of guiding events is found," he wrote to the Führer, arguing that the more reasonable course would be disarming and "opening up avenues of international trade to the end that every nation of the earth may be enabled to buy and sell on equal terms in the world market as well as to possess assurance of obtaining the materials and products of peaceful economic life." These were, in Roosevelt's own words, the "essential problems."[99] He did not require that Hitler cease persecuting his political opponents, Jews, or other minorities. He asked only that Hitler signal the faintest willingness to join the liberal internationalist order US leaders were hoping to build—to play the game of foreign affairs according to rules as FDR saw them. Hitler proved Roosevelt's fears well founded by publicly scorning his appeal, mockingly reading the letter before the assembled Reichstag.

As these episodes reveal, the ideal of a single global economic order was still shaping FDR's concept of security. Germany represented danger, he told journalists, because it was "seeking a new economy other than that which has been pursued for centuries by the world in unrestricted trading between nations." Similarly, he worried that "the aggressor group" was paying lower wages and thus selling its goods more cheaply abroad. If this were allowed to continue, he argued, America could compete only by lowering wages or subsidizing its exports, which would mean higher taxes.[100] Inseparable from Roosevelt's efforts to prevent war was the self-reinforcing matrix of liberal internationalism, realism, and dualism that permeated his rhetoric, interpreting the Axis powers' actions in a way that accentuated the threat they posed to a stable, rules-based world order centered on trade and commercial development—and by extension, the threat they presented to the United States' economic recovery. Indeed, since the president promised to fight the Depression with the full fury of war and the aggressor nations impended either a closed global economy or another major conflict, it is little surprise FDR portrayed them as a threat to the United States. New York governor Herbert Lehman recalled talking to the president often about the prospect of war, later saying, "I'm convinced that as early as '38, he was certain in his own mind that we were bound to be involved in the War."[101]

In short, the logic of Roosevelt's foreign policy rhetoric during the New Deal era inexorably led to a conclusion of fear. If the entire world is one neighborhood, what other response could there be when "gangsters" threaten to burn down the home next door? If disarmament was the key to ensuring a peaceful world order, how should one respond in the face of rapid rearmament by revanchist dictators? Each element of the president's discourse played a role in framing the global environment in this manner. FDR's dualism, an extension of his political progressivism, divided the world into straightforward clashes of good versus bad. His realism, with its roots in the writings of Mahan and his days as assistant secretary of the navy, taught that strength was the only guarantee of security in a world where uncivilized threats may emerge from unexpected places. And his liberal internationalism, by casting the globe in economic terms, postulating the importance of unrestricted trade, and prioritizing stability above all else, rendered countries that deviated from these principles as irrational, lawless aggressors. Never a theorist, Roosevelt pragmatically blended all these streams into a broad narrative that by 1939 warned the nation of perils on every side. His penchant for such dire language and his preference for liberal internationalist policy prescriptions were two sides of the same coin—two expressions of the same paradigm shift in US foreign policy discourse over which he presided. But first he would have to convince the American people of his case, overcoming the objections of the anti-interventionist movement.

Conclusion

FDR's presidency began in the desperate throes of the Great Depression, a challenge he and many others compared to armed conflict. Soldiers and machine gunners silently guarded his swearing-in to the nation's highest office; one journalist compared the scene to "a beleaguered capital in wartime."[102] As actual war drew near, Roosevelt used the power of his language to elaborate on the kind of foe the civilized world, in his telling, now faced. He put even more emphasis on the threat fascism posed to morality, religion, and democracy itself, describing the aggressors in eschatological terms. "Storms from abroad directly challenge three institutions indispensable to Americans," he declared in his 1939 annual message to Congress. "The first is religion. It is the source of the other two—democracy and international good faith. . . . An ordering of society which relegates religion, democracy and good faith among nations to the background" could "find no place within it for the ideals of the Prince of Peace. The United States rejects such an ordering, and retains its ancient faith."[103] Faced with a crisis of authority at home (Depression) and abroad (aggression) FDR invoked biblical imagery, religious warrants, and transcendent values to, in the words of Mary E. Stuckey, "[authorize] new forms of collective action" previously unimaginable in an American context.[104]

Since the "God-fearing democracies of the world" were now threatened by "international lawlessness," Americans had to "prepare to defend, not their homes alone, but the tenets of faith and humanity on which their churches, their governments and their very civilization are founded. . . . To save one we must now make up our minds to save all."[105] Changing tone from the "good neighborism" of his first inaugural address, FDR instructed Americans to steel themselves for another world war in which all the values they held dear had been targeted for destruction. In March 1939, he directed his trusted aide Sumner Welles to draft a speech; Welles wrote these words along "the lines you had in mind as you indicated them to me": "The outlook is very dark. . . . Nowhere in the world today does any real feeling of security remain."[106]

Roosevelt cited the combination of aggressive intent and new technology as sources of danger. The advent of air war meant that "any possible attack has been brought infinitely closer than it was 5 years or 20 years or 50 years ago," he told journalists. To the Business Advisory Council he explained that the British fleet and French army had always been a buffer protecting the United States. Now that buffer was no longer secure; the Western Hemisphere could be attacked "infinitely faster."[107] As a result, the United States needed to build its own infinitely faster means of defense. Roosevelt's private words suggest that his fears were sincerely felt. For example, he told his son James that national security required rapid government action "in these modern times where distance has been annihilated."[108] In another letter, he complained to Ambassador Joseph Kennedy that Americans did not understand "the 'relativity' of world geography and the rapid annihilation of distance and purely local economics."[109]

To instill a sense of that understanding, and the implications it entailed, was now FDR's mission. He warned newspaper editor William Allen White of the "greater chaos" the war would bring, expressing a particular fear that Germany and the Soviets might ally and win the war to rewrite the rules of global conduct. Then "the situation of your civilization and mine is indeed in peril. Our world trade would be at the mercy of the combine." But he saw no national will to rally against the danger. In fact, not even the clergy supported him. As Stuckey observes, they stood united in their "demand that the United States remain free of 'foreign entanglements' . . . to the extent that this reflected national opinion, it reveals the scale of the task that Roosevelt faced as he sought to bring the nation into the international arena in response to events that were starting to simmer in Europe."[110] He aptly summarized the rhetorical challenge before him: "Public opinion over here is patting itself on the back every morning and thanking God for the Atlantic Ocean (and the Pacific Ocean). My problem is to get the American people to think of conceivable consequences without scaring the American people into thinking that they are going to be dragged into this war."[111] In the world of FDR's rhetoric, the United States was already entangled. The question, for him, was how to convince Americans of his viewpoint and vision for America's role in the world. And that was a question others were willing to answer as well.

PART III

5 | The Debate over Intervention

War finally did break out on September 1, 1939, when the German invasion of Poland plunged Europe into war. Roosevelt reacted immediately, wielding his influence as president to interpret the dire events taking place. On the first day of the war, he presented the Nazi attack as firm evidence for his two-sided framing of world events, quickly denouncing Hitler's "inhuman barbarism . . . [that] sickened the hearts of every civilized man and woman." Two days later, his fireside chat linked the defense of civilization with the defense of religion and home: "We have every right and every reason to maintain as a national policy the fundamental moralities, the teachings of religion. . . . Most of us in the United States believe in spiritual values. . . . We seek to keep war from our firesides by keeping war from coming to the Americas."[1] With that last turn of phrase, FDR broached the vital question the German invasion raised for his fellow citizens: Was this a war to defend democracy, and if so, would it demand US entry?

The president's words gave voice to widely felt fears; upward of two-thirds of Americans believed that the Nazis ultimately aimed to attack the Western Hemisphere.[2] While war gave new urgency to this matter, Roosevelt had long brought attention to the possibility of an invasion in his public utterances. He did so as early as April 1938, when he had warned journalists that "a Fascist revolution in Mexico" might give Germany air bases there, from which it would launch attacks on the US mainland: "Mexico is awfully close to us. . . . Iowa could be in danger." On other occasions FDR had placed those hypothetical German bases in Venezuela or Brazil and made Kansas City, New Orleans, or St. Louis the threatened locale. He also claimed there existed "a lot of evidences" that the Japanese were "thinking to a certain extend in terms of this continent"[3] John Murphy notes, Roosevelt repeatedly aimed to shrink the distance Americans felt between themselves as the frightening events overseas, stressing "the potential speed of modern attack" afforded by the advent of air power, long-range bombers, and U-boats.[4]

As the German (and Soviet) attack against Poland rolled on, world events seemingly conspired to confirm the warnings about aggressor nations Roosevelt had made for years. The administration's hopes for a new liberal internationalist order had been dashed upon the harsh realities of aggression abroad, and now it appeared that the United States might be next in the line of fire. Certainly, many Americans at the time, and most since, agreed that the president had good reason to believe that the United States itself was in danger. From the outbreak of war through the spring of 1940, public opinion polls showed a consistent majority of Americans (often nearly two-thirds) believing that Germany ultimately aimed to attack the United States, or at least the Western Hemisphere. Even among those who feared a German attack, though, there were many who would not accept the president's dualism as a framework for interpreting the war. While half of the public viewed the war, at its outset, as a fight to defend democracy, half saw it as merely another European squabble over power and wealth.[5]

Indeed, the war shattered whatever consensus existed beforehand. Hitler's conquests set off broader debates surrounding the nature of the American constitutional system, the role of power in politics, the influence of finance in democracy, and the moral foundations of society. To wit: T. S. Eliot declared, "Certainly there is a sense in which Britain and America are more democratic than Germany; but on the other hand, defenders of the totalitarian system can make out a plausible case for maintaining that what we have is not democracy, but financial oligarchy."[6] University of Chicago president Robert Maynard Hutchins cautioned that "we come much closer to Hitler than we may care to admit. If everything is a matter of opinion, and if everybody is entitled to his own opinion, force becomes the only way of settling differences of opinion. And of course if success is the test of rightness, right is on the side of the heavier battalions."[7] Niebuhr rejected these sorts of admonitions, publishing *Christianity and Power Politics* in 1940 to signal his support for the war effort. Writing years later, Arthur Schlesinger Jr. reflected on what he had learned from Niebuhr in the first years of the war: "Traditionally, the idea of the frailty of man led to the demand for obedience to ordained authority. But Niebuhr rejected that ancient conservative argument. Ordained authority, he showed, is all the more subject to the temptations of self-interest, self-deception and self-righteousness. Power must be balanced by power."[8] Others such as Frank Buchman, an American missionary in England, called for "Moral Re-Armament," claiming that the European crisis was "fundamentally a moral one. The nations must re-arm morally."[9] Intellectuals, like politicians, pastors, journalists, and everyday citizens, disagreed over how to best diagnose the new international situation.

The war catalyzed these discussions and many others. As the previous quotations illustrate, any historical account that presumes a broad American consensus on the war, its meaning, and the appropriate national course of action is misleading. In point of fact, John Bodnar writes that "the significance of the struggle was the source of a widespread political and cultural debate. . . . The controversy was lengthy and extensive—carried out in literary circles, movie theaters, museums, public parks, veteran organizations, and the inner recesses of private minds— because ultimately it was not so much about the war as about national identity."[10] The debate over whether the United States should enter the war was therefore not a merely deliberative question but pitted rivaling conceptions of American identity—expressed through differing visions of the United States' role in the world—against each other in a discursive melee that would determine the future of the nation and globe. That debate was typified by a clash of competing rhetorical interpretations, each laying claim to the inheritances and traditions of US foreign policy as they struggled to make sense of the bewildering world in which Americans now found themselves.

War, Metaphors, Economics, and the Roosevelt Administration

After the conflict began, FDR pursued a careful rhetorical strategy of articulating a policy of formal neutrality while weaving together themes of moral judgment, American innocence, and the danger posed by the Axis powers to the United States.[11] Roosevelt consciously broke with Woodrow Wilson's admonition for Americans "to be neutral not only in deed but in thought" made twenty-five years prior, instead telling his fellow citizens that "even a neutral cannot be asked to close his mind or close his conscience." He followed this statement weeks later by asserting the nation's moral goodness by virtue of its innocence in the conflict: "The disaster is not of our making. No act of ours engendered the forces which assault the foundations of civilization." He urged Americans to link these familiar premises with the broader liberal internationalist narrative he had advanced over the previous years: "When peace has been broken anywhere the peace of all countries everywhere is in danger. . . . Every battle that is fought does affect the American future."[12] Roosevelt's rhetoric paired declarations of neutrality with an assertion of American innocence, working to fix all the interlocking symbols of insecurity developed over the past six years—aggression, autarky, war, isolation—firmly upon Germany.

In terms of policy, FDR did what he could to prevent a total Axis victory in the short run. His approach increasingly blurred the difference between containing Hitler's triumphs and aiding Allied militaries.[13] Yet Roosevelt, whose election team literally invented the tracking poll, was aware that the public was not ready to support any kind of direct American involvement.[14] In the early months of 1940, the absence of fighting in Europe (the so-called "Phony War") had eroded the fatalistic feeling that the United States would inevitably be drawn into the war. Until the fall of France, as historian Lynne Olson has written, "most Americans had viewed the war in Europe as if it were a movie . . . that had nothing to do with their own lives."[15] Whatever his personal views, FDR would not lead a nation toward war with so little support. To demonstrate his ostensible commitment to neutrality, early in 1940 Roosevelt sent his trusted aide Sumner Welles to talk to Hitler. As the president told British ambassador Lord Lothian, however, he did so not in the hope of finding peace but only so that he could issue a statement when Welles returned "making it clear that Germany was the obstacle to peace" and the aggressor.[16]

FDR's early approach to the war therefore consisted of two broad, preventative goals: forestalling Allied defeat and avoiding US entry into the war as a combatant. Roosevelt's public rhetoric tracked closely with these aims while also priming the American public to view the Axis powers as enemies. He seemed sure they eventually would be. Within days of the Nazi invasion of Poland FDR expressed agreement with Democratic National Committee chairman Jim Farley, who deemed that "we are to all intents and purposes in a state of war."[17]

Throughout this time period a wide range of analytical viewpoints emerged within the administration. These internal deliberations over how best to understand the war and its potential ramifications for the United States, always haunted by the greater question of US intervention, generally reflected Roosevelt's prior utterances by coalescing around the themes of rearmament, economics, and civilization. Often these discussions were governed by the logics of his previous metaphors.

For example, Roosevelt at times sounded ready to fight, in line with the language of "gangsters." In mid-May he told Morgenthau the nation would be at war in "60 or 90 days." Weeks earlier, he had already told his secretary of agriculture (and soon to be vice president) Henry Wallace that he wanted soldiers to guard the District of Columbia to prevent an enemy from burning it, as the British had done in 1812.[18] Another time FDR reportedly told Wallace that "the Germans had definite designs on our hemisphere." To resist those designs, he said, the United States needed only a strong air force and navy and an army just big enough to win "in Brazil—or some similar country—in case of invasion."[19] He confided in his secretary of state as well; "The only thing the Germans understand," he told Hull, "is a reply in kind."[20]

Reflecting the hopefulness of the good neighbor metaphor, others in the administration placed their hope in the economic balance underlying the conflict. Officials at the Departments of State and Commerce predicted that the German people may revolt due to resource shortages, stating that "there was trouble brewing in Germany."[21] Chief of naval operations Betty Stark reported in March, "Either oil or finances, or both, may be deciding factors. . . . Any one or combination of these could bring on peace without a definite military decision having been reached."[22] As late as July 1940, newly appointed secretary of war Henry L. Stimson argued that the "war was going to be decided by fuel and that Germany was really very short of fuel," forecasting German oil supplies "would be exhausted . . . in the autumn."[23] Secretary of the navy Frank Knox revived these hopes in a November 1940 speech. As he said, "Europe has insufficient supplies" of food and oil; there thus rested a "chance for ultimate success" with a (relatively bloodless) blockade.[24]

Regardless of metaphor, economics often served as the lens through which the German threat was understood. FDR told Senator Josiah Bailey that "if the Germans do dominate the world," Americans would lose "our own safety, the security of our own trade, the future of our own crops, the integrity of our own continent, and the lives of our own children." He asked Wallace to investigate what could be done for American farmers "if England and France were completely wiped out and we lost the entire European market."[25] He composed a speech that emphasized the dire commercial risk if Germany conquered Britain. Should Hitler vanquish Britain, a draft read, Americans "would be faced with competition by government-controlled and government-subsidized trade," which would diminish the US economy and eventually lead to state controls here at home.[26] In fact, in a letter to Senator David Walsh, Roosevelt actually downplayed the possibility that a future clash with Germany would be military in nature: "We are not going into war anyway unless Germany wishes to attack us." If the Germans wanted to make war on the United States, he added, they would easily find a trumped-up excuse.[27]

Many major figures echoed FDR's economic focus. Dean Acheson, assistant secretary for economic affairs, vocally mourned the decline of the prosperous world order preserved by the "Pax Britannica." Economic advisor Herbert Feis warned that the rules of "steady, ordinary development" were now gone due to Hitler's threat to Britain.[28] Hull feared that German control of Europe "would prevent any Europeans from trading with us except on conditions which Berlin lays down," perhaps even leading to "the disappearance of free enterprise." A group of top corporate executives worried in January 1940 over "whether or not the American capitalist system could continue to function if most of Europe and Asia should abolish free enterprise in favor of totalitarian economics as a result of this war." Stimson, like others in the administration, saw in the German blitzkrieg a challenge that was not only economic and geopolitical but civilizational: "Our civilization . . . the Caucasian civilization of Europe . . . is hanging by a thread."[29] Getting planes to the Allies, he said, "may mean the saving of our civilization."[30]

Like in Roosevelt's previous rhetoric, civilization emerged as a common *topos,* or place of invention, around which he composed his appeals. He decried the leaders of the Soviet Union as a threat to civilization after the Soviet invasion of "liberal, forward-looking" Finland in late 1939, declaring Stalin's "dictatorship as absolute as any other" on earth.[31] He wrote to Joseph Grew, his ambassador in Tokyo, that the Japanese "idea of civilization and human happiness is so totally different from ours," meaning they could represent yet another menace "if the Japanese government were to fail to speak as civilized twentieth century human beings." In a letter he praised the interventionist Committee to Defend America by Aiding the Allies as a "very great movement for saving America by helping to save our type of civilization and government."[32] When he decided to give Churchill fifty American destroyers in exchange for rights to British bases, he told his secretary: "Congress is going to raise hell about this. But even another day's delay may mean the end of civilization. . . . If Britain is to survive, we must act."[33] For FDR, saving Britain was conflated with saving civilization, an association he had long been taught.

Yet aid could only get the Allies so far, especially in the face of growing Japanese power in east Asia. "We cannot lay down hard-and-fast plans," Roosevelt wrote to Ambassador Grew.[34] Without greater freedom to substantially counteract the Axis threat—an impossibility without a corresponding change in public opinion—Roosevelt would find himself politically hamstrung to pursue measures that he thought would provide the nation with the security it needed. Reflecting his frustration, he wrote to the US High Commissioner for the Philippines that the outcome of any conflict with Japan and Germany "will depend far more upon what they do" than anything else.[35] The problem facing FDR was therefore rhetorical, as he needed to convince Americans to support more interventionist measures if he was to be empowered to effectively safeguard the nation's security. Otherwise, in the face of severe domestic resistance to US entry into the war, the administration could do little more than it already had: help the Allies within the confines of neutrality while vigorously debating how best to understand and respond to the world conflict.

For many Americans, the great turning point of history came not in September 1939 but in the late spring of 1940, when the German blitzkrieg swept across France and the Low Countries, leaving only a short boat ride between Hitler and the conquest of Great Britain, which would give him total domination of Europe. According to the liberal internationalism FDR had preached for years, US security rested on its economic interests, the superiority of its (Anglo-American) civilization, and a stable, lawful international order. Each of those elements was now grievously vulnerable to Axis aggression. Roosevelt's rhetoric consequently primed US citizens to view German and Japanese advances as ominous threats to the United States—which, if one accepted his interpretation of world events, they were.

As German armies swept across France and Japanese troops advanced in the Far East, it seemed easy to see this theory turning into reality. Media outlets like *Time* magazine encouraged their readers to view events through Roosevelt's lens of American innocence, powerlessness, and insecurity. "The U.S. felt defenseless," *Time* wrote, in words that helped create the mood it described: "The hurricane that had swept Europe, the gathering clouds in the Three Easts, had come, with nightmare speed, close, real and threatening. The reaction was profound—broad and deep. As in few times of peace the nation spoke as a whole and the voice came clear to Congress: Arm. Arm the U.S. for what may come."[36]

Looking back, Geoffrey Perrett described the public mood in the summer of 1940 in similar terms: "Nearly all believed now that Britain would soon be defeated and that when it was, their own country would find itself in grave danger." Yet Perrett added a crucial exception: "Nearly all, that is, except the staunchest isolationists."[37]

Anti-Interventionism: A Rival Interpretation

For Roosevelt, the isolationists—or more precisely the anti-interventionists, those who opposed all military intervention abroad—could not be lightly dismissed. Although anti-interventionism did not possess the popularity it once had by the spring of 1940, it remained a formidable political force. Both the Republican and the Democratic parties still included anti-intervention planks in their 1940 platforms.[38] Frontrunner for the GOP presidential nomination Thomas Dewey cautioned Americans that "there is no fever so contagious as war fever" in a May 28 campaign speech in Dallas, and his chief foreign policy advisor John Foster Dulles dismissed Hitler as a "passing phenomenon."[39] The *Wall Street Journal* mocked ads for "Stop Hitler Now!" and ran an editorial titled "A Plea for Realism" on June 12 that declared: "Our job today is not to stop Hitler."[40] University students around the nation held peace demonstrations; ten thousand students marched in New York City, 88 percent of Columbia University students objected to the war, University of Michigan students raised a swastika-emblazoned flag on the campus flagpole, and at the University of Chicago students brandished protest signs that read "The Yanks Are Not Coming!"[41]

Of course, the anti-interventionist vision went unrealized. Historians of the movement, such as Wayne Cole, have argued that structural changes in the world and American domestic life inevitably made anti-interventionism untenable by the 1940s.[42] Be that as it may, the Roosevelt administration's foreign policy was not inevitable, nor was it demanded by objective facts—as Nietzsche observed, "Facts are precisely what there is not, only interpretations."[43] Its structural imperatives were mediated by the particular way Hitler's conquests were interpreted through the lens of Roosevelt's foreign policy narrative that synthesized elements of dualism, realism, and liberal internationalism. And that interpretive framework was neither automatic or, logically speaking, necessary. As Denise Bostdorff contends, "Because of the symbolic nature of our political world, the issues that presidents discuss are not objective, independent entities, but linguistic constructions. Cities, weapons, the elderly, wildlife, and oil fields certainly exist; meaning, however, does not lie in these entities themselves, but in the language used to interpret them and the events in which they are involved."[44] Because citizens do not encounter political phenomena independent of the symbols used to describe them, we hold alongside Murray Edelman that "political language *is* political reality."[45] FDR, as a uniquely powerful rhetorical actor endowed with the strategic advantages of the presidency, offered an interpretation of world events that was compelling and, as it turns out, ultimately winsome. It does not follow that his account was necessarily objective, inevitable, or correct.

Eventually Roosevelt's view did become widely accepted as simple common sense, an obvious response to obvious facts. But he won that victory by purveying a complex blend of selective perceptions and subjective interpretations, the elements of which reinforced each other to form a single narrative that pointed to a set of conclusions that saw the Axis powers as enemies and American intervention as necessary. But until December 7, 1941, those conclusions were sharply contested. Looking back decades later, historian Arthur Schlesinger Jr. remembered the clash over intervention as "the most savage political debate in my lifetime," more intense than even the debate over the Vietnam war.[46]

Met with a rapidly changing international environment, it is no surprise that some Americans arrived at different interpretations of events and thus propounded alternative conclusions about US foreign policy than the president. The loud (and cacophonous) anti-interventionist voice was there in 1940, reminding the nation that quite different perceptions and interpretations were equally available, which would point to quite different conclusions than those of the administration. As a movement, then, anti-interventionism is worthy of scholarly attention not because we wish to reopen the debate over whether the United States should have fought Hitler or because the reasons FDR gave for American entry into the war were somehow wanting or false. Rather, the arguments advanced by the anti-interventionists are of interest because, as political rivals of the president, they influenced the rhetorical choices made by Roosevelt to advance his foreign policy vision, a vision whose foundational assumptions continue to influence American actions in the world today.

The anti-interventionists represented the last major political expression of a way of life once taken for granted, one premised on American separation from the political intrigues and great power politics practiced by the rest of the world. FDR's rhetoric, since it was uttered at least partially in reply to anti-interventionist critiques of his foreign policy, was thereby refracted through the arguments advanced by this rival vision. Since this study takes as its subject the evolution and impact of Roosevelt's foreign policy discourse, it is worth exploring the anti-interventionist stance(s) so as to better understand the president's own rhetoric given in response.

The contrast between the two opposing camps was far from complete. Most opponents of intervention actually shared Roosevelt's premises. Many agreed with him that Nazism was a moral evil; some anti-interventionists were among the most vehement critics of Nazism and fascism in general. There was even broader agreement that the United States was, and had always been, a morally innocent nation. Indeed, anti-interventionism was often motivated by a traditional American sense of home and the homeland as intrinsically pure, cut off from the evils of the Old World, preserving the highest ideals of civilization. This line of reasoning hearkened all the way back to George Washington, who as president saw "divine beneficence toward us" at work in the United States' "exemption hitherto from foreign war" and "the calamities which afflict so many other nations."[47] Both sides of the intervention debate agreed that the United States stood blameless in the conflict at hand and bore no responsibility for the network of causation leading up to the war.

Many anti-interventionists also admitted that innocent nations were sometimes forced to resist aggression in order to protect their security. Many agreed with the president that no one could predict where and when the aggressors might strike. Most of them were willing, and sometimes eager, to build up US military forces. Case in point, a May 1940 poll showed fully 94 percent of Americans willing to spend whatever was necessary to make US defenses secure.[48]

More broadly, both sides were bent on reinvigorating national identity by mounting a new defense of democracy.[49] Both interventionists and anti-interventionists argued that democracy was endangered, but the difference lay in what symbol of insecurity they saw as placing democracy in peril. The anti-interventionists parted ways with the president because for them the war, not Germany, was the main source of danger to the nation and to its democracy. The centralizing policies that the country would be forced to adopt in order to effectively wage war to defeat Hitler would create, in the words of newspaperman Frank Gannett, a "Russianized economic system" even vaster than the New Deal, choking out the economic liberty and political freedom essential to democratic governance.[50] Most of them dismissed FDR's dire warning that the United States itself might soon be vulnerable to attack. As former president Herbert Hoover jibed, "Every whale that spouts is not a submarine."[51] Regardless of Hitler's aims or long-range intentions, Germany "could as readily send an army to Mars as to the United States," the noted writer Oswald Garrison Villard insisted. "The fundamental strategic factors that make up America's impregnability" had not changed, another critic wrote, despite the German triumphs in Europe. "Chances of a successful invasion of North America . . . are negligible," said a third.[52]

Though anti-interventionism certainly correlated with anti-Roosevelt sentiment, opposition to US entry into the war extended well beyond the Republican Party. For example, professional military men were some of anti-interventionism's strongest supporters. As late as August 1941, a British military aide who met with many of his US counterparts reported: "Not a single American officer has shown the slightest keenness to be in the war on our side."[53] A few of those officers spoke out and explained their views. Major General James K. Pearsons charged that "alarmists who think we are wide open to attack are merely the victims of nightmares of ignorance." Rear Admiral Stanford C. Hooper made the point that the Germans had no bombers that could reach the American mainland either from Europe or from Brazil. And the most famous of all the anti-interventionists, aviator Charles Lindbergh, pleaded before the American public: "Let us stop this hysterical chatter of calamity and invasion. . . . No one wishes to attack us and no one is in a position to do so."[54]

In another instance, Lieutenant Colonel Thomas R. Phillips, of the army's general staff corps, took Roosevelt's argument about the danger of long-range bombers and stood it on its head. Even if the Germans developed bombers that could reach the United States, he argued, the critical fact was that the military had its own long-range bombers, which "made the American coast impregnable to invasion," because they would destroy most German troop ships before they ever reached American shores. A top administration figure, Adolf Berle, agreed that "if there is anything like an adequate [US] air force, a naval invasion of the Western hemisphere is out of the question." Similarly, some argued that if Japan occupied Hawaii, US bombers could render the occupation useless by cutting the Japanese supply lines.[55]

Thus, the debate over intervention was not about whether the United States was insecure. Both sides thought the nation was at risk, and both sides articulated that risk as a threat to the American democratic way of life. Rather, the crux of the debate turned on the sources and symbols of insecurity each side adopted. For interventionists, Hitler and the Axis powers represented a totalitarian threat to American democracy; they generally characterized the danger to the nation as economic, military, or civilizational in nature. Anti-interventionists, by contrast, disagreed far more over what should be done about Hitler, but they found common ground in rejecting war on the grounds that intervention would harm democracy at home and risk irreversibly entangling the United States in the affairs of faraway places abroad. As Senator William Borah said, "War is always the eternal enemy of democracy, the friend of communism, and the father of fascism."[56] Consequently, the bitter dispute between the administration and its critics did not center mainly on empirical facts that might prove or disprove whether Germany and Japan actually threatened the United States—the ostensive subject of debate—but on the interpretation of those facts. The rhetorical battle between Roosevelt and the anti-interventionists over the nation's rearmament program and preparations for military conflict served as surface manifestations of a much deeper dispute over the political future of the United States.[57] As the "Great Debate" over intervention progressed, each side turned to its chosen symbols of security and insecurity to make its case over the airwaves, in the newspapers, and across public discourse. To display these differences, it is worth outlining the anti-interventionist case in greater detail.

The Anti-Interventionist Case

The debate about intervention was ultimately a conflict between competing narratives about change and the future. Both sides agreed that the world of the early 1940s was caught up in a maelstrom of change that threatened the foundations of American life. The disagreement was about what sort of change was most dangerous and how it might best be controlled. From the president's point of view, the United States was now thoroughly embedded in a tangled web of international economic and political processes. With the fall of France, the entire web was threatened by the newly emerging power blocks in Europe and Asia. "Certainly we had hoped to live out our own lives under conditions at least somewhat similar to the past," Roosevelt wrote poignantly to Norman Thomas: "Today I am not so sure that even you and I can do that."[58] For liberal internationalists such as the president, instability was already an unavoidable fact. Therefore, the question was how to how to use the fact of entanglement to the nation's best advantage, to hopefully fend off the violent change being attempted by the Axis powers and build a new global system after the war's end. Collective security, underwritten by American-led economic and military alliances, would win the current war and then theoretically deter aggression, preventing future wars.

Anti-interventionists saw this drastic redefinition of America's global role, and the resulting transformation of US foreign policy, as itself the main change to fear. Most of them assumed that American interests could still be assessed independently of the rest of the world. It therefore made sense for them to argue that things at home were, and should remain, fundamentally stable. This perception of invulnerability was embedded, as both a cause and an effect, in the broader anti-interventionist viewpoint. In their dominant narrative, as Cole summarizes it, "The United States could more effectively lead the world to the good life by building and sustaining democracy, freedom, and prosperity at home than it could through military involvement in foreign wars. They opposed any American efforts to police the world or to rebuild the world in an American image."[59] Anti-interventionists, because they tended to measure security by the nation's fidelity to its founding ideals, largely calculated the state of the nation's safety without much recourse to the international setting.

In fact, many anti-interventionists doubted that efforts to rebuild the world could succeed in any event, given the huge differences they perceived between the United States and the rest of the world. It was useless to try to reform foreign peoples and habits, they warned. In the words of the America First Committee (AFC), "Why lend a hand to an alien band whose dreams we can never change?"[60] The prominent anti-interventionist writer Stuart Chase argued that such conversionary efforts would harm life at home as well as abroad: "Any attempt by the United States to forcibly impose a pattern on the Old World will not only fail, but almost certainly shatter the American pattern. This will leave the world without stability and without hope, anywhere." Among those who felt the firm hand of American control, many, "perhaps most of them, won't like it," he added, which would only lead to further conflict: "When in due course new Hitlers arise, we shall have to do it all over again."[61]

Astute anti-interventionists like Chase recognized the underlying structure of Roosevelt's response to change. In order to build a secure world, it would first be necessary to have a dependable policing system that could keep potential aggressors ("new Hitlers") at bay, and any such system would require the United States to serve as a police officer. Hence, the matter of dispute was how to define the areas that were critical to US security and within which the nation would act. In a reprise of the debates over US imperialism four decades before, this question served as a microcosm for competing visions of the nation's future. Like President McKinley, who in his last public utterance instructed Americans on "how near one to the other is every part of the world" since "distances have been effaced" by technology, interventionists in the mold of FDR argued that aggressors might threaten American interests from anywhere, necessitating US attention and potential action to offset aggression wherever it may be.[62]

For the majority of anti-interventionists, alternatively, there was already a clear line separating the secure from the insecure that ran along the coastlines of North America (though some might extend it to the whole Western Hemisphere). The America of ordinary homes and neighborhoods lay safely sheltered behind that line, and attempts to redraw it elsewhere would result in ever more American entanglement overseas. In this respect, the anti-interventionists echoed the turn-of-the-century arguments made by William Jennings Bryan against imperialism: "The destiny of this Republic is in the hands of its own people, and upon the success of the experiment here rests the hope of humanity. No exterior force can disturb this Republic, and no foreign influence should be permitted to change its course."[63] Like Bryan, anti-interventionists argued that Americans' exceptionality—and therefore security—was grounded on the choices made by their forefathers, and the nation risked abandoning that inheritance should it embark on military missions abroad. A strong security buffer confined to the nation's coastline could keep war and its attendant insecurity away from American shores. As long as it stayed that way, domestic life would remain stable and secure indefinitely.

Critics of Roosevelt's foreign policy advanced this argument against what they saw as the president's deliberate courtship of insecurity. As one critic in the anti-interventionist newsletter *Uncensored* (where most articles were anonymous) complained, FDR's talk of aggressors "still leaves the boundaries of 'American vital interests' undefined. . . . If we do not know where our vital interests begin, how can we decide intelligently what our defense needs are?" The influential anti-intervention leader Norman Thomas agreed. By mid-1940, he wrote, "Our eastern frontier, pushed back from the Rhine, became the English Channel; our western frontier was somewhere between Shanghai and Singapore. If neither the President nor the people was ready to answer explicitly the question 'What shall we defend?' it is no wonder that they were even vaguer in answering the second question 'How shall we defend it?'"[64] The anti-interventionists argued that a foreign policy containing no fixed line defining "vital interests" robbed Americans of their sense of security; it made defense needs unpredictable and allowed a virtually unlimited number of sources of insecurity to potentially demand the nation's attention. It made more sense to define the security perimeter close to home, see that it was secured, and then go about one's business feeling relatively safe. As Lindbergh put it, "National strength must be built within a nation itself and cannot be built by limiting the strength of others."[65]

In a particularly probing (though never published) essay, the anti-interventionist writer Lawrence Dennis highlighted the difference between a positive policy—"to build over here"—and a negative policy of limiting the strength of others by restraining them behind a constantly shifting line abroad:

> America has the chance to try to build a new order in this hemisphere without having to fight for such a chance. . . . If we fought outside this hemisphere, we should not be fighting for an opportunity to build a new order here; we should be fighting to prevent another power from building a new order over there. If we won that fight, the gain, if any, would be purely negative. We should not, thereby, have built another and better order abroad or at home. We should thereby have weakened and impoverished ourselves for the building of a new order at home.[66]

Dennis's bifurcating logic reveals the set of oppositions characteristic of anti-interventionist appeals: fighting versus not fighting, "here" versus "there," preventative measures versus constructive measures, national impoverishment versus (in contemporary parlance) nation-building at home.

Though it was rarely stated so clearly, the rival definitions of security at work served as the decisive issue whenever any particular aspect of the intervention question was discussed. For interventionists, national security required the power to resist the baneful effects of geopolitical change. For their opponents, the meaning of security went beyond such negative efforts overseas. As one *Uncensored* writer put it, "[Security] rests on many things that have very little to do with Hitler or the war."[67] The privileging of an anti-interventionist conception of security over a liberal internationalist understanding can be seen in five particular areas of public dispute: the hemispheric threat, economics, imperialism, the morality of the war, and the nation's future.

First, the most obvious arena in which the two rival views of security clashed was over the likelihood of an Axis invasion of Latin America. In addition to FDR's aforementioned claims that Germany sought to establish air bases in Brazil, which the anti-interventionists rejected, the administration was also concerned about the Axis powers' corporate footprint in the Western Hemisphere. These worries led the Roosevelt administration to infiltrate Transocean (a German news agency) offices in Latin America. FBI director J. Edgar Hoover was "convinced" that the company was a cover for Nazi agents.[68] In any case, historians have largely concluded that the anti-interventionists had the better case when it came to the possibility of hemispheric invasion. Hitler apparently did have secret plans to build bases in northwest Africa and the Atlantic and to use them as launching pads for attacks on the Western Hemisphere, but scholars studying German documents have concluded that the interventionists' case exaggerated the Germans' long-range air capability and threat to the Americas.[69]

Latin America also figured in arguments over the economic threat posed by Germany and Japan. Roosevelt made the case that Axis domination of the Old World would plunge the United States into financial calamity. The most influential anti-interventionist organization, the AFC, responded by highlighting the importance of South America to US trade: "There is no raw material so indispensable that we need fight outside this hemisphere for it. . . . As long as we are able to control most of South America Hitler cannot strangle the really essential part of our foreign trade."[70] Lindbergh likewise contended that the United States was "strong enough to defend Western hemisphere and could make advantageous trade treaties with whomever might control Europe & the eastern hemisphere."[71] Rather than see American economic interests in need of protection around the globe, as liberal internationalists did, anti-interventionists tended to reframe the economic threat in terms of access, then argue that specific resources would still be available even in the event of an Axis-dominated international order.

Liberal anti-interventionists, a small but vocal part of the larger movement, particularly made their case in economic terms. Adherents of this view typically saw war as an exclusively destructive endeavor and wanted the United States to wait until the combatants exhausted each other, then lead the way toward global prosperity. Villard, for example, proposed that the United States should offer "a plan for world union . . . military and economic disarmament and economic justice for all peoples." Stuart Chase reiterated this point: "Our material superiority, our splendid geographical isolation, give us the clear responsibility to take first place in finding a solution to unemployment and insecurity."[72] The AFC, as an organization, sometimes took a similar stand, though in more nebulous language. After the war, one of its flyers read, "When the peoples of Europe, Asia, and Africa . . . turn to Peace at last, America's strength will help rebuild them and bring them back to health and hope."[73]

For these anti-interventionists, global poverty was the main source and clearest symbol of insecurity. In their view, the surest route to security would be a broad public effort to improve the quality of life for all peoples. Norman Thomas charged that the failure of capitalism was "most immediately and obviously made apparent to the common man by the insecurity under which he suffers, and the poverty of which he is a victim. . . . Given the advance in modern technology, this poverty is more and more unnecessary. But private capitalism of its own volition offers no cure."[74] A prominent New Deal official, Jerome Frank, supported the liberal anti-interventionist focus on global poverty. In his book *Save America First* he argued that free-trade policies would not work until all countries were on a roughly equal economic footing: "To try to force free trade on the world, or on any single country, until that time, is not only impossible but would invite disastrous consequences." Moreover, "the belief that extensive world trade means world peace is a dangerous piece of wishful thinking. Not only has the struggle for markets caused war, but—certainly as far as America is concerned—war has been an important stimulant of foreign trade."[75]

Other liberal anti-interventionists, reflecting the tradition of US anticolonialism, criticized intervention on the grounds that war would benefit the economies of the United States and its allies. Pacifist leader A. J. Muste called the war a battle between "satiated powers determined to hang on to the 85 percent of the earth's vital resources which they control, even if that means plunging the world into another war, and another set of powers equally determined to change the imperialist status quo."[76] Thomas predicted that if the United States got into the war, whatever the outcome, "many American generals, admirals, munitions maker and imperialists—yes, and workers—will have or think they have a stake in maintaining conscription and armament economics. It will be easy to find an enemy to fear. Stalin or his successors will be around. Even Britain may provoke our armed rivalry."[77] Entangling alliances would lead to more militarization, the argument went. And a more militarized nation would be more likely to interpret conflicts—or any political change abroad—as situations calling for military intervention.

Opposition to imperialism served as the rhetorical vehicle for many anti-interventionist appeals. Typically these criticisms attempted to reverse the logic of Roosevelt's metaphors by demonstrating that the war could not be clearly divided between good neighbors and devious aggressors. Case in point, one *Uncensored* author argued that "the war actually is imperialist (with the USSR included). It is a war for markets, raw materials, and—incidentally—for the control of native populations of Africa, Asia, and Europe. That is the basis of empire. . . . If Britain goes down, Germany and Japan and Italy will gain large chunks of the older empires. But this would probably not alter the principles of empire economics." Thus the war, in stark contrast with FDR's rhetoric, was merely a "temporary falling out among thieves."[78] Empire and conflict were inextricably connected, Muste argued: "We must recognize that we too are a war-like and imperialist nation." Americans, he continued, inhabit "a civilization under a political-economic system of which your nation and the enemy nation are alike a part. . . . Its foundations were largely laid in greed and injustice and violence. . . . [War] is both an outgrowth and an expression of that decay and an agent for terribly accelerating it." Similarly, Norman Thomas flatly declared: "We reject the notion of trying to defend 'our interests' or 'our trade' by military force all around the world."[79]

Roosevelt's rhetoric associated Britain with civilization and thus stressed shared cultural ties. Indeed, FDR called the British Empire "the spearhead of resistance to world conquest."[80] By contrast, anti-interventionist rhetoric frequently portrayed Britain as a rapacious imperialist power and cautionary tale. Britain had no clear war aims, one critic charged: "Most Englishmen dodge the issue by saying that the aim is victory. But victory is a word of many meanings, and the peace is an inevitable function of the means and the extent by which victory is attained." Given Britain's long imperial past, it was easy to suspect that the undefined "victory" the British wanted was really a continuation (if not expansion) of their empire. Since Roosevelt was unclear about what he meant by helping Britain, many anti-interventionists suspected that he wanted to bring the United States into the war to achieve victory in a way that would create "a seven-seas empire, run from Washington."[81] In place of imperialism, many anti-interventionists dreamed of a more equitable postwar distribution of global power. "Anti-interventionists (misnamed isolationists) recognize," an *Uncensored* author wrote, "that the U.S. must ultimately share in the development of international institutions free from domination by any nation or set of nations."[82] Attempts at domination inevitably provoked resistance, which brought conflict.

Thomas carried this line of reasoning one step further by equating imperialism with fascism and accusing Roosevelt of purposefully cultivating fear:

> The lovers of Great Britain for her own sake and the sincere internationalists . . . would be astonished at the immense preponderance of sheer fear in popular support of "aid to Britain" as I have tested it in all parts of the country. Moreover, men who when pressed deny that they really fear direct attack on us, in speeches and radio comment consciously and unconsciously cultivate precisely that fear. It does not build a good morale for saving democracy.

For Thomas, there was little distinction between German fascism and British imperialism (or US intervention). As he declared, "It was our own fear which had made us turn toward our own fascism as a protection against foreign fascism."[83]

Again, the worry expressed by anti-interventionists was that the United States would sacrifice its values if it entered the war. Thus they made their case by positioning themselves as being opposed to fear and insecurity. As Charles Lindbergh said: "I do not believe that we will ever accept a philosophy of calamity, weakness, and fear."[84] Jerome Frank agreed that fear was a root of fascism and a danger to the American public: "Fascism, as a fear reaction of the economic dynasts in Europe, is explicable. . . . But there is no good objective reason for an outbreak of that reaction here. . . . To stop the sickening cycle that leads to Fascism and civil war, it is necessary that false fears be promptly eradicated."[85]

Anti-interventionists expressed skepticism about any alliance with the "economic dynasts" in London in part because they were skeptical about British innocence. It was as guilty as any other nation of pursuing selfish interests, they claimed. "Any power with as large an empire as Britain has cannot afford to be too sincere about thoroughgoing world collaboration," one *Uncensored* writer contended. By the end of 1940, some even feared the British might be aiming for "a negotiated peace [that] would leave the empire intact and British naval power would survive." Ultimately "an Anglo-German working harmony in Europe . . . might well be directed against the Americans."[86]

In addition to bashing the ethics of going to war to preserve the British empire, anti-interventionists also questioned the morality of the conflict by invoking the traditional idea of American inculpability in the troubles plaguing the rest of the world. In short, they lamented that their nation was sacrificing its traditional innocence by going to fight overseas for debatable reasons, and they accused the Roosevelt administration of maneuvering to bring the nation into the war. As Lindbergh charged, "We have participated in the intrigues of Europe and not always in an open 'democratic' way."[87] If FDR was ultimately successful, the argument went, then the United States could no longer claim to be a powerless, innocent victim of circumstances.

There were only two outcomes of war that were certain, anti-interventionists insisted. One was a dangerous growth of the power of the president and the executive branch. "We in the United States in wartime sacrifice many essentials of democracy," a memo from the AFC warned: "In a long and unpopular war, the sacrifice might well become permanent." Much anti-interventionist writing shared the dire tone of Oswald Garrison Villard's prediction: "We would jeopardize the very existence of the Republic."[88] The centralizing dictates of exercising global authority would weaken US commitment to democracy at home and abroad.

The other predictable outcome was a postwar America entangled in military alliances. The anti-interventionist formula was simple: alliances increased insecurity by multiplying the number of potential conflicts into which the United States might be drawn. Anti-interventionists feared the prospect of "entangling alliances" and they opposed entry into war precisely because it would permanently ensnare the United States in world affairs.[89] As Oswald Garrison Villard warned: "We may be led into overseas policies utterly at variance with our original policy of no entangling alliances. It would inevitably plunge us deep into the power-politics game being played abroad and make the temptation to use the Army and Navy as an element in the pursuit of diplomatic ends greater than ever." More specifically, Villard argued, "Since no military and naval officers the world over are ever satisfied with their armaments or believe that they have reached the ultimate in national defense, the tendency is to develop defense methods and alliances beyond the borders of the country."[90] This cycle of fear and readiness for war would have a predictable result, progressive senator George Norris foresaw: "We would become warlike, and when we had become warlike, there would be no doubt that we would soon be fighting with somebody."[91]

Roosevelt and the interventionists often depicted the struggle to resist aggression as a simple battle of good against evil. Anne Morrow Lindbergh spoke for most anti-interventionists when she wrote: "To so many people . . . it is clearly a case of the forces of evil vanquishing the forces of good. I cannot simplify it to that." Anti-interventionists in her mold saw no clearly defined moral differences between the European rivals, instead viewing the war as an old-fashioned Old-World struggle among amoral nation-states, all bent on enhancing their power. On this point most anti-interventionists shared the worldview of "realism" and its theoretical underpinnings, affirming that nation-states vie with others to increase their power. However, for them these premises led to the conclusion that to bifurcate the world into good and bad nations was simply unrealistic.[92] As Senator Gerald Nye put it, the administration was "marching us straight into a war of European power politics."[93]

These warnings ultimately revolved around a concern not only for what the nation's global involvement would look like after the war but also over what kind the future the war would create in the United States. "No longer can any one power be said to control all the seas of the world and probably no power ever will," an *Uncensored* author cautioned. Since naval hegemony was no longer possible, an unreasonably massive number of land troops would be needed to pursue the project. As General Pearsons argued: "If we are going to stretch the Monroe Doctrine to include Singapore and Shanghai and South America, we will need an army of millions."[94] A military buildup on such an enormous scale would also carry the seeds of major change in domestic budget priorities. In fact, Oswald Garrison Villard eventually resigned from the AFC because of what he saw as its excessive acceptance of defense spending: "I believe it carries within it the seeds of death for our democracy."[95] Norman Thomas pinpointed this danger in the article "The American Century," which he called "Henry Luce's widely publicized screed in favor of an Anglo-American empire with us as *senior* partner. . . . If by a miracle we should win the power Mr. Luce covets, we should have to maintain it by a military establishment, and probably by wars great and small, at a ruinous cost. A national income that might be used to raise the standard of living would be absorbed in large part by this imperialist gamble."[96] For these reasons, most anti-interventionists held that it was often better to negotiate compromises than to take the risk of war and huge standing armies. As Senator Burton K. Wheeler proclaimed, "We should know whether it is possible to have a negotiated peace. We should know the terms of peace demanded by both sides."[97]

Needless to say, no negotiated peace was forthcoming. According to presidential speechwriter Robert Sherwood, FDR's "greatest fear then and subsequently was a negotiated peace, another Munich." The president acknowledged that economic motives played a major role in his decision: a negotiated peace "would be only another armistice, leading to the most gigantic armament race and the most devastating trade wars of all history." And even if negotiation were desirable, he contended, it was not possible with a monster like Hitler.[98] Hence, although FDR shared anti-interventionists' concern over transforming the United States into a garrison state, his different definition of security led him to the opposite policy conclusion—he flatly refused to pursue the subject of peace talks. British diplomats in Washington reported Roosevelt "would never consent to any proposals which would allow Germany to preserve the status quo."[99]

The anti-interventionist case ultimately rested on a deep skepticism that the United States could maintain the political features that had made it, in the words of Abraham Lincoln, the "last best hope of earth" while also going to war and permanently inserting itself into the moral maelstrom of great power global politics. For that reason, even liberal anti-interventionists, who shared much of FDR's internationalist framework, thought the war a bad idea. Stuart Chase, the liberal anti-interventionist par excellence, summarized the danger of intervening on the grounds provided by the administration: "If we fight it will not be to serve the national interest, but because our emotions are aroused—fear, hate, pity. We have no enemy to fear. . . . Let us watch our emotions as never before. Let us beware of ideological crusades to march out and make the world safe for something, such as liberty or democracy, or *against* something, such as aggression or the rule of force. We cannot force liberty down the throats of another people. Trying to, we lose our own."[100] Perhaps when Chase italicized the word *against* he meant to underscore FDR's tendency to define security in the negative terms of forcible resistance to perceived threat. Regardless, Chase—along with other anti-interventionists—intentionally positioned themselves as opponents of fear in a callback to Roosevelt's first inaugural address.

Weakness of the Anti-Interventionist Cause

Of course, anti-interventionism had major weaknesses, which its opponents (including Roosevelt) would ruthlessly exploit. First, the movement was unable to advance a positive vision of world affairs after the war to rival the interventionists. As the very term *anti-interventionism* suggests, the cause was defined by what its adherents opposed—not only armed intervention in the European war but the whole new way of understanding American security propounded by FDR. Ironically, although anti-interventionists were able to perceive the shift to a negative, defensive focus in US foreign policy, they suffered from their own inclination to cast their position in negative, defensive terms. And since the anti-interventionists had no unified, alternative view of foreign policy to offer, the initiatives came, for the most part, from the president. Roosevelt was thus able to set the agenda of the debate, forcing his opponents to respond to his agenda rather than setting one of their own.[101]

In the spring of 1941, Chester Bowles, a prominent supporter of America first (and later undersecretary of state), lamented anti-interventionists' "lack of interest or discussion about the new world which will follow the war."[102] He offered an explanation for the movement's impotence at the time, identifying its second major weakness: "Perhaps that is because the membership of the America First Committee is distinctly varied," he wrote to AFC chair R. Douglas Stuart Jr., "and it will be difficult for us to get any agreement among the different elements."[103] Bowles was certainly correct about the makeup of the AFC and the entire anti-interventionist movement, which possessed several large, fissiparous factions.

Conservatives (centered in the Midwest) generally argued that what had worked in the past would still work just fine. Old-school progressives (mostly Republicans from the Great Plains across the Rocky Mountains to the Pacific Coast) alternatively argued that change was still needed, but all the changes that really mattered should happen domestically. The third, and smallest, wing of the movement were the internationalist anti-interventionists. Most were liberals, though many urged economic and political changes more radical than any that Roosevelt and the Eastern establishment internationalists would consider.

Among all anti-interventionists, the liberal internationalists were most likely to make their case in terms of systemic structures. The other factions in the coalition were more inclined to accept what has been called "the devil theory of war," blaming individuals for the move toward intervention: the munitions makers, the military leaders, and above all the president. Only the liberals explained how Roosevelt's global capitalist vision and the cultural fear of change were both leading toward intervention and war. They offered the public choices among future economic structures and future interpretations of the meaning of security.

In the public eye, the broad areas of agreement among anti-interventionists obscured their divisions, creating the impression of a relatively unified movement. And despite its many internal differences, the movement was held together by a consensus on what it stood against—not merely that war must be avoided, and that intervention would lead to war, but that FDR's vision would lead to a fundamental restructuring of American foreign policy and national identity for the worse. As a group they shared this broad alternative view, although there were many different variants of it and no one person ever articulated an "official" version. Still, as a broadly understood "political vocabulary," it was a formidable opponent of FDR's ambitions.

In response, Roosevelt did what he could to play the movement's factions against each other. He cemented good relations with liberal anti-interventionists by appointing one of their number, Henry Stimson, as his secretary of war. FDR simultaneously courted big business and finance elites centered in the Northeast to build support for the tremendous investments it would take to build up the military, siphoning succor from the traditional backers of the Republican Party.[104] In return, Roosevelt placed many domestic reforms on the back burner as the armed forces expanded under Stimson, these marriages of convenience leaving domestic policy increasingly undebated as the US military arsenal grew. As he would later put it, Dr. New Deal was already becoming Dr. Win the War. But the work of public persuasion was just beginning.

Conclusion

In the years just preceding American entry into World War II, the eventual direction of public opinion was still far from certain. The anti-interventionist movement posed a major political obstacle for Roosevelt's goal of reorienting US foreign policy around his understanding of the crisis. Public opinion was unpredictable, volatile, uncertain, and ambivalent. A majority continued to express a strong desire to avoid war. Yet a growing plurality favored taking steps to protect Britain, a step that many believed would lead directly to war.[105] As a result, the American electorate could reach no clear consensus on what security might mean in 1940—much less how to achieve it. Ever the pollster, Roosevelt could take no guidance from such contradictory feelings, nor could he predict how Americans' temperament might change.

However, the swaying public mood and the fierce debate it yielded did provide the president with one major benefit: the affordance of a flexible response. If the political problem confronting Roosevelt was indeed one of public persuasion, then the uncertainty surrounding US intervention also gave him the rhetorical leeway that he prized so highly in any situation. As Frank Costigliola has suggested, "Gusts for and against military intervention enabled him to tack in his own direction, to change course as he wanted."[106]

Eventually, though, he had to win the domestic political battle if he were to gain the ability to reshape US foreign policy in accordance with his interpretation of national—and, by extension, global—security. In order to keep all options open, he had to win overwhelming public support so that he could pursue whatever policy options would help him realize his vision. The anti-interventionists posed a formidable impediment to that goal because they raised so many doubts about FDR's narrative, kept those doubts so central in public discourse, and offered alternative narratives that had significant public appeal.

6 | Roosevelt's Rhetorical Victory, 1940
Arsenal of Democracy

To fend off his domestic opposition, Roosevelt relied upon the one tool over which he wielded total control: his words. As Vanessa B. Beasley and Deborah Smith-Howell record, "Public address was so central to Roosevelt's leadership style that Eleanor Roosevelt first used the phrase 'no ordinary time' to prepare supporters for an upcoming period of uncharacteristic silence from their president."[1] FDR would deploy his oratorical ebullience throughout 1940 to commandingly interpret not only the events taking place abroad but also to frame his own actions as chief executive so as to win the battle of competing narratives at home. By the year's end, he would have reframed the debate over intervention on his terms, winning an unprecedented third term as president and helping Britain survive the German onslaught in the process.

However, the task that lay before him immediately prior to and after the Nazi conquest of France was more complicated than his previous rhetorical endeavors, since it involved striking a delicate balance between confidence and fear. In order to maintain public backing for his rearmament program and his administration's efforts to help the Allies within the legal confines of neutrality, FDR needed the American electorate to be sufficiently alarmed to support the policies he might chart. Yet he could not afford to utterly terrify the nation or appear to be a warmonger lest he strengthen the hand of his domestic opponents, the anti-interventionists, thereby rendering any effort to help the Allies politically impossible. FDR's job was therefore to build a "public façade of optimism and defiance," because if he revealed his "private fears and even despair," as Frank Burt Freidel argues, the citizenry "would have panicked and insisted that the nation retreat into Fortress America," effectively ending the political contest.[2]

To achieve this delicate balance, as it turned out, Roosevelt did not need to create a new pattern of discourse. He merely applied the rhetorical structure he had developed over the preceding years of his presidency, adapting elements of his previous New Deal and foreign policy discourse to persuade Americans to embrace his view of the global crisis. Eleanor herself pointed out the deep consistency in FDR's tactics and rhetoric; she judged that his course in 1940 was "only a continuation of the line of action he had begun to follow as far back as 1936."[3] To win the battle for public opinion, he would legitimate his ever more martial policies by appealing to the public's desire for security, a value he had done more than any other to elevate as a chief value of public life. He then deployed a fleet of metaphors and biblical allusions to argue that his policies advanced American security on political, economic, and moral grounds.

For example, in his 1940 Annual Address, FDR argued that the United States was not immune from the effects of the war by reference to John 8:32 ("the truth shall set you free"):

> We must look ahead and see the kinds of lives our children would have to lead if a large part of the rest of the world were compelled to worship a god imposed by a military ruler, or were forbidden to worship God at all; if the rest of the world were forbidden to read and hear the facts—the daily news of their own and other nations—if they were deprived of the truth that makes men free. We must look ahead and see the effect on our future generations if world trade is controlled by any nation or group of nations which sets up that control through military force.[4]

In this speech and others, FDR carefully laid the groundwork for a more flexible foreign policy over the course of 1940. As Mary E. Stuckey notes, "FDR conflated the political, the economic, and the ideological. . . . American freedom depended upon access to facts, religion, and trade. Endangering one endangered them all, and in a world where these were under threat, no amount of isolation could protect them at home."[5] He sought to unify the American people on his terms.

There was a striking parallel between the endeavor he confronted now and the challenge he faced in the early days of the New Deal. In both cases, he was pursuing policies "pasted together with conflicting politics and cultures," as Frank Costigliola states, but "FDR understood that with both ventures people had to believe the framework made sense. It all boiled down to the need for structures of meaning and promise even if the construction was ad hoc and in part an illusion."[6] As he had already shown on the domestic front, Roosevelt was skilled at constructing believable ad hoc structures of meaning and making those structures seem to fit together seamlessly. In 1940, he would exercise his masterful ability to construct mythology to new effect—winning the interpretive battle over US intervention in World War II. Starting in the early summer and continuing past his reelection in November, FDR escalated the intensity of his clash with the anti-interventionists, ending the year with his "Arsenal of Democracy" address.

FDR's Opening Move: The Address at Virginia

On June 10, 1940, twelve days before the French surrender, the president and his aides frantically rewrote the commencement address he had prepared to give that day at the University of Virginia Law School (Franklin Jr. was one of the graduates). Earlier that morning they had received word that Italy had formally declared war upon the Allies, and during the ride down from Washington, FDR and Eleanor debated how he should respond.[7] The president chose to seize the moment and detail his case for a more active US foreign policy. The local newspapers had announced that Roosevelt would be making an important announcement, and as rain began falling that afternoon the president encountered an expectant audience packed into the campus gym. His address was broadcast over the three major radio networks and across the world.[8]

Roosevelt opened his speech by conforming to the generic standards of a commencement address, acknowledging that every generation "has questions to ask the world." He quickly used this device to segue into his larger topic: the nation's response to the global conflict. "But every now and again," the president said, underlining specific words for emphasis, "in the history of the republic a *different* kind of question presents itself—a question which asks, not about the future of an individual, or even of a generation, but about the future of the *country*, the *future* of the *American people*." He then listed three epochs in the nation's life that conformed to this description: the revolutionary period at the country's beginning, the "endless years" that comprised "the War Between the States" and "again today." By arguing that the present moment constituted a particularly opportune time for national transformation, FDR invoked the notion of *kairos*, or "the critical moment" of ethical, persuasive, or political opportunity.[9] As Sharon Crowley and Deborah Hawhee observe, "Kairos suggests a special notion of space and/or time" in which an audience may be persuadable that was not before, since "rhetorical situations create the available arguments" for orators to deploy.[10] In choosing the address at Charlottesville to make his case against the anti-interventionists, Roosevelt signaled that he believed the entry of Italy into the war and the impending French surrender had changed the political calculus to the extent that argumentative breakthrough was now possible with the American public.

Roosevelt next articulated the "question" that was being asked "with even greater anxiety" by the students assembled before him. By asserting that the anxiety felt belonged to his immediate audience, not him, FDR obliquely suggested that worry was an appropriate response to the unfolding situation in Europe while avoiding expressing that feeling himself, thereby using fear to emotionally prime his domestic audience for the appeals he would soon deliver. The "question," he declared, asked "what the future holds for all peoples and all nations that have been living under democratic forms of government—under the free institutions of a free people." By stating the "question" in this way, Roosevelt framed the issue as one of freedom versus unfreedom or democracy versus autocracy; he evaded a geographic, legal, or strictly national framing of the conflict. Since Hitler was already at war with several democracies, this portrayal papered over the fact of American neutrality. By abstracting the conflict into one pitting "this philosophy of force" against "the ideal of individual liberty, the ideal of free franchise, the ideal of peace through justice," FDR's rhetoric deftly elided the issue of US noncombatant status—American ideals, if not the actual country, were under attack.

Such dualistic logic directly undermined legal, diplomatic, and economic arguments for anti-interventionism by depicting the war as a transcendent battle between two (and only two) sides. This "new philosophy" of aggression, Roosevelt admonished his hearers, was diametrically opposed to "the way of life or the way of thought of a nation whose origins go back to Jamestown and Plymouth Rock." Like the anti-interventionists, FDR claimed that he was seeking to preserve the American way of life from harmful influences, but instead of locating the potential harm in the war itself, he attributed the threat to national life to a poisonous "belief in force." That philosophy, the president said in a callback to his anti-elitist New Deal rhetoric, placed control in the hands of "infinitely small groups of individuals who rule without a single one of the democratic sanctions." In addition to being antidemocratic, this system was amoral and therefore anti-American as well: "Such mastery abandons with deliberate contempt all of the moral values to which even this young continent for more than three hundred years has been accustomed and dedicated." FDR's phraseology metaphorically substituted place—this young continent, Plymouth Rock, Jamestown—to stand in for the "American way of life," allowing him the strategic ambiguity to avoid having to lay out exactly what he thought that way of life entailed. He thereby sidestepped anti-interventionist claims that entering the war would render elements of American life irrecoverable while also depicting the war as a binary conflict pitting good against evil.

Moving into the heart of his critique of anti-interventionism, the president narrowed his focus to the Western Hemisphere. He again articulated his warning in the language of fear, again in a way that demurred on whether the fear was his own: "Perception of danger to our institutions may come slowly or it may come with a rush and a shock as it has to the people of the United States . . . danger has come to us clearly and overwhelmingly; and we perceive the peril in the world-wide arena—an arena which may become so narrowed that only the Americas would retain the ancient faiths."[11] This paragraph contained the main elements of the president's internationalist narrative. The danger confronting the United States was global in scale; it was a war religious in intensity; the menace was total and overwhelming and urgent, not discountable or distant; and the security of the Western Hemisphere was conflated with that of the United States, which existed under terrific threat. Moreover, this perception was, according to FDR, universal. Although some may need more time, all will realize the danger's proximity.

With the nation so imperiled, Roosevelt lampooned the anti-interventionist position as fundamentally unserious. As he stated, writing by hand the words of the final sentence,

> Some indeed still hold to the now obvious delusion that we of the United States can safely permit the United States to become a lone island in a world dominated by the philosophy of force. Such an island may be the dream of those who still talk and vote as isolationists. Such an island represents to me and to the overwhelming majority of Americans today a helpless nightmare of a people without freedom, a people lodged in prison, hand-cuffed, hungry and fed through the bars from day to day by the contemptuous, unpitying masters.[12]

These sentences are stunning for their starkness and symbolism. Argumentatively, FDR's words reflect the realist dimensions of his foreign policy, as the "obvious" interpretation of world events offered by his administration was juxtaposed with the "delusion" proffered by isolationists. Deprecating the anti-interventionist outlook as a fanciful delusion or "dream," Roosevelt asserted that "the overwhelming majority of Americans" viewed events from the presumably more sober-minded perspective of the commander in chief, seeing hemispheric isolation as a "nightmare." Additionally, FDR's description of America as a "lone island" invited Americans to compare themselves to the actual island nation—Britain—that would soon be alone in the fight against the German Luftwaffe. By implicitly comparing his country's position to that of Britain, Roosevelt's rhetoric tacitly suggested that the United States would not be left to its own devices "in a world dominated by the philosophy of force." Elements of kairos were at work in this passage also, as it was "now" obvious with the entry of Italy that the anti-interventionists were wrong about the war.

Furthermore, FDR's image of Americans as a people "without freedom" struck mythic, resonant chords of national identity. As Samuel P. Perry notes, freedom and notions of the frontier have long been intertwined in the US context, providing "a definition of American identity predicated on the conquering of the unknown; material spaces become the ground for proving one's identity as an American."[13] In contrast to the archetypical American experiencing freedom on the boundless territorial space of the frontier, Roosevelt's language created the impression of a confined people cramped onto an island. His words also contrasted freedom (and related concepts of sovereignty) with prison, evoking the image of a shackled inmate helpless before "contemptuous, unpitying masters." Critically, these masters express their cruelty by withholding food, leading their "prisoner" to starve—a figurative counterpart to the economic arguments made by Roosevelt that a world under Axis sway would be a danger to US commerce. Taken together, these metaphoric images furnished by FDR's rhetoric worked as visual, affective complements to the more didactic claims with which he began his speech, and they functioned to rebut the anti-interventionist case on emotional as well as rational grounds. He followed these rhetorical flourishes with a call for Americans to rally behind him: "Let us not hesitate—all of us—to proclaim certain truths. We, as a nation, and this applies to all the other American nations, are convinced that military and naval victory for the gods of force and hate would endanger the institutions of democracy in the western world." Like his cousin Theodore, whom Leroy G. Dorsey credits for redefining the frontier as a site of "spiritual regeneration," FDR merged the mythic image of the American frontier with religious appeals to amplify the danger posed by the Axis powers.[14]

The president then explicitly addressed the actions of Mussolini, stating that his administration viewed the dictator's decision to enter the war "with the utmost regret and grave disquiet." He followed this condemnation by retracing the diplomatic steps that had led to Mussolini's decision and "the still greater enlargement of the scene of the conflict in the Near East and Africa," telling his audience that he had personally attempted to sway Italy from joining Hitler's side. By relating the story in this way, FDR affirmed a central tenet he shared with the anti-interventionists—belief in American innocence—and showed how the Italian government "has manifested disregard for the rights and security of other nations; for the lives of the peoples of those nations which are directly threatened by this spread of war." Italy, like Germany, turned down FDR's vision of a peaceful, liberal internationalist order, making them both aggressors.

In short, Roosevelt's narrative confirmed his dualistic depiction of the conflict, his account of Italy's decision working as an expository aside detailing the grim motivations of a new villain. He piercingly communicated the Italians' duplicity with a sentence he wrote by hand: "On this tenth day of June, 1940, the hand that held the dagger has struck it into the back of its neighbor." The metaphoric inversion of this sentence—everting years and years of FDR's "good neighbor" talk—distilled the treachery of Mussolini, now revealed to be a murderous housebreaker, more capably than any discussion of treaties or declarations could have done. With a reference to "the first great American teacher of democracy," Thomas Jefferson, the president paired this portrayal of Punic faith with a prayer for "those beyond the seas who are maintaining with magnificent valor their battle for freedom." The dissimilarity with which FDR described the Axis (backstabbers) and Allied (valorous freedom fighters) powers could not be missed. As *Time* magazine wrote after the address, "With Roosevelt's speech . . . the U.S. had taken sides. Ended was the myth of U.S. neutrality."[15]

In response to the aggressors' perfidy, Roosevelt concluded his address by outlining his plan of action followed by a call for "effort, courage, sacrifice, devotion" on the part of his hearers.[16] In a practical declaration of war upon anti-interventionism, he proclaimed, "In our American unity, we will pursue two obvious and simultaneous courses: we will extend to the opponents of force the material resources of this nation and, at the same time . . . use of those resources in order that we ourselves in the Americas may have equipment and training equal to the task of any emergency and every defense." Again invoking realism ("obvious"), FDR stated in no uncertain terms that his administration's policy was to economically aid the Allies and militarily prepare for war. By framing his rearmament policy as an attempt to prepare for whatever dangers may come, he undercut anti-interventionist arguments that his administration was acting imprudently. More broadly, he positioned his policy as the natural conclusion to the narrative he had spun over the course of his address. If the present was an exceptional time because there existed a heretical enemy devoted to conquest, that enemy had backstabbed its neighbor, and the enemy would delight in emaciating America, then supporting friends that were fighting said enemy would seem to be a reasonable course of action. Faced with such an urgent situation, he was not interested in a debate: "We will not slow down or detour. . . . Full speed ahead." Indeed, he would unrelentingly reiterate these arguments through the year's end.

The US media reacted to FDR's speech in different ways, although most analyses were sympathetic. The *Atlanta Daily World* labeled the speech "a happy occasion" for "all those bonafide Americans and believers in the principles of free government."[17] The *Christian Science Monitor* called Roosevelt's performance an "Intimate Message" that marked "an American scene in every aspect."[18] Cleveland's *Plain Dealer* editorialized that FDR "has done much to shatter the remnants" of anti-interventionism; the *Des Moines Register* stated that the president "decided it . . . in the way that the vast majority of Americans wanted it decided"; and even the Republican-leaning *Pittsburgh Post-Gazette* declared, "This (speech) may not be neutrality in the strictest sense, but the fact is the overwhelming majority in this country supports the President's position fully."[19] Even so, some discordant voices remained. The *Chicago Tribune* analogized FDR to Neville Chamberlain, who promised to defend Poland though "it was obvious that the allies could not re-enforce the Polish army or supply it. Similarly, with Paris in the gravest danger of capture, Mr. Roosevelt announces his determination to support France," concluding: "He encourages the nation to believe that its preparation is far more complete than in fact it is."[20] And journalist James MacDonald, reporting from London, related that most Britons "believed he had gone as far as he possibly could to help the Allies."[21]

As a whole then, FDR's "Dagger" address (as it came to be called), as powerful an opening shot as it was, did not by itself rally the nation to his side. Instead, it marked a shift in Roosevelt's presidential rhetoric as he began making the case for intervention more stridently. The speech signaled to the American public that the administration thought the status quo was unacceptable and that change, of some sort, would soon be coming—an inevitability, the president claimed, given the entry of Italy and dire straits of France. The compelling narrative Roosevelt crafted in this address placed the anti-interventionists on the defensive, and he would combine this narrative with a rhetorical strategy over the course of 1940 that systematically undercut the case for neutrality, putting his "ruthless political savvy" on full display.[22]

FDR's Strategy: Argumentative Appropriation

Following the address at Charlottesville, FDR's masterstroke was to use the language and underlying values of the anti-interventionists to defeat them. In every way he could, he insisted that he agreed with their purely defensive stance, their belief in American exceptionalism, and the traditional ways of life in the United States they sought to preserve. The debate, the president clearly held, was only about the best methods to achieve the goals that all Americans shared. "By emphasizing the defensive advantages to the United States," as Robert Dallek has noted, "he was able to defuse the war question more effectively than even he had dared hope."[23] In short, the president won by agreeing, ardently, with his political opposition.

From a rhetorical vantage, stasis theory can help explain how the president was able to reframe the debate as one concerned with methods instead of values. Stasis theory was developed by classical figures such as Hermagoras, Cicero, and Quintilian as a series of questions (stases) one may ask to discover relevant points of dispute between two parties. Stasis thus serves as a diagnostic tool to locate the proper ground of argument so as to prevent disputants from talking past each other (i.e., it is little use arguing over the best evacuation route with someone who refuses to flee a hurricane). As Ryan Weber observes, "Stasis helps avoid an asymmetry where opposing arguments cannot find resolution because they fail to ask and argue the same questions."[24]

Although the exact phrasing of the questions of stases vary, many scholars work from a sequence that distills them into four questions pertaining to fact, definition, quality, and policy:

Fact: Does or did a thing exist?
Definition: What is the thing that exists?
Quality: What is the nature of the thing and how should we value it?
Policy: What should be done about the thing?[25]

While the clash between FDR and the anti-interventionists played out in multiple arenas, they occupied common ground on a number of questions regarding the war. Roosevelt's brilliance was to weaponize this agreement into powerful rhetorical appeals, turning the debate on its head. And there were plenty of areas in which the two sides agreed.

For example, on the level of fact all parties acknowledged that a war was taking place and who the combatants were. In terms of definition, all agreed on where the various theaters of combat were located—although FDR soon began referring to the war as "a world conflict," thereby imposing narrative unity on the various hostilities taking place from North Africa to Nanjing.[26] The anti-interventionists deeply disagreed among themselves, much less with the Roosevelt administration, over what the war represented, what caused it, and how best to understand it (questions of quality). But the clearest point of departure between the anti-interventionists and the administration was over policy—whether to intervene or not intervene. As a result, FDR homed in on other questions, even minimizing American aid to Britain, so as to repeatedly redirect the debate toward areas where he could claim that his administration and the anti-interventionists shared the same ground. By asserting that he and his critics believed the same things, Roosevelt appropriated anti-interventionist talking points. He transformed the debate into one of policy—how, pragmatically, to best defend the American people. To convince his audience, Roosevelt incessantly contended that he agreed with his critics on the underlying values they sought to preserve.

This dynamic played out repeatedly over the next six months. FDR specifically co-opted anti-interventionist arguments surrounding defense and American innocence, combining these rhetorical touchstones with the reinvigorated dualism displayed in his "Dagger" address to justify his increasingly warlike policies. Above all, he gained support by joining the anti-interventionists in defining security primarily as a quality of domestic life in the United States. He promoted American rearmament along with military aid for Britain as necessary measures to ultimately keep the American homeland, and every American home, secure.

Defensive Measures: Destroyers, Britain, and the Draft

After his address in Charlottesville, Roosevelt applied the term "defense" to whatever policy he championed whenever possible. If the nation wanted to ensure that "liberty and justice will survive and be secure," he preached, then "ours must once again be the spirit of those who were prepared to defend as they built, to defend as they worked, to defend as they worshipped." In another instance he declared, "The core of our defense is the faith we have in the institutions we defend."[27] In transforming *defense* into a god-term in his public statements, however, the president broadened the scope of that word immensely. His rhetoric framed the defense of the homeland as part of a much larger project, which involved protecting the Western Hemisphere, Britain, and civilization itself. Roosevelt tied these elements into a single tapestry, arguing that defending the United States entailed these commitments as well.

The president used this formula to successfully reach an agreement to transfer fifty aging destroyers to Britain that fall. Since the start of the German blitzkrieg against the Low Countries and France on May 10, Churchill had asked Roosevelt to sell these warships to Britain. On May 16, the same day he gained an additional $1 billion in defense funding from Congress, the president replied that he could not perform this action without legislative approval. Domestic support for the transfer was hardly forthcoming. In addition to the anti-interventionists and skeptical legislators, military leaders, including George Marshall, opposed such a deal on the grounds that Germany might capture the ships and the supplies they carried. By late July, with the Battle of Britain and German submarine raids growing more intense, Churchill desperately wrote Roosevelt: "I must tell you that in the long history of the world this is a thing to do *now*."[28]

FDR concurred. He seized upon the idea of trading the destroyers in exchange for leasing rights to British bases in the Caribbean and North

Atlantic. During an early September trip to West Virginia—a stop on his "noncampaign campaign" for president—he shocked reporters by not only telling them he had reached an agreement to transfer the warships, but also that he was not going to seek congressional approval.[29] Incensed, anti-interventionists argued that this deal was a clear step toward war. Republican presidential nominee Wendell Willkie called it "the most arbitrary and dictatorial action" a president had ever taken.[30] By focusing on the president's apparent arrogation of power over Congress, FDR's opponents framed the deal as evidence of their central claim—that the governmental changes that would accompany the march to war were themselves the threat to the American way of life.

Roosevelt deftly parried the anti-interventionists' attack by claiming that his only motive was their own goal of defending the United States. Indeed, he proclaimed that the deal was "the most important action in the reinforcement of our national defense . . . since the Louisiana Purchase." In portraying his actions as an important defensive measure on par with doubling the size of the country (an undoubtedly exaggerated valuation of old destroyers and several naval outposts), FDR's words achieved their purpose. As Dallek recounts, "The response in the United States was widely favorable" to his appeal.[31]

A similar dynamic played out at the same time, more fiercely, over the passage of the Burke-Wadsworth Bill. A potential law to introduce the nation's first-ever peacetime draft, the proposal had support from both sides of the congressional aisle (a Gallup poll found Democrats nationwide supported it by a 3-1 margin, Republicans by 3-2).[32] After some agonizing over the political risk—he had prevaricated on conscription all summer—Roosevelt decided to endorse the bill. Anti-interventionists were enraged; major figures such as senators Robert La Follette Jr. and George Norris came out heatedly against the president's endorsement. But through the long-winded debate, public opinion gradually shifted toward support for the measure. The peacetime draft eventually won a narrow victory in Congress on September 16. Upon signing the bill into law, Roosevelt again labeled the draft a defensive measure: "It is a program obviously of defensive preparation and defensive preparation only." He justified it as the best way "to fend off war from our shores" but then quickly added, "We must and will prevent our land from becoming a victim of aggression."[33]

In sum, Roosevelt deployed the word "defense" to defang actions like drafting young men for war and sending warships to Britain. This rhetorical strategy was a favorite of his on the campaign trail, and even led him to overpromise. As he would unequivocally state in a speech in Boston days before the presidential election, "Your boys are not going to be sent into any foreign wars."[34] Willkie reportedly cursed this speech as the moment the Republicans lost the 1940 campaign.[35]

The president continually equated his program for giving all aid to Britain short of war with the anti-interventionists' goal of defending the nation against war: "The nub of the whole purpose of your President is to keep you now, and your children later, and your grandchildren much later, out of a last-ditch war for the preservation of American independence."[36] Aid to Britain became a central thread in the mythic web that Roosevelt was weaving, linking homes, neighborhoods, nation, allies, global capitalism, and civilization itself as inseparably fused symbols of security. The counterpoint to his abstraction of the war to the plane of transcendent ideals, he presented all these elements as embodiments of the same set of timeless values, all to be preserved by a single policy of defense. By this logic, the United States could protect democracy at home only by defending democracy in Britain and everywhere else, which meant that a threat to democracy anywhere represented a source of insecurity to the nation as well.

Therefore, the only rational choice, it seemed, was to mount an "all-inclusive defense," a "total defense," as the president described it. "We are building a total defense on land, on sea, and in the air," the president told one audience, extemporaneously repeating the phrase "a total defense" for emphasis, then explaining its meaning: "sufficient to repel total attack from any part of the world."[37] Such words smuggled in a tacit premise that the United States could mount a "total defense" only by being permanently involved in events all over the globe, since any place might erupt in conflict at any time. As he had at Virginia and before, FDR collapsed the distinction between defending the Americas and fighting overseas, instead redrawing the line between aggressors and those who resist them. He implored Americans to "ask, not only what the future hold for this republic, but what the future holds for all peoples and all nations. . . . The world—and the world includes our own American hemisphere—is threatened by forces of destruction."[38] Again, in his rhetoric the threat was not geographically located but rather, like an evil spirit, the "philosophy of force" scoured the earth in search of victims: "Forces of evil which are bent on conquest of the world will destroy whomever and whenever they can destroy." FDR drove home his point, lamenting the many Americans "who closed their eyes, from lack of interest or lack of knowledge; honestly and sincerely thinking that the many hundreds of miles of salt water" would protect them from the Axis aggressors.[39] Distance, in his telling, provided Americans no safety from the inferno engulfing Nazi-occupied Europe. The answer was *defense.*

Roosevelt sketched this frightening picture to promote his program for aiding the defense of Britain: "Overseas success in warding off invasion by dictatorship forces means safety of the United States," he insisted. To strengthen his case, he appealed to common moral ideals that, he contended, the United States and Britain shared. Both nations were full of "ordinary, self-respecting men and women" who, like good neighbors, could settle any dispute in a reasonable peaceful fashion.[40] After his reelection, when he hit upon the idea of "lend-lease" as a way to get military supplies to Britain, he explained to reporters that it was the obvious thing to do, employing the tried-and-true metaphor of the good neighbor to convey his message: "Suppose my neighbor's home catches fire, and I have a length of garden hose. Since both my neighbor's house and my own are in danger, I don't talk about cost. I just give him the hose." After the war, he explained, "we would get repaid in kind sometime, thereby leaving out the dollar mark in the form of a dollar debt and substituting for it a gentleman's obligation to repay in kind. I think you all get it."[41] Any gentleman, any decent neighborly person, would "get it," he implied.

American Innocence: "Duty Imposed from Without"

Most of the anti-interventionists did not "get it." One of their leaders, Senator Robert Taft, scoffed that "lend-lease" would be "a good deal like lending chewing gum—you certainly don't want it back." After the measure's approval, Senator Arthur Vandenberg lamented, "We have torn up 150 years of traditional American foreign policy. We have tossed Washington's Farewell Address in the discard. We have thrown ourselves squarely into the power politics and power wars of Europe, Asia, and Africa. We have taken the first step upon a course from which we can never hereafter retreat."[42] Even before Roosevelt proposed the "lend-lease" plan, the question of aid to Britain had become a crucial symbolic battlefield in the political war between the administration and its opponents. To win that war, the president kept much of what he actually did to help Britain secret. "I am doing everything possible—though I am not talking very much about it," he explained to Lewis Douglas, because the anti-interventionist press would "pervert it, attack it, and confuse the public mind."[43]

If the goal was to weaken anti-interventionism, a repeated public emphasis on saving Britain specifically could do more harm than good. For anti-interventionists, aid to Britain was the primary symbol of insecurity. They could easily argue that Britain (almost always the "British Empire" in their parlance), with its long record of colonialism, hardly represented the values Americans should fight for. As Norman Thomas stated, "If the survival of any empire is vital to our interest and security, then our democracy is in a bad way."[44]

To counteract this appeal, Roosevelt worked to convince the public that he was not trying merely to save one foreign nation, an imperialist nation at that. Rather, he insisted that while aid to Britain was vital, it was merely a particular case at hand exemplifying a universal moral principle.[45] As he did in the "Dagger" address, he abstracted the conflict into the realm of values, stating, "We defend and we build a way of life, not for America alone, but for all mankind."[46] FDR was thereby able to portray US aid to Britain (to the extent he acknowledged it) as a manifestation of American virtue, affirming the nation's altruistic motivations in foreign affairs. As he said in his address accepting the Democratic presidential nomination, the conflict was an ideological battle between "democratic forms of government" and the "philosophy of force" propagated by aggressors who serve "gods of force and hate."[47] In that fight America stood on the side of the angels, as demonstrated through its military and economic aid to Britain. Thus reconceptualized, the war material FDR sent to Britain was not strictly about the war at all but was instead merely the outworking of the United States' moral character. This abstraction co-opted the anti-interventionist argument that US involvement in the war would sacrifice the nation's virtue by rhetorically transforming the administration's involvement in the war as evidence of the nation's virtue, which was consistent with its democratic inheritance.

This way of speaking carried many of the same assumptions that were foundational to anti-interventionist understandings of the United States. America was an innocent nation whose exceptional virtue had to be protected from the taint of foreign threats. Because of the nation's unique moral character, it could pursue its self-interest—whether profiting from weapon transfers or remaining staunchly neutral—while also adhering to the highest ethical standards, with no contradiction between the two. As a democratic, civilized, and moral nation, the United States was a model that the whole world should, and eventually would, want to emulate.

FDR consistently equated democracy with the American way of life in politics and society. As Geoffrey Perrett has pointed out, there was "a confusion of what was American with what was democratic and a confusion of what was political with what was social."[48] By positing the specifically American form of democracy as the transcendent universal value, the president could speak about democracy in the language of faith, which in turn made it easier to describe his administration's decisions as attempts to preserve the nation's moral virtue. At times this language became explicit: "That spirit—that faith—speaks to us in our daily lives. It speaks to us in our counties, in our cities, in our towns, and in our villages. It speaks to us from the other nations of the hemisphere, and from those across the seas."[49] A similarly religious theme did make its way into the final version of his third inaugural address: "If the spirit of America were killed, even though the Nation's body and mind, constricted in an alien world, lived on, the America we know would have perished." Editing a draft of that address, Roosevelt found the final sentence—"we go forward, in the service of our country, with the guidance of God"–and changed "with the guidance" to "by the will" of God.[50]

Roosevelt overtly linked this moral framework to his New Deal policies, arguing that the same motivation that inspired him to aid Americans in need underwrote his foreign policy of helping the Allies now. The "one consistent thought" underlying all his domestic programs and the aid to Britain was the same: "a constantly growing sense of human decency."[51] This conflation of the New Deal with the administration's foreign policy after the fall of France also worked in the other direction—dangers from overseas were now articulated as threats to the socioeconomic gains achieved by the New Deal reforms. Roosevelt reassured the public that there would be no step backward, saying, "We must make sure . . . that there be no breakdown or cancellation of any of the great social gains we have made in the past years. . . . We still insist on the need for vast improvements in our own social and economic life."[52] His strategy for protecting the New Deal was to combine domestic and foreign symbols of insecurity into a single rhetorical package—"All our domestic problems are now a part of the great emergency"—and to promote his domestic reforms as "a component part of national defense itself."⁵³ Threats to FDR's foreign and domestic policies became gradually more interchangeable. Every worker who desired the nation's protection against poverty had to protect his nation in time of war.

Roosevelt was urged to take this tack by a future secretary of state, Dean Acheson, who advised him to "give a rousing speech tying America's ideals at home to the survival of those ideals around the globe. The great freedoms secured by the New Deal must be linked to the threat to freedom arising from fascism." Roosevelt was "delighted."⁵⁴ A few weeks later, he invited Acheson to join the administration as assistant secretary of state for economic affairs. By integrating the New Deal's constellation of appeals into his foreign policy discourse, FDR flattened distinctions between domestic and foreign policy while also importing the divisive moral framework—a tiny exploitative elite set against the common masses—intrinsic to the domestic rhetoric of his past seven years in office. He applied this framework to warn against war profiteering: "Our present emergency and a common sense of decency make it imperative that no new group of war millionaires shall come into being in this nation as a result of the struggle abroad."⁵⁵ He used this language to alert the nation to potential fifth columnists, who used dissent to undermine the "singleness of national purpose," leading to "political paralysis, and, eventually, a state of panic."⁵⁶ In the spirit of the New Deal, the president urged all citizens to be vigilant in watching for these agents of insecurity and reporting them to the government for swift action, so that all Americans could be kept secure. As he warned, the adversaries of decency lurked within as well as abroad: "The evil forces . . . are already within our own gates."⁵⁷

But Roosevelt's coup de maître was to equate the anti-interventionists with the domestic enemies of his New Deal discourse. Misguided anti-interventionists joined "economic royalists" as new symbols of domestic insecurity: "We guard against the forces of anti-Christian aggression, which may attack us from without, and the forces of ignorance and fear which may corrupt us from within."⁵⁸ Here, as so often, he equated "decency," his generic term for all civilized values, with Christian religion, turning the anti-interventionist critique on its head. Instead of Roosevelt acting as the agent of moral corruption by centralizing government power in preparation for war, it was now the anti-interventionists who, by resisting the president's attempts to demonstrate the nation's virtue, were the enemies of American innocence.

All citizens had to choose, Roosevelt implied: either defend their nation or let it fall into the clutches of the "forces of destruction." Anyone who wanted to keep the United States pure—and retain a view of America as a morally superior land that needed to be defended—would have to be willing to take global responsibility for keeping civilization secure everywhere. And the only way to do that in 1940, Roosevelt maintained, was to do everything possible to help Britain win the war. The war would be the bulwark protecting moral decency. Anyone who did not become part of this cause by actively supporting Britain would, by default, be assisting the spread of evil in the present and the reign of evil in the future.

Ultimately, though, Roosevelt's stark depiction of these alternatives functioned to persuade Americans that they really had no choice. The United States had done nothing to provoke aggression, the president repeatedly insisted. "The duty of this day has been imposed on us from without," he said when inaugurating the nation's first peacetime draft.[59] The nation was innocent in the hostilities erupting worldwide, yet those hostilities still loomed over the United States' future nonetheless. Since events and threats around the world were now all bound together, moral privilege and duty were also bound together: "In the face of the danger which confronts our time, no individual retains or can hope to retain, the right of personal choice. . . . He has a first obligation to serve in defense of our institutions of freedom . . . in whatever capacity his country finds him useful."[60] FDR's emphasis on American innocence, an appropriation of his opponents' worldview that no doubt helped him defeat them in the court of public opinion, contained within it a call to arms to act in defense of the freedom and democracy Americans held dear thanks to the third element of his discourse—dualism.

Dualism: "Decency versus the Firing Squad"

The linchpin of the president's rhetorical structure was his familiar either-or thinking. Whereas this feature of FDR's discourse was used in his past foreign policy utterances in a descriptive capacity—interpretively dividing the world into civilized/uncivilized, altruistic/aggressive, and economically open/closed pairs—he now deployed a morally charged dualism to prescriptive ends, the sheer force of his portrayals giving way to action. Adapting the rhetorical structure he had used in the past (with its roots in his progressivism), Roosevelt advanced a binary view of world affairs as a justification for his administration's 1940 policies.

On the one side stood the United States, the guardian of spiritual values and civilized principles. "Life's ideals are to be measured in other than material things," he proclaimed in his third inaugural address. "Most vital to our present and our future is . . . the spirit—the faith of America."[61] As described above, the president extended these amorphous attributes to cover fellow democracies. Like in his "Dagger" address, he equated Allied soldiers with defenders of freedom. On the other side stood the Axis powers, reduced to a cohesive monolithic force threatening US interests everywhere around the world. Of course, this depiction papered over serious differences within the Axis camp, which was far from a monolith. The Germans did not even bother to tell the Japanese about their plan to attack the Soviet Union beforehand, demonstrating, in Reynold's words, the "hollowness" of "the Berlin-Tokyo Axis."[62] But FDR's rhetoric erased the peculiarities among the Axis powers, and this minimization served as the fulcrum around which his dualism swung.

This binary vision was acted out in specific, concrete policies. Some were widely noticed and debated, like the draft. Others attracted less attention, like the decision to reinforce the American military presence in the Philippines. "This policy shift," one author notes, "was testimony to the intensifying ideology of all-or-nothing global war, in which retreat was tantamount to defeat."[63] The president framed the war as an apocalyptic battle waged in what he called a "world-wide arena."[64] His framing of the situation was total: "Civilization as we know it versus the ultimate destruction of all that we hold dear—religion against godlessness; the ideal of justice against the practice of force; decency versus the firing squad."[65] FDR's dualism imposed a familiar narrative structure, making sense of the complex and frightening events taking place abroad and serving as the rationale justifying his chosen courses of action.

The central theme of his narrative was the threat to the United States itself. It was an "illusion" to go on believing that geographical isolation would make America "secure against dangers," Roosevelt insisted.[66] But when it came to defining the exact nature of that peril, he remained studiously vague. Yet here too the administration co-opted anti-interventionist lines of argument, this time seizing upon their fears of state control. Within the administration, it was commonly assumed that if the United States were cut off from substantial foreign trade while being forced to spend huge sums on the military, it would have to adopt a rigidly state-controlled economy. Under a state-controlled economy, as anti-interventionists were quick to point out, individual freedoms would be radically curtailed. Thus, according to FDR, the United States defended Britain to preclude policies of centralization, which would be necessary to stave off economic strangulation. Hull made that point dramatically when he warned that the Reciprocal Trade Agreements Act had to be renewed to prevent "the disappearance of free enterprise."[67] FDR argued the same in a more optimistic register, telling Congress that "open[ing] up the trade channels of the world . . . [is] an indispensable part of the foundation of any stable and enduring peace."[68]

Increasingly, the president spoke as if "America" encompassed the entire Western Hemisphere: "Unless the hemisphere is safe, we are not safe."[69] He drew the link between his own nation and the hemisphere most clearly when he talked about the economic threat of Nazi conquest. He laid the main emphasis on the economic threat to hemispheric free trade. German leaders intended "to enslave the whole of Europe, and then to use the resources of Europe to dominate the rest of the world" economically. "Most important of all," they wanted to seize "the vast resources and wealth of this American Hemisphere [which] constitute the most tempting loot in all the round world."[70] Defending his plan to give Britain destroyers in return for British bases, he said little about aiding Britain, but rather insisted that "the value to the Western Hemisphere of these outposts of security is beyond calculation." The president went beyond the Monroe Doctrine, which declared that any threat to the postcolonial hemispheric status quo would be construed as a threat to the vital interests of the United States; he even went further than his "Cousin Teddy," who issued the "Roosevelt Corollary" claiming exclusive international policing powers in the affairs of Latin American nations for Washington. FDR asserted that any menace to the hemisphere's economy ("enslavement") threatened the personal safety—which he had long defined in expansive, economic terms—of every American home.[71]

Although Roosevelt's discourse was built on this apocalyptic description of the problem, he did not call for the classic apocalyptic solution: an all-out war to destroy the forces of evil. Rather, in keeping with the rhetorical strategy of appropriating anti-interventionist lines of argument, he asserted that he instead wanted to invest in building an impregnable defense against the threatening danger. He justified the nation's rapidly growing military preparation by insisting that it was only a way of "safeguarding our institutions" "to protect and to perpetuate the integrity of democracy."[72]

Any nation helping to defend the world against the monolithic evil was, by definition, on the side of America and thus of the good. The only alternative was to be ruled by criminals, practitioners of the "philosophy of force," who would constantly oppress the global community. In such a dichotomous world, the logic of Roosevelt's dualism indicated, there could be no meaningful neutrality. Consequently, the whole world became a single battlefield, pitting the interlinked and interchangeable symbols of security against the equally linked and interchangeable symbols of insecurity. The two rhetorical chains were represented by two global camps, separated by not only geopolitical borders and military front lines but also ideological chasms. Anyone who did not actively support the side of democracy and security would, by default, be supporting the philosophy of force that controlled the other side. Throughout 1940 FDR made this case compellingly, winning more and more Americans to his side as he disarmed one anti-interventionist argument after another.

Conclusion: The Arsenal of Democracy

President Roosevelt's 1940 rhetorical campaign against anti-interventionism resulted in three primary effects. First, his efforts helped safeguard US policies to support Britain, thereby securing for the administration an immediate victory in the short term. Buoyed by American support, London held out under the Luftwaffe's bombing blitz and remained in the war. To blunt the appeal of anti-interventionism, FDR had to define victory as effective defense and nothing more. So, he proclaimed the survival of Britain as the United States' first victory. Staving off evil—keeping it contained behind a defensive perimeter—became the equivalent of defeating evil, at least in Roosevelt's 1940 utterances. Despite the resistance of Taft and other anti-interventionist politicians, FDR kept the munitions flowing to Britain and the public on his side.

Second, the president won reelection by an electoral college landslide, serving to validate his expansion of federal and executive power not only in domestic affairs but also in foreign policy. Roosevelt's rhetoric increasingly blurred the line between the New Deal reforms and his dualistic understanding of international affairs, globalizing the argument that new structures of security were needed to keep the old values secure from self-aggrandizing aggressors. FDR saw his 1940 reelection as an endorsement of this new way of thinking and speaking. He could point to a poll showing some 80 percent of the public approving the lend-lease plan, the surest sign yet of the burgeoning triumph of his political outlook over that of the anti-interventionists.[73]

Yet at the same time, he won his third term with only about 55 percent of the total votes. Some historians have concluded that he was not reelected because voters thought he would keep them out of war, nor because they agreed with his strategy for leading them into war or with his postwar vision. Indeed, there was widespread uncertainty about just where he was leading the nation. Americans were "like a leaderless army," *Life* magazine explained, waiting "to be given their marching orders."[74] Rather, it seems likely that Roosevelt won because those 55 percent of the voters trusted him most to give them their orders no matter what happened and to guide the nation if (or when) it got into the war. The president was the great symbol of stout resistance to the vaguely articulated and ultimately unpredictable threats of which he himself constantly warned.[75] In that sense, then, the president's appropriation of anti-interventionist values—a defensive orientation, concern over centralization, and an appreciation of American uniqueness and virtue—proved successful, as he was able to win reelection in a way that did not constrain his freedom of action going forward. Most Americans elected him to an unprecedented third term in the Oval Office because of their trust in him, a belief that would soon be tested.

Third, Roosevelt's public arguments that worked to confound the anti-interventionist cause served as inventional devices for his future rhetoric. While FDR's appropriation of his opposition's talking points can, within the narrow confines of 1940, be seen as an imaginative debate tactic that helped stifle resistance to his policies, his rhetoric also worked to longer-lasting effect. By weaving together a mythic constellation of appeals combining dualism, freedom, Christianity, innocence, apocalypticism, democracy, defense, protection, and security, FDR developed rhetorical resources for describing the American war effort. Although he shied away from making a positive case for US entry into the war at this time, the president would turn to these themes when he needed to make such an appeal. One significant aspect of his rhetorical victories over the anti-interventionists in 1940, therefore, is that this argumentative clash before the American public helped Roosevelt generate the inventional resources for talking about US involvement in military efforts overseas in a way that avoided backlash like the kind that felled his political mentor, Woodrow Wilson. Regardless of his intent, FDR's rhetorical victory of 1940 set in motion a new long-term direction for the nation in its foreign affairs.

All these threads came together in FDR's "Arsenal of Democracy" address, a fireside chat given on December 29, 1940. This speech is commonly understood as a turning point in American neutrality, as the president overtly called upon the nation to arm the remaining Allied nations in their fight against the Axis powers. In actuality, this address— while still an important rhetorical event—was simply one of many moments in which the president stringently made his case against the anti-interventionist position following the fall of France. Viewed along a continuum from June, Roosevelt's call for the United States to become the "Arsenal of Democracy" at year's end punctuated his successful campaign against the strict neutrality advanced by the anti-interventionists.

In the address, FDR expressed insecurity in economic language blended with geopolitical considerations, blurring his liberal internationalist and realist sensibilities into a combined package. FDR's dualism funneled these elements into an entreaty for the nation to embrace its identity as a martial democracy. Echoing the address at Virginia, FDR described the threat arrayed against the United States as a civilizational challenge. As he stated in an early draft of the "arsenal of democracy" speech he wrote by hand: "We are the heirs of twenty centuries of [as an afterthought he added "Christian"] faith in the fatherhood of God and the brotherhood of man. On that belief have been founded our families, our communities, and our nation. This year for the first time in our history that Christian civilization is in danger."[76] In calling Americans to become "the great arsenal of democracy," he insisted that "never before since Jamestown and Plymouth Rock has our American civilization been in such danger as now."[77]

According to the administration, Axis military and economic power imperiled not just democracy but also the American homeland itself. Cabinet members testifying to the House Foreign Affairs Committee "expressed fear of an invasion of the United States if the British Navy was beaten or taken." In handwritten notes for the fireside chat, which explained why America had to be "the great arsenal of democracy," FDR wrote that Germany, Japan, and Italy had agreed on an "expansion program—world control." (In the final text of that speech, he merely mentioned briefly that the aggressors were motivated by a racist ideology that spurred them on to conquest.)[78] In any case, he proclaimed to the American people that a German triumph over Britain would imprison the United States: "All of us . . . would be living at the point of a gun—a gun loaded with explosive bullets, economic as well as military. . . . To survive in such a world, we would have to convert ourselves permanently into a militaristic power on the basis of war economy."[79] Germany aimed to achieve this goal, he explained, by conquering Britain and its preeminent navy, gaining control of the seas, and thus dominating the world's channels of trade.

Roosevelt characteristically turned to metaphor to communicate the intensity of the Axis threat. Opposed to Britain stood "the evil forces which have crushed and undermined and corrupted so many," he warned in vivid language. Germany and its allies comprised an "unholy alliance of power and pelf to dominate and enslave the human race." The aggressors were like "a gang of outlaws [that] surrounds your community and on threat of extermination makes you pay a tribute."[80] Moving beyond metaphors of criminality, heresy, and belligerency, he employed animalistic and mechanistic labels; the enemies, having no moral values and knowing no reason but force, were like "a tiger" or "an incendiary bomb." There was no reasoning with them, no middle ground to be had.[81] In these ways Roosevelt utilized the power of metaphor to facilitate assent and foreclose contestation of his foreign policy vis-à-vis the war.[82]

Yet Roosevelt still held back. Knowing that public opinion remained broadly uneasy about US entry into the conflict, and seeking to avoid the fate of Wilson before him, FDR did not call for war. The opening lines of his address explicitly disavowed this goal, as he assured Americans, "This is not a fireside chat on war." Rather, he insisted in a contorted turn of phrase: "It is a talk on national security; because the nub of the whole purpose of your President is to keep you now, and your children later, and your grandchildren much later, out of a last-ditch war for the preservation of American independence and all the things that American independence means to you and to me and to ours." Indeed, "preparation" and the construction of an "all-inclusive defense" were not the same as a request to Congress for a declaration of war. Even as he proclaimed that all the things Americans held dear lay vulnerable, including independence itself, he demurred from pushing further. Roosevelt's restraint speaks to the monumental challenge that still lay before him: to articulate a positive case for entry into the conflict. While he had generated the materials for that argument, its assembly into a cohesive set of war aims would have to wait another year.

7 | Roosevelt's Rhetorical Victory, 1941
The Four Freedoms

Flush with electoral victory, Roosevelt entered 1941 on a political high. He was popular. His approval ratings reached a record height of 72 percent after his inauguration that January.[1] He was winning the intervention debate. A poll the previous October had shown that an even higher 76 percent of military-age men were willing to serve in the armed forces if called upon.[2] At the same time, Harvey J. Kaye observes, "his triumph was shadowed by the question of what was to be done . . . he knew the country was not yet prepared for military action, physically or otherwise."[3] Even though FDR's persuasive efforts had begun bearing fruit in opinion polls, American entry into the world conflict remained a distant political possibility. As Robert Divine notes, "Rarely do people respond positively to a simple query about entering a major conflict."[4] Hence, as the president embarked upon his ninth year in office, the nation's foreign policy stood in a place of tension—opposed to Axis aggression, sympathetic to Britain, committed to hemispheric defense, yet still formally neutral and inflexibly opposed to proactive US entry into the war.

Roosevelt's discourse reflected this volatility, as his political battle with the anti-interventionists pulled him in two opposing rhetorical directions. To circumvent their objections, he embraced "defense" as the rationale for his rearmament program and equated victory with impenetrable national defenses in the face of alarming threats. But his words also sounded expectant notes, linking domestic security with hope for a reconstructed global order. "Never have free men been satisfied with the mere maintenance of any status quo," he said: "We have always held to . . . the conviction that there is a better life, a better world, beyond the horizon." The United States would aid the defense of Britain in order to create a free postwar world, where "the human spirit may find fulfillment" through a "free [i.e., capitalist] and productive economic system."[5] This confident optimism reflected the evolving beliefs of the liberal internationalists, who were now coming to hold that war might be a moral imperative that was necessary to move society toward higher social and economic development.[6] Roosevelt's rhetoric was torn between settling for a politically savvy defensive emphasis and offering a concept of a better world that would arise from the ashes of war. These two impulses could not coexist indefinitely.

Consequently, FDR did not seek to merely consolidate the rhetorical gains made the previous year against the ani-interventionists. Polls demonstrating American readiness to defend the homeland were not enough. After all, Woodrow Wilson also had public opinion on his side when he led the nation into war, only to see his foreign policy collapse alongside his presidency a scant two years later. The Roosevelt administration, as Elizabeth Borgwardt writes, was "planning the peace while the war was still raging . . . the instructive failure of Wilsonian diplomacy taught that negotiating positions tended to harden quickly after an armistice, and nations soon turned inward. . . . A corollary of these first two prescriptions was to work actively to bring public opinion along as well, ideally in ways that could be measured and heard by the Senate."[7] Susan Butler likewise records that FDR kept a portrait of Wilson in the room where he crafted speeches with his aides. As the president's biographer and friend Robert E. Sherwood recounted, "The tragedy of Wilson was always somewhere within the rim of his consciousness. Roosevelt could never forget Wilson's mistakes."[8] FDR was determined to avoid making the same errors his mentor made.

To accomplish that aim required Roosevelt to craft a positive case for intervention, not simply rely on "defense" as a rhetorical justification for his policy of "aggressive neutrality."[9] Over the course of 1941 he would articulate the outlines of such a vision, providing Americans a glimpse of a future postwar world as he prepared the nation to enter the conflict. Relying on appeals to nostalgia, freedom, democracy, and security, FDR adapted elements of his previous discourse to reframe the prospect of war as something consistent with American self-understanding. By year's end he would have effectually won the debate with the anti-interventionists, his various arguments coalescing into a positive case for US entry into the war *before* the attack on Pearl Harbor. He started his effort a week into the new year.

The Four Freedoms

Roosevelt began the shift toward articulating a positive postwar vision in his annual message to Congress on January 6, 1941. In that speech, which was soon dubbed the "Four Freedoms" address, he wholeheartedly rejected the "new world order" of the Axis powers, submitting in its place the "the moral order" of the future. He enumerated the marks of the civilized postwar society he wished to establish, framing his endeavor (like the New Deal) as an exercise in securitization: "In the future days, which we seek to make secure, we look forward to a world founded upon four essential human freedoms." Both the eschatological language of the biblical prophets ("future days") and the reference to security were added by the president himself to the text. Even as he offered a foretaste of the world after the war, FDR relied on the familiar keynotes of apocalypticism, religiously charged language, and an emphasis on security. Evincing his faith in human progress, the president announced that the consummation he described was "no vision of a distant millennium" but was capable of being realized now: "It is a definite basis for a kind of world attainable in our own time."[10]

Throughout the address he accentuated defending the good that already existed rather than transforming the world to make it better. The future FDR envisioned would bring nothing radically new: "Let us say to the democracies: We are putting forth our energies, our resources, and our organizing powers to give you the strength to regain and maintain a free world."[11] *Regain* was a key word here, for it suggested that the new world order would bring only a more secure guarantee that the fundamentals of old, which seemed to be eroding around the world, would be preserved. As in his New Deal rhetoric, Roosevelt synthesized nostalgia with a call for a new course. He had made this connection for some time, equating a defense of the old and the building of the new in foreign affairs. He stated in 1940, for instance, "We defend and we build a way of life, not for America alone, but for all mankind."[12] He thus blurred the distinctions between transforming the world and preserving the American way of life by making them merely two different ways of expressing the nation's mission. FDR continued to link these pursuits in his third inaugural address. He quoted George Washington, saying, "The preservation of the sacred fire of liberty . . . [is] finally, staked on the experiment intrusted [*sic*] to the hands of the American people," and then added: "If we lose that sacred fire, we shall reject the destiny which Washington strove so valiantly and so triumphantly to establish."[13] Again, the future ("destiny") was conflated with the past, in this case the very origin of the nation.

Roosevelt expended considerable effort in the Four Freedoms address to demonstrate the consistency of his administration's foreign policy with past American actions. "It is true that prior to 1914 the United States often had been disturbed by events in other Continents," he stated, referencing French aggression under Napoleon and Napoleon III, the Spanish–American War, the War of 1812, and "a number of undeclared wars" over US commercial rights abroad. What these experiences amounted to, he said, was "the historic truth that the United States as a nation has at all times maintained opposition . . . to any attempt to lock us behind an ancient Chinese wall while the procession of civilization went past." By using the metaphor of a wall to convey isolation and (in line with Roosevelt's view of racial hierarchy) civilizational stagnation, the president's words simultaneously asserted the continuity of his foreign policy with US precedent and also the atmospheric stakes of the current conflict. In the logic of this depiction, the United States risked losing its identity by falling behind the rest of the world.

Roosevelt's speech framed the conflict as one of competing ideals. Months prior in his "Stab in the Back" speech at Charlottesville, he had elevated hostilities to the realm of abstractions to impose a dualistic interpretation of the war. As he had said then, the Axis powers rendered the whole world insecure because they "abandon with deliberate contempt all of the moral values to which even this young country for more than three hundred years has been accustomed and dedicated." Now America's mission was to defend moral values—above all, freedom— for the whole world. As Luke Glanville notes, Roosevelt's speech foregrounded "the need for a future peace to be founded on the protection of 'freedom' worldwide."[14]

The Four Freedoms speech became the most famous of Roosevelt's optimistic visions. Tacked on to the end of the 1941 annual address, these lines were composed as a discrete rhetorical unit, handwritten on a separate piece of paper by speechwriter Samuel Rosenman (who said he was taking dictation from the president) and titled "peroration."[15] Like the overall vision, each of the freedoms was firmly embedded in the liberal internationalist agenda FDR had promoted since the 1920s as a way of safeguarding traditional values: "The world order which we seek is the cooperation of free countries, working together in a friendly, civilized society." He endorsed freedom of speech, the first of the four, as a sine qua non of democracy. He had always linked the tradition of democratic freedoms with capitalism. In the 1920s he had traced the origins of democracy and all its political rights back to the growth of an entrepreneurial middle class in the Middle Ages.[16]

Freedom of religion fit naturally with his long-standing claim that democratic capitalism was the political-economic expression of eternal spiritual truths. A global liberal internationalism would have to be nurtured by an active spiritual life, based on a return to those age-old truths. Roosevelt framed this element of his foreign policy as an expansion of New Deal values: "Just as our national policy in internal affairs has been based upon a decent respect for the rights and the dignity of all of our fellow men within our gates, so our national policy in foreign affairs has been based on a decent respect for the rights and the dignity of all nations, large and small. And the justice of morality must and will win in the end."[17]

Roosevelt explained that freedom from fear (a few months later he would call it "freedom from terrorism") "translated into world terms, means a world-wide reduction of armaments to such a point and in such a thorough fashion that no nation will be in a position to commit an act of physical aggression against any neighbor—anywhere in the world." This formulation had been percolating for some time. As early as November 1939, he reportedly told some White House visitors that he wanted to guarantee four freedoms, including "freedom from fear of aggression."[18] Disarmament had long been a foundation of his vision of a pacific internationalist world system, safeguarding traditional civilized values and directing would-be empire-builders into the productive realm of commerce.

Privately, though, FDR told both Churchill and Sumner Welles about one proviso he thought necessary for global safety: the demand for disarmament would not apply to the United States and Britain. They would need modern weapons to police the world system of democratic capitalism and enforce the disarmament of all other nations. All nations would enjoy "complete economic and commercial and boundary liberty, but America and England would have to maintain the peace. . . . Smaller powers might have rifles but nothing more dangerous."[19] As a benevolent nation, so the argument went, other countries had little to fear from the United States; Roosevelt would say months later, "The aggression is not ours. Ours is solely defense."[20] The president's vision for a disarmed world, and by extension "freedom from fear," rested on a belief in intrinsic American innocence from the machinations of great power politics.

Lastly, FDR promised "freedom from want." He explained what this meant: "[When] translated into world terms, [it] means economic understandings which will secure to every nation a healthy peacetime life for its inhabitants—everywhere in the world." Those last four words were added by the president himself in the editing process.[21] In the Hullian faith of the administration, the only kind of "economic understanding" that could ensure "a healthy peacetime life" was a fully liberalized and fully global trade system. The history of the speech and the phrase confirm that this is what the president had in mind. In a November 1939 report from the White House, one of the freedoms was identified as "freedom to make a living." And an early draft of the speech suggested that the president should close by supporting the rights of workers against their capitalist bosses. In the United States, it read, freedom meant that "no class is made sacred. No property system is made superior to human rights." FDR softened that final definition to say, more vaguely, that "freedom means the supremacy of human rights everywhere."[22] He set this idea in a broader context when he told a press conference that "freedom from want" meant "the removal of certain barriers between nations, cultural in the first place and commercial in the second place."[23] He thereby reasserted economic doctrines central to his foreign policy since the 1920s in redeveloped form, framing them as a form of individual liberty that was part and parcel with the freedoms surrounding speech, religion, and fear.

The Four Freedoms represented the skeleton of FDR's vision for a postwar liberal internationalist order, which would preserve the highest moral values of old and incorporate Germany along with all other nations. In effect, Roosevelt was aiming to avoid Wilson's mistakes in World War I by taking the exact opposite route: planning for victory but controlling the postwar settlement by announcing, well in advance, war aims that were idealistic yet broad and general. In articulating these aims, FDR introduced little that he had not said before. He made the same demands of Germany that he had stipulated all along—to become a full, and fully disarmed, participant in a global liberal internationalist system—and his emphasis on nondiscriminatory trade and disarmament were well established by 1941. Hence, the Four Freedoms served as his ultimate fusion of traditional American values and hopes for a transformed world.

The critical movement in this speech, however, was Roosevelt's rhetorical construction of the United States as a heroic moral agent in the conflict. Rather than merely cheer on and support the gallant Allied soldiers defending liberty, as he had in the "Dagger" address, here FDR issued an edict on what the war's settlement would entail. As James J. Kimble notes, the "address worked to construct a heroic nation that could intervene in international affairs to save the victim (democracy) from the immoral villain (the Axis powers) . . . this narrative description of world affairs—especially given its traditional roots in American discourse—would have been compelling for many in Roosevelt's various audiences."[24] Building on his description of the United States as democracy's "arsenal" a month before, FDR portrayed his country as a major character in the global drama that was unfolding. While he still described the American role in the war in defensive terms—editing a draft of the speech, when he came across the claim that "an unprepared America" could not "defeat the whole world" he changed "defeat" to "hold off"—the president had now introduced the idea of the United States as the decisive actor in the conflict.[25]

It remains unclear whether Roosevelt was an idealist crusading for moral values, a realist who recognized the dangers of aggression, a capitalist maneuvering to enrich his country, or a politician aiming to win a political victory. Historians have debated his true motives endlessly.[26] What is clear is that FDR's public and private words sketched a loose narrative that mixed the ideas of upholding democratic civilization, creating a new economic order, and holding the forces of aggression in check. Only this combination, he conveyed, would protect moral values. And, as he tacitly claimed in his address, the United States alone was both willing and able to lead that effort. If the values underlying a civilized order were to be American values, then the United States was now called upon to provide the moral guidance, economic coordination, and military power necessary to establish that order. From the address's very first sentences, the president announced that the nation faced an "unprecedented" threat to its security and its "continued independence." "At no previous time has American security been as seriously threatened from without as it is today," he warned bluntly.[27] That peril had engulfed the entire globe: "Every realist knows that the democratic way of life is at this moment being directly assailed in every part of the world." Since the aggressors would accept nothing less than the "total surrender" of all civilized people, "the future and the safety of our country and of our democracy are overwhelmingly involved in events far beyond our borders."[28] He made all these connections seem obvious, in the process conveying a sense of threat as well as a glimpse of the war's purpose that more directly involved the United States.

Anti-Interventionist Resistance

If the Axis powers demanded the "total surrender" of democracy, as FDR insisted, then those who equally insisted that the United States could stay out of the fight were part of the problem. He thus cast "isolationists," who thought that America alone could "hold off the whole world" as not only imprudent but also untrue to American ideals. Just two weeks later, in his third inaugural address, Roosevelt made a revealing slip of the tongue. Where his printed text read that it was time "to rediscover what we are and what we may be. If we do not, we risk the real peril of inaction," he misspoke on the last word. As his own handwritten note on the reading copy explains: "I misread this word ['inaction'] as 'isolation,' then added 'and inaction.' All of which improved it!"[29]

FDR cautiously downplayed the concrete, specific details in his hopeful postwar vision as a strategy meant to isolate the anti-interventionists. By phrasing his foreign policy aims as attempts to spread the benefits of American-style freedom to the rest of the world, Roosevelt backed the anti-interventionists into a rhetorical corner—in rejecting the president's proposals, they implicitly opposed the freedoms he espoused. He used their determination to reject his postwar vision against them. For example, Roosevelt called Lindbergh a "copperhead" that April, leading the pilot to become so enraged that he renounced his commission in the US military granted for his transoceanic aviation; in response, the administration wasted little time in wondering why he was so quick to resign his position at home but reluctant to criticize Nazi actions abroad.[30] In addition to cornering the anti-interventionists, FDR's ambiguity had the added benefit of avoiding a replay of the end of World War I, when the hopes raised by Wilson's fourteen points led to a postwar disillusionment that in 1920 cost Roosevelt the vice presidency.

Indeed, some liberal anti-interventionists claimed that the Four

Freedoms were merely propaganda to promote his imperialist program. Roosevelt wanted to "fill the four corners of the earth with four freedoms," they charged: "Having failed to bring his Four Freedoms to the United States, our president seems to feel that he can bring them to five-sevenths of the world." This seemed to be clear evidence of an "empire mind. . . . Once this empire is accepted, it need have no limits."[31] Though the Rooseveltian vision of world transformation seemed to be packed with symbols of security, most anti-interventionists (conservative as well as liberal) described it as one huge symbol of insecurity, a surefire recipe for embroiling the United States in future conflicts around the world. The president could get more political mileage by wrapping his idealistic vision in his own package of symbols of insecurity and persuading the public that he was in the best position to assess the true threats to the nation's security and its values.

Despite this resistance, however, Roosevelt's rhetorical strategy did seem to be winning at home. His position was buoyed days after the inaugural, when Hitler reciprocated Roosevelt's harsh rhetoric by threatening to sink any ship bound for Britain, including those from the United States.[32] Support for the Lend-Lease Act grew sufficiently to ensure its passage in March 1941. However, polls at that time showed only about 60 percent of the public supporting the measure. If FDR aimed to educate the American public to a new way of thinking, one that would survive the cataclysm of contact with the enemy, then he still had significant work to do.[33] The narrative structure he would use to pursue that long-term goal—and, in the short run, to ensure public support for more aid to Britain—was rounding into form. Now he needed only to persuade a larger majority to view the world situation through its lens.

"Unlimited National Emergency"

Roosevelt's next step was another major radio address on May 27, 1941, which garnered his largest audience yet. His speech had two aims. The first, according to one of its authors, was simply "to scare the daylights out of everyone." In this address the president declared "a state of unlimited national emergency," doing so "primarily for its psychological effect," as his attorney general said.[34] To achieve this purpose, FDR used vivid images of peril. The Nazis were waging "world war for world domination," he proclaimed.[35] If they obtained air bases close to the United

States through either war or negotiated peace, they would use them to bomb American soil: "The safety of American homes even in the center of our country has a definite relationship to the continued safety of homes in Nova Scotia or Trinidad or Brazil." Therefore, Americans should act to defend those distant homes "just as much as we would to fight for the safety of our own homes."[36] There was little new in the way of argument here. By 1941 Roosevelt had focused on the emerging technologies of aerial warfare to claim that America faced a direct risk of attack for decades, and he used that image to incite fear.

Second, the speech also aimed to clarify the president's view of the war. Up to that point he had kept his analysis studiously vague, as usual. Journalist Raymond Gram Swing commented that Roosevelt would not take a public stand on naval convoying, for example, because any stand would "compromise fatally his position at the center of national unity: he would destroy himself as the symbolic figure around whom a solid national opinion could cohere."[37] However, a government survey of newspapers suggested that the president now needed to take clearer stances in respect to the war if he wished to further shape national opinion. The survey found many editorials blaming the public's "apathy, confusion, and timidity" on the president because, the editorial writers charged, he did not trust the citizenry to understand or adequately act upon the need to save Britain.[38] Thus, FDR sought to both frighten the public and make it feel that it was being well-informed of strategies the president was pursuing to ward off the Axis threat.

Consequently, the bulk of this speech offered his most specific military and geopolitical analysis to date. The longtime student of Mahan based the crux of his argument on a time-honored principle: "All freedom . . . depends on freedom of the seas." This framing thematically linked the "emergency" to the principles he had championed four months prior in the Four Freedoms address. According to FDR, the Axis powers' "supreme purpose" was to "obtain control of the seas, and to achieve it, they must capture Great Britain." Whether or not control of the seas was actually Germany's supreme purpose in 1941, it was certainly the supreme concern of the president. A few weeks earlier, he had privately urged Churchill to focus on sea defenses rather than land battle, because "in the last analysis Naval control of the Indian Ocean and the Atlantic Ocean will in time win the war."[39] Now, publicly, he claimed to know what was in "the Nazi book of world conquest": defeat Britain, seize control of the seas, "fasten an economic stranglehold upon our several nations" of the Western Hemisphere, and then ultimately (in a callback to the Charlottesville "Dagger" address) "strangle the United States of America."[40]

The danger, as he depicted, was chiefly economic: "The whole fabric of working life as we know it . . . would be mangled and crippled," necessitating "permanent conscription of manpower," all public resources poured into armament, and a nation "year in and year out, standing day and night watch against the destruction of our cities." FDR's close aide Sumner Welles had explained the economic danger more specifically in a speech a few months earlier: Since Latin American trade depended on exporting many of the same goods and crops produced in the United States, those countries had to sell their excess products to the Old World. If the Axis powers dominated all of Eurasia, then they could dictate the terms of global trade to the New World, including the United States.[41]

At the same time, Roosevelt's geopolitical analysis also incorporated the principles laid out in his Four Freedoms address to provide a basis for optimism. "If the Axis powers fail to gain control of the seas, they are certainly defeated," he contended: "[They] will suffer inevitable disaster." His prediction followed from the moral logic he imposed to frame the conflict. The Axis could not indefinitely suppress the universal human yearning for freedom he had so eloquently described in January: "Once they are limited to a continuing land war, their cruel forces of occupation will be unable to keep their heel on the necks of the millions of innocent oppressed people on the continent of Europe; and in the end their whole structure will break into little pieces."[42] While he had previously been wary of furnishing political ammunition for the anti-interventionists, FDR now announced his expectation that the nations of a liberated Europe would be reconstituted "as democracies" and thus more American (and less autocratic and less imperialistic).[43]

Although Roosevelt employed strident rhetoric in asserting executive power in declaring an "unlimited emergency," he did not follow this address with an explanation of what that phrase entailed or if he was implementing any new policies. Indeed, the speech did not clarify the exact nature of the Axis threat either.[44] The president signaled his "assumption of power to do something big and conclusive, but just what nobody knows," one anti-interventionist wrote at the time. "There may be simply nothing more to do."[45] FDR was imprecise as to what the state of emergency he had invoked meant in practical terms.[46]

For his purposes, however, vacuity was a political virtue; it left his critics with little to criticize. Having no definite plan of what policies he might propose (or institute), his goal was still to shape the public mood to accept whatever policies he might want to promote in the future. The "unlimited emergency" speech took him a step closer to that goal. Although FDR had no new policies to back up his words, and he predicted that he would "be lucky to get an even break" in public opinion, the response apart from the staunch anti-interventionists was almost completely favorable.[47] By collapsing the distinctions between a militarily attacked America and an economically strangled America, FDR's frightening mélange of threats worked to keep his political options open. Even as he revisited these themes, however, this speech amounted to a clear attempt to go beyond merely describing or framing the conflict taking place overseas and instead move public opinion in a direction where Americans would be more willing to support FDR's leadership. In offering his analysis of events and determining that they now constituted an emergency, Roosevelt built on his prior appeals and informed his audience that the United States, the world's beacon of freedom, virtue, and civilization, was (somehow) resisting the forces of evil. Correspondingly, the anti-interventionist argument that FDR's foreign policy would only multiply the sources of national insecurity fell on fewer and fewer ears.

Extending the Borders of Democracy:
The Soviet Union and China

In June 1941 the international situation changed dramatically when Germany invaded the Soviet Union, raising both a new specter of insecurity and new hopes for security. Though the Nazi regime seemed more irrational and aggressive than ever, the prospect of a long war drawing German troops and resources to the Eastern Front made the survival of Britain seem a much surer bet. But now FDR had to justify supporting not only the British—traditional allies whose war motives were still suspect in some quarters—but the Soviets, who were traditionally seen as suspect, at best, and in some quarters as outright foes. FDR expressing support for a totalitarian leader like Stalin, whom he had castigated as a dictator no better than Hitler only eighteen months prior, could easily cast doubt on all of his idealistic claims about his reasons for opposing the fascists.[48]

The Roosevelt administration began talks to extend Lend-Lease aid to Moscow days after the invasion and began delivering war material to the Soviets within three months.[49] FDR's main argument for extending aid to the Soviets rested on simple self-interest. Prolonging the war on the Eastern Front, he pointed out, would postpone the day that the United States might have to decide whether to enter the war.[50] His focus on this point demonstrated his continuing respect for the political power of anti-interventionism and underscored his aim of maximizing his future flexibility.

The public reaction reflected the ambiguities raised by the continuing debate over intervention. Polls suggested that most Americans would be glad to see Germans and Soviets destroy each other, and a majority doubted the Soviets would win.[51] Missouri senator Harry Truman echoed the view of many Americans when he said, "If we see that Germany is winning we ought to help Russia, and if Russia is winning we ought to help Germany, and that way let them kill as many as possible."[52] Nevertheless, over half of the respondents hoped for a Soviet victory because they believed (according to pollster George Gallup) that "Russia is not imperialistic, but Germany is. Russia, even if she won, would not invade the United States, whereas Germany probably would." Even if Soviet ideology was widely hated, Soviet power to disturb American life was not feared.[53] These polls showed that the American public largely accepted the interventionist fear that Hitler might well attempt to conquer the United States, but it also demonstrated major public backing for the central premise of anti-interventionism—that the primary goal of US foreign policy should be to find a way to keep Americans untouched by the complexities of Old World politics and culture.

Regardless, Roosevelt faced a problem of legitimation. His rhetoric for years had equated protecting the homeland with building a global system of liberal internationalism and open trade. In this new paradigm, any nation that refused to participate fully would be, by definition, outside the boundaries of civilization and thus a dangerous aggressor. According to the dualistic liberal internationalist logic advocated by FDR up to this point, the United States staunchly opposed undemocratic nations that isolated themselves and sought to modify these countries' behavior. As a result, Roosevelt faced the rhetorical problem of how to reconcile a huge anticapitalist nation becoming an ally (or at least a nation that merited millions of dollars of US military aid), no matter his personal hopes or "wishful thinking" in regard to the Soviet Union.[54]

The president was now constrained by his previous schema, which had steadfastly divided the world into aggressors and victims of aggression. To embrace a third category would undermine his entire case against the anti-interventionists over the necessity of aid to Britain.[55]

FDR's rhetorical solution was to create a victimhood narrative for the Soviet Union. As Yassin al-Haj Saleh writes, "Victimhood narratives do not invent injustices per se, but they depict these injustices as systematic targeting of an 'innocent' community by an 'antagonist' other."[56] FDR had long traded in the language of victimhood in his description of Axis aggression, and now he used this device as a discursive vehicle to place the Soviets on the side of the Allies and all their attendant moral values. Roosevelt now described the Soviet system as a good neighbor, even claiming that it guaranteed freedom of religion. He often spoke in generalities. Days after the German invasion, for instance, he declared in a radio broadcast that "the fundamentals of 1776 are being struck down abroad and definitely they are threatened here."[57] He later described Russia as a victim of German aggression, no different than any other land Hitler had attacked.[58] Despite the rich reservoir of anti-Soviet and anticommunist sentiment in American public opinion, the president's reframing of the Soviets was soon more or less accepted, giving further evidence that his appeals were succeeding. Any nation under Nazi attack was now part of the United States' line of defense, contributing to the ultimate defense of the American homeland.[59] This solution, as Mary E. Stuckey notes, "masked" the "inherent contradiction" in allying with the Soviet Union, with FDR's good neighbor metaphor papering over divisions without reconciling them.[60]

A similar phenomenon played out with China during this period as well. While the Roosevelt administration had dispatched a few volunteer officers to help the Kuomintang fight the Japanese army in mainland China since 1937—the beginnings of the famed "Flying Tigers" pilot squadron—it significantly increased US aid to China during 1941. Urged by secretaries of state Cordell Hull and William Franklin Knox, FDR approved a $100 million loan to Chiang Kai-shek's government and transferred the first $50 million on February 2.[61] In an address on March 15 he analogized China's need for aid to that of Britain and Greece, each commitment furnishing evidence that "our country is going to be what our people have proclaimed it to be—the arsenal of democracy."[62] George Marshall established an American military mission to China on July 3, 1941, and an additional $630 million in Lend-Lease aid was approved in August.[63]

While China and Kai-shek had long been viewed sympathetically in the United States, few on the ground would have classified his government as a democracy. Nevertheless, in a June 10 report to Congress on Lend-Lease, Roosevelt portrayed China in exactly that way: "Beginning with the outbreak of the war the American public began to realize that it was in our own national interest and security to help Britain, China, and other democratic nations," and: "We have supplied, and we will supply, planes, guns, ammunition, and other defense articles in ever-increasing quantities to Britain, China, and other democracies resisting aggression."[64] As with the Soviet Union, FDR redescribed China in more favorable terms to maintain narrative fidelity with his two-sided depiction of international affairs.

Throughout the summer of 1941, Roosevelt's foreign policy discourse progressively lumped the less-than-democratic nations fighting the Axis powers, most prominently the Soviet Union, into the United States' camp of civilized democratic allies. More clearly than ever, then, the line between security and insecurity could be drawn anywhere, potentially placing it everywhere. The same arguments FDR made for aiding the British, the Chinese, and the Soviets could apply all around the world. By classifying all victims of aggression together, regardless of their political, historical, geographical, or ideological proximity to the United States, Roosevelt's rhetoric expanded the limits of his dualism to theoretically encompass every country on earth. His discourse thereby situated American interests—defined in terms of civilization, democracy, or economics—across the globe in a manner unmatched by any previous president.

The Atlantic Charter

The next step in the evolution of Roosevelt's foreign policy discourse took place in early August. To allay concerns that he supported dictators and to overtly reinforce his commitment to the ideals of democratic civilization, the president agreed to meet with Churchill at Argentia, Newfoundland, where they issued an Anglo-American statement of war aims. Roosevelt initially told Churchill that he wanted the two to issue a short statement couched in vague generalities, saying only that they "had discussed certain principles relating to the civilization of the world."[65]

In the event, a much longer and more detailed document emerged, dubbed the Atlantic Charter, affirming global moral principles as war aims. The president's purpose in issuing the eight-point document, signed by Churchill as well himself, was to reassure Americans that they were not aiding Britain merely to preserve its empire against an upstart imperial rival. It would furthermore assure them that a president allying with a communist regime was not abandoning the principles of democracy.[66] These domestic goals were important enough to him that he wrote out the version of the charter presented to Congress in his own hand.[67] Following his strategy of avoiding Wilson's mistakes, FDR's actions functioned to establish broadly agreed-upon objectives (before the United States even entered the conflict) that would help secure consent for a postwar settlement organized along the lines of his internationalist principles.

In that sense, the Atlantic Charter served as a strategic document for FDR. It signaled to American audiences that the president had not abandoned the ideals he had advanced for years despite his persistent use of dualism to frame a conflict fought along increasingly blurry ideological lines. Though the document sounded on its face like a series of vague generalities, it was a critical step in converting the Four Freedoms—and, more broadly, the foreign policy vision advanced by FDR as president—into concrete war aims. Like the Four Freedoms, it was premised upon the total defeat of Nazi Germany and the other Axis powers. Unlike the Four Freedoms, it spelled out an actual program. It stated, in idealistic terms, the new norms of international politics the Roosevelt administration aspired to inaugurate after the war's end. The document thus served as a practical response to public concerns over his administration's foreign policy direction following the extension of military aid to nations other than Britain. When Roosevelt presented it to Congress, he called for "a peace which will afford to all nations the means of dwelling in safety within their own boundaries."[68] For American audiences, at least, this was reassurance that the United States would support Britain, and perhaps eventually enter the war, only in order to make its own borders once again safe.

Yet the same sentence went on to call for a peace "which will afford assurance that all the men in all the lands may live out their lives in freedom from fear and want." That phrase reaffirmed Roosevelt's constant theme that US borders would be secure only if the whole world were re-shaped according to his administration's political and economic vision. While the charter reemphasized that the highest goal of foreign policy was to keep the nation safely sheltered behind impenetrable defenses, it simultaneously reaffirmed the familiar premise that insecurity or aggression anywhere in world could make Americans insecure at any time. All references to boundaries or borders, ostensibly the prime symbols of security, thus became at the same time symbols and reminders of insecurity when distilled through FDR's rhetorical matrix.

Roosevelt's promise of "freedom from fear" was fleshed out in the Atlantic Charter's insistence on "abandonment of the use of force." As it read, "nations which threaten, or may threaten, aggression outside of their frontiers" would have to be disarmed, "pending the establishment of a wider and permanent system of general security." The document likewise gave a more specific interpretation of Roosevelt's call for "freedom from want." The United States and Britain would "endeavor to further the enjoyment by all States . . . of access, on equal terms, to the trade and to the raw materials of the world." This sentence further muddied the distinction between a Hullian universal trading system and a universal set of moral ideals.

Indeed, these issues of trade and international norms revealed the second way in which the charter was a strategic document. In the Atlantic Charter, Roosevelt for the first time imposed his blend of liberal internationalism and "good neighborism" on the other Allied powers. In fact, the original draft of the charter was written entirely by Secretary Hull's State Department. As David Kaiser writes, "While the Army and Navy planned for war, the State Department had been laying plans for the eventual peace," aiming to achieve a "Wilsonian world without great armaments or trade barriers."[69] The charter thus represented the first step in Roosevelt's attempt to articulate war aims for the entire anti-Axis alliance in the idiom of his administration, and his ability to foist his perspective on Britain before the United States even entered the war serves as evidence of the tremendous power he wielded already. Churchill needed a continuing flow of US war material at virtually any cost, so he implicitly committed Britain to ending the preferential treatment accorded to members of the empire. That would be the true repayment for the Lend-Lease materials.[70] Consequently, the Atlantic Charter served as a doubly strategic document for FDR by not only signaling to domestic audiences his commitment to liberal ideals but also by binding the British to war aims his State Department had originally written. Beyond that, it also reinforced the message of the Four Freedom speech that (unlike at Versailles) there would be no punitive or invidious postwar settlement.

To be sure, the Roosevelt administration compromised as well. It allowed the proviso "with due respect for their existing obligations" as a concession to the British hope of retaining some kind of imperial closed trading bloc. However, when the British suggested that the United States should lower its own existing trade barriers, the American representatives simply ignored them. "Hull and his allies in the State Department knew who the sinner was," Warren Kimball writes, "and eliminating imperial preference had become a neoreligious quest."[71] The British diplomats saw no choice but to accede to the State Department's ardent demands. One of their officials involved in the Argentia meeting concluded that "FDR has only one clear idea about the peace and that is that America shall emerge . . . as the strongest Power in the world."[72] Nevertheless, by signing the Atlantic Charter Churchill gave his blessing to the Rooseveltian synthesis of national security and liberal internationalism. For the president, the Atlantic Charter therefore constituted a strategic success, especially considering that over thirty Allied nations would eventually sign it.[73] Above all, it established that the United States, even before it became an active belligerent, would play the leading role in shaping the postwar world.

Some critical observers at the time in the United States suggested ways in which the Atlantic Charter served the goals of political realism and, by implication, represented the greater enmeshment of the United States in great power politics. The liberal journal *Commonweal* complained that the document aimed at merely "restoring the status quo"—precisely the words Hans Morgenthau would later use to define the realist notion of peace—a status quo that gave much advantage to American and British interests. John Foster Dulles agreed that the charter's unifying conception was "that the postwar world should reproduce and stabilize the political organization of the prewar world." The ultimate goal of innovation for the future was still to preserve the essences—and the advantages—of the past.[74]

Anti-interventionists saw this goal plainly and decried it loudly. Senator Gerald Nye charged that Roosevelt and Churchill planned "to disarm the world, except that part of the world which these two men will dominate . . . because the task is forever to be ours of policing the world, inflicting our ideologies and our wishes upon the world." The America First Committee said the same, telling its members that "the *heart* of Point Eight means an *Anglo-American world police force.*" And America First recognized the long-term implications: "Projecting an Anglo-American police force makes it seem likely that many more strategic parts of the earth will have to be occupied to make secure military control everywhere in the world. And this may be true even though the Anglo-American Union protests that it does not 'seek' territorial aggrandizement. . . . Economic reasons may necessitate the seizure of additional territory."[75] The idealist language of the Atlantic Charter, anti-interventionists argued, simply masked the permanent extension of American power onto the global stage.

From its more liberal perspective, *Uncensored* made similar claims. The charter promised that all nations would dwell in safety within their own boundaries because "nations that have enough and are fighting for the status quo ante bellum obviously have no interest in territorial changes." The eighth point called for disarmament, one writer argued, because "realists in Washington are also thinking about world organization. . . . What occupies these realists today is a plan to control the world by controlling the world's raw materials. . . . [The United States] would dispense raw materials as it saw fit." Inverting FDR's good neighbor metaphor, this writer analogized the United States to a parsimonious utilitarian, dispersing resources only to those neighbors that proved useful. Of course, he or she noted, the United States would need a "huge standing army" and an equally large navy to stop "bad nations" from aggression. *Uncensored* found validation for its fears when secretary of the navy Frank Knox later said that the United States and Britain should have "sea power for the next 100 years," and press secretary Stephen Early confirmed that this was the administration's view.[76] Indeed, before the United States even entered the war the administration had broached the idea of a postwar international police force with the British government behind closed doors.[77]

After the Roosevelt–Churchill shipboard conference ended, the president tried to downplay these critical concerns by focusing public attention on the "visible performance, not the tangible text" of the meeting.[78] He had good reason. While he had been gone, Congress voted to extend the service of military draftees by only a single vote, 203–202.[79] Rather than focus on the specific policy issues discussed, FDR sought to emphasize the image of democratic civilization's leaders at prayer. He told journalists that the high point of his meeting with the prime minister was not the written agreement but "the very remarkable religious service on the quarterdeck of the Prince of Wales last Sunday morning . . . a deeply moving expression of the unity of faith of our two peoples," in contrast to the values of Hitler.[80] He thus reinforced his framing of the war as a battle of fundamental ideals, pitting civilized people who (by definition) pray on Sunday against dictators who (by definition) preyed upon civilized, praying folk. In promoting this image Roosevelt was quite successful; a poll taken five months later showed that few people could recall any of the specific commitments in the Atlantic Charter.[81]

In sum, Roosevelt promoted an internationalist vision of the future with new global economic and political institutions modeled on the American way. Although few Americans saw that as something worth fighting for, they were much more ready to combat the moral evils Roosevelt wove into his larger foreign policy message surrounding national security. FDR's narrative of 1940 and 1941 was mostly successful in shaping a new public climate, fusing idealism with the defense of national self-interest and setting that traditional American blend in the new context of globalized insecurity. If, as Stuckey holds, "the effects of presidential rhetoric may be subtle and delayed rather than dramatic and immediate," then the efficacy of FDR's discourse of national security, slow-acting as it was, would soon be revealed by the "Undeclared War" with Germany.[82]

The Undeclared War

When he returned from Newfoundland, the president continued to downplay policy and highlight the transcendent symbolism of the meeting. At a press conference he read, approvingly, a letter from Supreme Court Justice Felix Frankfurter: "We live by symbols and we can't too often recall them. And you two in that ocean . . . in the setting of that Sunday service, gave meaning to the conflict between civilization and arrogant, brute challenge."[83] FDR undoubtedly knew that Frankfurter had recently used that turn of phrase in a ruling upholding a compulsory rite of patriotism and national pride. Writing for the Supreme Court, the justice insisted that schools could compel all children to recite the "Pledge of Allegiance," regardless of their religious scruples, because "the ultimate foundation of a free society is the binding tie of cohesive sentiment. . . . 'We live by symbols.' The flag is the symbol of our national unity, transcending all internal differences, however large."[84] Like Frankfurter's opinion, FDR's foreign policy rhetoric highlighted the value of unity by its consistent emphasis on transcendent symbols and ideals.

Frankfurter's ruling pointed to a crucial factor influencing public opinion in the autumn of 1941. As Michael Sherry records, "Patriotic rituals and symbols only lately invented now seemed timeless (and required) for Americans . . . [a] spirit of regimentation shaped the mobilization of fear in particular." FDR's words did much to create this "spirit," as Sherry continues: "Roosevelt himself sounded the alarm. . . . It flowed logically from his conception of national security."[85] The president worked hard to uphold the unifying image of a war fought for national defense and democratic ideals. He had engineered a domestic revolution in his first two terms in the White House, then extended the rhetorical framework used to apply New Deal themes to international affairs. Unlike economic reforms, however, he recognized the political difficulty of leading the nation into war without virtually unanimous support. As Stuckey notes, FDR "sought to align political forces at home in such a way that war, if and when it came, could be fought on the basis of shared principles and would be prosecuted by a unified nation."[86] And in early autumn 1941, about one-fifth of the American populace still stubbornly supported anti-interventionism, enough in his estimation to keep the nation out of the war.[87]

Faced with anti-interventionist persistence, Roosevelt took a calculated risk as summer turned to fall. On September 4, the USS *Greer*, a naval destroyer, became the first American ship to engage in hostilities with a German submarine, which, as Roger Daniels records, enabled FDR to go "on the offensive."[88] A week later, the president declared over radio that "the blunt fact [is] that the German submarine fired first upon this American destroyer without warning, and with the deliberate design to sink her." He announced that US warships would now shoot German naval vessels on sight. This measure was both defensive and essential, he asserted: "This is the only step possible if we would keep tight the wall of defense which we are pledged to maintain around this Western Hemisphere." FDR in turn linked this policy with his narrative, combining the military defense of the hemisphere with a set of timeless moral-religious values, declaring that Americans protected "with Divine help and guidance . . . their democracy, their sovereignty, and their freedom . . . [against] an enemy of all law, all liberty, all morality, all religion."[89] Roosevelt now deployed his rhetorical framework of inter-locked symbols of (in)security to justify his most martial policy yet, an undeclared war with Nazi U-boats in the North Atlantic.

Predictably, anti-interventionists saw the matter quite differently. They retorted that the "shoot-on-sight" policy was another step in Roo-sevelt's intentional path to (declared) war. One *Uncensored* article stated, "Since 'national defense' is the shibboleth on which the president's policy is based, it was essential that the Greer incident be presented to Americans with an air of injured innocence."[90] As this writer recognized, the president's narrative would be compelling only if America were the wholly innocent, and thus wholly virtuous, party in the conflict.

Roosevelt's calculated risk and insistence on "injured innocence" paid off. By mid-September, polls showed the public supporting the shoot-on-sight policy in the Atlantic by roughly two to one. When the USS *Kearney* was attacked in October, FDR leveraged the event into a repeal of the Neutrality Act, taking credit for "an American policy of infinite patience."[91] One month later, a leading political pollster, Had-ley Cantril, found that "our morale is probably higher than during any other critical period the nation has faced." Indeed, one poll at the time found fully 75 percent of Republicans supporting the president's for-eign policy and fewer than 20 percent identifying as isolationists.[92] But ambivalence remained. In that same poll, 75 percent to 80 percent of respondents opposed the idea of the United States declaring war against Germany. Furthermore, even those who were willing to go to war hardly seemed to relish the prospect. One liberal anti-interventionist observed: "What worries the Administration as much as enthusiastic opposition is the fact that its support is almost always unenthusiastic. The real en-thusiasm for war comes from those who believe it is the duty of the United States to destroy Hitler under any circumstances, rather than to destroy Hitler only if he crosses an imaginary line which the President might draw in the Atlantic."[93] This was the main thrust of the liberal anti-interventionist case. They, like many Americans, were only willing to countenance force if it would, like the New Deal, lead to a better future for themselves and for the world; they were not content to go to war to corral dangerous forces and preserve the injustices of the ante-bellum political order. As another writer contended, the "defense of an unsatisfactory status quo is not enough to touch off the winning spirit of a people."[94]

As winter drew nearer, FDR's foreign policy had coalesced into a two-part strategy. First, he had accomplished the difficult rhetorical task of creating a positive framework through which to understand American war aims. In speech after speech, from the Four Freedoms to the Unlimited Emergency to the Atlantic Charter to all the fireside chats and press conferences in between, Roosevelt united elements of his previous discourse to generate a coherent case for US entry in World War II. His discourse moved from merely descriptive to prescriptive, legitimizing his progressively warlike policies and offering the American public a nascent vision for the postwar world. This rhetorical approach gave Roosevelt several advantages. It allowed him to recognize that few Americans truly wanted war, even as the public moved gradually toward accepting war as an inevitability. Such widespread ambivalence testified to the lingering power of the anti-interventionists; as late as November, Congress barely passed a measure allowing US merchant ships to be armed and enter belligerent ports despite FDR's full backing for it. Carol J. Jablonski records that although antiwar groups like the Catholic Worker Movement had been weakened, a zealous core committed to "unrelenting pacifism" steadfastly remained.[95] Thus, Roosevelt continued to describe the war in strong—but not too strong—of terms. If he initiated military intervention, he risked validating anti-interventionist claims that war had been his aim all along.[96]

This dilemma led to the second part of his strategy. Having created an interpretive framework that presented intelligible American reasons for entering the conflict and maneuvered (with the Kriegsmarine's help) the United States into an undeclared naval war with Germany, Roosevelt then waited for an exigence to occur that would compel a declaration of war. He had privately articulated this strategy as early as May, when he confided to Morgenthau that he was just "waiting to be pushed into this situation" by a provocation from Hitler. Secretary of War Henry Stimson noted in confidence that "the President shows evidence of waiting for the accidental shot of some irresponsible captain on either side to be the occasion of his going to war." FDR said much the same thing to diplomat William Bullitt.[97] Churchill claimed later that summer that Roosevelt had promised "he would become more and more provocative. . . . He would look for an 'incident' which would justify him in opening hostilities. . . . Everything was to be done to force an 'incident.'" By November the president was telling advisors: "The question is how to maneuver them into firing the first shot without too much danger to ourselves."[98] If, deep in his heart, the president truly did not want war, then his words belied that inmost feeling.

In summation then, FDR developed the interpretive schema for the American public to make sense of the conflict *before* the attack on Pearl Harbor. If an Axis attack came, he could maintain his political advantage only if he were able to claim, believably, that his nation was a reluctant victim of unprovoked aggression. In return, he got a nation more open to the possibility of war as soon as an enemy attack of sufficient size triggered it. The fact that the nation rallied so quickly to war and FDR's leadership following the Japanese attack—rather than interpret such an attack as a confirmation of years of anti-interventionist warnings—serves as a testament to Roosevelt's rhetorical strategy, effort, and genius.

Until then, the nation occupied an unstable position. Several historians have commented on the uncertain, insecure public mood in the prelude to Pearl Harbor. Sherry chronicles a widespread sense of fatalism: "Most Americans must have felt scarcely more control over their own government's course than they did over the global crisis into which fate seemed to have sucked them."[99] Frances Perrett describes a prevalent state of anxiety, "a widespread fear that the country was about to be put to a severe test and perhaps it would fail. . . . This was a people that did not want to step straight into war but preferred to be pushed, pulled or kicked into it. An odd sight . . . of people, singly or together, adrift for lack of sure purpose on which to attach their will." The famous anthropologist Margaret Mead corroborated this view at the time when she wrote that the United States had put a chip on its shoulder, "a special American form of aggressiveness; so unsure of itself that it has to be proved."[100]

Years later another president, Bill Clinton, would say that in such times of doubt and insecurity the American people would rather have a leader who is strong and wrong than one who is weak and right.[101] Roosevelt avoided that choice by presenting himself as both strong and right by adopting a posture of "aggressive innocence."[102] He kept his bellicosity in check, lest he be accused of warmongering, and he never publicly wavered in his characteristic self-confidence. To preserve his— and the nation's—air of innocence, FDR waited for others to act. And his symbolically charged language thus played a crucial role in creating the conditions for the enduring transformation of American life that began on the morning of December 7, 1941.

Conclusion

Two years after Roosevelt issued them, Norman Rockwell delivered to the public his famous illustrations of the president's Four Freedoms. Rockwell's paintings became classic depictions of the American home and neighborhood as a familiar, comforting, and safely enduring environment. His inspiration for freedom of speech, he recalled, was a town meeting in which one dissenting person was allowed to "have his say" despite everyone else's disagreement with him. The message of "Freedom from Fear," according to Rockwell himself, was "Thank God we [Americans] can put our children to bed with a feeling of security, knowing they will not be killed in the night." "Freedom from Want" was not depicted as "the foundation of a global New Deal," Robert Westbrook has noted, "but rather as the defense of the familial surfeit during a peculiarly American holiday," Thanksgiving.[103] Only in his portrayal of freedom of religion did Rockwell even hint at racial or ethnic diversity.[104] The artworks suggested that the president had called Americans to defend their private freedoms in their local settings and that the new global context of US foreign affairs need not entail reciprocal interaction with foreign lives and values. Global engagement was instead only a matter of projecting American life onto the rest of the world while preserving freedom at home. The paintings implied that the president wanted the world's future to be precisely what white America's past, at its best, had always been.[105]

Roosevelt's global context was absent in Rockwell's pictorial translation, as was the idea of a transoceanic menace to the nation. Though the frightening specter of Axis aggression remained in the background of Rockwell's paintings, insecurity was very much in the foreground of Roosevelt's discourse. Over the course of 1941 the president elaborated on this foundational vision, his rhetoric gradually coalescing into a positive case for American entry into World War II. Once the United States entered the conflict, FDR would draw upon the vision he had sketched to fully voice a new understanding of the nation's role in the world—to lasting rhetorical effect.

PART IV

8 | Administration and Public War Aims

On December 7, 1941, when Franklin Roosevelt met with Harry Hopkins to discuss the shocking news of the bombing of Pearl Harbor, they talked about the worst-case scenarios, such as a Japanese offensive inland and across the Rocky Mountains.[1] When the president asked Congress for a declaration of war, though, he showed no hint of these worries. He promised that "the American people in their righteous might will win through to absolute victory."[2] The next day, in a fireside chat, he repeated the point in the same defiant tone: "The United States can accept no result save victory, final and complete."[3] All other concerns would be subordinated to that overriding goal, including domestic reforms. By placing victory above all other priorities, the president forestalled (whether intentionally or not) political debate about war aims. When he concluded his first wartime fireside chat by saying, "We are going to win the war and we are going to win the peace that follows," he left unanswered the question of what exactly it meant to "win the war" and the more vexing question of what it would mean to "win the peace."[4] Debates over US foreign policy now shifted from the issue of intervention to the question of what victory would look like for the United States. "War is an attempt to achieve political objectives by fighting," as William C. Bullitt, the US ambassador to Moscow, reminded FDR, "and political objectives must be kept in mind."[5] What was the nation's aim in fighting the war?

Months earlier Henry Luce had asked that very question. In his famous editorial, "The American Century," he put it this way: "We would like to know what war we are trying to win—and what we are supposed to win when we win it."[6] Unlike the populations of other major powers, Americans had no tangible enemy to repulse from their mainland or skies, and thus the answer to Luce's question was neither straightforward nor simple. Americans were free to answer Luce's question, and more broadly to imagine the meaning of the war as well as its aftermath, in myriad ways. Because of this, as John Morton Blum puts it, Americans "in most cases and at most times were fighting the war on imagination alone."[7] Three and a half years at war would see much imagining and many answers as various voices battled over America's aims in war. Since everyone was fighting on the same side, against the same enemy, it was natural to assume that everyone was fighting for the same thing— *victory*. This illusion would play a major role in creating memories of World War II as, in Thomas Sanders's words, "the last good war."[8]

Yet the president, with his eye on worst-case scenarios, was not at all sure how long unanimity would last. As with the rise of fascism and debate over intervention, however, interpretations of what constituted "victory" for the United States in World War II diverged sharply. Roosevelt worried that public support for the war, more broad than deep, might soon shrink if there were no military successes. For this reason, he might have found little to disagree with in the words of Archibald MacLeish, whom he appointed the first assistant secretary of state for public affairs: "The principle battleground of this war . . . is American public opinion."[9] Given the deep disagreements that took place even within the administration over specific policy or military decisions—Secretary of War Henry L. Stimson, for example, called FDR's decision to launch the Operation Torch landings in North Africa "evil" and likely to "ripen into immediate disaster" behind closed doors—it is unsurprising that Roosevelt would express concern over his ability to maintain national unity over the course of the conflict.[10] Combined with his aspirations to reshape the international order in the United States' favor at war's end, the divergent interpretations of American war aims circulating in public discourse presented him with a rhetorical challenge, a challenge epitomized by the sharp differences between the administration and the public when it came to the meaning of the war, its goals and purposes, and the postwar world it would produce.

In this chapter, we explore the varied interpretations of "victory" voiced in the Roosevelt administration and public discourse during the war. FDR and his subordinates drew and diverged from his prewar constellation of liberal internationalism and realism—sometimes disagreeing vehemently about particular strategies or policy decisions—but the main constant was a concern that whatever else the postwar world may be, it would be secure. As the president debated issues of trade, disarmament, colonialism, communism, and civilization with his cabinet members, he emphasized that the primary focus of the war would be to create a secure global environment to prevent chaos. More than democracy, the administration prized stability as its chief war aim. At the same time, many Americans' desires revolved around defending (or getting back to) their individual homes, families, and economic pursuits. Most of all, they wanted to put the war—and the outside world that had caused it—behind them, never to imperil or interrupt their lives again. These divergences orbited around competing constellations of symbols of security and insecurity that provided differing ways of making sense of the war's purpose and victory's meaning.

Administration War Aims: Victory as "Survival"

Keeping with his strategy of avoiding Wilson's fate, FDR maintained a consistent focus on planning for the peace settlement while the battle still raged. As Harry Hopkins related, Roosevelt "regarded the postwar settlement so to speak as being his particular preserve."[11] The president's central concern was that the United States be in a position to dictate the terms of the peace. As early as the end of 1939, the president told the British ambassador, Lord Lothian, that he hoped to be "a kind of umpire," to "lay down the conditions for an armistice."[12] By 1940 the State Department, with help from the Council on Foreign Relations (CFR) and other parties, was drawing up detailed plans for rearranging the world in the postwar era.[13] FDR followed the work of the State Department planners with keen interest; by 1943, he met with them weekly.[14]

Occasionally, Roosevelt and his subordinates voiced Wilsonian enthusiasm. Reflecting on the opportunities opened up by global planning, he could wax prophetic: "Something 'big' will come out of this war: a new heaven and a new earth."[15] After the Yalta Conference, Hopkins spoke for himself and his boss: "We really believed in our hearts that this was the dawn of the new day we had all been praying for and talking about for so many years. We were absolutely certain that we had won the first great victory of the peace—and, by 'we,' I mean all of us, the whole civilized human race."[16] Hull fleshed out this eschatological hope when he told Congress that after the war "there will no longer be need for spheres of influences, for alliances, for balance of power, or any other of the special arrangements through which, in the unhappy past, the nations strove to safeguard their security or to promote their interests."[17] Commenting to columnist Joseph Alsop on the far reach of American military operations (in Africa, Asia, and Polynesia), FDR gushed: "What a privilege it is to be alive in this particular day and age!"[18]

Despite periodic outbursts of rhapsody, administration officials more often defined their mission as one of safeguarding the nation against dangers that they saw looming on the horizon. Their depiction of the perils of the postwar world drew heavily from the same old sources and symbols of insecurity that had shaped Roosevelt's prewar discourse. FDR told Democratic Party chairman Robert Hannegan that he would run for a fourth term because the nation's "future existence and the future existence of our chosen method of government are at stake."[19] In 1944 he told his new secretary of state, Edward Stettinius, that the issue was not whether the United States could make the world safe for democracy but whether democracy could make the world safe from another war.[20] Words like these suggested that the Allies' true war aim was not victory but survival; in fact, at one point FDR himself suggested calling World War II "the survival war."[21] While such language may seem strange coming from the lips of the only major world leader whose country's mainland had been spared from attack, Roosevelt conflated the survival of the United States with the expansion of its economic system, democracy, global reach, and way of life. Understood in this way, "survival" became a term that communicated the need to reform the postwar world so that these aspects of American life could last into perpetuity.

Others at the top of the elite establishment echoed the president in making this point. Henry Luce's aforementioned editorial was an especially influential example. It was widely interpreted as an optimistic vision of American-led change that would transform the world. But Luce presented the transformations he proposed as ways to protect values America already held against unpredictable threats in an uncertain future. The real purpose of the war, he wrote, was to shape "America's [global] environment." The only way to "make democracy work successfully" at home, he argued, was to create "a vital international economy and . . . an international moral order. . . . Only as we go out to meet and solve for our time the problems of the world revolution, can we know how to re-establish our constitutional democracy." Without a new "American century . . . there is not the slightest chance of anything faintly resembling a free economic system prevailing." In that situation, he concluded, "this nation cannot truly endure," and Roosevelt would be "the last of the American Presidents" unless all Americans resolved "to create the first great American Century."[22] Luce called for the projection of US power to reshape the world's economic system, and if the nation failed to do so then it could not "truly endure." Luce, like FDR, described the United States' war aims in the language of survival.

Others articulated similar sentiments. Stimson feared "that the country might be left powerless" if it did not successfully "cope with the conditions of the world."[23] Walter Lippmann said much the same, lamenting that the hallmarks of civilization—"order, security, and well-being"— could no longer be taken for granted. Lippmann sounded similar notes to the president; as Warren Kimball comments, "It could have been Franklin Roosevelt speaking."[24] His words joined with the voices of many other members of the foreign policy establishment and the administration to frame the war as a fight for survival, defined as the continuance of the American way of life in a dangerous world. This basic rhetorical structure fleshed itself out most clearly in various administration discussions surrounding a successor organization to the League of Nations, disarmament, trade policy, colonialism, the Soviet Union, and civilization.

Roosevelt Administration War Aims: Symbols of Security

An important piece of Roosevelt's plan to shape the postwar world in a way that protected the United States (and all its elites held dear) was a United Nations organization, or UNO. Early proposals featuring the language of "United Nations" were a direct extension of the principles laid down in the Atlantic Charter. On January 1, 1942, the United States alongside the other twenty-five nations fighting the Axis powers signed the Declaration of the United Nations, a document that articulated Allied war aims in the idiom of Roosevelt's liberal internationalism. Reflecting his dualistic abstraction of the conflict, it stated that the signatories "are now engaged in a common struggle against savage and brutal forces seeking to subjugate the world," and they dedicated themselves "to defend life, liberty, independence and religious freedom, and to preserve human rights and justice in their own lands as well as others lands."[25] Critically, Luke Glanville observes, this formal statement of Allied war aims carried the implication that FDR's Four Freedoms, now framed as human rights, "should be enforced not only domestically but internationally."[26] The Roosevelt administration adapted the language of this statement and developed it into the idea of a successor organization to the League of Nations.

One of the key questions surrounding the new UNO was whether it would play the role of international police power. As the concept of a UNO gained popularity during the war, the question of whether it would have its own military force sparked a major political debate. The idea had significant support among liberal internationalists; even Sumner Welles, as close to Roosevelt as anyone on foreign policy matters, supported it.[27] But FDR recognized the domestic fear that an international military force would limit the United States' freedom of action abroad, and he was keenly aware that Wilson's failure could be directly attributed to Article X of the Covenant of the League of Nations, which called on "all Members of the League" to act "against external aggression" directed at any other member, opening the door to endless foreign entanglement.[28] Roosevelt feared reversals in public opinion, confiding in Churchill at one point later in the war, "We may be heading before very long for the pinnacle of our weakness."[29]

Roosevelt sketched out a hazy plan to enforce the peace in his idea of "four policemen." The United States, Britain, the Soviet Union, and China together would run the UNO's Security Council, while each kept order in its own quarter of the world. By the end of 1943, the State Department had drawn up a plan to implement this idea after the war's end.[30] FDR explained his thoughts in more detail to Grace Tully and Samuel Rosenman. Not only "aggressor nations" but "the rest of the world would have to disarm. . . . Inspection would be arranged by the four policemen in all the countries to see that they did not begin to arm secretly," and if they were found to be arming they "would be threatened first with a quarantine and if the quarantine did not work they would be bombed."[31] This language was merely the latest iteration of Roosevelt's neighborhood metaphor; the United States had gone from a friendly neighbor lending a hose to a policeman enforcing communal amity.

As Roosevelt's comment would suggest, the supposedly invincible power of aerial bombardment emerged as another major symbol of security within the administration. Before the war FDR had done more than anyone to make this new technology a powerful symbol of insecurity. By the time he developed his plan to use aerial bombing to keep the peace, that technology was widely (though wrongly) believed to be turning the tide of war in the allies' favor, proving its worth as a symbol of security that could maintain the stability of the world after the war.[32] His reevaluation of air power and his willingness to use it to pummel enemy populations reflected broader trends. In 1943, one British air strategist wrote: "It should be emphasized that the destruction of houses, public utilities, transport and lives; the creation of a refugee problem on an unprecedented scale; and the breakdown of morale both at home and at the battle fronts by fear of extended and intensified bombing are accepted and intended as aims of our bombing policy. They are not by-products of attempts to hit factories."[33]

While American air strategists insisted that their targets were either bottlenecks of war production or the enemy's industrial fabric as a whole, they similarly attributed Allied victory in war to the bombing campaigns. Paul Nitze, future architect of Truman's Cold War policy, argued in 1945: "It seems clear that, even without the atomic bombing attacks, air supremacy over Japan could have exerted sufficient pressure to bring about unconditional surrender and obviate the need for invasion."[34] Now the president expected to use air power after the war as the ultimate guarantor of US security, in time complementing this capability with the atomic bomb.[35]

The UNO and air power operated as symbols of security in administration discourse. The discussions surrounding these symbols reveals that FDR and his subordinates prized the safety they hoped these innovations could bring to the postwar world. More than democracy or freedom, their war aims revolved around plans to create a stable international environment after the war. Their anxieties over symbols of insecurity—trade, colonialism, the Soviet Union, and "civilization"—equally reveal how *stability* operated as the chief war aim in the administration.

Roosevelt Administration War Aims: Symbols of Insecurity

One of FDR's biggest fears was that the postwar world would relapse into another Great Depression. If that happened, he told secretary of state Edward Stettinius, it would "make another war possible in twenty years."[36] From the beginning of his time in office, Roosevelt had demanded that Germany become a full, and fully disarmed, participant in a global, liberal, American-fashioned system of open trade. That system, kept politically stable and thus safe for investment capital, was a primary symbol of security in the parlance of the administration. After all, FDR originally framed the Axis powers as gigantic symbols of insecurity not only because they sought to overthrow the global political order but because they also closed themselves off from economic interaction with other nations. As FDR related to Hull, "I just can not [*sic*] go along with the idea of seeing the British empire collapse financially, and Germany at the same time building up a potential re-armament machine to make another war possible in twenty years."[37]

FDR's postwar economic agenda was designed to ward off another depression as well as future aggression, which elevated instability (both economic and political) as a major symbol of insecurity. When world leaders met at Bretton Woods in 1944 to hammer out a postwar economic arrangement, he told them: "Commerce is the lifeblood of a free society. We must see to it that the arteries are not clogged again."[38] Rhetorically, he still defined autarky as the critical link between the twin threats of aggression and depression. When the Bretton Woods agreement was drafted, he urged Congress to ratify it because "the world will either move toward unity and widely shared prosperity or it will move into necessarily competing economic blocs."[39] His treasury secretary and close friend Henry Morgenthau acknowledged the same principle in his speech to the Bretton Woods Conference: "The only genuine safeguard for our national interests is international cooperation."[40] Like in his prewar discourse, multilateral foreign trade served as FDR's solution to the economic danger of a depression in the postwar world.[41] As columnist Arthur Krock put it, FDR's policy for preventing war was "economic freedom for all."[42]

The administration's definition of security blended economics and geopolitics, which was evident in its approach to colonialism as well.[43] Privately, FDR described the colonies held by the European powers as multifaceted symbols of insecurity. "The question of dependent territories was an issue of security as much as economics," he told advisors.[44] Describing the emerging plan to turn European colonial holdings into trusteeships under UN supervision, Sumner Welles explained that "everything is designed to promote world security. The project is motivated not by altruism or idealism but solely by considerations of security."[45] As Welles's statement attests, while on the surface the administration may have stressed ideals like victory, democracy, and freedom, underneath lay a common framing of the issue at hand: security.

Roosevelt predicted that ending colonialism after the war would create a more stable and prosperous world based on American ideology and favorable to American interests.[46] He resisted his military advisors' call to keep some Pacific Islands as US territories (rather than trusteeships) because he worried that any move toward colonialism would undermine plans for an open liberal trade system.[47] At the same time, FDR was keen on using some US trusteeship areas as military sites for air bases, again blending his economic and geopolitical objectives. Applying his "policemen" metaphor, he told one group of diplomats that "peace must be kept by force. There was no other way and world policemen would be necessary who would need certain places from which to exercise their functions without bringing up questions of changes in sovereignty."[48] Roosevelt instructed the State Department to begin negotiating for places that he saw as strategically crucial for US air bases, such as the coast of Africa, South America, and small islands in the Atlantic and the Pacific Oceans.[49]

When it came to the future of Europe, FDR likewise prioritized safety over unpredictability and order over democracy. For example, when US troops invaded Italy and liberated Rome, leading to Mussolini's removal from power, Roosevelt desired a figure who could maintain firm control. Rather than risk a power vacuum, he told Churchill, he would deal with any new ruler who could "best give us first disarmament and second assurance against chaos."[50] Governance of Italy then went to Mussolini's former chief of staff, Pietro Badoglio. Justifying what seemed to be a continuation of fascist rule, the president told reporters that it was imperative "to avoid anarchy. In a country that gets into a state of anarchy, it is a pretty difficult thing to deal with, because it would take an awful lot of troops." Self-determination was "a long-range thing."[51]

The same fear of chaos shaped postwar planning for the rest of Europe and for Asia, which reflected the administration's ideological proclivity for the old progressive value of order. Early in 1943, discussing the future of Germany with Roosevelt and Eden, Hopkins expressed a fear that "either Germany will go communist or an out and out anarchic state would set in; that indeed the same kind of thing might happen in any of the countries in Europe." Hopkins advocated planning with Britain and the Soviet Union to prevent anarchy, and according to his notes, "the president agreed that this procedure should be followed."[52] Roosevelt simultaneously told Eden that the postwar order needed China as a great power, and "anarchy in China would be so grave a misfortune that Chiang Kai-Shek must be given the fullest support."[53]

The Dumbarton Oaks Conference powerfully illustrated how the administration prioritized maintaining order after the war, regardless of the idealistic trappings of wartime rhetoric. FDR told the diplomats who gathered at Dumbarton Oaks in 1944 to create the UNO, that their task was not to design a democratic body but that they were "planning the great design of security and peace." Security—not freedom—served as the president's rhetorical touchstone. Hence, as Paul Gordon Lauren writes, "The diplomacy at Dumbarton Oaks and the strategic positioning of armed forces around the globe revealed that the Great Powers already were seeking to mold the postwar world in particular ways that had little to do with the wartime promises of peace and justice for all people. In fact, their actions gave every appearance of having everything to do with geopolitics and almost nothing to do with normative values about peacemaking and human rights."[54] In Roosevelt's formulation, security was the key to peace and the antidote to chaos. Because the administration defined security elastically, achieving this aim required the channeling of the vagaries of the geopolitical and economic future into a stable, predictable, orderly pattern that would protect the world against the threat of chaos.[55]

The Soviet Union, to say nothing of the rhetorical contortions demanded by the US–Soviet alliance, confounded policy-makers. The Joint Chiefs of Staff were among the most concerned. If the defeat of Germany left the Soviets in control of most of Europe, they stated, "we would have to conclude that we had lost the war."[56] As for Roosevelt himself, he was "realistic" enough to believe that the Soviet Union was going to control most if not all of Eastern Europe after the war. In a memorandum to Hull, he explained why it was politically imprudent to make any formal protest of Soviet domination of Eastern Europe: "In their occupied territory they will do more or less what they wish."[57] "So better give them gracefully," he wrote to Cardinal Francis Spellman: "What can we do about it?" Another time he voiced hope that, with time, "European influences would bring the Russian to become less barbarian."[58] Of course, Stalin secretly surveilled Hopkins, FDR, and the other US diplomats at Yalta, perhaps illustrating the naivety of such hopes as well as appeals to "friendship and world harmony" directed at the communist regime.[59]

Near the end of his life, Roosevelt seemed to be trying to balance the contradictions of the US alliance with Stalin as well as the broader framework he understood him through. He wrote to Churchill: "I would minimize the general Soviet problem as much as possible because most of these problems, in one form or another, seem to arise every day and most of them straighten out. . . . We must be firm, however, and our course thus far is correct."[60] This advice—to exude confidence and moral certainty in the face of challenge—had been part and parcel of Roosevelt's political persona since his days in Albany, and he now applied this approach to the uncertainty surrounding the Soviet Union's postwar status vis-à-vis the United States. Most of all, he told Churchill, "We must not permit anybody to entertain a false impression that we are afraid."[61]

Liberal internationalists like Roosevelt generally equated economic and political stability with civilization itself. It is therefore not surprising that their sense of vulnerability extended beyond specific military, geopolitical, and economic threats to a more vague and pervasive set of anxieties about the future of civilization. The *New York Times* spoke for many when it called World War II "the greatest threat ever to world civilization."[62] Cordell Hull pronounced the war "the gravest crisis in human experience."[63] An Allied victory would be "a triumph of civilization itself over barbarism," said Sumner Welles.[64] Roosevelt adopted this framing when he told Stimson that "the German people as a whole must have it driven home to them that the[ir] whole nation has been engaged in a lawless conspiracy against the decencies of modern civilization."[65]

But much attention was focused on the continuing threat to civilization after the allies won the war as well. The famed historian Henry Steele Commager warned that the only alternative to world peace would be the collapse of civilization.[66] Proponents of the UNO often supported their proposal by depicting the dangers of a future war.[67] And many agreed with Senator Joseph Ball that "civilization won't survive continued war" and "may perish in World War III."[68] The Committee to Study the Organization of the Peace, established by the American League of Nations Association and headed by the ardent peace advocate James T. Shotwell, warned that "the old landmarks are disappearing" and that the challenge to peace was "a challenge to civilization itself" at this "most critical time since the dawn of history. . . . The fate of civilization is at stake."[69] Across the administration and literate society, Americans phrased their fear in the language of civilizational threat. With the future seeming so uncertain, clouded by doubt and despair, many in learned society urged caution, lest the dark impulses that had already done so much damage be unleashed again and overwhelmed the battered ramparts of civilization.[70] As Roosevelt told Felix Frankfurter, following his journey to Teheran, "I realized on the trip what a dreadful lack of civilization is shown in the countries I visited—but on returning I am not wholly certain of the degree of civilization in *terra Americana.*"[71]

At root, FDR and others in the administration worried that the evils unleashed in Germany might claim another society, possibly even their own, someday after the war was over. The president told Perkins, "I have never been able to make out why people who are obviously human beings could behave like that. They are human, yet they behave like demons."[72] Other Christian thinkers, like FDR, also acknowledged the potential for demonological influence in bringing about the war yet also recognized the possibility that their own societies "could let loose terrible demonic forces."[73] These fears provided the animating force behind the postwar plans of the Roosevelt administration and explain why it prioritized stability over other ideals such as democracy or freedom throughout the contest. As Warren F. Kimball notes, FDR wished to "prevent global 'monsters' from intervening and destroying the peaceful American system."[74] It might be more accurate to say that Roosevelt was in fact advocating global intervention by the United States but only (or principally) in order to stop future "monsters" from destroying the globalized American system; his was a preventative interventionism. His primary concern was the threat that evil nations posed to two sets of interests—those of his own nation and those of virtuous, civilized people everywhere—which he treated as two sides of a single coin.[75] The American United Nations Association expressed this view quite clearly: "Democracy needs an organized world. America is the last best hope to do it."[76] The administration's war aims were to realize that world, using American power as its chosen instrument.

Roosevelt's fragmentary vision of the postwar world was far from complete. But one of its foundational assumptions was that only global engagement—first a victorious "world war" and then a long-term, strictly enforced world peace—could protect a United States whose interests were now worldwide. A nation with global economic interests would need global military logistical capabilities too.[77] So defending American territory, American geopolitical power, and American economic interests were now merely different facets of the same project. That defensive project provided a single rationale for both a liberalized global trade system and a global network of US military bases.[78] Combined with the language of insecurity ("survival"), this rhetoric collapsed distinctions that other Americans, most notably the anti-interventionists, relied on to distinguish vital from peripheral US foreign policy aims. British foreign secretary Anthony Eden, recalling a meeting with Roosevelt in 1943, wrote: "He seemed to see himself disposing of the fate of many lands, allied no less than enemy. He did all this with so much grace that it was not easy to dissent. Yet it was too like a conjuror, skillfully juggling with balls of dynamite, whose nature he failed to understand."[79] Like a stick of dynamite, Roosevelt voiced anxieties that an explosion anywhere might set off a much larger chain reaction everywhere.

Since the Roosevelt administration was firmly committed to postwar policies of liberal internationalism, which would require American engagement everywhere in the world, all of these symbols of insecurity would, accordingly, have to be faced simultaneously and perhaps permanently. While little suggests that FDR consciously cultivated such a view—his "four policemen" scheme, despite its inconsistencies, would suggest otherwise—his transposable definitions of security virtually demanded such a national posture. Elizabeth Borgwardt has concluded, in our view correctly, that "the core idea in international diplomacy to emerge from WWII for American policy planners was the conviction that security was indivisible: political, legal, and economic developments supported (or undermined) one another in myriad direct and indirect ways."[80] Anything that might erode security in one realm or region would, within this Rooseveltian narrative, erode security everywhere. By 1945 a sense of vulnerability was, as John Lewis Gaddis writes, "basic" to the policy-makers' view of the world.[81]

Public Opinion, Operation Torch, and the Home Front

Most Americans defined "victory" quite differently than the administration. Public opinion over the purpose of the war, far from unitary, gave Roosevelt good reason to worry—especially in the first year of US direct participation in the conflict. Polls showed about 30 percent of Americans still supporting the anti-interventionists' purely defensive approach to the conflict, limiting US military operations to the Western Hemisphere.[82] Among the majority who did support an active war effort, there was a widespread view that Japan was the real enemy, since only Japan had attacked American soil. Roosevelt's rhetorical focus on the home front might be explained, in part, by the often-overlooked fact that only 18.1 percent of American families had one or more of their members in the military.[83]

Some seven months after Pearl Harbor, with no American troops yet in ground action, FDR feared that public support might wane for involvement in the European front. Against the opinion of his military advisors, FDR directed the army's chief of staff George Marshall to prepare to invade North Africa. Marshall later recalled that "the main thing about the Mediterranean operation was something occurring at an early date, and that was the only thing we could think of that could be done at an early date." The operation was meant to provide an early success, solidifying public support for the war against Germany. "The President considered it very important to morale," Marshall explained, "to give the country a feeling that they are in the war."[84] Indeed, Roosevelt and the Democrats worried that the Republicans, campaigning on policies that would reduce wartime rationing and mandatory service, would take back control of Congress in the 1942 elections. One active Democratic figure wrote FDR, "Democrats [will] lose control of Congress at the coming election, barring a military victory by the United States."[85] Roosevelt even cabled Churchill that he wanted the amphibious landing in North Africa to be accomplished "by an exclusively American ground force," and when delays pushed the operation until November, he reportedly pleaded with Marshall, "Please make it before Election Day!"[86]

Though Operation Torch was a resounding success, it was not completed until five days after the vote. It showed. Republicans scored major gains in the 1942 elections, and Roosevelt's Democratic majority in Congress shrunk massively. Regardless, public investment in the war at that time appeared oddly minimal, and issues of war and peace played a relatively minor role in the campaigns. Some observers saw this as evidence that many Americans wanted to ignore the nation's sudden immersion in world affairs. *Fortune* magazine commented that "the victorious candidates . . . were almost entirely normalcy men, quiet, churchgoing, family men, not quite prohibitionists, men whose outlook was limited to their states and their regions."[87] The grand questions of foreign policy that so gripped the administration featured little in the 1942 elections, despite propagandistic attempts to convince everyday Americans that they were in the line of fire—as the very first "This is War!" episode declared after reporting on a desperate scene of carnage, "*You* too are in it, you and your family and your friends and your church."[88]

Nevertheless, to the extent the American people cared about the war at that point, it was not to FDR's political advantage. A government-commissioned poll in June 1942 found that over half of all Americans said they still did not know clearly what the war was all about or what the ultimate goal was, beyond the vague term *victory*. A third of Americans wanted a separate peace with Germany.[89] Among those who claimed to understand the war, only a very small percentage could name key points of the Atlantic Charter, supposedly the clearest statement of war aims. Few Americans wanted the armed forces risking their lives for foreigners' political freedom or matters of grand strategy.[90] A December Democratic Party election postmortem succinctly reported, "Opinions given very generally indicated dissatisfaction with the conduct of the war."[91]

Thus, even after a string of victories in North Africa and Italy, FDR continued to fret about the danger of public complacency and a resurgence of anti-interventionism. A year after Operation Torch, speechwriter Samuel Rosenman gave the president this summary of public opinion, much of which stood in direct opposition to the stances held by the administration's liberal internationalists: "People are almost twice as much interested in domestic affairs as international affairs. Two-thirds of the people think we should not give aid to foreign countries after the war if this would lower our own standard of living. Almost half the people think that if we do aid foreign countries after the war our own standard of living will be lowered."[92] Even as the war neared its end, newspaper editorials reflected little public support for internationalism, widespread resentment of US allies for playing power politics, and a lack of trust in the Soviets or even the British to cooperate with the United States after war.[93] In sum, if the enemy's remote proximity forced Americans to go to war on the basis of imagination, then Roosevelt consistently struggled to capture that imagination and channel it toward the ends he and his team envisioned.

This difficulty stemmed from a deeper issue: there were so many different answers to Luce's question: "What we are supposed to win?"[94] Although every American was theoretically free to imagine the meaning of the war in their own way, many individual imaginings drew on the resources provided by the culture; in John Morton Blum's words, "The war could signify only what the culture ordinarily endorsed."[95] Most of the adult public could still remember World War I, and the memory was generally a sour one. There existed great skepticism about idealistic images of a crusade to forge a Wilsonian new world order, a skepticism that the president had recognized and respected in all of his rhetoric since the 1920s. FDR maintained his fear of anti-interventionist sentiment, which he feared might revive at any time. "Anybody who thinks that isolationism is dead in this country is crazy. As soon as this war is over, it may well be stronger than ever," he told Sherwood as late as the autumn of 1944, with Allied troops advancing steadily to victory.[96]

The wartime research of polling pioneers Hedley Cantril and Jerome Bruner confirmed that Americans cared much more about domestic than foreign issues. Most people said that the United States was fighting for freedom and democracy, but they really believed, Bruner found, that "we went to war because our security demanded it. To us this war is a crusade to regain that security and the freedom it gives us."[97] Americans' understanding of the war thus revolved around their views of security and freedom, and on the face of it, the administration's plans to realize these goods through an internationalist agenda were not likely to be popular with the electorate. Consequently, as Roosevelt articulated the nation's war aims, he was constrained by the political need to appeal to the mass public and so had to shape his rhetoric, and to some extent his policies, to satisfy the concerns of that public. Of course, that is not to say there existed a unitary public view of the war. Far from it. The American public, however defined, articulated fragmentary and at times contradictory purposes behind US involvement in World War II. Broadly considered, these myriad understandings of the war coalesced around several main symbols that Americans associated with the freedom and security for which they fought: economic opportunity, family, home, and the American way of life.

Public War Aims: Symbols of Security

Following the New Deal's reforms, many Americans defined security in terms of their own individual economic future. As Bruner explained, "The payoff is what happens right here at home and what is likely to happen. . . . A good job is still the bench-mark for the best of possible worlds." In a 1943 poll, most Americans said that the greatest national concern was jobs and the economy; only 13 percent named world peace. In another poll, 53 percent expressed greatest interest in domestic issues like full employment; only 16 percent said their greatest interest was international problems like a new league of nations.[98] In the words of one Kansan letter writer, "The grandiose promises of the Atlantic Charter are but a gesture of good will for health, wealth, prosperity, and long lives for everyone everywhere. But justice, like charity, begins at home."[99]

The advertising industry, which grew immensely during the war, was all too happy to reinforce this yearning for domestic prosperity. Magazines targeting female readership were flooded with appeals for women to work in numerous roles, telling them, according to one expert, that "whatever they did—be it produce ammunition or save tin—was valuable and vital to the war effort."[100] The War Advertising Council organized "mass marketing patriotism" to reach all sectors of the home front. The council stressed to copywriters that "the industrial worker" literally was "the soldier in overalls," and its leader, Chester J. La Roche, argued, "We must create a *civilian* mass army—an army that man for man and woman for woman will beat Germany and Japan at their own game."[101] Other ads depicted the Axis powers as enemies of free enterprise and equated victory with the renewal of consumer choice.[102] The idea that victory in war would bring a consumer paradise in peace was implied in a great many ads and spelled out literally in some. For instance, one advertisement for Royal typewriters trumpeted, "WHAT THIS WAR IS ALL ABOUT": the right to "once more walk into any store in the land and buy anything you want."[103]

Such advertising, coupled with an intensive campaign to promote war bonds, may have convinced some Americans that money and commerce, more than military battles, were the key to winning the war. Scholars and reporters who have studied the war on the home front agree. According to Michael Adams, the advertising atmosphere communicated that "buying a war bond was a contribution on a par with military service."[104] Distinguished author and journalist Eric Sevareid observed at the time, "Wars are won by buying and selling, not by killing and dying." And as a radio dramatist put it during the war, the nation fought for "the house I live in, a plot of earth, a street, the grocer and the butcher."[105] This vision was both a product and a vindication of Roosevelt's public rhetoric, which wrapped all kinds of political and economic ideology in the trappings of home, neighborhood, and the security of traditional values.

A war for private good created one symbol of security that the Roosevelt administration shared: postwar prosperity. But for most Americans it was the prosperity of self and family that mattered, not the national gross domestic product, and certainly not the globalized system of open trade that State Department planners theorized about. For example, one letter (published in the profree trade *Wall Street Journal*) asserted that the government should plan "for a broad basis of production" after the war, "which will not only create employment but will maintain it."[106] As a result, a good, steady job and a home full of modern consumer goods became more specific symbols of security and a major concern of those fighting the war and on the home front. Indeed, one writer to the *Baltimore Sun* complained that "at this very moment labor, farmers, contractors, and a large section of our population, regardless of our danger, of their danger, are doing their utmost to advance their selfish interests at the peril of national security."[107] Individual advancement, more than the gross national product or international standards of living, served as the primary war aim for a great many Americans during World War II.

This focus on private and domestic prosperity often extended to the troops overseas, as few soldiers cited elements of FDR's liberal internationalism among their reasons for fighting the war. In the recollection of Audie Murphy, one of the most decorated US infantrymen of World War II, soldiers variously pursued sex, drinking, violence, or silence out of a simple desire to escape the "constant peril" of the battlefield and return home.[108] In fact, the young playwright Arthur Miller visited several army bases (researching the script for a film called *G. I. Joe*) and remarked on "the near absence among the men . . . of any comprehension of what Nazism meant." Japan, he noted, was seen as the prime enemy: "We were fighting Germany essentially because she had allied herself with the Japanese who had attacked us at Pearl Harbor."[109] An official survey of army air corpsmen in 1944 found that there was "very little idealism . . . not much willingness to discuss what we are fighting for."[110] In mid-1943, poet Randall Jarrell estimated that "99 of 100 people in the army" still hadn't "the faintest idea" what the war was about: "Their two strongest motives are (a) nationalism . . . and (b) race prejudice—they dislike Japanese in the same way, though not as much, as they dislike Negroes."[111] More than visions of global prosperity or stability, the troops found enthusiasm for the war in more personal motives.

Race and ethnicity, to be sure, factored into the reasoning of many soldiers. For example, Paul Douglass, a future Illinois senator, volunteered for the marines "to get myself a Jap."[112] Racial prejudice played a significant role in motivating Americans on the home front as well. As one Kentuckian who grew up during the war later recalled, "If we wanted to be in big trouble, we'd get angry and call the other kid a dirty Jap rat. That was the filthiest thing you could say."[113] And, of course, racial motivations played out in more positive ways as well. Stephen Ambrose recounts an exchange between an American soldier and a German prisoner of war, with the GI telling his captive, "We are fighting to free you from the fantastic idea that you are a master race."[114] Many African American soldiers saw the war as an opportunity to advance the cause of civil rights, and despite the continued segregation of the armed forces, there were several significant advancements in labor and military integration during the war.[115]

Overall, most soldiers did not share the president's global focus. Ernie Pyle reported of those at the front: "They say that if they ever get home, they never want to see another foreign country." Rather than fuel internationalist sentiment, American soldiers' experiences overseas often left them more assured of their own nation's exceptionalism. In the remembrance of William Manchester, a marine who served in the Pacific theater, soldiers' experiences in battle fueled "patriotic identification" more than any other emotion.[116] When the Senate ratified the establishment of the UNO, Pyle observed that there was little reaction among the troops: "They didn't see it as their business." Many soldiers came away less than impressed with the people of other lands. Encountering strangers around the world, their number one question was, according to Paul Fussell: "Why can't everybody be like them?"[117] Rather than fight to inaugurate a new world, many of them simply endured combat for a much more practical reason: for the chance to return home. A poem in the *Infantry Journal* summed it up well: "The more we rub out, the sooner we're through / To return where they wait for a soldier."[118]

According to the *New York Times*, the typical soldier simply thought that "the war must be finished quickly so that he can return to take up his life where he left it." Ernie Pyle also found that "the one really profound goal that obsessed every American" was going home. As for positive war aims, GIs would generally admit only to wanting to protect their buddies—"The Marines didn't know what to believe in," Robert Sherrod reported from Tarawa, "except the Marine Corps"—and to protect the American way of life.[119] For many Americans in uniform, the purpose of the war had little to do with liberal trade policy or fear of international aggression. They simply wanted to go back home.

Indeed, many Americans at home and abroad actually derided the administration's official pronouncements that the war would transform the world for the better as a hunk of "globaloney."[120] Others mocked the State Department as a supposed "citadel of virtue" or "shrine of prosperity."[121] In a letter to the *Wall Street Journal*, for instance, a reader argued for skepticism in respect to the administration's purported idealism: "It is too often assumed that with the overthrow of Hitler and the purging of the Nazis, democratic force in Europe will come at once to the fore and the rebuilding of that continent will then follow the lines we want. . . . We are apt to think of Europe as being latent with democracy, whereas in many parts of that continent that is utterly untrue."[122] Americans were quick to express incredulity in the face of idealistic claims to make the world better through an Allied victory over the Axis powers.

Rather than fight, sacrifice, and potentially die for the ideals of the Four Freedoms, most citizens supplied personal motivations for their participation in the war effort. In this regard, they were encouraged by the Office of War Information (OWI), a federal agency created in 1942 to maintain public morale and persuade the public of the administration's war aims. In one scholar's estimation, the agency's most effective appeal was not to parrot liberal idealism but rather its ominous depictions of "what would happen to some loved one if Hitler took over."[123] This domestic propaganda effort was reflected in public attitudes toward the war, as many Americans expressed that their motivation for fighting was to protect family and home.

This impulse to defend one's home expressed itself in a variety of other ways.[124] From apple pie and baseball to marriage and family, various images of home dominated discourse concerning the war's purpose (this tendency even extended to the pinup girls preferred by US servicemen overseas).[125] In temporal terms, the war was not imagined as a transformative event for the nation, much less the world, but as a temporary violation of the normal rhythms of life. Most Americans saw the war as an aberration, a (hopefully brief) interruption in their normal peacetime lives, a nasty job to be finished as quickly as possible so that all could return to normal, ordinary life.[126] Indeed, one letter to the *Boston Globe* decried this tendency, arguing that more attention needed to paid to the inevitability of US global involvement after the war:

> Too many waiting women as well as fighting men see the future only in rosy terms of "what it is all over." . . . It is not going to be pure romance, however, and they will both be happier if they realize this now. We cannot wrap ourselves up in cocoons and let events roll past. We are all involved. We will all be involved in the peace just as certainly as we are in the war.[127]

For many Americans, home was a dominant symbol of security attached to family, love, and locality. Home, like the meaning of the war, was a product of imagination. It was envisioned as the place where a securely monogamous love (consecrated by marriage) would last forever and a wider circle of loving relatives and friends would gather for good times. In that home all would be untouched by sources of danger, especially danger from abroad. On a more abstract level, home symbolized a longing to restore inviolable boundaries between home and violence abroad. Often these desires expressed themselves as a wish that the war would end in such a way that the United States would not be forced to fight again. As one Atlantan wrote, US war aims should be "to win the peace of this war and prevent World War III."[128]

Other opinions notwithstanding—public opinion was hardly uniform, after all—for most Americans the primary goal of the war was to restore regularity, normality, and some sense of enduring secure boundaries that Americans associated with the traditional image of home. To wit, a Gallup poll found that 58 percent of Americans opposed numerous changes in the United States after the war.[129] Nor was it surprising that, for many Americans, the desire to escape change meant more than merely preserving the good, and the goods, of the present. It meant returning to what they remembered (or imagined) as a better pre-Depression past. The OWI informed Roosevelt that when Americans visualized a postwar world, most assumed it would be "compounded largely of 1929 values and the economics of the 1920s"—an economics of seemingly endlessly rising prosperity.[130] People wanted, it seems, not merely to prevent but to roll back change to realize a supposedly simpler time.[131]

A similar longing for the past pervaded the US military around the world. The ordinary soldier was "the people's hero," Blum observed, because "like them, he had little visible purpose but winning the war so that he could return to a familiar, comfortable America, to what an earlier generation meant, more or less, by 'normalcy.'"[132] One *Baltimore Sun* article summarized the "hundreds of letters" the paper had received from American troops abroad, describing their desire to simply return home and not be asked to fight again: "The millions of men in our armed forces are discussing the kind of peace we must make. They insist that the final purpose of this war is not this time to 'make the world safe for democracy,' but to produce a lasting peace no matter what the ideologies of the world may be."[133] For those who fought, peace meant, above all, a return to the domestic tranquility that they felt had once pervaded their homeland, where all could pursue the American dream undisturbed by depression and, even more, by foreign conflicts. A popular cliché had it that the soldiers overseas were "seven million isolationists."[134]

These longings for a simpler prewar existence bears a striking resemblance to the ideas articulated by the anti-interventionist movement prior to American entry into the war. The rejection of globalism; the suspicion of foreigners, even allies; the enduring sense of American exceptionalism; the longing for home and family and all the stability they represented; the single-minded pursuit of domestic prosperity; the wish to return to a cherished (even if imaginary) past; a defensive stance to protect enduring geographical, social, and moral boundaries—these had all been sources and symbols of security for most of the anti-interventionists. Thus, the inchoate mythology that emerged to make sense of the war drew heavily on, and overlapped in many ways with, the mythology that had dominated the anti-interventionism movement. For example, one Annapolis, Maryland, resident expressed more worry over the government's seizure of power at home than the enemy abroad, echoing anti-interventionist fears that the war itself threatened the American way of life: "I maintain, seriously, that if [Maryland] Governor O'Conor or any other man or men are going to rule by decree we should bring back every soldier overseas, make the best peace terms possible and end the war which we say is being fought to preserve the American way of life and government."[135]

None of these concerns would have been any surprise to Franklin Roosevelt. He remained exquisitely attuned to public opinion, and thus he feared a resurgence of "isolationism" much like that which had destroyed the presidency of Woodrow Wilson. After all, he had not won his prewar battle with the anti-interventionists because he convinced the public to support a call for long-term American engagement around the world. A world-class politician, he knew that whatever else they wanted, Americans had little enthusiasm for the values of liberal internationalism as a whole. On the contrary, the public had responded to his insistence that he cared only about defending the United States. He won the political debate by creating compelling images of national insecurity meant to prove that there was indeed something to fear and to protect. His words functioned to make the threat to the nation seem so tangibly imminent that Americans would rally to defend their country and way of life as they—in all their complex and contradictory ways—understood it.

Public War Aims: Symbols of Insecurity

The combination of a nebulously defined official war aim—victory—and the nation going to war on the basis of imagination created an ironic paradox. On one hand, the United States was the least vulnerable of all major combatants. Outside of several isolated submarine attacks and sabotage attempts, the American mainland went practically unscathed over the course of the conflict. On the other, the American people, by all indications, felt increasingly insecure as the war progressed. Indeed, the National Association of Broadcasters prohibited programs "which might unduly affect the listener's peace of mind" for 1942, when the war's outcome was still far from certain, as part of the effort to reduce Americans' anxieties.[136]

Obviously, for those engaged in combat, the danger of the battlefield posed a major source of insecurity. Yet the experience of combat was less straightforward than presumed. Many soldiers who fought in World War II, like Paul Fussell, rejected the "moral simplification" of the war into a contest between good guys nobly pitted against villainous aggressors.[137] A number of veterans "were generally disillusioned by their encounters with military authority and mechanized warfare and troubled by a moral outlook that sanctioned indiscriminate killing," John Bodnar observes: "Thus, the stories they told—in novels, memoirs, and fact-based reports—not only stressed the tragic costs of the war more than the gains but to a surprising extent rendered a harsh judgment on the character of the Americans themselves and their political and military leadership."[138] The risks of combat deeply affected those exposed, and soldiers' experiences on the battlefield were far from uniform. But the disquietude expressed by veterans who returned from the war frequently had as much to do with the insecurity generated by their interactions with the US military as much as being fired upon by enemy weapons.

In similar fashion, civilians on the home front expressed high amounts of insecurity that had little to do with the physical threat of an actual enemy attack.[139] Even before the United States entered the war, Roosevelt received (and kept in his safe) a report from pollster Elmo Roper documenting the public's deep sense of insecurity. It began, "The American here appears convinced that the sun will never shine as brightly after the storm as it did before. . . . The American sees nothing so good as the world he left behind him. . . . He is overwhelmingly sure of victory in the field, but defeat at home."[140] As speechwriter Robert Sherwood commented, this was "the first war in American history in which the general disillusionment preceded the firing of the first shot."[141] Rather than fear of the Axis enemy, then, it seems fair to conclude that the symbols of insecurity that affected the home front most had to do with the ancillary effects of the war, the changes sweeping American society as it prosecuted total war. For example, it was (ironically) more dangerous to spend the war working in the United States in a factory than fighting on the battlefield. Geoffrey Perrett records, "With an overall death rate of 5 per 1,000 the military was a safer place to be than at home, where the death rate was more than twice as high and where the death and injury rates were higher still in war industries. . . . There were 17,000 military amputees. Industrial accidents in the war years produced over 100,000 more."[142] Even soldiers abroad were reportedly "worried sick about postwar joblessness," according to *Fortune* magazine.[143] Industrialization, the workplace, and economic anxiety for the future, so it seemed, became a major source of insecurity for a nation that had until recently still been short of work.[144]

Nevertheless, most people were happy to have jobs after so many years of economic depression, and they went to where the jobs were. Through the war years, while inflation grew by 27 percent, average earnings went up 65 percent.[145] But this new economic security had its downsides. The lure of better jobs led to massive internal migration throughout the nation, dislocating families and displacing communities. Millions of uprooted Americans found themselves working and living alongside strangers over the course of the war, often people of different ethnic and racial backgrounds. Social and cultural patterns of many kinds were disrupted, creating new conflicts. Hedley Cantril, trying to promote enmity toward the enemy, predicted that "fearful people, if not brought together by a common hatred, are apt to hate each other."[146] To some extent, his prediction proved true. For example, in Orange, Texas, a shipbuilding town near the Louisiana border, racial and sexual tensions rose as the population tripled to meet the demands of wartime production. Yet in the memory of one resident, "There was nothing you could do about it" since all the changes stemmed from forces outside the control of the town's residents.[147]

Many Americans feared moral breakdown engendered by the war as well. Women were working, many of them full time, in significantly greater numbers than ever before, raising new tensions with the men of their households. Teenagers now found steady work and money in their pockets, making it possible to create distinct teen marketplaces and cultures, opening up more of a generation gap and a corresponding rise in juvenile delinquency. New freedoms and new possibilities generated, for many, a sense of declining family values, symbolizing the "massive disruption of American society" taking place on the home front.[148] By 1945 a favorite topic on radio talk shows was: "Are we facing a moral breakdown?"[149] As Michael C. C. Adams sums it up, "America in the war was wrenched by change. . . . Despite the myth that all Americans were well adjusted back then, many felt great anxiety about their society and its future."[150]

Most of all, the war seemed to instill pessimism about the ability of the United States to remain untouched by war going forward. Just five or six years earlier there existed a widespread assumption that the United States need never fight another war. But during the first year of active warfare, a poll showed 60 percent of the public saying that there will always be wars and that the United States would be in another war within fifty years. Only 25 percent said war could be avoided. Another poll near the end of the war found: "When asked if they expected the country to be at war again within 25 years, Americans, by a margin of two to one, answered yes."[151] These dramatic shifts in attitude, no less than the sweeping changes racing across American society, were a testament to the war's effect on the electorate.

In this sense, the main rhetorical effect of the war was to strengthen the longing that most Americans felt for a secure family, home, and nation, longings for boundaries permanently safe from the dangers of war—the same longings that had driven the passions of the anti-interventionist movement. Those longings had been co-opted by Roosevelt in his rhetorical campaign against the anti-interventionists, recast as symbols of security in service to his more economically minded internationalist vision. The "old man in the White House," as the 1944 Republican campaign denigrated him, had reconfigured the nation's political discourse just as he (and the war effort he commanded) had transformed the conventions of American life.[152] It was now his challenge to weave together a winning narrative that could make sense of all the various symbols of security and insecurity circulating in administration and public discourse. Out of the interaction among those conflicting images, Roosevelt developed a winning rhetorical synthesis, blending public and administration war aims into a new package of appeals. When FDR passed away shortly before the war's end, he bequeathed to his successors not a unified vision but a panoply of rhetorical fragments that they would use to make sense of the United States' new global role. At the center of it all was an overriding focus on security, which would help lay the rhetorical foundation for the Cold War to come.

Conclusion

Americans possessed many different interpretations of "victory." For Roosevelt and his team, the administration's war aims came into focus as they articulated an interconnected set of priorities, ideals, and plans to shape the postwar world. Each of these strands—revolving around civilization, Stalin, order, chaos, free trade, air power, the UNO, and "policemen"—contained its own conception of security that operated at the center of discourse as it responded to powerful symbols of insecurity, from high tariffs and weapons buildups to the Soviet Union and the decay of civilization. As they blended together, these links cohered into an interpretive framework that prized stability as the chief objective and would guide policy-makers' discussions over the aims of US foreign policy during World War II and, ultimately, beyond. Just as the debate over intervention established the basic structure within which the administration deliberated war aims, so the various (and interchangeable) definitions of security that evolved over this period influenced the nation's path after the war's end.[153]

The language used to develop this foreign policy framework hearkened back to the Progressive Era and the New Deal. Liberal internationalism called for the progressive spirit of rational planning, conducted by experts, to spread throughout the world. Postwar planners expected to translate that spirit, which at root sought to combat various forms of insecurity as conceptualized by the administration, into concrete institutionalized reality. On the economic front, global organizations like the World Bank, the International Monetary Fund, and other trade establishments would be erected to ensure the free flow of goods and services around the world. Politically, international relations among nations would be mediated by reasoned dialogue in the UNO, where the vehicle of disputes would be voices instead of weapons. The national borders and the production of armaments that might threaten those borders would be controlled by the "four policemen." The movement of colonies toward independence would be superintended by trustees who would educate their leaders on the political responsibilities of independence. More broadly, administration planners equated the growth of civilization with predictability so as to ward off the various sources of insecurity they feared might imperil civilization. The challenge, as FDR and his subordinates framed it, was to forge a postwar peace that left the United States unshakably secure, in the process midwifing America's emergence as a global superpower.

For Roosevelt and most of the foreign policy elite, the turn to liberal internationalism tinged with "realism," the decision for war, and the plans for future peace were all ultimately in the service of protecting domestic tranquility—the "survival" of the American way. During the war, they applied the framework developed over the preceding years to engineer a new way of talking about American national security that prioritized order, great power politics, open trade, and an "organized world." All of these aims and their related symbols became tools to help forge, in the title of Walter Lippmann's wartime bestseller, the "shield of the republic." The elite vision of an "American Century" was not only (or even mostly) a reflection of confident enthusiasm about transforming the world. It was, more obviously, a plan for avoiding dangers that had threatened in the past, still threatened in the present, and might well persist into the future.

Theirs, however, was not the only way to talk about American war aims. After all, the United States only entered the war after the attack on Pearl Harbor; up until then, nearly a fifth of Americans still wished to remain out of the conflict and vastly more opposed a US declaration of war. While the public held far from unitary views as to the war's ultimate aims, comparatively few members of the electorate cared about international politics to the extent of the Roosevelt administration, much less shared the aims of its postwar planners. FDR thus needed a way to persuade the public to accept the administration's path while creating the appearance that the administration was merely pursuing goals in line with predominant public opinion. He sought to achieve what Mary E. Stuckey and Leroy G. Dorsey label "interpretive dominance" over the nation's war aims.[154]

The solution to this dilemma was readily at hand: merely recast, for wartime conditions, the message he had proffered so successfully to prepare the nation for war. Ever aware that the winds of public opinion might shift against him, as they had Wilson, Roosevelt sought to frame his discourse in a way that undermined arguments advancing a vision contrary to his own, thereby persuading Americans that any threat to the emerging global liberal international order would be a threat to their own homes, families, and lives. Thus comprised FDR's final rhetorical challenge: convince the American people of the need for liberal internationalism as he saw it, with the attendant concepts of security and the United States' interventionist, active, and (to a critical eye) entangled role in world affairs that came with it. With the anti-interventionist movement's collapse, there was no organized political voice to express resistance to the proposals of the administration and foreign policy elite. As a result, the president was relatively free to pursue war aims in line with his preferences and explain his choices to the public in whatever words would appeal best to them. And those were, above all, words about security.

9 | Roosevelt's Winning Synthesis

During the war, the president's greatest political achievement was to skillfully promote his internationalist message by blending his own agenda with the various values held by the public through a subtle interplay of symbols of security and insecurity. Following the attack on Pearl Harbor, the administration moved quickly to frame the war in terms of its vision for the postwar world. Roosevelt's rhetoric operated alongside Office of War Information (OWI) propaganda, a cooperative Hollywood, publishing industry campaigns, and patriotic commercialism to create an environment that would convince the American public to support the administration and foreign policy elite's war aims.[1] Given FDR's political stature as the nation's only four-time elected president and his unequaled rhetorical leadership, his words played a vital role in advancing a new understanding of the United States' role in the world over the course of the conflict.

Roosevelt drew on the whole panoply of symbolism that he had used so effectively before the United States entered the war. But he gave that symbolism a more complex meaning by attaching it to, and expressing it through, two new symbolic terms that came to dominate the public understanding of America's war aims: "the United Nations Organization" (popularly known as "the UNO") and "unconditional surrender." These terms operated as "condensation symbols," or terms that evoke a specific (often vivid) image, supply instant categorization, and carry "intense emotional and effective power."[2] The effective use of those symbols was the key to gaining public support for the administration's wartime program and plans for the postwar world. By the time he died, Roosevelt had achieved a thoroughly dialectical triumph: a foreign policy discourse based on a foundation of symbols of security that camouflaged the permanent extension of American power (and with it, vulnerability) onto a global stage.

Roosevelt won his rhetorical victory in part because he was so skilled at casting his interpretation of events in dramatic narrative form. "In human affairs, the public must be offered a drama," he told Charles

De Gaulle (who hardly needed to be taught this lesson).[3] War gave the president the opportunity to make his rhetoric more dramatic than ever. But the desire to dramatize influenced strategy as well as language. For example, he decided not only to push for an amphibious landing in North Africa before the 1942 elections but also chose to postpone a direct invasion of Europe until success was virtually assured, and according to air force general Henry Arnold FDR "was insistent" that the military find a way to strike mainland Japan immediately after Pearl Harbor, resulting in the Doolittle Raid on Tokyo.[4] George Marshall learned a lesson from his commander in chief: "The leader in a democracy has to keep the people entertained."[5] Whether one called it entertainment or something else, FDR captured the public's imagination with his words. Roosevelt, like Richard Lanham, viewed rhetoric as an instrument for encouraging "people to attend to what we would like them to attend to," effecting persuasion along the way.[6] FDR began his effort to capture the wartime attention, emotions, and assent of the American people by dramatizing the meaning of the war soon after the bombs finished falling on Hawaii.

Response to Pearl Harbor: Narrative, Security, and Threat

Roosevelt responded to the Japanese surprise attacks on Pearl Harbor and the Philippines with a nationally broadcast fireside chat. He indicated the global direction his wartime narrative would take when he edited a draft of that talk, amending a proposed line that stated the aim of the war as "We are now fighting to maintain our right to live among our neighbors in peace and freedom and common decency." FDR made two significant additions. He inserted the word "world" before "neighbors," again suggesting that the goal of US foreign policy was to turn the whole world into a tranquil neighborhood. And after "decency" he added "without fear of assault," emphasizing that the aim would be to create a world in which aggression—or at least aggression directed toward America—was only a memory.[7] With these amendments, FDR subtly suggested that the postwar world would be one in which even the possibility of "assault" by another nation would become a pipe dream, bringing into focus the chief objective of his administration's war policy: absolute security.

The rest of the chat focused primarily on the dangers of defeat and similarly borrowed from FDR's previous foreign policy metaphors. "Powerful and resourceful gangsters have banded together to make war upon the whole human race," he said, describing the Axis enemy in the language of criminality. Like wrongdoing, FDR warned, the enemy could now appear anywhere: "The attack at Pearl Harbor can be repeated at any one of many points in both oceans and along both our coast lines and against all the rest of the Hemisphere. . . . The Nation is fighting for its existence and its future life."[8] Roosevelt repeated his familiar refrain. The entire world, though aspiring to be one safely decent neighborhood, was actually under terrific threat.

Roosevelt took the opposite route from Wilson, who had raised high expectations during World War I only to see them dashed in the postwar settlement. FDR instead focused on fears in the present more than hopes for the future, seeking more to manage public sentiment rather than inflame it. As John Morton Blum notes, "The President tried to prevent his rhetoric from whipping up emotions he could not control. He would have preferred to employ no propaganda at all, and the little he endorsed for home consumption spoke more to the dangers of defeat than to the opportunities of victory."[9] This assessment, like FDR's opening fireside chat, illustrates a principal narrative emphasis on threat, defense, and danger in Roosevelt's wartime rhetoric. Most administration propaganda similarly avoided concrete descriptions of the postwar world in favor of vague idealism or fear appeals stemming from the threat posed by the enemy.[10]

At a press conference two months later, Roosevelt took the same path, describing the dangers he foresaw in vivid detail: "Enemy ships could swoop in and shell New York. Enemy planes could drop bombs on war plants in Detroit. Enemy troops could attack Alaska." Asked whether the military could repel such assaults, he replied flatly, "Certainly not."[11] Throughout the war, Roosevelt's fireside chats and other speeches continued to focus on his preeminent message of keeping American homes secure from attacks that might come from anywhere.[12]

In the same respect, Roosevelt tied the safety of individual homes to US involvement in battles around the world. He insisted that the majority of citizens who remained stateside as civilians were just as deeply involved in the war effort as the soldiers at the various fronts thousands of miles away. Preparing a radio address, he suggested a line to that effect: "War has to be conducted by the entire population. You cannot draw a line between the man or woman in uniform and the man or woman in civilian clothes."[13] He made this point publicly at a press conference a few days later: "You can't take a piece of paper and draw a line down the middle of it and put the war abroad—or the war front—on one side of the line, and put the home front—so-called—on another side of the line, because it all ties together."[14] He repeated the argument that all citizens, not just soldiers, were firsthand participants in the war in a 1942 fireside chat honoring Washington's birthday. He asked his hearers to look at a world map as he explained the challenges of "a new kind of war" involving "every continent, every island, every sea, every air lane in the world."[15] While his proximate goal was to coax Americans into seeing the European and Pacific conflicts as interlocked theaters of a single war, his words also had the effect of erasing the distinctions—and, tacitly, the dangers—between the home front and front line.[16]

In addition to this depiction of the war as a total conflict engulfing multiple continents, FDR also continued to frame the conflict as one of transcendent ideals. As he told speechwriter Samuel Rosenman, "I'm going to speak about strange places that many of them never heard of—places that are now the battlefield for civilization."[17] Geographer Alan Hendrikson has suggested that by linking the words *battlefield* and *civilization*, FDR "set out a geospatial framework—a worldwide one—for the higher, longer-term, even planetary 'goals' of the war. . . . His *global* thinking, on a geographical plane, reemerged as *universal* thinking on an ideological plane."[18] His continued depiction of the war as a battle for civilization itself reinforced the idea (already foreshadowed in Roosevelt's prewar rhetoric) that the war was not so much about Germany and Japan as it was about an ongoing, universal battle between civilization and its foes.

Roosevelt had worked hard for years to make universal terms like "civilization" synonymous with the secure home of the individual American. But never before had he, or any president, symbolized so starkly the idea that the physical security of every American was entwined with and imperiled by violent events and ideological conflicts in every corner of the globe, no matter how remote. Although he was talking about security in the present, Roosevelt was also preparing the public to accept the same link between domestic and global geopolitical security—and thus, also, insecurity—in the future. He made this clear in his 1943 State of the Union Address. He stressed the importance of "victory in the peace" and equated that victory with "striving toward the enlargement of the security of man here and throughout the world" in the future as well as the present: "It is of little account for any of us to talk of essential human needs, of attaining security, if we run the risk of another World War in ten or twenty or fifty years." FDR emphasized this point in animalistic language: "We have learned that we can never dig a hole so deep that it would be safe against predatory animals. We have also learned that if we do not pull the fangs of the predatory animals of this world, they will multiply and grow in strength—and they will be at our throats again once more in a short generation."[19] With words like these, Roosevelt's public utterances extended his narrative of security and threat, set in a global context, into the future, laying the discursive foundation for a more internationalist foreign policy after the war that would seek to defang the monsters abroad.

Viewed rhetorically, FDR's public utterances created a narrative with dueling notions of security and threat at its center. His focus on fear was strategic, as he highlighted manifold symbols of insecurity to keep public expectations in check (unlike Wilson), reflecting, as Michael Dobbs notes, the degree to which he "obsessed" with averting a public backlash.[20] He borrowed heavily from his previous metaphors of aggression but now employed them to identify specific military threats. At the same time, he argued that the United States was engaged in a total war in which there were no meaningful distinctions between the contributions of soldiers abroad and civilians at home. Combined with the geospatial dimensions of his rhetoric, this premise suggested that all Americans everywhere existed in a shared state of constant peril from the global conflict. Consequently, the only way to achieve peace now and sustain it in the future would be to support an internationalist (if not interventionist) US foreign policy so as to prevent another world war. One of the principal symbols FDR would develop to reinforce this narrative was the UNO.

Securing the Postwar World: The United Nations Organization

In the 1943 State of the Union speech, Roosevelt publicly introduced the idea of a new postwar institution, the United Nations Organization. With this idea FDR also introduced a new purpose for his words about long-term military and geopolitical security. His rhetoric was not de-

228 | CHAPTER 9

signed to solely create an amorphous public mood of support for the war but also aimed to build popular support for a specific policy initiative: creating the UNO.

The term "United Nations," already familiar as the official name of the wartime alliance, now became the symbol of a continuing postwar coalition to protect against insecurity. The United Nations "can and must remain united for the maintenance of peace," FDR proclaimed in biblical language, "by preventing any attempt to rearm in Germany, in Japan, in Italy, or in any other Nation which seeks to violate the Tenth Commandment—'Thou shalt not covet.'"[21] He tied this scriptural reference to his postwar vision, elevating his administration's UNO plan to the realm of idealism: "The very philosophy of the Axis powers is based on a profound contempt for the human race. . . . The issue of this war is the basic issue between those who believe in mankind and those who do not—the ancient issue between those who put their faith in the people and those who put their faith in dictators and tyrants." In Roosevelt's formulation, to reject his idea of a postwar global organization would be to reject religion, democracy, and respect for humanity, all of which were needed to create "a better America."[22]

But the words "or in any other Nation" contained an obvious warning as well, insinuating the need for indefinite vigilance and international unity to oppose future aggressors. Roosevelt's grouping of the world into countries that "believe in mankind" and those whose faith was "in dictators and tyrants" neatly simplified the state of global affairs for his hearers. Yet this interpretation of the war through the lens of American values also increased the urgency of maintaining the current alliance after the war's conclusion, as the United States would need the support of allies to remain alert to the threat of future tyrants. While FDR's speech offered the UNO as one more symbol of global security, it did so at the expense of again obliterating any sort of a US defensive perimeter in favor of a resolve to stamp out potential threats wherever they may arise. The UNO quickly became one of the most powerful public symbols of postwar peace, but it remained popular in part because its ambiguity allowed Americans to project onto it whatever they wished. Therefore, the UNO also symbolized, though less obviously, the tensions and underlying contradictions inherent in FDR's concept of security.

FDR thereby transformed "the UNO" into a condensation symbol that strengthened his narrative about the purpose of the war. As Doris Graber writes, a condensation symbol is "a name, word, phrase, or maxim which stirs vivid impressions involving the listener's most basic values." Due to their flexibility—each listener projects their own definition of the value or feeling in question onto the symbol—condensation symbols are, she contends, "the most potent, versatile, and effective tools available to politicians for swaying mass publics."[23] Indeed, condensation symbols operate, as David S. Kaufer and Kathleen M. Carley write, as "seductive invitations to enter a house that has been designed without doors or windows."[24] Through their invocation, adoption, and repetition, such terms function much like a well-worn metaphor that literalizes with rote use and reuse, slowly concretizing into a fixed, "obvious" way of interpreting an issue until rival interpretations become inconceivable. Whatever course FDR charted after the war, it would surely require a much greater degree of global involvement than the public had ever accepted before. The UNO became the primary symbol of accepting that new internationalism.

In other words, the UNO became the primary marker of anti-interventionism's demise. As Robert Dallek puts it: "The portraits of an effective postwar peace-keeping body had as much to do with creating an internationalist consensus at home as with establishing a fully effective peace system abroad. . . . [They were] the means by which domestic opinion was to be put firmly behind a continuing American part in overseas affairs."[25] In that sense, Roosevelt's campaign for the UNO was the culmination of his political battle against the anti-interventionists, his administration successfully extinguishing the embers of anti-interventionist sentiment by fanning support for the UNO. Polls showed the UNO growing in popularity, and the 1944 election saw a number of leading anti-interventionists in Congress lose their seats. These results were interpreted as a sign of the solid bipartisan consensus that had emerged for postwar internationalism, of which the UNO was the primary symbol.[26]

It would be a mistake, though, to conclude that the administration had succeeded in creating a widespread public embrace of liberal internationalism. In the report FDR received from pollster Elmo Roper, three weeks before the Pearl Harbor attack, nearly 60 percent of the public agreed that after the war the United States should play a larger part in world affairs and "join a union of democracies in all parts of the world to keep order"—not to perfect the world, nor to enact free-trade policies, but only to protect America (and thus themselves) from a continuing threat of chaos.[27]

Just as he described the Axis powers as criminals, Roosevelt dressed the UNO in corresponding metaphors of law enforcement, as "a sheriff's posse to drive out outlaws."[28] If some nation "started to run amok, and seeks to grab territory or invade its neighbors," the UNO would "stop them before they got started."[29] "The Council of the United Nations must have the power to act quickly and decisively to keep the peace by force, if necessary," FDR said in another speech:

> A policeman would not be a very effective policeman if, when the he saw a felon break into a house, he had to go to the Town Hall and call a town meeting to issue a warrant before the felon could be arrested. . . . If we do not catch the international felon when we have our hands on him, if we let him get away with his loot because the Town Council has not passed an ordinance authorizing his arrest, then we are not doing our share to prevent another World War."

These words were crafted to build support for FDR's preferred UNO structure, with real power vested in a "Security Council" consisting of "four policemen" (a term he used only in private), while a relatively powerless General Assembly would give all other nations a chance to "blow off steam."[30]

Roosevelt's law enforcement metaphor operated on several levels. It asserted that the United States was a legitimate authority in international relations, and it presumed that its main responsibility was to impose order, by violence if necessary. The language of law enforcement also contained the premise that the United States would only resort to force in exceptional circumstances and that American police power enjoyed popular support among other nations. Lastly, the logic of FDR's metaphor worked to preserve American freedom of action abroad, as his "Town Council" reference suggested, since effective police operate with broad sanction. Moreover, Roosevelt softened the force of his law enforcement metaphor with a homey analogy, saying, "I live in a small town and I always think in small town terms, but this goes for small towns as well as big towns." Although he had not lived in a small town in quite some time, he never missed a chance to tie his global policy visions to the Rockwellian image of the small American town, with all the desires for so many kinds of security that it summoned. Here again, the president masterfully blended metaphors of locality, neighborhood, authority, and safety, his imagery working to "restrain the political imagination" of his hearers.[31]

However, when FDR promised that the UNO would keep the global neighborhood safe from outlaws, he never suggested that outlawry would disappear. He promised only that the weapons of collective security would prevent would-be aggressors from disturbing the stability of the civilized world. The UNO—or, more precisely, the Security Council with which the United States was identified—would preserve (and, if necessary, restore) the global status quo. The UNO would in effect protect the existing balance of power. The arguments for the UNO assumed that civilized people would always have to be on the lookout for, and on guard against, future outlaws. The State Department similarly acknowledged that the UNO would not be a perfect institution, but it claimed that it was the only alternative to "international anarchy," and it warned Americans that without the UNO the United States would be in a dangerously weak position.[32] Assistant Secretary of State Dean Acheson made it clear that the UNO, "the embryo of world order," might have to use military force in order to prevent another war.[33]

These words of promise and warning were calculated to build public support for the overall idea of a UNO. As his speechwriter Robert Sherwood noted, "The references to the Town Council and the local constabulary provided another evidence . . . of Roosevelt's ability to reduce an enormous and even revolutionary issue to the familiar scope of a small town."[34] FDR relied on that ability often, saying things like, "Today the more you travel, the more you realize that the whole world is one neighborhood. . . . Unless the peace that follows recognizes that the whole world is one neighborhood . . . the germs of another world war will remain as a constant threat to mankind."[35] This view was reinforced by the great success of Wendell Willkie's 1943 bestseller *One World*. "All round the world there are some ideas which millions and millions of men hold in common," Willkie wrote, "almost as much as if they lived in the same town."[36] *One World*, like FDR's UNO proposal, was popular because it depicted a safe and secure postwar world imagined in accordance with American cultural values, a world that would surely diminish the threat of future aggression against the United States.

Rather than fostering genuine internationalism, then, the UNO won approval on the basis that it offered the most effective defense of American homes, neighborhoods, and small towns and the way of life that went with them. Roosevelt generated support for protecting his "global neighborhood" from a vaguely defined sense of ongoing threat by emphasizing "neighborhood," not "global." By 1944, pollster Jerome

Bruner concluded that the public supported postwar internationalism because American self-interest demanded it.[37] His colleague Hedley Cantril agreed: "Our present 'internationalism' is not rooted in knowledge or analysis of facts. . . . Our fundamental attitude would seem to be one of self-interest."[38] By the war's end, polls revealed that two-thirds to three-quarters of the public agreed that a strong international organization was the best way to keep the United States out of future wars.[39]

Historians studying the question have generally concurred. Robert Divine, for example, writes that Americans largely supported the UNO not because it would make the world safe for democracy but because it would "make the world safe for the United States." They "yearned for a magic formula that would permit them to live in peace without constant involvement abroad."[40] Indeed, the State Department responded to this mood by stressing the limits on the UNO's power and appealing to the public's desire to avoid war.[41] The UNO symbolized the increasing connection between the concepts of peace and security on both the domestic and international scale, which helped blur all these conceptual divides in political discourse.

The pro-American focus of the UNO campaign was crucial for appealing to the former conservative anti-interventionists. Many of the old anti-interventionists found themselves accepting the broad public discursive frame of Rooseveltian internationalism on the basis that it preserved American freedom of action abroad. Geoffrey Perrett observes that "the emerging internationalism more and more appeared—especially where isolationism had once held sway—to be a new nationalism. It was fiercely anti-British and anti-Russian. Among conservatives its catch-phrase was 'national sovereignty.'"[42] Neil Smith likewise calls this new internationalism a "nationalist internationalism . . . some kind of global Monroe Doctrine" and notes "the central contradiction in that vision, namely, that its internationalism was simultaneously and fervently nationalist. . . . Conservative nationalism redirected American internationalism toward intense self-interest."[43] Although the mood that FDR called "isolationist" was not totally dead—it would emerge again after the war under the new title of "unilateralism"—resistance to internationalism of the sort he faced prior to entering World War II would never again play a decisive role in shaping US foreign policy over the course of the twentieth (and, thus far, twenty-first) century.

Yet the successful UNO campaign represented the final defeat of anti-interventionism as a distinct political movement precisely because it co-opted the lingering power of anti-interventionist values, now wrapped in internationalist language. That combination of old values and new language was tied together by the common agreement, on all sides, that the United States had to protect itself against postwar threats. The dwindling but persistent voices opposing the UNO insisted that the organization itself was a threat to the nation. The rising tide of support for the UNO praised it as a stout bulwark against future perils. The very logic of the pro-UNO argument required the assumption that those perils would indeed arise, a premise articulated again and again in Roosevelt's presidential rhetoric. As the UNO became a popular symbol of security, then, it reaffirmed a framework that assumed a natural state of insecurity, signaling the need for eternal postwar vigilance against continuing dangers to the nation. If the UNO was meaningful only because the story that Roosevelt told to promote it rested on the need to fend off future insecurity, then he affirmed his commitment to defeating insecurity in the present with repeated calls for a second condensation symbol: unconditional surrender.

Securing the Postwar World: "Unconditional Surrender"

In January 1943, a few days after giving the State of the Union Address, Roosevelt flew to Casablanca, Morocco, to meet Winston Churchill. At the meeting's end, he announced publicly that the United States would accept nothing less than the "unconditional surrender" of its foes. This should not have come as news to the American people. From the very first day of the war (and even before), Roosevelt had described the conflict as a crusade to defeat malevolent powers and principalities run amok in the world. The Axis enemy, therefore, had to be defeated unconditionally because it was unconditionally evil. The president's call for "unconditional surrender" mixed his rhetoric of dualism with apocalypticism.

On December 8, 1941, as FDR asked Congress for a declaration of war, he used words he had written in his own hand: "No matter how long it may take us to overcome this premeditated invasion, the American people in their righteous might will win through to absolute victory."[44] According to speechwriter Robert Sherwood, he resisted suggestions from his aides to soften his absolutist tone. He was even more emphatic the next day in his fireside chat: "The United States can accept no result save victory, final and complete. . . . the sources of international brutality, wherever they exist, must be absolutely and finally broken."[45] A few weeks later, in his 1942 State of the Union Address, the president placed that pledge in the explicit context of biblical eschatology. He stated, "We are inspired by a faith that goes back . . . [to] the Book of Genesis: 'God created man in His own image.' . . . Those on the other side are striving to destroy this deep belief. . . . There never has been—there never can be—successful compromise between good and evil. Only total victory can reward the champions of tolerance, and decency, and freedom, and faith."[46] FDR's rhetoric rejected even the idea of a qualified peace, and this speech became a main blueprint for domestic propaganda efforts undertaken by the OWI.[47]

The highly publicized declaration at Casablanca reminded the nation of these earlier words, concentrated them into a simple two-word label, and inserted them into the foreground of discourse about the war. The term "unconditional surrender" reconfirmed the popular picture of the war as an apocalyptic crusade for civilization against totalitarian barbarism, operating as yet another condensation symbol in Roosevelt's rhetoric. This rigid dichotomy was supported by a flood of racist imagery, directed especially against Japan. The popular media constantly echoed the sentiment FDR expressed when he assured reporters that American soldiers could defeat the Japanese because "it is the difference between our type of civilization and our type of fellow and theirs."[48] This civilizational, racial language reinforced the image of the war as a crusade on behalf of the (white, democratic) American way of life.

Constant talk of the battlefield and its dangers, coupled with widespread invocations of God's blessing on and help for "our boys overseas," echoed aspects of Christian apocalyptic traditions. Wartime religious imagery often compared battlefield sacrifices to the Crucifixion.[49] For much of the American public, steeped in Christian imagery, the rhetoric of unconditional surrender conjured up notions of global devastation, judgment, and renewal reminiscent of the biblical Apocalypse—chaos as a path to a fresh start in an expiated world now cleansed of evil.

Yet Roosevelt carefully avoided fleshing out the implications of his language with any specific commitments to building a grandiose future. So, the apocalyptic promise conjured by the words "unconditional surrender," like the UNO, created a blank slate onto which everyone could project their own vision of the postwar world. More subtly, FDR's declaration of unconditional surrender diverted attention away from the war's end altogether. This phrase suggested that once the Axis powers were defeated there would be few obstacles toward world peace and therefore all issues not directly connected with winning the war could be deferred or ignored.[50]

As a result, the famous declaration at Casablanca served the administration's domestic purposes well. It helped avoid, or at least postpone, any open confrontation between the goals of administration planners and the American public's views of the war. While evidence suggests that the primary strategic purpose of the statement was to assure Stalin that the United States and Britain would open a second front in Europe, it is hard to imagine a politician as astute as FDR being unaware of how his words might impact folks back home. As Russell F. Weigley argues, "The American way of war" typically requires at least a symbolic image of total victory.[51]

Moreover, "unconditional surrender" implied a clear endpoint to US involvement in the bloody affairs of the outside world. Gaddis Smith explains this point in depth: "The idea of unconditional surrender allowed Americans to assume that once world peace was restored they could fully withdraw from European political engagements. . . . Americans assumed that the enemy's existence was the principal cause of insecurity. When all nations were freed from enslavement and fear of Axis aggression, they would embrace American ideals of democracy and peaceful conduct. Win the war, and all else would be easy."[52] Many Americans naturally fell prey to the expectation that once the Axis was defeated, there would be few obstacles in the way of establishing the peace of the world. This conclusion flowed directly from the apocalyptic paradigm, which suggests that once the eschatological suffering ends, peace and fulfillment follow permanently. Americans were generally willing to imagine the United States as the most powerful nation in a postwar world, but they remained reluctant to commit the nation to keeping the peace abroad. Thus, the words "unconditional surrender" helped buffer the impact of anything the president said about the United States' role in the postwar world, suggesting that whatever this vaguely defined role might be, it would demand little of the average American.

Roosevelt and the elite voices supporting his foreign policy often called for unconditional surrender and a postwar UNO in virtually the same breath. This constant conjunction masked the obvious contradictions between the two. The language of unconditional surrender suggested a world permanently cleansed of all evil. Yet the UNO was desperately needed, according to its boosters, to protect the world from the continuing menace of evil aggressors. Given many citizens' desire for a postwar return to "normalcy," with Americans free to disengage from the rest of the world, the Roosevelt administration's plans to usher in a new US-led world order risked sparking a political backlash that could undermine the president's entire postwar agenda.

The task facing the president was therefore to resolve, or at least obscure, these contradictions by making the two sets of war aims symbolized by the UNO and unconditional surrender seem wholly compatible. The key to his success was synthesizing two common threads that ran through all of his wartime discourse. One was American exceptionalism, the traditional view that the United States was a unique, morally superior nation. The other thread was a continuation of his previous rhetoric of insecurity, stressing America's vulnerability to foreign enemies. By tying these threads together in his discourse, FDR added new dimensions to his foreign policy narrative that would endure through the war and complete the narrative.

American Exceptionalism and Vulnerability

Roosevelt consistently hammered the simple message that democracy, civilization, and the American way were opposed by totalitarian fascism in the form of the Axis powers. Few members of the general public took much interest in the theoretical divisions between democracy and fascism, nor did the president take much time to elaborate on those differences. However, these caricatured depictions painted a clear image of moral separation, marking the United States as a pure nation fighting evil. This portrayal affirmed the United States' inherent peacefulness and goodness, both central pillars of traditional American exceptionalist discourse. In addition to promoting public support for unconditional surrender, since evil could not be negotiated with, this moral separation also resonated with Americans' widespread expectation that after the war life would return to normal. War, for many Americans, represented a temporary immersion in the dirty world of power politics. The separation of wartime from peacetime thus reinforced the idea of a moral gulf between the United States and the rest of the world.

The implicit hierarchy common to American exceptionalist discourse also helped bridge the gap between liberal internationalists, who wanted an activist foreign policy, and the bulk of the American public, whose focus was to achieve private domestic tranquility. A prominent assumption in public discourse was that all people ultimately yearned to be Americans because of the superiority of the American way of life. Hence, once the unnatural obstacle of totalitarianism was removed, there would be little need to actively promote US values abroad since people everywhere would leap at the chance to embrace the American way. The creation of a postwar world in the United States' image would, in line with this mode of thinking, require little active exertion on the part of the average citizen, thus resolving the paradox of a foreign policy premised on both a worldwide mission and aloofness from global affairs.

The assumption that the rest of the world would, if given the chance, become like the United States also played out in discussions surrounding the UNO. Many identified the UNO with US political aims; the proponents of the UNO promoted it enthusiastically as a vehicle for American ideals; and as most Americans envisioned it, the organization served as a projection of the US political system and its democratic spirit writ large.[53] State Department pamphlets promised that the UNO would require "no surrender of American traditions." On the contrary, the state portrayed the new international institution as a "classic expression of American liberalism," a new way to bring the American way of life to the world.[54] Thus the UNO, ostensibly a proposal to offset power differentials among nations through a democratic forum, was framed as a lasting peace consonant with the essence of American exceptionalism (and public expectations).

Reflecting the ambiguity of FDR's rhetoric, relatively few Americans felt that the UNO would require the United States to sacrifice its freedom in foreign policy. Polls bore this out. As Jerome Seymour Bruner found, "When people were asked which country should have the greatest say in the peace that was to come, four people out of five said the United States should. About half the country openly agreed that this was America's century and wanted the world to be organized accordingly."[55] For many Americans, apparently, the UNO was actually (in the words of one historian) "a disguise for invincible national advantage."[56] The UNO became the most prominent symbol representing the new blending of internationalism and American unilateralism.

The open-ended nature of the UNO as a symbol of postwar foreign policy also helped allay criticism from ardent liberal internationalists as well. They wrapped the idea of a UNO in their own apocalyptic vision of "one world," a unified political order bringing democracy and abundance to all, a world where the causes of war would simply disappear and conflicts would be resolved through (presumably) rational discourse alone. When combined with a commitment to the unconditional surrender of all enemies, their rhetoric created a classic apocalyptic narrative: the world would briefly be plunged into chaos, but out of the ashes a pure and perfected new world would arise, cleansed of evil. That narrative was deeply rooted in a rich tradition of political discourse that lay at the root of American exceptionalism: the tradition of the "redeemer nation," God's chosen agent for global transformation.[57]

Even if Roosevelt was trying to avoid endorsing this tradition, he used language that called it to mind. He coupled his demand for unconditional surrender with a promise that his policies would provide "the beginnings of a permanent structure of peace."[58] All member states of the UNO, he declared, would have "a common devotion to the cause of civilization and a common determination to build for the future a world of decency and security and, above all, peace." "There can be no middle ground here," he proclaimed: "We shall have to take the responsibility for world collaboration, or we shall have to bear the responsibility for another world conflict."[59] Roosevelt's presidential rhetoric alluded to the hope of a postwar, apocalyptic peace even if he remained studiously vague and uncommitted as to its niceties. He never went out of his way to explicitly deny those resonances, and he never tried to refute the idealists' apocalyptic portrayal of the conflict. American exceptionalism, however, resolved this tension in his rhetoric. To the ears of everyday Americans, the eschatological echoes of FDR's rhetoric reaffirmed the nation's exceptional role as the champion of civilization and peace in the world. His words encouraged the nation to interpret calls for a future, permanent peace as an affirmation of American uniqueness, not as plans for an internationalist revamping of foreign policy.

American exceptionalism served as the rhetorical vehicle for defusing the symbolic tension between the proposed UNO and calls for unconditional surrender in other ways as well. If the nation possesses a unique democratic mission inherited from its founding ideals, then it follows that each generation of Americans faces the difficulty of rising to the challenge of this high calling. As William Kristol notes, this interpretation of the United States' purpose can be found in the federalist writings of Hamilton and Madison:

This kind of American Exceptionalism—the idea of American Exceptionalism as a task or duty to try to live up to the claim that we are capable of good government by "reflection and choice"—is an inducement in *The Federalist* to moderation, not to pride or vainglory. . . . Rather, Americans can succeed by being prudent and taking into account these laws of politics and not having reckless or foolish dreams about the character of human nature.[60]

FDR's rhetoric, imbued with progressivism, frequently interpreted the challenge to live up to the founders' ideals as a call to care for common man in America. In similar fashion, he framed the persistence of insecurity in the postwar world as a challenge for the nation to overcome, but he framed the insecurity that threatened in economic terms that drew upon his previous New Deal discourse. This rhetorical maneuver unfolded in three steps.

First, FDR acknowledged that Americans were vulnerable and would remain so in the world after the war. This admission was subtle but present in his calls to "win the war and win the peace" (as one increasingly popular phrase put it) and his other statements.[61] Editing a draft of his 1943 State of the Union Address, the president found "We must not wait until the war is ended and then attempt to improve a system of social security overnight" and changed "social security" to the less political, more folksy phrase "personal and family safety."[62] Though this passage was eventually deleted, it indicated his intention to focus his wartime rhetoric not on any promise of postwar abundance but on the promise of personal and family security for all. In that speech he acknowledged that he had "been told that this is no time to speak of a better America after the war" but declared defiantly: "I dissent. If the security of the individual citizen, or the family, should become a subject of national debate, the country knows where I stand."[63] By positing that the safety and security of individual Americans was a matter of debate, even implicitly, Roosevelt suggested that the United States and its citizens remained vulnerable to forces outside their control.

Second, Roosevelt conflated this vulnerability with economic insecurity, a comparison he had made since the first hour of his presidency. During the Depression the prevailing wisdom had been economist Alvin Hansen's "stagnation theory," which assumed a permanently limited US production capacity. Within this schema, government's role was to stabilize the economy by directing the limited fund of private resources through central planning. By 1941, Hansen had decided that he was wrong; there was no limit to American economic capacity: "We have reached a stage in technique and productivity which a few years ago no one believed possible. All of us had our sights too low."[64] The chief engine of this growth was the production of war materiel, which grew the economy and made for fewer US deaths on the battlefield.[65] Americans on the home front endured wartime rationing and demanding labor conditions as they outproduced the combined Axis powers singlehandedly.[66]

However, many feared that once the war was over the United States would return to a state of economic depression. The correlation between military spending and economic boom was obvious enough, so it made good sense to assume that the end of the war would bring a sudden economic collapse. Roosevelt capitalized on this anxiety and interpreted it through his New Deal framework that equated economic well-being with security, granting him an opening to talk candidly about planning for the postwar era. While he was preparing his State of the Union message in January 1943, he told Canadian leader Mackenzie King: "I am proposing to speak of jobs and further security for the post-war period. This is contrary to nearly all political advice I receive; nevertheless, it is bound to be an issue and we might as well get on the right side of it now."[67] He had written to his subordinate David Lilienthal months prior about "those boys in Guadalcanal and Africa," asking him, "Does this Congress propose to tell them they are going to come back to fear about jobs, fear about the things a man can't prevent, like accident, sickness, and so on?"[68] A few months later Roosevelt personally wrote down a list of proposed GI benefits on the transcript of an address he gave, including, "In case no job is found after diligent search, then unemployment insurance if the individual registers with the U.S. employment service."[69] The president addressed the question of joblessness head-on, again discussing it in terms of security, fear, vulnerability, and assurance in his wartime correspondence and public speech.

Third, Roosevelt publicly argued that it was the nation's duty to address the economic insecurity of individual citizens as well as the world. Drawing on his New Deal rhetoric, he endorsed "the right to full employment . . . for all able-bodied men and women in America who want to work" and promised "assurance against the evils of all major economic hazards . . . from the cradle to the grave." Even as he positioned himself as working to protect individual Americans' economic prospects, however, he darkened this statement by acknowledging the inherent insecurity each citizen faced, stating that Americans were "eager to face the risks inherent in our system of free enterprise."[70] He therefore did not deny that the postwar world would contain insecurity. Instead, he focused attention on the individual economic component of this threat—the specter of unemployment, perhaps the most fearsome of all symbols of insecurity in American political discourse at this time—and argued that the nation, led by him, would defeat it after the war as it had done during the New Deal.

Roosevelt carried this argument further and contended that the United States should take it upon itself to secure economic prosperity, not only for its citizens but also for the entire world. This rhetorical move subtly inserted the basic premise underwriting his administration's liberal internationalist postwar agenda—that the United States should construct an interconnected global economic system after the war—into political discourse, camouflaging the assumption that the world needed free trade with the rhetoric of American exceptionalism. The State Department paved the way for this claim by planting an article in the November 1942 edition of *American Mercury* that bluntly told the American people, "You are going to be given a try at running the world. . . . American leadership in world affairs, looking toward a pacific and prosperous epoch, is the ultimate goal of those in Washington who are endeavoring to design the shape of things to come."[71] By defining the age of "American leadership in world affairs" as a "prosperous epoch" before other descriptors, the State Department article promoted a primarily economic lens by which to view the postwar, American-led world.

FDR's presidential rhetoric did much the same. For the most part, he relied on the same kind of rhetoric he had already been using, packed with words broad and vague enough to mean all things to all people while at the same time deploying the language of prosperity to describe his postwar vision. For example, he began 1943 with a very brief New Year's Day "Statement on War and Peace," pointing out "the supreme necessity of planning what is to come after—and of carrying forward into peace the common effort which will have brought victory in the war," so that "mankind may enjoy . . . the unprecedented blessings which Divine Providence through the progress of civilization has put within our reach."[72] By emphasizing providence, blessings, and progress in his plans for "what is to come after," Roosevelt foregrounded the importance of economics to the domestic *and* global context. When editing the draft of another speech later that month, he made clear the interrelation between these two goals. He found the line: "We must co-operate in helping each nation in its efforts to attain for its own people the highest standard of life that can be made possible." In case anyone should miss the crucial link, he added by hand: "And in this we include the highest standard of living for our own American people."[73] FDR thereby combined the imperative to economically care for individual Americans after the war with the pursuit of global economic prosperity in the postwar world, framing each of these endeavors as demonstrations of American exceptionalism.

Critically, this rhetorical tactic acknowledged the reality of continuing insecurity in the postwar world but addressed it in a manner that helped resolve the inherent tensions in the president's foreign policy discourse between symbols of absolute security (unconditional surrender) and continuing insecurity (UNO). Roosevelt framed the persistence of insecurity in the postwar world, interpreted by him as individual economic vulnerability in a callback to the New Deal, as a challenge for Americans to overcome by living up to the nation's ideals. This formulation thus used American exceptionalism in concert with a particularly economic understanding of American vulnerability as a means for assuaging the contradictions present in other aspects of FDR's foreign policy discourse.

Of course much of the president's speech during the war was devoted to the immediate imperative of winning the conflict. Roosevelt's story of the war was built around the dramatic battle between the Allies and the Axis. At a deeper level, though, the plot of his story turned on the equally dramatic and even more basic battle between security and insecurity. He suggested that there would be little point in talking about individual security as long as national security was in jeopardy.[74] On the symbolic level, then, economic and military security, like national and personal security, became two sides of the same coin as FDR conflated different notions of insecurity and security into a larger dualistic drama between good and evil. Within the terms of this drama, American exceptionalism demanded that the nation secure the economic future of its citizens and, as a manifestation of the United States' unique calling, extend the blessings of "Divine Providence" around the world. This narrative did not abrogate or censure American self-interest but rather seamlessly interlaced the increasing economic prosperity of the United States into the new understanding of the nation's global leadership role.

Roosevelt's Winning Synthesis: The Narrative of American Security

Roosevelt's wartime discourse united economic considerations with the nation's safety, connecting fears of future economic trouble with military insecurity as twin challenges facing the nation. Viewed in terms of drama, these challenges operated as conflicts driving FDR's foreign policy narrative that prioritized national security above all else. Early in 1943, the president highlighted two salient symbols of insecurity in his public utterances: the risk that foreign aggressors might militarily defeat the United States and the possibility of a postwar economic depression at home. His presidential utterances linked these two symbols of insecurity and made them inseparable from a third: the possibility that, once this war was won, other aggressor nations would threaten America in the future. In a rhetorical maneuver Wilson D. Miscamble likens to a magic trick, Roosevelt tied these three threats together, bundled them into a single discursive package, and depicted his own postwar policies, whatever they might be, as the only way to ward off the whole panoply.[75]

Case in point, the 1943 State of the Union speech linked military victory directly to a vision of postwar economic security not only on the home front but throughout the world: "Let us remember, too, that economic safety for the America of the future is threatened unless a greater economic stability comes to the rest of the world. We cannot make America an island in either a military or an economic sense. Hitlerism, like any other form of crime or disease, can grow from the evil seeds of economic as well as military feudalism."[76] In characteristic fashion, FDR colorfully deployed metaphors of criminality, illness, time, geography, and agriculture to elevate the conflict to a transcendent level. Continuing the line of reasoning exhibited in his "Dagger" address, he now defined the enemy to consist not only of dictators like Hitler in the present but also "Hitlerism," an abstract phenomenon that might spring up anywhere, at any time, in the future. It was a symbol of enduring economic as well as military insecurity, and this formulation positioned the United States as the defender of the postwar status quo.

In this speech the danger of future aggressors was tied closely to the danger of a future depression. The implication was clear enough: engagement with every corner of the globe was not just a temporary wartime adjustment; it was now a permanent fact of life, an inescapable response to the new fact that potential peril—economic as well as military—lurked everywhere. Thus, Roosevelt prepared the nation to face a future filled with endless uncertainty, always in danger of losing both peace and prosperity. By the spring of 1943, Roosevelt had established the three pillars of his wartime vision of the postwar world: (1) unconditional surrender, followed by (2) postwar economic security at home, and (3) global security through the UNO. As FDR spoke of all three, though, he made it clear that they all depended on the United States accepting the obligations that came with its exceptional status: assuming primary responsibility for protecting military, geopolitical, and economic security around the world, indefinitely. For the rest of his life he would interweave these three themes in his public rhetoric. The common thread linking it all together was the word *security*.

The question of economic security was a major theme in presidential speeches throughout the war. In a statement issued on the second anniversary of the signing of the Atlantic Charter, FDR stated that the principle for which the nation fought was "the object of security for all; of improved labor standards, economic adjustment, and social security."[77] He declared months later, "When victory comes there can certainly be no secure peace until there is a return of law and order in the oppressed countries, until the peoples of these countries have been restored to a normal, healthy, and self-sustaining existence. This means that the more quickly and effectually we apply measures of relief and rehabilitation, the more quickly will our own boys overseas be able to comes home."[78] In the same press conference he assumed the moniker "Dr. Win-the-War," he said that "it seems pretty clear that we must plan for, and help to bring about, an expanded economy which will result in more security, more employment, in more recreation, in more education, in more health, in better housing for all of our citizens, so that the conditions of 1932 and the beginning of 1933 won't come back again."[79] His statement from the Dumbarton Oaks Conference announced the aim of the war to be "first to defeat the enemy, assure that he shall never again be in position to plunge the world into war and then to so organize the peace-loving Nations that . . . no other would-be aggressor or conqueror shall even get started."[80] Near the end of his life, he issued a similar message to Congress on the Bretton Woods Conference:

> I have recommended for your consideration the immediate adoption of the Bretton Woods Agreements and suggested other measures which will have to be dealt with in the near future. They are all parts of a consistent

whole. That whole is our hope for a secure and fruitful world, a world in which plain people in all countries can work at tasks which they do well, exchange in peace the products of their labor, and work out their several destinies in security and peace. . . . The point in history at which we stand is full of promise and of danger. The world will either move toward unity and widely shared prosperity or it will move apart into necessarily competing economic blocs.[81]

In his 1944 State of the Union Address, to cite another example, FDR said that the goal of the war "could be summed up in one word: Security. . . . That means not only physical security which provides safety from attacks by aggressors. It means also economic security, social security, moral security—in a family of nations."[82] Yet when he added details to this abstract formulation with a list of specific proposals, he spoke only of benefits for Americans, labeling his program "a second Bill of Rights," again conflating domestic and foreign threats to the nation's safety. "All of these rights," he proclaimed, "spell security," because "true individual freedom cannot exist without economic security and independence."[83] Again and again, Roosevelt's rhetoric expanded the domain of "security" to encompass more areas of life as it had during the New Deal era, with the result being a politically winsome synthesis between the extension of American power abroad with the impulse to secure Americans' lives at home.

The political battle over the "Second Bill of Rights" offers yet another example of the dialectical interplay between FDR's symbols of security and insecurity. Essentially an enhanced New Deal set of policies, it reflected Roosevelt's new globalized understanding of security; in short, the military threat to security from abroad became an important motivation for revising and strengthening economic security at home.[84] By affirming the federal government's ability to shore up security at home, this proposal softened the expected persistence of insecurity abroad implicit in FDR's other postwar proposals such as the UNO. Moreover, efforts to get economic protections enacted into law had to overcome a rising conservative sentiment that gave the Republicans major gains in the 1942 election. One of the great spurs to this shift to the right was the growing fear that a stronger state—like the New Deal state—could easily lead to a totalitarian state. It was the president, more than anyone else, who had taught the American public to fear totalitarianism in its foreign forms and urged the nation to arm, then go to war, against it.

Now this particular fear, which he had said so much to foster, came back to weaken the appeal of his own domestic policies.[85] Consequently, even as he faced political resistance, FDR met rhetorical victory as his conflation of domestic threats and foreign ones, typified by the symbol of totalitarianism, was echoed by his political opponents.

Perhaps the greatest testament to Roosevelt's rhetorical success can be found in how he converted several prominent anti-interventionists to his interpretation. Senator Vandenburg, one of FDR's staunchest rivals in the debates of 1940 and 1941, gave a half-hour speech endorsing the president's vision on January 10, 1945: "I do not believe that any nation hereafter can immunize itself by its own exclusive action. Since Pearl Harbor, World War II has put the gory science of mass murder in to new and sinister perspective. Our oceans have ceased to be moats which automatically protect our ramparts."[86] This speech, perhaps more than any other single example, epitomizes the triumph of Roosevelt's political vocabulary over that of his rivals.

The reverberative effect of Roosevelt's rhetoric was evident in other arenas as well. For example, the president's vague insistence that the postwar world would be one of prosperity for all Americans was reflected in advertisements from the time. A continuing deluge of ads promised that victory would usher in a paradise in which all those on the side of good would enjoy whatever commodities their hearts desired.[87] Just as the president declared that America would achieve the total defeat of evil abroad, so commercials proclaimed the total defeat of material want at home. And many of these ads made it clear that America's exceptional virtue, proven through wartime heroism and technological innovation, gave the United States the right to become *the* land of unparalleled comfort and abundance.[88] Since Roosevelt frequently paired his demand for "unconditional surrender" with a call to protect prosperity in the postwar world, advertisements that assured abundance for all after the war symbolically complemented his and his administration's official rhetoric. The message would work the other way around too: the enemy was never far from the domestic tranquility of the American home; the United States' exceptional potential for creating material abundance would always be at risk; those who wanted to enjoy life in a prosperous America would continually need to remain vigilant against threats from abroad. While Roosevelt never issued a statement quite to that effect, his words could easily take on meanings that he never intended. After all, he was the dominant political figure of his age, setting the tone for American public discourse for over a decade.

In sum, FDR's wartime language combined all of these incongruous images of conflict, peace, and the postwar world into a story that served, more than any competing interpretation, to give meaning to the war effort. In his telling, the absolutely virtuous nation was fulfilling its destined mission by quickly exterminating absolute evil and then letting the world go, for the most part, on its way while the United States turned back to its primary concern—promoting and securing its own economic well-being. Once the evil had vanished, the story continued, the way the world went would inevitably be the American way, and if any nation went too far to resist this trend, the United States could always employ the UNO to provide gentle pressure and goad errant states back toward the path of democracy and progress (the president never publicly advanced his "four policemen" plan). The postwar world hinted at by FDR was one in which all nations would advance together in a globalized economy with the United States at its center. Critically, as Miscamble notes, the president failed to translate this story into a set of commonly accepted and "realistic policies to guide his nation in the postwar era." Rather, he bestowed a story—a story Walter Lippmann called FDR's "evangel of Americanism," a story his successors would adapt to meet the challenges of the world after the war, a story with security at its heart.[89]

Conclusion

By the time Franklin Roosevelt died, the American public as a whole had largely accepted his story as the best—indeed, for many, the only plausible—interpretation of the new situation. The story seamlessly fused the apocalyptic language of a redemption that was at once both national and global with the defensive language of safety from military, geopolitical, and economic threats. It fused Wilsonian internationalist discourse and the anti-interventionist worldview into a new mode of public discourse that blurred the differences between the two and rendered them both largely irrelevant as independent political forces. Most Americans could accept this wartime narrative because it so skillfully blended liberal internationalist, realist, unilateralist, and millennialist language, stringing all these traditions into the common thread of

American exceptionalism and making all serve the overriding promise of postwar security.

Because it embraced all these discursive strands, this story could give a unified meaning to the war and the immense American war machine it created. Instead of a threat to the nation's democratic inheritance, the changes wrought by the war effort now served as the path to personal as well as national security and the fulfillment of the United States' exceptional mission. This meaning could unite most of the American public, providing a multilayered framework for public discourse about the nation and its proper foreign policy course. Roosevelt's narrative served narrower political ends as well, giving the administration freedom to plan, pursue, and implement policies guided by its own elite constellation of realism and liberal internationalism.

FDR's wartime synthesis was able to gain such success because it so closely mirrored the fundamental themes and structure of his prewar narrative. The supreme objectives of the UNO, unconditional surrender, and postwar economic planning, as Roosevelt described them, was the same as the supreme objective of his pre–Pearl Harbor efforts to aid England and, before that, the New Deal: security. This common thread united discourse across his presidency. Throughout the war, he returned again and again to the familiar rhetorical strategy he had used throughout his political career. FDR identified symbols of insecurity, presented them as interlinked or even interchangeable parts of a single danger, stressed that this danger imperiled every American home, and insisted on his own favored policies as the only effective antidote to the threat.

This loose narrative thinly papered over the contradictions among its constituent images of peace and security. Those contradictions remained apparent for those who cared to see them. The nearly universal support for the war as seen through the lens of the Rooseveltian narrative indicates that few people did. As Leroy G. Dorsey describes, narratives of the sort FDR proffered exhibit political force in how they "bridge differences and promote commonality among human beings by framing their everyday reality in an almost mystical way."[90] World War II, with all of its emotional urgency and potency, cemented Roosevelt's narrative synthesis as a new, dominant foundation of political discourse concerning the nation's role in the world. It remained up to future inhabitants of the oval office what to do with the paradoxical narrative he created as they, in the timeless words of William E. Leuchtenburg, presided in his shadow.[91] In foreign policy discourse as in so many other arenas of American life, FDR set the parameters of what would succeed him. He bequeathed to the nation many somethings to fear.

Conclusion
A Still Unfinished History

On the evening of September 11, 2002, New York mayor Michael Bloomberg read aloud Franklin Roosevelt's 1941 annual address. He listed the "Four Freedoms" identified by FDR in that speech, reissuing the call of the thirty-second president of the United States for "a world founded upon four essential human freedoms" of speech, of worship, from want, and from fear. Juxtaposed with the patriotic gravity of the one-year anniversary of the 9/11 terrorist attacks, Bloomberg's recitation of Roosevelt's "Four Freedoms" address evoked comparisons to the nation's experiences in World War II, particularly the attack on Pearl Harbor. This analogy, repeated by news commentators ad nauseum in the year following the attacks, worked alongside Bloomberg's overall performance to color the deaths of thousands of helpless civilians in the destruction of the nation's largest financial center in a more patriotic light. Rather than nameless white-collar workers, many of whom were not US citizens, FDR's words allowed Bloomberg to symbolically transform the victims of the attacks into American martyrs. While they had not died as soldiers, a more traditional display of national virtue, this "weird symbolic substitution" portrayed them as heroes of a different sort. According to the speech's logic, they gave their lives in service to one of the principal values contained within the wider mission of American life as articulated by FDR: to realize freedom from material want.[1] Roosevelt's discursive blend of economic, political, and military notions of security, rearticulated by the billionaire mayor of New York, would still seem to exert persuasive power many decades after their utterance.

This episode offers just one overt moment in which the long shadow of FDR's rhetoric can be seen at work in American public life. Other examples abound. President Joe Biden placed FDR's portrait in the Oval Office and compared his own legislative proposals to the New Deal.[2] Hillary Clinton launched her 2016 presidential campaign on New York City's Roosevelt Island, announcing her "Four Fights" for American citizens and proclaiming her dedication to "Franklin Roosevelt's enduring vision of America, the nation we want to be."[3] More relevant for our purposes, Roosevelt's continuing influence can commonly be found in the mundane assumptions operative in US foreign policy discourse. For example, in 2019 conservative commentator David French argued that the 2003 invasion of Iraq was justified on the basis that "there were few greater instruments of instability in the world than Saddam Hussein," a line of reasoning that directly hearkens back to Roosevelt's language of aggressor states and friendly neighborhoods.[4] The July 4, 2020, edition of *Economist* magazine praised then candidate Biden, who had already compared himself to FDR, as someone who would "return to multilateral engagement in foreign policy . . . which could begin to steady a chaotic world."[5] As Bradford Vivian observes, Rooseveltian logic is at work whenever American politicians (like Bloomberg, Biden, and Clinton) or commentators (like French or *Economist*) announce their "fidelity" to fundamental US liberties while at the same time advocating the "unceasing enlargement" of those liberties worldwide.[6]

One does not have to scour recent commentary to find evidence of Roosevelt's impact on political discourse, of course. FDR's influence was appreciated in his own time. Five days after his death, Winston Churchill eulogized the president before the House of Commons, recounting Roosevelt's successful campaign to prepare for war while fending off critics of intervention: "There is no doubt that the President foresaw the great dangers closing in upon the pre-war world with far more prescience than most well-informed people on either side of the Atlantic, and that he urged forward with all his power such precautionary military preparations as peace-time opinion in the United States could be brought to accept. There never was a moment's doubt, as the quarrel opened, upon which side his sympathies lay." In Roosevelt, he memorialized, the British people lost "the greatest American friend we have ever known and the greatest champion of freedom who has ever brought help and comfort from the new world to the old." However, the prime minister reassured the assembled parliamentarians that FDR's legacy was carefully preserved in the Atlantic Charter, "which will, I trust, long remain a guide for both our peoples and for other peoples of the world." Moreover, Roosevelt's vision was safeguarded by the people he had appointed: "He has left behind him a band of resolute and able men."[7] The internationalist reorientation FDR fashioned in US foreign policy, according to Churchill, was doubtful to be reversed, a standing tribute to his political significance.

While Churchill's prediction has proved correct—the United States has not withdrawn into anything resembling "isolationism" since FDR's departure—the transformation he oversaw was less immanently sweeping than it would appear on the surface. Case in point: shortly after the United States joined the United Nations a research survey found that 30 percent of American citizens were "uninformed" and an additional 27 percent were "poorly informed" concerning the newly chartered global forum.[8] The same study also discovered that internationalist stances on postwar issues correlated with being better informed on the United Nations, with 76 percent of the "better-informed" respondents believing that "America should take an active part in world affairs" as compared to only 41 percent among the "uninformed." The poll found similar divides over the questions of whether increased foreign trade would benefit individual citizens and whether international problems ranked "among the most important confronting the United States."[9] Indeed, the same year, poet W. H. Auden labeled the era "the age of anxiety," expressing fear over the direction the nation and world were taking.[10] These myriad responses belie a simple understanding of FDR's effect on US foreign affairs. John Bodnar's survey of veterans' attitudes further affirms this point, recording that many "saw in the forceful calls for national defense and power a retreat from the liberal dreams articulated by Franklin Roosevelt and the spirit of the Four Freedoms."[11]

Therefore, it seems fair to say that Roosevelt presidency precipitated a complex shift in American foreign policy that defies any straightforward historical account organized along a linear isolationist-to-interventionist national trajectory. Indeed, FDR's legacy in global affairs has been ambiguous and contested from the second he left office. Rather, these findings point to a deep equivocality in public opinion on the subject of foreign affairs in the aftermath of the Roosevelt presidency. This ambivalence, we contend, can be traced in part to the ambiguities and contradictions embedded in FDR's presidential rhetoric, which drew from realist, racial, progressive, nostalgic, apocalyptic, liberal-internationalist, and American exceptionalist discourses with little consideration for the possible inconsistencies this paradoxical brew might contain. To help explain the development of these overlapping elements of FDR's discourse, we have shown how Roosevelt's rhetorical victories built on one another, each success drawing from the constellation of appeals that preceded it. Thus, we have examined a series of thematic snapshots encompassing his entire political career, seeking to capture the progression of his discourse from a wide-angle perspective starting with his first campaign for state senator in New York and culminating with his defeat of the anti-interventionist movement and instantiation of a new way of talking about America's role in the world during World War II.

Our aim has not been to fully explain the success of Roosevelt's rhetoric or the broader transformation of American attitudes toward foreign affairs between the mid-1930s and early 1940s. That process was far too complex for any single explanation to suffice. Rather, we have sought to shed light on how Roosevelt's words as president played a role in that shift and how his political discourse evolved over the course of his career, with notions of security playing a central role in his utterances from his earliest days in Albany to his final moments as president.

Roosevelt first entered office as a New York State legislator riding the twin waves of progressive politics and his own name recognition. Although his political predilections were unoriginal, he articulated his preferences with vivid language and a bevy of brilliant metaphors. He wasted little time following the footsteps of his cousin Theodore into the office of assistant secretary of the navy, where he positioned himself as an advocate for rearmament and the projection of naval power within the Wilson administration. After losing in the 1920 election as the Democratic vice-presidential candidate and being stricken with polio the following year, FDR reinvented himself as an advocate for disarmament and international trade. He won the governorship of New York and then the presidency, vowing to offer the nation a "new deal" while adopting the demeanor and language of a military commander fighting a foreign foe.

Rhetorically, his progressivism and Mahanianism predisposed him to emphasize economic issues, which lay at the heart of the nation's concern as the Great Depression intensified. During the New Deal years, he perfected the metaphors of home, military language, and moral appeals he deployed in his famous 1933 inaugural address, wedding them to a liberal internationalism in foreign affairs that stressed the importance of stability, unrestricted trade, and disarmament. He wrapped all of his proposals in the language of security, frequently equating the term with economic prosperity at home and political order abroad. Roosevelt influenced public opinion so greatly because he (and his speechwriters) could pull those fragments together with powerfully effective narratives. He was a masterful storyteller, among the greatest ever to reside in the White House. His stories drew upon, expressed, and in some ways reshaped the cultural foundations and values of the American people.

The New Deal, and indeed his whole political career, prepared the way for Roosevelt's response to the war. Confronted by a global arena recalcitrant to his internationalist vision of ever-advancing commercial prosperity through unrestricted trade, FDR began to decry the abstract forces of aggression, imperialism, and economic nationalism. These critiques gave way to a corresponding synthesis in Roosevelt's own rhetoric that merged elements of dualism, realism, and liberal internationalism, resulting in a constellation of appeals that framed resistance to open trade and rearmament as threats to US security. As the descent to war grew closer, Roosevelt encountered the limits of his persuasive powers, with the American public resistant to any calls for international involvement. In the face of a powerful anti-interventionist movement, FDR adapted elements of his New Deal discourse to argue that civilization stood in danger from apocalyptic threats overseas. Over the course of 1940 and 1941, he made the case against anti-interventionism by first appropriating his political opponents' value structure to disarm their critiques and then assembling those values into a positive case for war, casting an inchoate vision of the postwar world in his "Arsenal of Democracy" fireside chat, "Four Freedoms" address, "Unlimited National Emergency" speech, press conferences, and other public communication.

Ultimately, it was the Japanese attack on Pearl Harbor that sealed Roosevelt's victory in the political battle over intervention. An overwhelming majority of Americans assumed that war was the only possible response to the attack, a testament to FDR's persistent preaching. But that interpretation of events was not inevitable. It prevailed because the president won over such a significant proportion of the public to his way of viewing and talking about the world situation. He won this political victory largely through building his rhetoric on the basic, almost universal, premise that no American wanted to go to war, thereby creating a new kind of public discourse that combined the ideals of liberal internationalism with a powerful desire for peace and security. If Roosevelt had argued for American entry into the conflict only on pragmatic grounds, casting Germany as a military and/or economic threat, he likely would have lost the debate. The actual evidence of a military threat to the American homeland was doubtful, and relatively few citizens were willing to go to war to alter the contours of the global economy.

Consequently, Roosevelt laid out his vision of the postwar settlement well in advance. Always aware of Woodrow Wilson's failure to obtain

American entry to the League of Nations, FDR feverishly checked the pulse of public opinion throughout the war. He dramatized events, crafted an absolutizing narrative of good versus evil, depicted the conflict as a battle for civilization, and asserted the unlimited danger posed by the "gangsters" who threatened the global neighborhood. Because, as Blum contends, the US public fought the war on the basis of imagination, the Roosevelt administration expended great effort in shaping the American people's conception of the conflict. FDR's words operated alongside official pronouncements, Office of War Information propaganda, and prowar messages from a compliant private sector to market the administration's postwar agenda in terms palatable to public opinion. Roosevelt incorporated new symbols of security such as the United Nations Organization and calls for "unconditional surrender" into his winning synthesis of appeals, ultimately articulating all these various elements of his discourse as interconnected issues of security and insecurity.

Although Roosevelt's responsibility for the Cold War that followed him is the subject of endless debate—he simultaneously considered the Soviet Union one of his "four policemen" while also withholding information about the atomic bomb from Stalin—there can be little doubt that Roosevelt played a predominant role in creating the discursive framework that would shape the United States' Cold War world. By positioning security as a primary political virtue in American civic life while also defining security in all these variegated ways, FDR set the stage for the escalation and expansion of security concerns that would occur under his successors' watch. As Mark Stoler has written, "The very concept of national security policy as defined in the years immediately following the end of World War II"—a concept that residually influences discourse and policy-making about national security today—"institutionalized a view of the world and a response to threats that echoed in many ways the views and policies of the Roosevelt administration from 1940 to 1945."[12] While his rhetorical conflation of American commercial and foreign policy interests was not new, Roosevelt added to this mixture an emphasis on security variously articulated as a defense of the international status quo, the promotion of trade, a call to maintain the independence of the Western hemisphere, preserving the moral values of the past, the protection of a vaguely defined global neighborhood, and safeguarding the economic well-being of individual American homes. By defining security in such amorphous and transposable ways, Roosevelt's words elevated national security to a primary value in American political discourse while also undermining the nation's ability to ever fully realize (much less maintain) security in all these various manifestations.

Therefore, Roosevelt's contribution to the Cold War should be understood in primarily rhetorical terms, as his structure of discourse became the default idiom through which American politicians deliberated foreign policy concerns in the wake of his passing. This contention does not mean that we believe FDR's rhetoric necessarily led to the United States' bipolar rivalry with the Soviet Union or that his words determined the decisions of his successors—far from it.[13] Rather, our argument is that Roosevelt's role in the Cold War should be viewed through the lens of rhetorical invention—"the creation or discovery of speech materials"—as he generated the symbolic resources by which future presidents would make sense of the United States' postwar role (along with its responsibilities) on the global stage.[14] Farrell, analyzing Roosevelt's 1933 inaugural address, discerns that "Roosevelt invented and empowered a meaningful rhetorical constituency," arguing for a view of "Roosevelt's discourse . . . as a piece in a larger frame, a frame that even Roosevelt may not have glimpsed completely at the time. To sense invention at work here is to suggest the profound interplay of these mysterious factors and the way they came together to produce a unique utterance, an utterance that crystallized and animated the power of a still unfinished history."[15]

A still-unfinished history. Farrell's turn of phrase appositely captures FDR's rhetorical relevance for American political culture writ large, as echoes of the longest-serving commander in chief can still be heard every time a president adopts a personalist leadership style, uses media technology innovatively, invokes a state of crisis, or imposes his (or her) interpretation of world affairs in public discourse. In our view, Farrell's words aptly encapsulate the multilayered effect of Roosevelt's foreign policy discourse covered in this book. As Paul Chilton describes, there exist certain "cognitive structures" that "guide thinking about security and international relations in a fashion that may be independent of the detailed and often technical rationales given by specialists themselves. The presence of semantic and conceptual connections is not arbitrary or accidental, but has arisen from the historical evolution of discourses during which modern states constituted themselves in an international system."[16] We have sought to shed light on one such period of "historical evolution" that, like the evolutionary theory of punctuated equilibrium, witnessed a rapid transformation of the discourses that shaped and continue to shape US foreign policy. Viewing FDR from this broad perspective of rhetorical invention, we argue that his rhetoric accomplished three primary effects.

First, Roosevelt's security-laden rhetoric worked alongside other elite voices and Office of War Information propaganda to generate political support for the administration's war policies, the final step in a pattern of instrumentally using appeals to security to accomplish political ends. Early on, Roosevelt's words galvanized the nation to support his administration's reform efforts by compressing his policies into a single term—the New Deal—that reinterpreted the biting economic collapse as a crisis of security afflicting individual American homes, thereby rendering the sustenance of those homes the responsibility of the federal government. His rhetoric inaugurated a new civic culture and set in motion a revolution in citizens' relationship to their president through the use of radio, his fireside chats deployed as a tool to manage public anxiety about the Depression and war through an image of intimacy and warmth. Roosevelt's discourse mediated and made sense of the United States' transition to superpower status for the American people, with all its dislocating power. And his words framed World War II in terms that were intelligible to the public, as his rhetorical synthesis rallied the nation to battle while also generating political support for the administration's plans for the postwar world.

Throughout this process, FDR consistently linked national security to a healthy, expanding economy. He had often talked about boundless possibilities for commercial productivity and expansion before 1929, and during the World War II years he presented himself, both publicly and privately, as defending the gains already made. By connecting economic and geopolitical concerns, Roosevelt was able to portray his hopes for the postwar future as a continuation of the New Deal imperative to secure American homes, itself supported by nostalgia for a romantic American past. This winning rhetorical synthesis rallied the nation to conflict, kept the nation engaged in both major theaters of combat, and maintained support for the administration's war policies. While it might be tempting to assume that the American public would have supported Roosevelt's command of the war effort regardless of his rhetoric, it is worth remembering that the Democrats suffered major losses in the

1942 midterm elections—precisely why Roosevelt attempted to execute the Operation Torch landings in North Africa before the vote was held. Any evaluation of Roosevelt's wartime rhetoric should not discount the instrumental utility of his discourse for ensuring public support for the war effort as well as garnering legislative approval for the administration's war policies.

Understood as a form of rhetorical invention, FDR's strategic use of rhetoric to generate public support for his war and postwar aims demonstrated the utility of appeals to security. In his discursive complex, an elastically defined national security sat enthroned as the highest value of American politics. But Roosevelt articulated this value in a manner that made it inseparable from a more traditional US commitment to preserving freedom as well as peace, moral purity, and national innocence. When he applied this framework to events happening on an international scale, the boundary between America and the world was blurred, perhaps in some minds even erased. This tactic held a distinct advantage: since domestic tensions and conflicts were now projected on a foreign screen, global action aimed at resolving international conflict thus worked to generate the appearance of protecting the United States.[17]

But there was on obvious price to be paid. The tensions and conflict themselves, when projected on a global scale, were immensely magnified. And they were now tied directly to fears of military or economic conquest by foreign aggressors. Consequently, Roosevelt's discursive constellation of security and insecurity contained within it the unavoidable conclusion that the United States could not and should not escape deep involvement in affairs around the globe, and thus Americans would have to accept the fact they were inescapably embedded in world politics. This conclusion has served as a foundational premise for every president's foreign policy since. As mentioned to at the beginning of this book, Roosevelt's elevation of security to the pantheon of American political values has not been undone; if anything, the twenty-first century has only confirmed the enduring viability of fear appeals in US political discourse. Consequently, FDR's instrumental use of symbols of security and insecurity has itself become a pattern oft-repeated by many an American politician. While he obviously did not invent the exploitation of fear appeals, Roosevelt used symbols of (in)security perhaps more effectively than any other US president to accomplish political ends.

Second, FDR's rhetoric advanced a static and reactive conception of the United States' role in the world, helping mediate the nation's transition to a "status quo" power. In addition to enshrining security as a chief value in US political life, Roosevelt's rhetoric also revamped the broad thematic contours of American foreign policy debate. The preceding chapters display the various symbols of security and insecurity progressively adopted in FDR's presidential rhetoric, exhibiting his penchant for accumulating various images of safety, security, home, and their opposites. Everything from air power to apple pie was conscripted into his broad drama pitting the interconnected forces of security against the equally interconnected forces of insecurity. All these shared elements served to reassure the public that Roosevelt was hard at work protecting the United States—individual Americans, their homes, their neighborhoods, and even their hemisphere—from future harm and suffering.

Even the impulse to avoid war, expressed most clearly in the anti-interventionist movement, was repurposed by Roosevelt in this schema. Many anti-interventionists believed in the traditional principle that Americans could draw hard lines between themselves and the rest of the world physically, politically, and ideologically; their stance signified the hope that the oceans could continue to keep the nation safe from all the risks entailed by foreign entanglement. In the hands of FDR, this impulse to avoid war instead became a symbol of America's reluctance to enter the conflict, a reluctance made tragic by the inevitable advance of aggression abroad. Thus, even as Roosevelt vigorously agreed with his critics that Americans did not want war, his policies and words transformed this desire from a realistic policy stance of nonintervention into proof of American faultlessness in the conflict, which morally paved the way for the United States to enter the war as a nation possessing only pure motives. In time, this belief in American innocence gave way first to widespread feelings of resignation surrounding eventual US entry into the war and then to an all-embracing sense of outrage in the aftermath of Pearl Harbor.

By tying together so many discursive strands, the president's rhetoric made it easy to imagine that the United States stood united as a nation by unshakably permanent, universally accepted, and unquestionably good values. However, these were also, the president repeatedly said, distinctively American values. His mythology created an image of Americans bound together not merely socially and politically but through a common set of value commitments that he presented as immutable foundations of the nation's life.[18] His skillful use of religious language made those values seem even more ageless and incontrovertible. Yet this blurring of domestic and international symbols of security, combined with the persistence of dangers abroad and the assertion of American values, correspondingly worked to escalate the urgency of even remote dangers, since those dangers now represented threats to a vaguely defined American way of life. By creating such powerful, mutually reinforcing images of unity and certainty, FDR's interplay of symbols could raise the very anxiety that it was meant to assuage.

Throughout World War II, the president guided the public's imagining of both the war and the postwar world. In each case he created vivid images of enemies that had to be defeated at all costs, requiring vigilance to stamp out other nations' aggression, rearmament, or autarky wherever they may arise. Whether conceptualized within the terms prescribed by his "four policemen," the US-centric global trading system established at Bretton Woods, the future UNO, or a potential "Security Council," Roosevelt's foreign policy plans envisioned a United States endowed with the responsibility of regulating the global postwar balance of power. Thusly endowed with such a duty, US foreign policy would henceforth be defined by seeking out and confronting potential usurpers of the international order. As exemplified by his support of the Badoglio regime in Italy, FDR consistently prioritized order over democracy in his wartime foreign policy. His rhetoric reflected this arrangement by portraying the United States not as an international force for the spread of democracy as in the days of Webster or even Wilson but instead as the world's chief law enforcer. The tacit message of the Roosevelt administration was that the chosen nation's mission was now to detect, react to, and control threats to a global order articulated as synonymous with American values.

This understanding diverged from previous presidential rhetoric concerning America's role in the world. For example, Warren G. Harding's inaugural address, like FDR's presidential rhetoric, described World War I as a "great storm" and similarly framed that conflict as one of abstract values, noting that "liberty . . . and civilization are inseparable." However, he argued that the storm had now passed, leaving "our Republic unshaken," and "though both [liberty and civilization] were threatened we find them now secure."[19] What made FDR's discourse different from that which preceded it was the pattern of interpreting so many phenomena through the lens of security, combined with an emotional, moral urgency and an elastic definition of insecurity.

In Chilton's terms, there existed a clash between the metaphors used by FDR to describe his postwar vision. As he notes, "Roosevelt had imaged world affairs within a conceptual framework that was undermined by the events of the war and the behavior of the Soviet Union in its aftermath." Specifically, the president adopted symbols of openness—unrestricted trade, the UNO, abstracting the conflict to the realm of values—while also articulating his war aims in the language of security, "a concept based essentially on closure."[20] Chilton mentions this inherent contradiction, observing that

> "'national security" was an uncommon phrase until the 1940s. It established itself following the Japanese attack on Pearl Harbor in December 1941 (a traumatic penetration of the American security space) and in the wake of the atomic attacks on Japan. The new thinking about security was in large measure an effort to come to terms with the central implication of modern weaponry: no state can be an invulnerable, impermeable sanctuary in the age of the strategic bomber and weapons of mass destruction. Under these conditions there could be no "defence" in the traditional sense.[21]

Indeed, Robert L. Ivie argues that the "fear-inducing" features of George Kennan's discourse are what made his "Long Telegram" and "X Article" effective articulations of Cold War strategy in the wake of World War II.[22] FDR's tendency to interpret change through the lens of insecurity, combined with the prevalence of security in all its symbolic guises in his rhetoric, encouraged a view of world affairs that equated change with danger, thus promoting a reactive foreign policy disposition that located safety in the status quo.

Third, Roosevelt's rhetoric generated images, inventional resources, and an overriding emphasis on security that all populate the foreign policy discourse of his presidential successors. In short, FDR instantiated a new way of articulating America's role in the world, at least in the realm of presidential rhetoric. Although different aspects of his rhetorical constellation can be found in the utterances of his predecessors—Theodore Roosevelt's voyage of the "Great White Fleet" encouraged an internationalist perspective, Wilson had spoken of dire threats overseas necessitating American action, and even Harding admitted the "inescapable" nature of the United States' "relationship to world affairs"—under FDR these various elements came together to form a powerful framework that saw the world in terms of globalized security and insecurity with America at its center.[23]

Cognizant of Wilson's failure, Roosevelt propounded a vision for the postwar order organized around disarmament, trade, civilization, and security. Encapsulated in texts such as the "Four Freedoms" address, "Day of Infamy" speech, Charlottesville "Dagger" address, and the Atlantic Charter, FDR relentlessly advocated aims that would unequivocally break from the nonentanglement principle that had overshadowed American foreign policy debates since the days of Washington. He overcame the resistance of peace advocates and anti-interventionists to articulate a new rationale for American engagement abroad, that the United States did not fight "for the purpose of power, or land, or prestige, or influence, but for the improvement of human freedoms across the world."[24] The spread of those freedoms he identified with his multitudinous symbols of security, thereby bequeathing to his successors a mixed rhetorical inheritance by which to make sense of the nation's budding rivalry with the Soviet Union and frame the task of constructing a postwar international order.

If, as Ronald Krebs argues, "dominant narratives" of national security exercise influence by delimiting "the contours of legitimate debate" in subsequent exchange, thereby structuring "argumentation and policy outcomes," then the force of Roosevelt's rhetorical revolution can be measured by his presidential successors' tendency to adopt his security-centric framing of US foreign policy.[25] And, the evidence shows, Roosevelt's unique interpretive cocktail of realism, dualism, and liberal internationalism found life long after his presidency ended.

In the immediate aftermath of the president's demise, Hogan notes, policy-makers were guided by the foreign policy convictions FDR spread such as the need for constant vigilance, permanent global involvement, entangling alliances, and clear symbols of security/insecurity; so guided, they "began to discard the last remnants of the country's prewar isolationism," "used the phrase 'national security' more frequently than before, and engineered a rapid expansion of American power into every nook and cranny of the world."[26] The failure of Progressive Party candidate Henry Wallace in the 1948 presidential election fittingly encapsulated this shift toward an interventionist, realist foreign policy paradigm that quickly became Cold War common sense. In the early 1950s Senator Robert Taft led a powerful faction (in some ways heir to the anti-interventionist movement) arguing for a scaled-back military presence abroad. But Taft and his followers never questioned the basic prioritization of security present in Roosevelt's rhetorical constellation. They argued only about how best to implement it.[27]

Eisenhower was also inclined to view dangers on a magnified scale. Indeed, he was proud that long before the attack on Pearl Harbor, his prediction that the United States would enter the war had earned him the nickname "alarmist Ike."[28] From the first days of his presidency, Ike spoke of the threat to the nation in apocalyptic terms. He stressed in public as well as in private that his overriding foreign policy goal was to defend the American way of life, which he saw as gravely imperiled. He warned his National Security Council that the country was unprepared for an enemy attack and therefore "we could eventually lose our existence as a free nation."[29]

Eisenhower never seriously considered an apocalyptic war to destroy the force he saw as the root of global evil: communism. Rather, he assumed that he could use his steely resolve—and teach the nation to maintain a steely resolve—to continue Harry Truman's foundational policy of containing communism. Yet Eisenhower resisted Truman's idea that the United States was in a "moment of peril." Rather, he told the nation, "Our danger cannot be fixed or confined to one specific instant." Instead, he stated, "We live in an age of peril."[30] Consequently, Eisenhower sought to establish cost-effective and morale-sustaining ways for the United States to go on indefinitely containing and managing the apocalyptic threat of communism. As part of that basic strategy, he advanced peace as a primary value of US foreign policy. But when Ike spoke of peace, he more often meant stability, resulting in a focus on maintaining the global status quo. At times, this meant restraining imprudent allies, such as during the Suez Crisis. At other times, achieving stability meant dispatching marines to prevent the overthrow of a friendly government or to stop communism from making inroads in new global spheres such as the Middle East.

By the end of the Eisenhower presidency, the basic interpretive structure introduced by FDR had become the nearly unquestioned foundation of American discourse and foreign policy. Indeed, on the day Eisenhower left office, John F. Kennedy charged that Ike and the Republican Party had not taken the permanent threat to the nation seriously enough, because the United States now faced its "hour of maximum danger."[31] The bipartisan consensus was confirmed—security was now fixed, undeniably, as the highest value in American foreign policy discourse. To confront that danger, Kennedy ordered a massive increase in the US military arsenal and the dispatch of more and more troops to the faraway land of Vietnam.

Lyndon B. Johnson turned that military mission into a full-scale war, in the process confirming the apotheosis of (absolute) security in the value hierarchy of US foreign policy. His words before the United Nations echoed FDR's confidence in the force of liberal rationality and his conflation of various notions of security: "The United States wants sanity, and security, and peace for all, and above all. President Kennedy, I am sure, would regard as his best memorial the fact that in his 3 years as President the world became a little safer."[32] He launched a massive military engagement—ironically, just the kind of policy response that FDR had worked so hard to avoid in fears of replicating Wilson's mistakes—and within a few years of the Gulf of Tonkin incident, huge public uproar arose over the Vietnam War. The national turmoil over the war, coupled with rapid social changes taking place at home, combined to create a pervasive sense of peril for many Americans whether they were at home or stationed somewhere in Southeast Asia.

Ronald Reagan tried mightily to use the "bully pulpit" of the presidency to restore a sense of national confidence. Yet as Reagan began his second term, the venerable diplomat and keen observer George Kennan could write: "A half-century ago people in this country had a sense of security vis-à-vis their world environment such as I suppose no people had ever had since the days of the Roman Empire. Today that pattern is almost reversed—our national consciousness is dominated at present by a sense of insecurity."[33] Indeed, it would seem the one constant in US political life after World War II is that Americans continually feel afraid. Throughout the Cold War era, as two historians recount, "talking up the threat, perpetuating the politics of insecurity, became the mission" of "the politicians and operators in Washington."[34] From the capital, that pervasive sense of insecurity rippled out to editorial rooms, barrooms, and living rooms across the nation. On a rhetorical level, Truman, Eisenhower, Kennedy, Johnson, Reagan, and the other Cold War presidents drew on foreign policy frameworks originally articulated by Roosevelt. Like FDR, their appeals saturated the public sphere with symbols of security and insecurity, further cementing a security-centric interpretive paradigm through which to view international affairs.

While the specific strategic approaches changed from administration to administration—from Ike and Dulles's "New Look" to Kennedy and LBJ's "Flexible Response" to Nixon and Kissinger's pursuit of Détente— the basic framing of American Cold War foreign policy as a realist story of two superpowers occupying opposite poles of world politics remained constant.[35] Throughout this period, "national security," understood as the protection of American homes and neighborhoods, was commonly the most effective justification for any foreign policy decision. Writing more closely to the present time, Maureen Dowd observes that "every election has the same narrative: Can the strong father protect the house from invaders?"[36] That was indeed the dominant question of virtually every presidential election from 1932 to the end of the Cold War, and it has enjoyed a second lease on life in the post-9/11 era. Therefore, it seems accurate to credit Roosevelt, who elevated security to unseen heights of interpretive power, with establishing the primacy of security in US political discourse in the twentieth century and as a consequence reshaping the deliberative contours of American foreign policy decision-making.

Reverberations of FDR can be found in many places. The tendency to identify the United Nations as possessing a mission wholly overlapping with the aims of US foreign policy, powerfully witnessed in the Korean War, Eisenhower's rhetoric, and in America's recent Middle East engagements, hearkens all the way back to Roosevelt's description of the UNO as a symbol ensuring US security after World War II. Widespread public disinterest in international affairs, a constant lament of American educators, foreign policy professionals, and news media, marks another constant between FDR's time and our own. Roosevelt's monolithic description of the Axis powers was repeated practically verbatim to describe American enemies in the Cold War and war on terror (and now China), as communists and terrorists came to occupy the office of chief symbol of national insecurity in turn—and occasionally, as under Reagan, at the same time.

Indeed, commentary in some circles following the 9/11 terrorist attacks expressed—alongside shock and horror at the carnage—an almost welcome return of the familiar, as though the presence of an enemy provided necessary direction to American foreign policy. After all, the chairman of the Joint Chiefs of Staff, Colin Powell, had warned the nation in the 1990s to start worrying about "the crisis nobody expected, nobody told us about," explaining that "the real threat is the unknown, the uncertain."[37] Shortly after the attack Vice President Dick Cheney explained that the new conflict would, like the Cold War, be a permanent fact of American life, stating, "There's not going to be an end date when we're going to say, 'There, it's all over with.'" On another occasion, he said that "it may never end. At least, not in our lifetime."[38] Looking back on that moment, one media commentator recalled in a 2019 interview,

9/11 happened and everyone I knew had this sense that like decadence was over. It was like there was six months to four years, depending on your perspective, where there was this feeling like of okay we had the Cold War and then we had [a] little period that we called the end of history that was decadent and now we have an enemy again, now we have a challenge again, now we have a reason to fight and seek greatness and all these things.[39]

The allure of a simple division of the entire world into good and bad, rational stability versus irrational aggression, and interconnected rival networks of symbols distilling security and insecurity has long outlasted its presidential progenitor.

Overall, looking back over the all years since the mid-1930s, we feel it is fair to ask: What freedom from fear? Sociocultural movements that were not based on fear flourished briefly—especially in the late 1960s and early '70s—but they have never taken hold as dominant political trends. Even the confident rhetoric of Ronald Reagan, one of the few occupants of the oval office capable of matching Roosevelt's oratorical brilliance, operated on the foundational assumption of an existential national threat located in Moscow. In short, fear, anxiety, and insecurity have been signature keys of US political discourse and culture at least since FDR's second term, the unique product of Roosevelt's complex rhetorical synthesis that worked to such stunning political, economic, and military effect.

On May 26, 2017, secretary of the Department of Homeland Security John Kelly said that the American public would "never leave the house" if they knew about the terrorist threats on which he was daily briefed. "It's everywhere. It's constant. It's nonstop," Kelly insisted. "It can happen here almost anytime."[40] He did not mean that the United States, or its citizens, should stay home, avoiding international commitments. No one with any significant political power in the United States has made that case since 1941. Rather, the head of Homeland Security—an office whose very existence would have been unimaginable before the presidency of Franklin D. Roosevelt—was implying that ordinary citizens would do well to let the government do its global work, most importantly its work of protecting the American people from threats that are everywhere around the world and might strike at any moment if given half a chance.

There is no evidence that FDR ever intended to confer upon his nation a future filled with such fear. Indeed, the documentary record does not allow us to say with any certainty what kind of future he intended to create; on this issue his well-known reticence to divulge his true views served him well. But the record strongly suggests a rather consistent aim throughout his political life: to create a world where all nations could trade openly with each other, with none giving any other favored trade rules, wherein no nation would advance its aims by militarily attacking another. He articulated these priorities by drawing on the same security-laden rhetorical formula he had used to build support for the New Deal; his example, as we have briefly suggested here, has been followed by and large ever since.

By articulating new US foreign policy aims and defeating the anti-interventionists in the way he did, FDR ordained a dually amorphous and transposable concept of security as the chief aim of the United States in World War II. He generated the inventional resources his immediate successors would use to make sense of the nation's new global role in the Cold War world, thus laying the groundwork for a broad foreign policy consensus and narrative that has lasted since the transformative days of his presidency. The ultimate paradox is that the discursive practice of homeland security provides a sense of security only because it replicates and reinforces the dualistic cultural categories and interpretive boundaries that, in many respects, generated the insecurity in the first place.[41] The intensified practice of homeland security hence perpetuates and heightens the sense of homeland insecurity, with its belief that there is indeed an enemy bent on destroying us and that we have good reason to feel frightened every day.

There are signs that the entrenched, realist understanding of American foreign policy that predominates in Washington may be reaching its expiration date some eight decades after FDR. Donald Trump's 2016 campaign, whatever else his presidency represented, revealed the waning strength of the narrative that has guided US foreign policy for nearly a century. In an analysis of Trump's victory, *Washington Post* journalist Greg Jaffe noted, "For years, the foreign-policy establishment has preached the importance of sustaining the U.S.-led, rules-based, international order—an exhortation that, at best, was meaningless to most Americans. At worst, it smacked of soulless globalism."[42] Trump's "America First" slogan even inspired some media commentators to come to a renewed defense of the America First Committee, long derided as a profascist organization in mainstream public discourse.[43] There are also glimpses of hope across the party aisle. Many Democrats have called for a future without "forever wars," a line that drew applause in the 2020 Democratic presidential primary debates.[44] New progressive as well as right-wing populist think tanks are emerging to combat the broad consensus that has guided US foreign policy since Roosevelt's final days. Perhaps by better appreciating how that consensus was forged by the rhetoric of the nation's longest-serving president, Americans can better imagine alternative, more peaceful paths for the United States to trod in the world.

Notes

Introduction: None Who Can Make Us Afraid

1. Walter Lippmann, *Public Opinion* (New York: Penguin Books, 1946), 81.
2. Eisenhower speaking to the speechwriter who coined the phrase, "I like that fine." Dwight D. Eisenhower, "Radio Address to the American People," *Public Papers of the Presidents: Dwight D. Eisenhower, 1953*, 307–14, Emmet John Hughes Diary, Emmet John Hughes Papers, box 1, Seeley G. Mudd Library, Princeton University. Hereafter cited as John Hughes Papers.
3. Thomas Paine, *Common Sense* (Philadelphia: W. & T. Bradford, 1792), 1.
4. Robert W. Tucker and David C. Hendrickson, *Empire of Liberty: The Statecraft of Thomas Jefferson* (Oxford: Oxford University Press, 1990), ix.
5. Alexander Hamilton, "Federalist No. 1," October 27, 1787, Founders Online, accessed march 15, 2023, https://founders.archives.gov/documents/Hamilton/01-04-02-0152; Stephen F. Knott and Tony Williams, *Washington and Hamilton: The Alliance that Forged America* (Naperville, IL: Sourcebooks, 2015), 155.
6. John C. Fitzpatrick, ed., *The Writings of George Washington from the Original Manuscript Sources 1745–1799*, vol. 35. (Washington, DC: United States Government Printing Office, 1939), 58. See also Lamont Colucci, *The National Security Doctrines of the American Presidency: How They Shape Our Present and Future*, vol. 1. (Santa Barbara, CA: Praeger, 2012), 28–29.
7. Maureen Groppe and Sarah Elbeshbishi, "Exclusive Poll: Overwhelming Majority Say the US Faces a Mental Health Crisis," *USA Today*, January 8, 2022, https://www.usatoday.com/story/news/politics/2022/01/08/mental-health-americans-see-crisis-amid-ongoing-covid-pandemic/9135532002/?gnt-cfr=1; Tori DeAngelis, "Depression and Anxiety Escalate during COVID," *Monitor on Psychology* 52, no. 8 (2021): 88.
8. Daniel R. Coats, *Statement for the Record: Worldwide Threat Assessment of the US Intelligence Community* (Washington, DC: Senate Select Committee on Intelligence, 2019), 21; "Disinformation: A Primer in Russian Active Measures and Influence Campaigns," Senate Committee Intelligence Hearing, US Government Publishing Office, March 30, 2017, https://www.intelligence.senate.gov/hearings/open-hearing-disinformation-primer-russian-active-measures-and-influence-campaigns-panel-i#; Jarrod Hayes and Janelle Knox-Hayes, "Security in Climate Change Discourse: Analyzing the Divergence between US and EU Approaches to Policy," *Global Environmental Politics* 14 (2014): 82–101.
9. See Edward Schiappa, *Defining Reality* (Carbondale: Southern Illinois University Press, 2003); Jeremy Engels, *Enemyship: Democracy and Counter-Revolution in the Early Republic* (East Lansing, Michigan State University Press, 2010); Chaïm Perel-

man, *The Realm of Rhetoric,* translated by William Kluback (Notre Dame, IN: University of Notre Dame Press, 1982), 53–80.

10. David Zarefsky, "Four Senses of Rhetorical History," in *Doing Rhetorical History: Concepts and Cases,* edited by Kathleen J. Turner (Tuscaloosa: University of Alabama Press, 1998), 20.

11. Barry Buzan and Ole Wæver, *Regions and Powers: The Structure of International Security* (Cambridge: Cambridge University Press, 2003), 491.

12. Lynn Boyd Hinds and Theodore Otto Windt Jr., *The Cold War as Rhetoric: The Beginnings, 1945–1950* (New York: Praeger, 1991), xx. See also Martin J. Medhurst, "Introduction," in *Critical Reflections on the Cold War: Linking Rhetoric and History,* edited by Martin J. Medhurst and H. W. Brands (College Station: Texas A&M University Press, 2000), 3–7.

13. Celeste M. Condit and John L. Lucaites, *Crafting Equality: America's Anglo-African Word* (Chicago: University of Chicago Press, 1993).

14. Mary E. Stuckey, "The Great Debate: The United States and the World, 1936–1941," in *World War II and the Cold War: The Rhetoric of Hearts and Minds: A Rhetorical History of the United States,* vol. 8, edited by Martin J. Medhurst (East Lansing: Michigan State University Press, 2018), 1.

15. Eric Grove, "Sea Power in the Asia-Pacific at the Turn of the Millennium," in *Asia-Pacific Economic and Security Co-operation: New Regional Agendas,* edited by Christopher M. Dent (New York: Palgrave Macmillan, 2003), 96.

16. We use the term *idiom* to communicate that specific articulations of security rhetoric contain meaningful "information that cannot be computed as a sum of the units composing the construction." That is, security utterances take place in cultural contexts that provide necessary background information to fully make sense of their content. See William N. Salmon, "Formal Idioms and Action: Toward a Grammar of Genres," *Language & Communication* 30, no. 4 (2010): 211–224.

17. David M. Kennedy, *Freedom from Fear: The American People in Depression and War, 1929–1945* (New York: Oxford University Press, 1999).

18. Matthew Dallek, *Defenselessness Under the Night: The Roosevelt Years and the Origins of the Homeland Security* (Oxford: Oxford University Press, 2016), 17–34.

19. Ira Katznelson, *Fear Itself: The New Deal and the Origins of Our Time* (New York: Liveright, 2014), 34, 38.

20. Katznelson, *Fear Itself,* 30.

21. For an example, see Steven M. Gillon, *Pearl Harbor: FDR Leads the Nation into War* (New York: Basic Books, 2011), xv.

22. Davis W. Houck and Amos Kiewe, *FDR's Body Politics: The Rhetoric of Disability* (College Station: Texas A&M University Press, 2003); Davis W. Houck, *Rhetoric as Currency: Hoover, Roosevelt, and the Great Depression* (College Station: Texas A&M University Press, 2001); Mary E. Stuckey, "FDR, the Rhetoric of Vision, and the Creation of the National Synoptic State," *Quarterly Journal of Speech* 98, no. 3 (2012): 297–319; Craig, *Fireside Politics: Radio and Political Culture in the United States, 1920–1940* (Baltimore, MD: Johns Hopkins University Press, 2003); Halford Ross Ryan, *Franklin D. Roosevelt's Rhetorical Presidency* (Westport, CT: Greenwood Publishing, 1988); Amos Kiewe, "Introduction," In *The Modern Presidency and Crisis Rhetoric,* edited by Amos Kiewe (Westport: Praeger, 1994), xv–

xxvii; Mary E. Stuckey, *Voting Deliberatively: FDR and the 1936 Presidential Campaign* (University Park: Pennsylvania State University Press, 2015); Davis M. Houck, *FDR and Fear Itself: The First Inaugural Address* (College Station: Texas A&M University Press, College Station, 2002); Jonathan W. Stone, "Listening to the Sonic Archive: Rhetoric, Representation, and Race in the Lomax Prison Recordings," *Enculturation: A Journal of Rhetoric, Writing, and Culture* 19 (2015), http://enculturation.net/listening-to-the-sonic-archive; Earnest Perry, "We Want In: The African American Press's Negotiation for a White House Correspondent," *American Journalism* 20, no. 3 (2003): 31–47; Elvin T. Lim, "The Lion and the Lamb: De-Mythologizing Franklin Roosevelt's Fireside Chats," *Rhetoric & Public Address* 6, no. 3 (2003): 437–464; Keiko Aoki, "A Study of Franklin Delano Roosevelt's Persuasive Communication within the Fireside Chat: An Analysis of Language and Style," *Human Communication* 9, no. 1 (2006): 71–81; Donovan Bisbee, "Driving the Three-Horse Team of Government: Kairos in FDR's Judiciary Fireside Chat," *Rhetoric & Public Affairs* 21, no. 3 (2018): 481–521; Harold P. Zelko, "Franklin D. Roosevelt's Rhythm in Rhetorical Style," *Quarterly Journal of Speech* 28, no. 2 (1942): 138–141; Marouf Hasian Jr., "Franklin D. Roosevelt, The Holocaust, and Modernity's Rescue Rhetorics," *Communication Quarterly* 51, no. 2 (2003): 153–173; Mary E. Stuckey, "Franklin D. Roosevelt, 'Address of the President to the Congress of the United States Broadcast from the Capitol, Washington, D.C.,'" *Voices of Democracy* 12 (2017): 1–15; Bryan Blankfield, "'A Symbol of His Warmth and Humanity': Fala, Roosevelt, and The Personable Presidency," *Rhetoric & Public Affairs* 19, no. 2 (2016): 209–243.

23. Thomas B. Farrell, *Norms of Rhetorical Culture* (New Haven, CT: Yale University Press, 1993), 88; Frank Costigliola, "Freedom from Fear," in *The Four Freedoms: Franklin D. Roosevelt and the Evolution of an American Idea*, edited by Jeffrey A. Engel (Oxford: Oxford University Press, 2016), 166; James J. Kimble, "Franklin D. Roosevelt, 1941 State of the Union Address ('The Four Freedoms') (6 January 1941)," *Voices of Democracy* 3 (2008): 77.

24. Ronald R. Krebs, *Narrative and the Making of US National Security* (Cambridge: Cambridge University Press, 2015), 2.

25. Francis A. Beer and Robert Hariman, "Realism and Rhetoric in International Relations," in *Post-Realism: The Rhetorical Turn in International Relations*, edited by Francis A. Beer and Robert Hariman (East Lansing: Michigan State University Press, 1996), 10–11.

26. Paul Chilton, *Analysing Political Discourse: Theory and Practice* (New York: Routledge, 2004), 5.

27. Zarefsky, "Four Senses of Rhetorical History," 30.

28. David Zarefsky, "The Presidency Has Always Been a Place for Rhetorical Leadership," in *The Presidency and Rhetorical Leadership*, edited by Leroy G. Darsey (College Station: Texas A&M University Press, 2002), 22–23.

29. Franklin D. Roosevelt, "Inaugural Address," March 4, 1933, American Presidency Project, accessed March 15, 2023, https://www.presidency.ucsb.edu/documents/inaugural-address-8; Vanessa B. Beasley and Deborah Smith-Howell, "No Ordinary Rhetorical President: FDR's Speechmaking and Leadership, 1933–1945," in *American Rhetoric in the New Deal Era, 1932–1945: A Rhetorical History of the United*

States, vol. 7, edited by Thomas W. Benson (East Lansing: Michigan State University Press, 2006), 2.

30. Martin J. Medhurst, "Afterword," in *Beyond the Rhetorical Presidency*, edited by Martin J. Medhurst (College Station: Texas A&M University Press, 1996), 220.

31. Mary E. Stuckey, *The President as Interpreter-in-Chief* (Chatham, NJ: Chatham House, 1991); Carol Gelderman, *All the President's Words: The Bully Pulpit and the Creation of the Virtual Presidency* (New York: Walker, 1997), 12.

32. See Leroy G. Darsey, "Introduction: The President as a Rhetorical Leader," in *The Presidency and Rhetorical Leadership*, edited by Leroy G. Darsey (College Station: Texas A&M University Press, 2002), 6–12.

33. Martin J. Medhurst, "Rhetorical Leadership and the Presidency: A Situational Taxonomy," in *The Values of Presidential Leadership*, edited by Terry L. Price and J. Thomas Wren (New York: Palgrave Macmillan, 2007), 61.

34. Damir Marusic, "Making Up Monsters to Destroy," American Interest, January 15, 2019, https://www.the-american-interest.com/2019/01/15/making-up-monsters-to-destroy/.

35. Both of us have studied how presidents used their rhetoric to help shape public opinion during the Cold War, showing how presidents framed the exigences presented by the superpower rivalry with the Soviet Union to expand American military involvement abroad. Ira argues that President Eisenhower's view of the Cold War led him to crystallize a defensive and conservative pattern of discourse—"apocalypse management"—that became the dominant pattern of US foreign policy rhetoric for decades following his presidency. This way of speaking highlights the irrationality of America's enemies, the United States' vulnerability in an interconnected world, and the endless search for global stability so that Americans may live in perpetual peace. Randall's work expands on this theme by showing how Eisenhower's conception of the Cold War led him to expand American influence in the Arab world, in the process underwriting a new understanding of the nation's role in the Middle East that continues to be used to authorize intervention in that region today.

36. Karlyn Kohrs Campbell and Kathleen Hall Jamieson, *Presidents Creating the Presidency: Deeds Done in Words* (Chicago: University of Chicago Press, 2008), 8.

37. Julian E. Zelizer, *Arsenal of Democracy: The Politics of National Security—From World War II to the War on Terrorism* (New York: Basic Books, 2010), 9.

38. Offner, "Liberation or Dominance? The Ideology of U.S. National Security Policy," in *The Long War: A New History of U.S. National Security Policy since World War II*, edited by Andrew J. Bacevich (New York: Columbia University Press, 2007), 3.

39. Mary E. Stuckey, "The Great Debate: The United States and the World, 1936–1941," in *World War II and the Cold War: The Rhetoric of Hearts and Minds: A Rhetorical History of the United States*, vol. 8, edited by Martin J. Medhurst (East Lansing: Michigan State University Press, 2018), 3, 12–13, 38.

40. Mary E. Stuckey, *Political Vocabularies FDR, the Clergy Letters, and the Elements of Political Argument* (East Lansing: Michigan State University Press, 2018), xvii, xix, 169.

41. Mary E. Stuckey, *The Good Neighbor: Franklin D. Roosevelt and the Rhetoric of American Power* (East Lansing: Michigan State University Press, 2013), 2.

42. Indeed, the generation of what Chaïm Perelman and Louise Olbrechts-

Tyteca would call "presence" was a critical component of FDR's rhetoric. John M. Murphy, "No End Save Victory: FDR and the End of Isolationism, 1936–1941," in *Making the Case: Advocacy and Judgment in Public Argument*, edited by Kathryn M. Olson, Michael William Pfau, Benjamin Ponder, and Kirt H. Wilson (East Lansing: Michigan State University Press, 2012),145; Chaïm Perelman and Louise Olbrechts-Tyteca, *The New Rhetoric: A Treatise on Argumentation* (Notre Dame, IL: University of Notre Dame Press, 1969), 116–117.

43. Frank Furedi, *How Fear Works: Culture of Fear in the Twenty-First Century* (London: Bloomsbury, 2018), 6. See also Gosling, "Mental Causes and Fear," *Mind* 71 (1962): 289–297.

44. Fear, like ideology, finds its material existence in textual circulation. By this we mean that although individuals undoubtedly contain thoughts of fear (like ideology) in their minds, their expressions of fear provide a reasonably accurate index of fear for scholarly analysis. Because fear, security, and insecurity are complex phenomena, they require the kind of in-depth analytic provided by rhetorical criticism to properly evaluate. See Michael Calvin McGee, "The 'Ideograph': A Link Between Rhetoric and Ideology," *Quarterly Journal of Speech* 66, no. 1 (1980): 3–5.

45. Furedi, "Fear Today," First Things, January 2019, 10, https://www.firstthings .com/article/2019/01/fear-today.

46. David Campbell, *Writing Security: United States Foreign Policy and the Politics of Identity* (Minneapolis: University of Minnesota Press, 1998), 1–4.

47. Gosling, "Mental Causes and Fear."

48. As Martin Luther King Jr. wrote in his "Letter from a Birmingham Jail," "But the judgment of God is upon the church as never before. If today's church does not recapture the sacrificial spirit of the early church, it will lose its authenticity, forfeit the loyalty of millions, and be dismissed as an irrelevant social club with no meaning for the twentieth century." Martin Luther King Jr., "Letter from a Birmingham Jail," April 16, 1963, African Studies Center, accessed March 15, 2023, https://www .africa.upenn.edu/Articles_Gen/Letter_Birmingham.html.

49. G. K. Chesterton, *What I Saw in America* (London: Hodder & Stoughton, 1922), 7, 12.

50. For related critiques of American civil religion, see Talal Asad, *Formations of the Secular: Christianity, Islam, Modernity* (Stanford, CA: Stanford University Press, 2003); William T. Cavanaugh: *The Myth of Religious Violence: Secular Ideology and the Roots of Modern Conflict* (Oxford: Oxford University Press, 2009); Stanley Hauerwas, *War and the American Difference: Theological Reflections on Violence and National Identity* (Grand Rapids, MI: Baker Academic, 2011); Raymond Haberski Jr., *God and War: American Civil Religion since 1945* (New Brunswick, NJ: Rutgers University Press, 2012).

51. Jason C. Flanagan, "Woodrow Wilson's 'Rhetorical Restructuring': The Transformation of the American Self and the Construction of the German Enemy," *Rhetoric & Public Affairs* 7, no. 2 (2004): 127, 115.

52. Woodrow Wilson, "Address on Flag Day," June 14, 1917, American Presidency Project, accessed February 11, 2023, https://www.presidency.ucsb.edu/doc uments/address-flag-day; Woodrow Wilson, "Address to a Joint Session of Congress Requesting a Declaration of War Against Germany," April 2, 1917, American Presi-

dency Project, accessed February 11, 2023, https://www.presidency.ucsb.edu/doc
uments/address-joint-session-congress-requesting-declaration-war-against-germany.

53. Wilson, "Address to a Joint Session of Congress."

54. Stephen J. Fowler, "'Caliphate' against the Crown: Martyrdom, Heresy, and
the Rhetoric of Enemyship in the Kingdom of Jordan," *Rhetoric & Public Affairs* 21,
no. 1 (2018): 121–126; Heidt, "Presidential Power and National Violence: James K.
Polk's Rhetorical Transfer of Savagery," *Rhetoric & Public Affairs* 19, no. 3 (2016):
365–396.

55. Leroy G. Dorsey, "Woodrow Wilson's Fight for the League of Nations: A Reexamination," *Rhetoric & Public Affairs* 2, no. 1 (1999): 110.

56. J. Michael Hogan, *Woodrow Wilson's Western Tour: Rhetoric, Public Opinion, and
the League of Nations* (College Station: Texas A&M University Press, 2006), 132.

57. Woodrow Wilson, "An Address in the City Auditorium in Pueblo, Colorado,"
September 25, 1919. Reprinted in Hogan, *Woodrow Wilson's Western Tour,* 14–15.

58. Hogan, 25, 168–171.

59. George C. Herring, *From Colony to Superpower: American Foreign Relations Since
1776* (Oxford: Oxford University Press, 2008), 436.

60. Andrew Johnstone, *Against Immediate Evil Evil: American Internationalists and
the Four Freedoms on the Eve of World War II* (Ithaca, NY: Cornell University Press,
2014), 2, 178.

61. FDR, "Address at Jackson Day Dinner," January 8, 40, PPA 1940, 25.

62. Murphy, "FDR and the End of Isolationism," 129.

63. Herring, *From Colony to Superpower,* 537.

64. David Reynolds, *From Munich to Pearl Harbor: Roosevelt's America and the Origins
of the Second World War* (Chicago: Ivan R. Dee, 2001), 10–11.

65. Edwin Black, *Rhetorical Criticism: A Study in Method* (Madison: University of
Wisconsin Press, 1978), ix–xiv.

66. We are mindful that many scholarly accounts of Roosevelt's presidential rhetoric and career have been derided as "hero worship of FDR's leadership." Mark J.
Rozell and William D. Pederson, *FDR and the Modern Presidency: Leadership and Legacy*
(Westport, CT: Praeger, 1997), 5; Beasley and Smith-Powell, "No Ordinary Rhetorical President," 5.

67. Maria Christina Ana Kabiling, "World War II in Popular American Visual
Culture: Film and Video Games after 9/11" (MA thesis, Georgetown University,
2010), ii. On court-packing, see Aaron Blake, "Pack the Supreme Court? Why We
May Be Getting Closer," *Washington Post,* October 9, 2018, https://www.washing
tonpost.com/politics/2018/10/09/pack-supreme-court-why-we-may-be-getting
-closer/?utm_term=.c983931a7745.

Chapter 1: Domestic Policy, 1912–1932

1. "Speech to the People's Forum," Troy, NY, March 3, 12, 1–2, box 1, Master
Speech File, Franklin D. Roosevelt Presidential Library & Museum. (Hereafter cited
as FDRL.)

2. "Speech to the People's Forum," 4–8.

3. Ernest Kidder Lindley, *Franklin D. Roosevelt: A Career in Progressive Democracy* (New York: Blue Ribbon, 1931), 322.

4. Belinda A. Stillion Southard, *Militant Citizenship: Rhetorical Strategies of the National Woman's Party, 1913-1920* (College Station: Texas A&M University Press, 2011), 6.

5. Richard Hofstadter, *The Age of Reform: From Bryan to F.D.R* (New York: Vintage Books, 1955), 5.

6. Mary Harris "Mother" Jones, "At a Public Meeting in Charleston," in *American Rhetorical Discourse*, edited by Ronald F. Reid and James F. Klumpp (Long Grove, IL: Waveland Press, 2005), 626.

7. See Ronald F. Reid and James F. Klumpp, *American Rhetorical Discourse*, 3rd ed. (Long Grove, IL: Waveland Press, 2005), 521-523, 535, 559; Walter Rauschenbusch, *Christianity and the Social Crisis* (New York: Macmillan, 1913), 349.

8. William Jennings Bryan, "Democratic National Convention Address," American Rhetoric, July 8, 1896, https://www.americanrhetoric.com/speeches /william jenningsbryan1896dnc.htm.

9. Tony Michels, *A Fire in Their Hearts: Yiddish Socialists in New York* (Cambridge, MA: Harvard University Press, 2005), 2.

10. Thomas Bender, *A Nation Among Nations: America's Place in World History* (New York: Farrar, Straus & Giroux, 2006), 255.

11. Reid and Klumpp, *American Rhetorical Discourse*, 586.

12. Albert J. Beveridge, "Policy Regarding the Philippines," January 9, 1900, Wendy Wolff, ed., *The Senate 1789-1989: Classic Speeches 1830-1993*, vol. 3. (Washington, DC: US Government Printing Office, 1994), 512.

13. Walter Nugent, *Progressivism: A Very Short Introduction* (Oxford: Oxford University Press, 2010), 2.

14. Jeffrey K. Tulis, *The Rhetorical Presidency* (Princeton, NJ: Princeton University Press, 1987), 107.

15. Leroy G. Dorsey, *Theodore Roosevelt, Conservation, and the 1908 Governors' Conference* (College Station: Texas A&M University Press, 2015), 41-42.

16. Ronald J. Pestritto and William J. Atto, "Introduction to American Progressivism," in *American Progressivism: A Reader*, edited by Ronald J. Pestritto and William J. Atto (Lanham, MD: Lexington, 2008), 2-3.

17. Vida Dutton Scudder, *On Journey* (New York: E. P. Dutton, 1937), 166.

18. "The Square Deal worked to balance competing interests to create a fair deal for all sides: labor and management, consumer and business, developer and conservationists. TR recognized that his program was not perfectly neutral because the government needed to intervene more actively on behalf of the general public to ensure economic opportunity for all." Sidney Milkis, "Theodore Roosevelt: Domestic Affairs," Miller Center, accessed January 17, 2023, https://millercenter.org /president/roosevelt/domestic-affairs.

19. Robert H. Wiebe, *The Search for Order, 1887-1920* (New York: Hill & Wang, 1967).

20. Woodrow Wilson, "Final Address in Support of the League of Nations," American Rhetoric, September 25, 1919, https://www.americanrhetoric.com/speeches /wilsonleagueofnations.htm.

21. See Gary Gerstle, "Race and Nation in the Thought and Politics of Woodrow Wilson," in *Reconsidering Woodrow Wilson: Progressivism, Internationalism, War, and Peace*, edited by John Milton Cooper Jr. (Baltimore, MD: Johns Hopkins University Press, 2008), 93–123.

22. John Dewey, *The Public and Its Problems* (Athens, OH: University of Ohio Press, 1980), 113, 142.

23. Regarding our terminology ("endless"), see Levari et al., "Prevalence-Induced Concept Change in Human Judgment," *Science* 360 (2018): 1465–1467.

24. FDR, *FDR: His Personal Letters, 1905–1928*, edited by Elliott Roosevelt, assisted by James N. Rosenau and Joseph P. Lash (New York: Duell, Sloan & Pearce, 1947–1950), 157.

25. Quoted in Ken Burns, *The Roosevelts: An Intimate History: The Fire of Life* (Walpole, NH: Florentine Films, 2014), 7:00–7:15.

26. "Acceptance of V.P. Nomination," Hyde Park, NY, August 9, 1920, pp. 1–17, box 2, Master Speech File, FDRL.

27. Deborah Dash Moore, *At Home in America: Second Generation New York Jews* (New York: Columbia University Press, 1981), 228.

28. FDR to Rep. W. C. Martin, July 20, 1925, Roosevelt, F.D.—Papers 1920–1928, box 3, "Martin, W. C."; see also FDR to Rep. William Oldfield, April 11, 25, Roosevelt, F.D.—Papers 1920–1928, box 3, "Oldfield, William A.," FDRL.

29. Speech to Democratic National Committee, May 29, 1919, in Kenneth S. Davis, *FDR: The Beckoning of Destiny 1882–1928: A History* (New York: Random House, 1993), 608.

30. Ward, *A First-Class Temperament*, 682.

31. "A Draft for 'History of the United States,'" in FDR, *FDR: His Personal Letters*, 2:546, 548.

32. Frances Perkins, *The Roosevelt I Knew* (New York: Viking Press, 1946), 153. On the relationship between Perkins and Roosevelt, see Atkinson, "The Rhetoric of Social Security and Conservative Backlash: Frances Perkins as Secretary of Labor," in *American Rhetoric in the New Deal Era, 1932–1945: A Rhetorical History of the United States*, vol. 7, edited by Thomas W. Benson (East Lansing: Michigan State University Press, 2006), 220–221.

33. Interview with Frances Perkins, vol. 3, pt. 1, 216, 219, 226, Columbia Center for Oral History Archives, Columbia University.

34. FDR, "Speech Nominating Smith," June 26, 1924, p. 6, box 4, series 1, Master Speech File, FDRL.

35. Dorsey, "Introduction: The President as a Rhetorical Leader," in *The Presidency and Rhetorical Leadership*, edited by Leroy G. Dorsey (East Lansing: Michigan State University Press, 2002), 9.

36. Walter R. Fisher, "Technical Logic, Rhetorical Logic, and Narrative Rationality," *Argumentation* 1, no. 1 (1987): 17.

37. Doris Kearns Goodwin, *No Ordinary Time: Franklin and Eleanor Roosevelt: The Home Front in World War II* (New York: Simon & Schuster, 1994), 46.

38. Franklin D. Roosevelt, *Franklin D. Roosevelt's Own Story: Told in His Own Words from His Private and Public Papers*, ed. Donald Day (New York: Little, Brown and Company, 1951), 108.

39. FDR, "The Age of Social Consciousness," *Harvard Graduate*, September 1929, 1-7; FDR, *Whither Bound?* (New York: Houghton Mifflin, 1926), 32.

40. "Speech to NY Democratic Convention," September 27, 1926, in Davis, *FDR: The Beckoning of Destiny*, 804; FDR, "The Age of Social Consciousnes."

41. FDR, *Franklin D. Roosevelt's Own Story: Told in His Own Words from His Private and Public Papers*, selected by Donald Day (Boston: Little, Brown, 1951), 118-119; David M. Kennedy, *Freedom from Fear: The American People in Depression and War, 1929-1945* (New York: Oxford University Press, 1999), 116, from FDR, *Franklin D. Public Papers and Addresses of Franklin Delano Roosevelt*, compiled by Samuel I. Rosenman (New York: Macmillan, 1938-1950), 1928-1932, 75-75, 15. (Hereafter cited as FDR *PPA*)

42. "Speech to Berkshire Bankers Association," June 20, 1921, in Davis, *FDR: The Beckoning of Destiny*, 636-637.

43. FDR, *Whither Bound?*, 15; FDR, "The Age of Social Consciousness," *Harvard Graduate*, September 1929.

44. Mary E. Stuckey, *Defining Americans: The Presidency and National Identity* (Lawrence: University Press of Kansas, 2005), 198.

45. FDR, "New York City, NY—Fur Club Luncheon," November 2, 1928, p. 437, box 6, series 1, Master Speech Files, FDRL.

46. FDR, "Elmira, NY—Campaign Speech," October 18, 1928, p. 34, box 5, series 1, Master Speech Files, FDRL.

47. FDR, *Whither Bound?*, 11, 5.

48. FDR, 11, 5.

49. Bradford Vivian, *Public Forgetting: The Rhetoric and Politics of Beginning Again* (University Park: Pennsylvania State University Press, 2010), 45.

50. Eleanor Roosevelt, "Foreword," *F.D.R. Columnist: The Uncollected Columns of Franklin D. Roosevelt*, ed. Donald Scott Carmichael (New York: Pellegrini and Cudahy, 1947).

51. Frank Burt Freidel, *Franklin D. Roosevelt: A Rendezvous with Destiny* (Boston: Little, Brown, 1990), 3; Robert E. Sherwood, *Roosevelt and Hopkins: An Intimate History* (New York: Harper, 1950), 9, 41, 385. For an analysis of the role of nostalgia in progressivism, see Kimberly K. Smith, "Mere Nostalgia: Notes on a Progressive Paratheory," *Rhetoric & Public Affairs* 3, no. 4 (2000): 505-527.

52. Quoted in "Home of Franklin D. Roosevelt," National Parks Service, accessed March 15, 2023, http://npshistory.com/publications/hofr/index.htm.

53. Geoffrey C. Ward, *A First-Class Temperament: The Emergence of Franklin Roosevelt, 1905-1928* (New York: Harper & Row, 1989), 271.

54. FDR, "Speech at Poughkeepsie 1933," *F.D.R. Columnist*, 74.

55. James MacGregor Burns, for example, summarizes what FDR learned from his childhood: "Men can live together only on the basis of certain simple, traditional ethical rules. . . . The turn of the century world seemed to validate these ideas; it was stable, secure, peaceful, expansive." James MacGregor Burns, *Roosevelt: The Lion and the Fox: 1882-1940*, vol. 1 (New York: Harcourt, Brace & World, 1956), 473.

56. "Reign of Law Sustained by Public Opinion 1925," box 41, FDRL; FDR, *Franklin D. Roosevelt's Own Story*, 123; Burns, *Roosevelt: The Lion*, 475. See other examples

in Fank Burt Freidel, *Franklin D. Roosevelt: Launching the New Deal*, vol. 4 (Boston: Little, Brown, 1952), 5-6.

57. Letter dated July 22, 1925, in FDR, *Franklin D. Roosevelt's Own Story*, 94; FDR to National League of Progressive Democracy, *F.D.R. Columnist*, April 9, 1925, 24; Roosevelt to W. C. Martin, n.d. [November 1925], Roosevelt, F.D.—Papers 1920-1928, box 3, "Martin, W. C.," FDRL.

58. "Nominating Alfred E. Smith, June 26, 1924," box 4, Master Speech Files, FDRL.

59. Ward, *A First-Class Temperament*, 537.

60. FDR to Louis B. Wehle, November 6, 1920, in Davis, *FDR: The Beckoning of Destiny*, 625.

61. FDR to Rep. Wm. Sirovich, May 14, 1930, in FDR, *FDR: His Personal Letters*, 2:119.

62. Rexford Guy Tugwell, *The Brains Trust* (New York: Viking Press, 1968), 295-296.

63. FDR, *Whither Bound?*, 6.

64. Leroy G. Dorsey, "Managing Women's Equality: Theodore Roosevelt, the Frontier Myth, and the Modern Woman," *Rhetoric & Public Affairs* 16, no. 3 (2013): 425.

65. Henry A. Wallace to Reverend Levy, February 6, 1956, Small Collections, FDRL.

66. Terry Golway, *Frank & Al: FDR, Al Smith, and the Unlikely Alliance that Created the Modern Democratic Party* (New York: St. Martin's Press, 2018), 67.

67. Franklin D. Roosevelt, "Statement on Religious Issues, 1928," June 18, 1929, *Boston Globe*, 15; FDR, "The Age of Social Consciousness."

68. Perkins, *The Roosevelt I Knew*, 139-142, 146. See also Henry A. Wallace to Reverend Levy, February 6, 1956, Small Collections, FDRL: "He liked the hymns to move briskly and hated it when they dragged." Democratic Party stalwart James A. Farley remembered FDR, explaining that initial inauguration day service by saying: "A thought to God is the right way to start off my administration. A proper attitude toward religion, and belief in God, will in the end be the salvation of all peoples." James A. Farley, *Jim Farley's Story: The Roosevelt Years* (New York: Whittlesey House, 1948), 36. But nothing else in the documentary record reflects any similar sentiment.

69. Robert H. Jackson, *That Man: An Insider's Portrait of Franklin D. Roosevelt* (Oxford: Oxford University Press, 2003), 74; FDR to Sarah Delano Roosevelt, Autumn, 1927, in FDR, *FDR: His Personal Letters*, 1:629.

70. "Annual Message to the Legislature," January 6, 1932, FDR *PPA*, 1928-1932, 124.

71. Dorsey, "Woodrow Wilson's Fight for the League of Nations: A Reexamination," *Rhetoric & Public Affairs* 2, no. 1 (1999): 110.

72. FDR to James Remick, January 23, 1925, Roosevelt F.D.—Papers 1920-1928, box 4, "Remick, James W.," FDRL.

73. Letter dated March 27, 1928, in FDR, *Franklin D. Roosevelt's Own Story*, 100.

74. "Houston Texas—June 27, 1928—Democratic National Convention—Placing Alfred E. Smith in Nomination," box 5, Master Speech Files, FDRL.

75. FDR, "Our Foreign Policy: A Democratic View," *Foreign Affairs* 6, no. 4 (1928): 575, 577; FDR to Robert W. Bingham, September 29, 1931, FDR, *Franklin D. Roosevelt: Selected Speeches, Messages, Press Conferences and Letters*, edited by Basil Rauch (New York: Holt, Rinehart & Winston, 1964), 65.

76. Burns, *Roosevelt: The Lion*, 476.

77. FDR, "Why We Need Politicians," *American Magazine*, April 1932, in Rosenau, *The Roosevelt Treasury* (New York: Doubleday, 1951), 374.

78. "Message Recommending Creation of Relief Administration," August 28, 1931, FDR *PPA*, 1928-1932, 458, 459; "The 'Forgotten Man' Speech," April 7, 1932, FDR *PPA*, 1928-1932, 625.

79. "An Address Before the State Charities Aid Association," January 17, 1930, FDR *PPA*, 1928-1932, 330.

80. Leslie Hahner, *To Become an American: Immigrants and Americanization Campaigns of the Early Twentieth Century* (East Lansing: Michigan State University Press, 2017), 7, 94.

Chapter 2: Foreign Policy, 1912-1932

1. Rogers M. Smith, *Civic Ideals: Conflicting Visions of Citizenship in U.S. History* (New Haven, CT: Yale University Press, 1997), 411.

2. FDR, "Speech before the Saturn Club, Buffalo, NY," December 23, 1911, box 1, file no. 12, Master Speech Files, Franklin D. Roosevelt Presidential Library & Museum. (Hereafter cited as FDRL.)

3. Alfred Thayer Mahan, *The Influence of Sea Power Upon the French Revolution and Empire* (Boston: Little, Brown, 1892), 402.

4. Mahan, *The Influence of Sea Power Upon the French Revolution and Empire*, 403-404.

5. Lawrence Freedman, *Strategy: A History* (Oxford: Oxford University Press, 2013), 116.

6. George C. Herring, *From Colony to Superpower: American Foreign Relations Since 1776* (Oxford: Oxford University Press, 2008), 303.

7. Sarah Delano Roosevelt, *My Boy Franklin* (New York: R. Long & R. R. Smith, 1933), 15; Geoffrey C. Ward, *Before the Trumpet: Young Franklin Roosevelt, 1882-1905* (New York: Harper & Row, 1985), 160.

8. Russell F. Weigley, *The American Way of War: A History of United States Military Strategy and Policy* (Bloomington: University of Indiana Press, 1973), 177-191.

9. Quoted in Eliot A. Cohen, *The Big Stick: The Limits of Soft Power & the Necessity of Military Force* (New York: Basic Books, 2016), ix.

10. "The White Man's Burden: The United States and the Philippines" was a poem by Rudyard Kipling urging the United States to assume the responsibility of empire like other white European nations. See Patrick Brantlinger, "Kipling's 'The White Man's Burden' and Its Afterlives," *English Literature in Transition* 50, no. 2 (2007): 172-191.

11. Leroy G. Dorsey, "Sailing into the 'Wondrous Now: The Myth of the American Navy's World Cruise," *Quarterly Journal of Speech* 83, no. 4 (1997): 451.

12. FDR, "Remarks at Watsonville, California," May 11, 1903, American Presi-

dency Project, accessed February 11, 2023, https://www.presidency.ucsb.edu/doc uments/remarks-watsonville-california.

13. FDR, "Fourth Annual Message," December 6, 1904, American Presidency Project, accessed February 11, 2023, https://www.presidency.ucsb.edu/documents /fourth-annual-message-15.

14. Serge Ricard, "The Roosevelt Corollary," *Presidential Studies Quarterly* 36, no. 1 (2006): 19.

15. Geoffrey C. Ward, *A First-Class Temperament: The Emergence of Franklin Roosevelt, 1905-1928* (New York: Harper & Row, 1989), 299; FDR, *Franklin D. Roosevelt's Own Story: Told in His Own Words from His Private and Public Papers*, selected by Donald Day (Boston: Little, Brown, 1951), 92.

16. William E. Leuchtenburg, "Franklin D. Roosevelt: The American Franchise," Miller Center, accessed January 17, 2023, https://millercenter.org/president/fd roosevelt/the-american-franchise.

17. See, eg, Frank Burt Freidel, *Franklin D. Roosevelt: The Apprenticeship*, vol. 1 (Boston: Little, Brown, 1952), 242, 246. In 1922, looking for projects to fill his recuperation time, he briefly considered preparing a "new and up date edition" of Mahan's famous book on the virtues of sea power, though he never pursued the idea. George Marvin to FDR, November 17, 1922, box 39, "Asia Magazine Article 1922-1923," FDRL.

18. Roosevelt to Chadwick, October 25, 1916, in Freidel, *FDR*, 260; FDR to Eleanor Roosevelt, August 2, 1914, in FDR, *FDR: His Personal Letters*, edited by Elliott Roosevelt, assisted by James N. Rosenau and Joseph P. Lash (New York: Duell, Sloan & Pearce, 1947-1950), vol. 2, 239.

19. Quoted in "Pledges Workers to Our Defense," *New York Times*, December 6, 1914, A4.

20. FDR, "Oswego, NY 'Montcalm's Victory'" September 30, 1913, box 1, file no. 24, Master Speech Files, FDRL.

21. Brian J. Auten, *Carter's Conversion: The Hardening of American Defense Policy* (Columbia: University of Missouri Press, 2008), 14-15.

22. Franklin D. Roosevelt article, "War at Sea and Its Weapons," published September 27, 1915, Writing and Statement File, box 40, folder 5, Franklin D. Roosevelt: Family, Business and Personal Papers, FDRL. See also Michael S. Bell, "The Worldview of Franklin D. Roosevelt: France, Germany, and United States Involvement in Europe" (PhD diss., University of Maryland, 2004), 143.

23. Greg Russell, "Theodore Roosevelt's Diplomacy and the Quest for Great Power Equilibrium in Asia," *Presidential Studies Quarterly* 38, no. 3 (2008): 433-435; Herring, *From Colony to Superpower*, 348-369; James Bradley, *The Imperial Cruise: A Secret History of Empire and War* (New York: Back Bay, 2009), 269-333.

24. FDR, "On Your Own Heads," *Scribner's Magazine*, April 1917, 413-416.

25. Freidel, *Franklin D. Roosevelt: The Apprenticeship*, 335, 260; "Speech on Preparedness," December 21, 1915, in FDR, *Franklin D. Roosevelt: Selected Speeches, Messages, Press Conferences and Letters*, edited by Basil Rauch (New York: Holt, Rinehart & Winston, 1964), 20.

26. Frank Freidel has called it "a sort of Mahan for the masses." Freidel, *FDR: The Apprenticeship*, 260.

27. Quoted in *Uncensored* (New York: Keep America Out of War Congress, 1939–1941), 2; and Allan Louis Benson, *Inviting War to America*, Vol. 20 (Girard, KS: Appeal to Reason, 1916), 18.

28. FDR, "The Navy Program and What It Means," *Nation's Business*, December 1915, 9.

29. FDR, "First Woman's National Defense Conference of the Woman's Section of the Navy League," November 16, 1915, box 1, file no. 45, Master Speech Files, FDRL.

30. William E. Leuchtenburg, "Franklin D. Roosevelt: Life Before the Presidency," Miller Center, accessed January 17, 2023, https://millercenter.org/president/fdroosevelt/life-before-the-presidency.

31. FDR to Eleanor Roosevelt, August 7, 1914, in FDR, *FDR: His Personal Letters*, 2:246; FDR to Eleanor Roosevelt, August 2, 1914, in FDR, *FDR: His Personal Letters*, 2:238; FDR to Josephus Daniels, Roosevelt, in FDR, *FDR: His Personal Letters*, 2:391. See also Freidel, *FDR: The Apprenticeship*, 267; Ward, *A First-Class Temperament*, 298.

32. Freidel, *FDR: The Apprenticeship*, 333; Michaela Höenicke Moore, *Know Your Enemy: The American Debate on Nazism, 1933–1945* (Cambridge and New York: Cambridge University Press, 2010), 28, 34.

33. Jeffery M. Dorwart, *The Office of Naval Intelligence: The Birth of America's First Intelligence Agency, 1865–1918* (Annapolis, MD: Naval Institute Press, 1979), 117, 119; FDR to Eleanor Roosevelt, July 19, 1917, in FDR, *FDR: His Personal Letters*, 2:351.

34. See Walter L. Hixson, *The Myth of American Diplomacy: National Identity and U.S. Foreign Policy* (New Haven, CT: Yale University Press, 2008), 121.

35. Woodrow Wilson, "Address to a Joint Session of Congress on the Severance of Diplomatic Relations with Germany," February 3, 1917, American Presidency Project, accessed February 11, 2023, https://www.presidency.ucsb.edu/documents/address-joint-session-congress-the-severance-diplomatic-relations-with-germany.

36. Woodrow Wilson, "Address to a Joint Session of Congress Requesting a Declaration of War Against Germany," April 2, 1917, American Presidency Project, accessed February 11, 2023, https://www.presidency.ucsb.edu/documents/address-joint-session-congress-requesting-declaration-war-against-germany.

37. Lloyd C. Gardner, *Safe for Democracy: The Anglo-American Response to Revolution, 1913–1923* (New York: Oxford University Press, 1984), 1; see also Frank A. Ninkovich, *The Wilsonian Century: U.S. Foreign Policy since 1900* (Chicago: University of Chicago Press, 1999).

38. James R. Andrews, "Presidential Leadership and National Identity: Woodrow Wilson and National Identity: Woodrow Wilson and the Meaning of America," in *The Presidency and Rhetorical Leadership*, edited by Leroy G. Dorsey (College Station: Texas A&M University Press, 2002), 141. See also Walter Russell Mead, *Special Providence: American Foreign Policy and How It Changed the World* (New York: Knopf, 2001), xvii, 147.

39. Underline written in original manuscript. FDR, "Liberty Loan Drive Speech to Bankers," November 1918, box 2, file no. 82, Master Speech Files, FDRL.

40. Freidel, *FDR: The Apprenticeship*, 260 (see also FDR, Liberty Loan Drive Speech to Bankers," 335); FDR to Eleanor Roosevelt, October 1914, in FDR, *FDR: His Personal Letters*, 2:257.

41. Ken Burns, *The Roosevelts: An Intimate History: The Fire of Life* (Walpole, NH: Florentine Films, 2014) , 1:28:00–1:28:20.

42. FDR, "More Wars Are Still to Come," May 29, 1918, box 1, file no. 76, Master Speech Files, FDRL.

43. FDR, "The National Emergency of Peace Times," *Journal of the Worcester Polytechnic Institute* 22, no. 4 (July 1919).

44. Henry Cabot Lodge, "The League of Nations Debate," 1919, in Ronald F. Reid and James F. Klumpp, *American Rhetorical* Discourse, 3rd ed. (Long Grove, IL: Waveland Press, 2005), 705.

45. Lodge, "League of Nations Debate," 705.

46. George Washington, "Farewell Address," September 19, 1796, American Presidency Project, accessed February 11, 2023, https://www.presidency.ucsb.edu /documents/farewell-address; Abraham Lincoln, "Second Annual Message," December 1, 1862, American Presidency Project, accessed February 11, 2023, https:// www.presidency.ucsb.edu/documents/second-annual-message-9.

47. Arthur M. Schlesinger Jr., *War and the American Presidency* (New York: W. W. Norton, 2004), 9.

48. "Acceptance speech for vice-presidential nomination," July 9, 1920, in FDR, *FDR: His Personal Letters*, 2:500, 507, 503.

49. Michael Osborn, *Michael Osborn on Metaphor and Style* (East Lansing: Michigan State University Press, 2018), 13.

50. Londa Schieberger, *Has Feminism Changed Science?* (Cambridge, MA: Harvard University Press, 1998), 147.

51. Francis A. Beer and Christ'l De Landtsheer, "Foreword," in *Metaphorical World Politics*, edited by Francis A. Beer and Christ'l De Landtsheer (East Lansing: Michigan State University Press, 2004), x.

52. Mary E. Stuckey, *The Good Neighbor: Franklin D. Roosevelt and the Rhetoric of American Power* (East Lansing: Michigan State University Press, 2013), 15, 28, 26.

53. "Campaign Speech," August 20, 1920, in Franklin D. Roosevelt, The *Roosevelt Reader: Selected Speeches, Messages, Press Conferences, and Letters of Franklin D. Roosevelt*, ed. Basil Rauch (Charlottesville: University of Virginia Press, 1957), 36.

54. Richard L. Merritt, "Woodrow Wilson and the 'Great and Solemn Referendum,' 1920," *Review of Politics* 27 (1965): 78; Andrew Sinclair, *The Available Man: The Life Behind the Masks of Warren Gamaliel Harding* (New York: Macmillan, 1965), 163-168.

55. Quoted in Willam E. Leuchtenburg, *The American President: From Teddy Roosevelt to Bill Clinton.* Oxford: Oxford University Press, 2015), 115.

56. Quoted in John F. Wilson, "Harding's Rhetoric of Normalcy, 1920-1923" *Quarterly Journal of Speech* 48, no. 4 (1962): 406. "Normalcy" was a major rhetorical touchstone for Harding. For another example, see Warren G. Harding, "Address Accepting the Republican Presidential Nomination," June 12, 1920, American Presidency Project, accessed February 11, 2023, https://www.presidency.ucsb.edu /documents/address-accepting-the-republican-presidential-nomination-2.

57. In fact, the United Stated provided almost 25 percent of the isolated communist pariah Soviet Union's imports in 1928. Katherine A. S. Siegel, "Technology

and Trade: Russia's Pursuit of American Investment: Russia's Pursuit of American Investment, 1917–1929," *Diplomatic History* 17, no. 3 (1993): 378–388.

58. Quoted in Eugene P. Trani and David L. Wilson, *The Presidency of Warren G. Harding* (Lawrence: University Press of Kansas, 1977) 136–137.

59. Ward, *A First-Class Temperament*, 559; FDR, "Our Foreign Policy: A Democratic View," *Foreign Affairs* 6, no. 4 (1928): 586; FDR, "A Plan to preserve World Peace," in Eleanor Roosevelt, *This I Remember* (New York: Harper, 1949), 353; FDR, "Statement on American Peace Award," in Frank Burt Freidel, *Franklin D. Roosevelt: The Ordeal*, vol. 2 (Boston: Little, Brown and Company, 1952), 129.

60. Freidel, *FDR: The Ordeal*, 236; FDR, "Our Foreign Policy," 579.

61. FDR, "Our Foreign Policy," 586; FDR to Armstrong, March 22, 1928, box 39, "Foreign Affairs Article 1928," FDRL. See also Hamilton Fish Armstrong to FDR, March 20, 1928, and FDR to Armstrong, April 17, 1928, box 39, FDRL.

62. Tami Davis Biddle, *Rhetoric and Reality in Air Warfare: The Evolution of British and American Ideas About Strategic Bombing, 1914–1945* (Princeton, NJ: Princeton University Press, 2002), 148.

63. *Macon Daily Telegraph* column, May 2, 1925, in FDR, *F.D.R. Columnist: The Uncollected Columns of Franklin D. Roosevelt* (Chicago: Pellegrini & Cudahy, 1947), 64.

64. Biddle, *Rhetoric and Reality in Air Warfare*, 157–159.

65. Priya Satia, "The Defense of Inhumanity: Air Control and the British Idea of Arabia," *American Historical Review* 111, no. 1 (2006): 32–33.

66. FDR to George Foster Peabody, October 10, 1922, box 39, "Asia Magazine Article 1922–1923," FDRL; FDR to Arthur Flavin, January 19, 1926, in Freidel, *FDR: The Ordeal*, 236. See also FDR to George Foster Peabody, September 26, 1923, FDR, box 39, "Asia Magazine Article 1922–1923," FDRL; FDR, letter to the editor, *Baltimore Sun*, August 13, 1923, FDR, box 39, "Asia Magazine Article 1922–1923," FDRL.

67. Freidel, *FDR: The Apprenticeship*, 232, 227, 232; Helen Keller, "Strike Against War," Gifts of Speech, January 5, 1916, http://gos.sbc.edu/k/keller.html.

68. FDR, letter to the editor, *Baltimore Sun*, August 13, 1923, FDR, box 39, "Asia Magazine Article 1922–1923," FDRL; *Macon Daily Telegraph* column, April 30, 1925, *F.D.R. Columnist*, 57, 58; *Macon Daily Telegraph* column, April 21, 1924, *F.D.R. Columnist*, 39, 38. As president, he would suggest that Venezuela encourage immigration "with the idea of developing a virile, democracy-loving white population over a period of four or five generations": Roosevelt to Gonzalez, June 3, 1938, in FDR, *Franklin D. Roosevelt and Foreign Affairs*, vol. 10, edited by Edgar B. Nixon (Cambridge, MA: Belknap Press, 1969–1983), 201–202. (Hereafter cited as *FDRFA*.) In contrast to his definite views about the Japanese, he was uncertain about Russians. "I wish someone would tell me about the Russians," he complained to Frances Perkins. "I don't know a good Russian from a bad Russian. . . . I like them and I want to understand them": Frances Perkins, *The Roosevelt I Knew* (New York: Viking Press, 1946), 86.

69. As the US Office of the Historian notes, "In actuality, the act protected U.S. assets in the area and prevented a possible German invasion." "U.S. Invasion and Occupation of Haiti, 1915–1934," Office of the Historian, accessed February 2, 2023, https://history.state.gov/milestones/1914–1920/haiti.

70. "Memorandum on Haiti 1922," box 41, FDRL. For a more recent and rather

different perspective on the US invasion of Haiti, see Brenda Gayle Plummer, *Haiti and the United States: The Psychological Moment* (Athens: University of Georgia Press, 1992). Some seventeen years later, Roosevelt did ask a group of journalists, "Have we a definite right to call any nation backward? . . . Are [Ethiopians] uncivilized people? I wonder": "Press conference with American Society of Newspaper Editors," April 20,1939, FDR, *FDRFA*, 14:387.

71. FDR, "Our Foreign Policy," 586, 584, 573; FDR, "Houston Texas—June 27, 1928—Democratic National Convention—Placing Alfred E. Smith in Nomination," box 5, Master Speech Files, FDRL.

72. John S. D. Eisenhower, *Intervention! The United States and the Mexican Revolution, 1913–1917* (New York: W. W. Norton, 1993), 75.

73. David W. Southern, *The Progressive Era and Race: Reaction and Reform, 1900–1917* (Wheeling, IL: Harlan Davidson, 2005), 47.

74. FDR to James Cox, December 8, 1922, in Freidel, *FDR: The Ordeal*, 122; FDR to Thomas Pendell, October 2, 1922, box 3, Roosevelt, F.D.—Papers 1920-1928, "Pendell, Thomas," FDRL; FDR, "Shall We Trust Japan?" *Asia* 23, no. 7 (July 1923); Leuchtenburg, *The American President*, 138.

75. See, e.g., *Macon Daily Telegraph* column, April 30, 1925, *F.D.R. Columnist*, 57ff, and FDR, "Shall We Trust Japan?"

76. FDR, "Memorandum on Leadership 7/8/28," box 42, FDRL.

77. FDR, *Whither Bound* (New York: Houghton Mifflin, 1926), 27.

78. FDR, *Whither Bound*, 28, 30, 31; *Macon Daily Telegraph* column, May 2, 1925, *F.D.R. Columnist*, 65; *The Standard* (Beacon, NY), September 20, 1928, *F.D.R. Columnist*, 132.

79. FDR, "Our Foreign Policy," 586; FDR, "Shall We Trust Japan?"; FDR to G. Hall Roosevelt, February 17, 1931, FDR: Papers as Governor of New York State, box 69, "Roosevelt, G. Hall," FDRL.

80. "Speech on Republican Attitude Toward War Debts," October 1926, in FDR, *Franklin D. Roosevelt's Own Story*, 96–98; FDR, "Speech—Syracuse, NY September 27, 1926," box 4, Master Speech Files, FDRL.

81. *The Standard* (Beacon, NY), September 20, 1928, *F.D.R. Columnist*, 136, 133; FDR to Mrs. J. Malcolm Forbes ("dear cousin Rose"), August 20, 1928, box 39, "Foreign Affairs Article 1928," FDRL.

82. Patrick J. Maney, *The Roosevelt Presence: A Biography of Franklin Delano Roosevelt* (New York: Twayne Publishers, 1992), 165.

83. "Radio Address," April 8, 1932, FDR, *Roosevelt Reader*, 68; "Radio Address," October 6, 1932, in FDR, *Memorable Quotations of Franklin D. Roosevelt*, compiled by Taylor E. Parks and Lois F. Parks (New York: Thomas Crowell, 1965), 174.

84. "Radio Address, 4/8/32," in FDR, *Roosevelt Reader*, 68; "Speech to New York State Grange," February 2, 1932, and "Campaign Speech," September 20, 1932, FDR, *Memorable Quotations*, 173; "Radio Address," October 6, 1932, FDR, *Memorable Quotations*, 174.

85. "Roosevelt, F.D. & Eleanor (1930–41)," box 6, David Gray Papers, FDRL.

86. Letter dated June 9, 1931, in FDR, *Franklin D. Roosevelt's Own Story*, 136; FDR, *Public Papers and Addresses of Franklin Delano Roosevelt*, compiled by Samuel I. Rosenman (New York: Macmillan, 1938-1950), 1928–1932, 75-75, 15, cited in David M.

Kennedy, *Freedom from Fear: The American People in Depression and War, 1929–1945* (New York: Oxford University Press, 1999), 116.

87. Quoted in James Chace, "The Winning Hand," *New York Review of Books*, March 11, 2004, https://www.nybooks.com/articles/2004/03/11/the-winning-hand/.

88. Quoted in Leuchtenburg, *The American President*, 139.

89. Quoted in Jean Edward Smith, *FDR* (New York: Random House, 2007), 709.

90. FDR, "Albany, NY—Radio Speech," April 8, 1932, p. 2, box 9, file no. 470, Master Speech Files, FDRL.

91. FDR, "Acceptance Speech on Receiving Nomination," July 2, 1932, box 9, file no. 483, Master Speech Files, FDRL.

92. Associated Press, "Farmers Besiege the Legislatures," *New York Times*, January 22, 1933, N1.

93. "Employment Fell 3.9% in January," *New York Times*, February 23, 1933, C30.

94. Quoted in William E. Leuchtenburg, *The FDR Years: On Roosevelt & His Legacy* (New York: Columbia University Press, 1995), 6.

95. Quoted in William E. Leuchtenburg, "Keynote Address: The Greenbelt Conference on New Towns," George Mason University Archival Repository Service, May 2, 1987, http://ebot.gmu.edu/bitstream/handle/1920/1887/638_01_01_04 .pdf?sequence=1&isAllowed=y.

Chapter 3: Economic Policy: The New Deal

1. FDR, "First Inaugural Address," March 4, 1933, in FDR, *Franklin D. Public Papers and Addresses of Franklin Delano Roosevelt*, compiled by Samuel I. Rosenman (New York: Macmillan, 1938–1950), 1933, 11. (Hereafter cited as FDR *PPA*.)

2. Immediate responses to the speech highlighted its emphasis on the military metaphor more than the "fear itself" line. Jonathan Alter, *The Defining Moment: FDR's Hundred Days and the Triumph of Hope* (New York: Simon & Schuster, 2007), 216–219.

3. Davis W. Houck, *FDR and Fear Itself: The First Inaugural Address* (College Station: Texas A&M University Press, College Station, 2002), 148.

4. Ronald Isetti, "The Moneychangers of the Temple: FDR, American Civil Religion, and the New Deal," *Presidential Studies Quarterly* 26, no. 3 (1996): 680; FDR, "First Inaugural Address," 15; William Manchester, *The Glory and the Dream: A Narrative History of America, 1932–1972* (Boston: Little, Brown, 1973), 77.

5. Patrick J. Maney, *The Roosevelt Presence: A Biography of Franklin Delano Roosevelt* (New York: Twayne Publishers, 1992), 49.

6. Quoted in Davis W. Houck and Miheala Nocasian, "FDR's First Inaugural Address: Text, Context, and Reception," *Rhetoric & Public Affairs* 5, no. 4 (2002): 650.

7. Robert Dallek, *Franklin D. Roosevelt: A Political Life* (New York: Penguin Books, 2017), 137–138.

8. Halford Ross Ryan, "Roosevelt's First Inaugural: A Study of Technique," *Quarterly Journal of Speech* 65, no. 2 (1979): 141, 143, 149.

9. Thomas B. Farrell, *Norms of Rhetorical Culture* (New Haven, CT: Yale University Press, 1993), 86, 90–91.

10. Houck and Nocasian, "FDR's First Inaugural Address," 674–675.

11. FDR, "First Inaugural Address."

12. Isetti also notes FDR "employed biblical rhetoric, especially the theme of driving out the moneychangers, as a means of defending, maintaining, and advancing a regulatory Progressive state based on political liberalism and Christian humanitarianism, which for Roosevelt were pretty much the same thing." Isetti, "The Moneychangers of the Temple," 685–686.

13. Houck, *FDR and Fear Itself*, 119–120.

14. Donald R. Richberg, "The New Deal's 'Revolution' Defended," *New York Times*, December 5, 1937, 159.

15. Philip Abbott, *The Exemplary Presidency: Franklin D. Roosevelt and the American Political Tradition* (Amherst: University of Massachusetts Press, 1990), 91.

16. Rexford Guy Tugwell, *The Battle for Democracy* (New York: Columbia University Press, 1935), 22; William E. Leuchtenburg, *Franklin D. Roosevelt and the New Deal: 1932–1940* (New York: Harper & Row, 1963), 345.

17. FDR, "Atlanta, GA—Oglethorpe University Commencement Address," May 22, 1932, p. 14, box 9, file no. 476, Master Speech Files, Franklin D. Roosevelt Presidential Library & Museum. (Hereafter cited as FDRL.)

18. H. W. Brands, *Traitor to His Class: The Privileged Life and Radical Presidency of Franklin Delano Roosevelt* (New York: Random House, 2008), 128.

19. Michael Hiltzik, *The New Deal: A Modern History* (New York: Free Press, 2011), 194.

20. Ellis Wayne Hawley, *The Great War: A History of the American People and Their Institutions, 1917–1933* (New York: St. Martin's Press, 1979), 198; Karl, *The Uneasy State*, 119.

21. Suzanne M. Daughton, "FDR as Family Doctor: Medical Metaphors and the Role of Physician in the Fireside Chats," in *American Rhetoric in the New Deal Era, 1932–1945: A Rhetorical History of the United States*, vol. 7, edited by Thomas W. Benson (East Lansing: Michigan State University Press, 2006), 35, 45.

22. Indeed, Jonathan Alter's history of FDR's early New Deal legislative victories begins with a chapter simply titled "Security." Alter, *Defining Moment*, 13.

23. "Radio Address on the Third Anniversary of the Social Security Act," September 15, 1938, FDR *PPA*, 1938, 481; Eric Frederick Goldman, *Rendezvous with Destiny: A History of Modern American Reform* (New York: Vintage Books, 1956), 289.

24. Leuchtenburg, *Franklin D. Roosevelt and the New Deal*, 335.

25. "Fireside Chat," April 14, 1938, in Russel D. Buhite and David W. Levy, eds., *FDR's Fireside Chats* (Norman, OK: University of Oklahoma Press, 1992), 115; "Message to the Congress Reviewing the Broad Objectives and Accomplishments of the Administration," June 8, 1934, FDR *PPA*, 1934, 288.

26. Robert E. Sherwood, *Roosevelt and Hopkins: An Intimate History* (New York: Harper, 1950), 65.

27. "Message to the Congress Reviewing the Broad Objectives and Accomplishments of the Administration," June 8, 1934, FDR *PPA*, 1934, 288; David M. Kennedy, *Freedom from Fear: The American People in Depression and War, 1929–1945* (New York: Oxford University Press, 1999), 245; "A Platform," box 52, file 1291, "acceptance speech 7/19/40," Master Speech Files, FDRL.

28. Charles C. Alexander, *Nationalism in American Thought, 1930–1945* (Chicago: Rand McNally, 1969), 7.

29. "Second Inaugural Address," January 30, 1937, FDR *PPA*, 1937, 1.

30. "A Message to the Congress on Social Security," January 12, 1935, FDR *PPA*, 1935, 46; "Fireside Chat," September 6, 1936, in Buhite and Levy, eds., *FDR's Fireside Chats*, 81; "Fireside Chat," March 9, 1937, in Buhite and Levy, eds., *FDR's Fireside Chats*, 86. Ward has offered a similar comment about Roosevelt's battle with polio: His goal was "to win that battle—which really meant simply not to lose it, not to allow his crippling to disable his career and destroy his future": Geoffrey C. Ward, *A First-Class Temperament: The Emergence of Franklin Roosevelt, 1905–1928* (New York: Harper & Row, 1989), 600.

31. Goldman, *Rendezvous with Destiny*, 279–280; Grace G. Tully, *FDR My Boss* (New York: C. Scribner's Sons, 1949), 323. See also James MacGregor Burns, *Roosevelt: The Lion and the Fox: 1882–1940*, vol. 1 (New York: Harcourt, Brace & World, 1956), 474.

32. Herbert Hoover, "Address at Madison Square Garden, New York City," October 31, 1936, American Presidency Project.

33. Quoted in Jonah Goldberg, *The Tyranny of Clichés: How Liberals Cheat in the War of Ideas* (New York: Sentinel, 2012), 58.

34. "Second Inaugural Address," January 20, 1937, FDR *PPA*, 1937, 6.

35. Tugwell, *Battle for Democracy*, 319; Goldman, *Rendezvous with Destiny*, 259; Leuchtenburg, *Franklin D. Roosevelt and the New Deal*, 338.

36. FDR, "Albany, NY—Radio Address re a National Program of Restoration," April 7, 1932, box 9, file no. 469, Master Speech Files, FDRL.

37. "Radio Address on the Third Anniversary of the Social Security Act," August 15, 1938, FDR *PPA*, 1938, 480; "Second Inaugural Address," January 20, 1937, FDR *PPA*, 1937, 6.

38. Mary E. Stuckey, *Voting Deliberatively: FDR and the 1936 Presidential Campaign* (University Park: Pennsylvania State University Press, 2015), 12. For an economic and political critique of the New Deal, see Jim Powell, *FDR's Folly: How Roosevelt and His New Deal Prolonged the Great Depression* (New York: Crown Forum, 2003).

39. "Second Inaugural Address," January 20, 1937, 5.

40. John H. Sharon, "The Psychology of the Fireside Chat" (BA thesis, Princeton University, 1949), 192.

41. "Radio Address on Brotherhood Day," February 23, 1936, FDR *PPA*, 1936, 86.

42. Houck, *FDR and Fear Itself*, 72.

43. FDR, "Statement to the Federation of Women's Clubs," December 14, 1933, American Presidency Project, accessed February 11, 2023, https://www.presidency.ucsb.edu/documents/statement-the-federation-womens-clubs.

44. FDR, "First Fireside Chat of 1934," June 28, 1934, FDR *PPA*, 1934, 316.

45. "Second Fireside Chat of 1934," September 30, 1934, FDR *PPA*, 1934, 422.

46. "Roosevelt to Felix Frankfurter," February 9, 1937, in FDR, *Roosevelt and Frankfurter: Their Correspondence, 1928–1945*, annotated by Max Freedman (Boston: Little, Brown, 1967), 382; William Randolph Hearst, *William Randolph Hearst: A Portrait in His Own Words*, edited by Edmond D. Coblentz (New York: Simon & Schus-

ter, 1952), 178. Roosevelt told his ambassador to Germany, William Dodd, in great detail about the scheme he believed Huey Long was employing to become "dictator" of the United States by 1941. See William Edward Dodd, *Ambassador Dodd's Diary: 1933–1938*, edited by William E. Dodd Jr. and Martha Dodd (New York: Harcourt, Brace, 1941), 213–214.

47. "Fireside Chat," September 30, 1934, in Buhite and Levy, eds., *FDR's Fireside Chats*, 57.

48. "Message to the Congress Reviewing the Broad Objectives and Accomplishments of the Administration," June 8, 1934, FDR *PPA*, 1934, 288.

49. FDR, "Fireside Chat #2—*Outlining the New Deal Program*," May 7, 1933, p. 5, box 14, file no. 627, Master Speech Files, FDRL.

50. Doris Kearns Goodwin, *No Ordinary Time: Franklin and Eleanor Roosevelt: The Home Front in World War II* (New York: Simon & Schuster, 1994), 319; "Address on the Occasion of the Fiftieth Anniversary of the Statue of Liberty," October 28, 1936, FDR *PPA*, 1936, 543.

51. Kennedy, *Freedom from Fear*, 365, 378, 247.

52. FDR, "Message to Congress on Small Home Mortgages," April 13, 1933, p. 1, box 14, file no. 624, Master Speech Files, FDRL.

53. FDR, "A Letter on the Improvement of Agriculture," December 8, 1933, American Presidency Project, accessed February 11, 2023, https://www.presidency.ucsb.edu/documents/letter-the-improvement-agriculture.

54. FDR, "Statement on the Extension of the Automobile Code," January 31, 1935, American Presidency Project, accessed February 11, 2023, https://www.presidency.ucsb.edu/documents/statement-the-extension-the-automobile-code; FDR, "Baltimore, MD—Address—National Conference of Young Democrats," April 13, 1936, p. 9, box 25, file no. 856, Master Speech Files, FDRL.

55. "Radio Address on the Third Anniversary of the Social Security Act," August 15, 1938, FDR *PPA*, 1938, 480.

56. Albert Marrin, *FDR and the American Crisis* (New York: Random House, 2015), 5.

57. Kennedy, *Freedom from Fear*, 371.

58. Warren F. Kimball, *The Juggler: Franklin Roosevelt as Wartime Statesman* (Princeton, NJ: Princeton University Press, 1994), 10.

59. Kennedy, *Freedom from Fear*, 372.

60. "First Fireside Chat of 1936," September 6, 1936, FDR *PPA*, 1936, 339; "President Enumerates the Gains under N.R.A. and Recommends its Extension for Two Years," February 29, 1935, FDR *PPA*, 1935, 82.

61. J. M. Keynes, open letter to Roosevelt, *New York Times*, December 31, 1933, cited in Leuchtenbeug, *Roosevelt and the New Deal*, 337.

62. "Fireside Chat," March 9, 1937, in Buhite and Levy, eds., *FDR's Fireside Chats*, 85.

63. "Fireside Chat," April 14, 1938, in Buhite and Levy, eds., *FDR's Fireside Chats*, 118.

64. Rexford Guy Tugwell, *The Brains Trust* (New York: Viking Press, 1968), 295.

65. "Annual Message to the Congress," January 6, 1937, FDR *PPA*, 1937, 636; see

also Barry Dean Karl, *The Uneasy State: The United States From 1915 to 1945* (Chicago: University of Chicago Press, 1983), 153.

66. "Acceptance of the Renomination for the Presidency, Philadelphia, Pa.," June 27, 1936, FDR *PPA*, 1936, 235.

67. Eric Foner, *Story of American Freedom* (New York: W. W. Norton, 1999), 209, citing FDR *PPA*, 1934, 292.

68. Foner, *Story of American Freedom*, 198.

69. "Fireside Chat on Present Economic Conditions and Measures of Being Taken to Improve Them," April 14, 1938, FDR *PPA*, 1938, 246.

70. Alter, *The Defining Moment*, 319.

71. "First Inaugural Address," March 4, 1933, FDR *PPA*, 1933, 14.

72. FDR, "Fireside Chat," April 14, 1938, in Buhite and Levy, eds., *FDR's Fireside Chats*, 118

73. FDR, "Message to Congress—The State of the Union," January 4, 1939, 4, box 43, file no. 1191-B, Master Speech Files, FDRL.

74. John A. Garraty, "New Deal, National Socialism, and the Great Depression," *American Historical Review* 78, no. 4 (1973): 925.

75. FDR, "Third Fireside Chat," July 24, 1933, FDR *PPA*, 1933, 301.

76. "Radio Address, Albany, N.Y.," April 7, 1932, FDR *PPA*, 1932, 625; "Speech at Pittsburgh," October 1, 1936, FDR *PPA*, 1936, 407.

77. Michael S. Sherry, *In the Shadow of War: The United States since the 1930s* (New Haven, CT: Yale University Press, 1995), 16; "Acceptance of the Renomination for the Presidency, Philadelphia, Pa.," 236.

78. William E. Leuchtenburg, "Analogue of War," in *Change and Continuity in Twentieth Century America: The 1920's*, edited by Robert H. Bremner, John Braeman, and David Brody (Columbus: Ohio State University Press, 1964), 82.

79. FDR, "Proclamation 2040—Bank Holiday," March 9, 1933, American Presidency Project, accessed February 11, 2023, https://www.presidency.ucsb.edu/doc uments/proclamation-2040-bank-holiday.

80. FDR, "Letter on Additional National and State Parks," May 26, 1937, American Presidency Project, accessed February 11, 2023, https://www.presidency.ucsb .edu/documents/letter-additional-national-and-state-parks.

81. "Address at Vassar College," August 26, 1933, FDR *PPA*, 1933, 345; "Address at the Dedication of the Samuel Gompers Memorial Monument," October 7, 1933, FDR *PPA*, 1933, 386. George Peek wrote that the New Deal, like war, was a venture in "nation-saving": George Nelson Peek and Samuel L. Crowther, *Why Quit Our Own?* (New York: D. Van Nostrand, 1936), 123. Using the language of wartime, NRA administrator Hugh Johnson told the AFL explicitly that strikes would be viewed as "subversive influences": Leuchtenburg, "Analogue of War," 131.

82. Mary E. Stuckey, *The Good Neighbor: Franklin D. Roosevelt and the Rhetoric of American Power* (East Lansing: Michigan State University Press, 2013), 144–145.

83. See Buhite and Levy, eds., *FDR's Fireside Chats*, xviii.

84. Elvin T. Lim, "The Lion and the Lamb: De-Mythologizing Franklin Roosevelt's Fireside Chats," *Rhetoric & Public Address* 6, no. 3 (2003): 455.

85. William Appleman Williams, *The Tragedy of American Diplomacy*, 2nd ed. (New

290 I NOTES TO PAGES 80-83

York: Dell Publishing, 1972), 173. See also Leuchtenburg, "Analogue of War," 130; and Lloyd C. Gardner, *A Covenant with Power: America and World Order from Wilson to Reagan* (New York: Oxford University Press, 1984), 31.

86. FDR, "Chapel Hill, NC—Address at University of North Carolina," December 5, 1938, 6, box 43, file no. 1185, Master Speech Series, FDRL.

87. Mary E. Stuckey, *Voting Deliberatively: FDR and the 1936 Presidential Campaign* (University Park: Pennsylvania State University Press, 2015), 8-12.

88. *New York Times*, November 13, 1932, quoted in James MacGregor Burns, *Roosevelt: The Soldier of Freedom* (New York: Harcourt Brace Jovanovich, 1970), 357 (see also Frank Burt Freidel, *Franklin D. Roosevelt: Launching the New Deal*, vol. 4 [Boston: Little, Brown, 1952], 5-6); Patrick J. Maney, *The Roosevelt Presence: A Biography of Franklin Delano Roosevelt* (New York: Twayne Publishers, 1992), 50; Schlesinger, *Coming of the New Deal, 1933-1935* (New York: Houghton Mifflin, 1958), 558; "Address at the Jackson Day Dinner, Washington, D.C.," January 8, 1938, FDR *PPA*, 1938, 39.

89. "Second Inaugural Address," January 20, 1937, FDR *PPA*, 1937, 5.

90. "Fireside Chat," April 14, 1938, in Buhite and Levy, eds., *FDR's Fireside Chats*, 122.

91. "Fireside Chat," July 24, 1933, in Buhite and Levy, eds., *FDR's Fireside Chats*, 34; "Campaign Address at Chicago, ILL.," October 14, 1936, FDR *PPA*, 1936, 483.

92. "Fireside Chat," April 28, 1935, in Buhite and Levy, eds., *FDR's Fireside Chats*, 65.

93. Warren F. Kimball, *Forged in War: Roosevelt, Churchill, and the Second World War* (New York: W. Morrow, 1997), 15.

94. FDR, "Message of the President of March 21, 1933 Relating to Unemployment Relief," March 21, 1933, 2, box 14, file no. 619, Master Speech Files, FDRL.

95. "Fireside Chat," October 12, 1937, in Buhite and Levy, eds., *FDR's Fireside Chats*, 105; "Fireside Chat," April 14, 1938, in Buhite and Levy, eds., *FDR's Fireside Chats*, 115.

96. Mary E. Stuckey, *Political Vocabularies: FDR, the Clergy Letters, and the Elements of Political Argument* (East Lansing: Michigan State University Press, 2018), 121.

97. "Message to Congress," March 21, 1933, FDR *PPA*, 1933, 80-81.

98. FDR, "Washington, D.C.—Annual Message to Congress," January 3, 1934, p. 10, box 17, Master Speech Files, FDRL.

99. "Fireside Chat," May 7, 1933, in Buhite and Levy, eds., *FDR's Fireside Chats*, 19, 24; "Fireside Chat," September 30, 1934, in *FDR's Fireside Chats*, 55; "Address on the Occasion of the Fiftieth Anniversary of the Statue of Liberty," October 28, 1936, FDR *PPA*, 1936, 543.

100. John F. Woolverton and James D. Bratt, *A Christian and A Democrat: A Religious Biography of Franklin D. Roosevelt* (Grand Rapids, MI: Eerdmans Publishing, 2019), 1.

101. "Fireside Chat," October 12, 1937, in Buhite and Levy, eds., *FDR's Fireside Chats*, 99; "Fireside Chat," May 7, 1933, in Buhite and Levy, eds., *FDR's Fireside Chats*, 20; Barry Dean Karl, *The Uneasy State: The United States From 1915 to 1945* (Chicago: University of Chicago Press, 1983), 104, 110. See also Zietsma, "Imagining Heaven and Hell: Religion, National Identity, and U.S. Foreign Relations, 1930-1953" (PhD diss., University of Akron, 2007), chapter 2.

102. See James K. A. Smith, *Awaiting the King: Reforming Public Theology* (Grand Rapids, MI: Baker Academic, 2017), 91–115.

103. FDR, "Philadelphia, PA—Acceptance of Re-nomination," June 27, 1936, p. 10, box 25, file no. 879-B, Master Speech Files, FDRL.

104. FDR, "Philadelphia, PA—Acceptance of Re-nomination," 10.

105. Eleanor Roosevelt, "My Day, October 5, 1936," *Eleanor Roosevelt Papers, Digital Edition*, 2017, https://www2.gwu.edu/~erpapers/myday/displaydoc.cfm?_y=1936&_f=md054453.

106. FDR, "Fireside Chat #8—Reporting on Drought Conditions," September 9, 1936, p. 13, box 26, file no. 912, Master Speech Files, FDRL.

107. Jeanne Fahnestock, *Rhetorical Style: The Uses of Language in Persuasion* (Oxford: Oxford University Press, 2011), 151.

108. Goldman, *Rendezvous with Destiny*, 286.

109. Alexander, *Nationalism in American Thought*, 23.

110. FDR, "Fireside Chat #9—Reorganization of Judiciary," March 9, 1937, 19, box 32, file no. 1041A, Master Speech Files, FDRL.

111. Marian C. McKenna, *Franklin Roosevelt and the Great Constitutional War: The Court-Packing Crisis of 1937* (New York: Fordham University Press, 2002), 354.

112. Trevor Parry-Giles and Marouf Hasian Jr., "Necessity or Nine Old Men: The Congressional Debate over Franklin D. Roosevelt's 1937 Court-Packing Plan," in *American Rhetoric in the New Deal Era, 1932–1945: A Rhetorical History of the United States*, vol. 7, edited by Thomas W. Benson (East Lansing: Michigan State University Press, 2006), 269.

113. Farrell, *Norms of Rhetorical Culture*, 86–87.

Chapter 4: Prewar Foreign Policy, 1933–1939

1. Thomas Jefferson, "First Inaugural Address," March 4, 1801, Avalon Project, http://avalon.law.yale.edu/19th_century/jefinau1.asp; Don Higginbotham, "The American Republic in a Wider World," in *The American Revolution: Its Character and Limits*, edited by. Jack P. Greene (New York: New York University Press, 1987), 169.

2. Quoted in George C. Herring, *From Colony to Superpower: American Foreign Relations since 1776* (Oxford: Oxford University Press, 2008), 289–290.

3. Campbell, "Trump's Protectionist Economic Plan Is Nothing New," *Atlantic*, January 9, 2017, https://www.theatlantic.com/business/archive/2017/01/trumps-protectionist-economic-plan-is-nothing-new/512585/; "US-China Trade War: Causes and Consequences," Foreign Policy Research Institute, April 24, 2019, https://www.fpri.org/event/2019/u-s-china-trade-war-causes-and-consequences/; Richard Aldous and Heidi J. S. Tworek, "Germany's Quest to Control the News," American Interest, April 9, 2019, https://www.the-american-interest.com/podcast/germanys-quest-to-control-the-news/, 2:30–7:30, 11:48–14:52; James Titcomb, "Germany Faces Losing US Intelligence If It Uses Huawei Equipment," Telegraph, March 11, 2019, https://www.telegraph.co.uk/technology/2019/03/11/germany-faces-losing-us-intelligence-uses-huawei-equipment/.

4. "First Inaugural Address," March 4, 1933, in FDR, *Public Papers and Addresses of*

Franklin Delano Roosevelt, compiled by Samuel I. Rosenman (New York: Macmillan, 1938–1950), 1933, 14, 13. (Hereafter cited as FDR *PPA.*)

5. FDR, "Second Fireside Chat," May 7, 1933, FDR *PPA,* 1933, 167.

6. Warren F. Kimball, *Forged in War: Roosevelt, Churchill, and the Second World War* (New York: W. Morrow, 1997), 102.

7. Beate Jahn, *Liberal Internationalism: Theory, History, Practice* (New York: Palgrave Macmillan, 2013), 2.

8. Patrick J. Hearden, *Roosevelt Confronts Hitler: America's Entry into World War II* (Dekalb: Northern Illinois University Press, 1987), 48; Warren F. Kimball, *The Juggler: Franklin Roosevelt as Wartime Statesman* (Princeton, NJ: Princeton University Press, 1994), 44.

9. Cordell Hull, *The Memoirs of Cordell Hull,* ed. Andrew Berding, vol. 1 (New York: Macmillan, 1948), 81; Tony Smith, *America's Mission: The United States and the Worldwide Struggle for Democracy in the Twentieth Century* (Princeton, NJ: Princeton University Press, 1994), 115. See also Richard N. Gardner, *Sterling-Dollar Diplomacy: Anglo-American Collaboration in the Reconstruction of Multilateral Trade* (Oxford: Clarendon Press, 1956), chapter 1.

10. Roosevelt to Schneider, June 22, 1938, FDR, *Franklin D. Franklin D. Roosevelt and Foreign Affairs,* edited by Edgar B. Nixon (Cambridge, MA: Belknap Press, 1969–1983), 10:311. (Hereafter cited as *FDRFA.*); Roosevelt to Hull, November 19, 1934, in Hull, *The Memoirs of Cordell Hull,* 1:372.

11. Interview with William Phillips (1933), p. 102, Columbia Center for Oral History Archives, Columbia University, https://oralhistoryportal.library.columbia .edu/document.php?id=ldpd_4073373.

12. FDR, "Address before the Inter-American Conference for the Maintenance of Peace," Buenos Aires, Argentina, December 1 ,1936, FDR *PPA,* 1936, 607.

13. "State Department Memorandum," February 11, 1936, Foreign Relations of the United States, Department of State (Washington, DC: US Government Printing Office), 1936, 1:636–637 (hereafter cited as FRUS); William Appleman Williams, *Tragedy of American* Diplomacy, 2nd ed (New York: Dell Publishing, 1972), 173; Roosevelt to Schneider, June 22, 1938, *FDRFA,* 10: 311.

14. Hearden, *Roosevelt Confronts Hitler,* 86; Robert Dallek, *Franklin D. Roosevelt: A Political Life* (New York: Penguin Books, 2017), 93.

15. FDR, "Annual Message to Congress," January 6, 1937, American Presidency Project, accessed February 11, 2023, https://www.presidency.ucsb.edu/documents /annual-message-congress-4.

16. Emily S. Rosenberg, *Spreading the American Dream: American Economic and Cultural Expansion, 1890–1945* (New York: Hill & Wang, 1982), 169, 180, 186. Rosenberg notes that Roosevelt and Hull wanted to give more power to the executive branch in controlling international economics. See also Frank Burt Freidel, *Franklin D. Roosevelt: A Rendezvous with Destiny* (Boston: Little, Brown, 1990), 215.

17. David M. Kennedy, *Freedom from Fear: The American People in Depression and War, 1929–1945* (New York: Oxford University Press, 1999), 188.

18. Hull, *Memoirs of Cordell Hull,* 1:537, 536; Lloyd C. Gardner, *Economic Aspects of New Deal Diplomacy* (Madison: University of Wisconsin Press, 1964), 64.

19. Hull, *The Memoirs of Cordell Hull,* 1:536

20. "An Appeal to the Nations of the World for Peace by Disarmament and for the end of Economic Chaos," May 16, 1933, in Dallek, *Franklin D. Roosevelt*, 43; FDR to King George V, May 16, 1933, in Frederick W. Marks, *Wind over Sand: The Diplomacy of Franklin Roosevelt* (Athens: University of Georgia Press, 1988), 23.

21. Hull to Roosevelt, February 14, 1935, *FDRFA*, 2:407; Gardner, *Economic Aspects of New Deal Diplomacy*, 40; FDR to Stimson, December 8, 1934, in FDR, *FDR: His Personal Letters*, edited by Elliott Roosevelt, assisted by James N. Rosenau and Joseph P. Lash (New York: Duell, Sloan and & Pearce, 1947–1950), vol. 3, 440.

22. David Reynolds, *From Munich to Pearl Harbor: Roosevelt's America and the Origins of the Second World War* (Chicago: Ivan R. Dee, 2001), 52; Frank Ninkovich, *Modernity and Power: A History of the Domino Theory in the Twentieth Century* (Chicago: University of Chicago Press, 1994), 121. See also the words of Walter Lippmann quoted in Kimball, *The Juggler*, 200.

23. Hull speech, November 1938, in Kimball, *The Juggler*, 44.

24. Freidel, *Franklin D. Roosevelt*, 211; "Address to the National Conference of Catholic Charities," October 4, 1933, FDR *PPA*, 1933, 2:379–380.

25. Gardner, *Economic Aspects of New Deal Diplomacy*, 44.

26. "Fireside Chat," October 12, 1937, in Russel D. Buhite and David W. Levy, eds., *FDR's Fireside Chats* (Norman, OK: University of Oklahoma Press, 1992), 104, 105.

27. FDR to Arthur Willert, June 16, 1937, *FDRFA*, 1937, 5:384 (see also Marks, *Wind over Sand*, 268); FDR to Dodd, August 30, 1937, *FDRFA*, 1937, 6:399.

28. FDR, "Letter to the Daughters of the American Revolution on National Defense," April 20, 1936, American Presidency Project, accessed February 11, 2023, https://www.presidency.ucsb.edu/documents/letter-the-daughters-the-american-revolution-national-defense.

29. FDR to Davis, June 26, 1934, FRUS, 1934, 1:277; FDR to Hull, November 24, 1934, FRUS, 1934, 1:193; FDR to Davis, August 30, 1933, FRUS, 1933, 1:208

30. Freidel, *A Rendezvous with Destiny*, 106.

31. Robert Dallek, *The American Style of Foreign Policy: Cultural Politics and Foreign Affairs* (New York: Oxford University Press, 1979), 120

32. See Reynolds, *From Munich to Pearl Harbor*, 172.

33. Preston, "Franklin D. Roosevelt and Roosevelt and America's Empire of Anti-Imperialism," in *Rhetorics of Empire: Language of Colonial Conflict After 1900*, edited by Martin Thomas and Richard Toye (Manchester: Manchester University Press, 2017), 77.

34. Preston, "Franklin D. Roosevelt and America's Empire of Anti-Imperialism," 77–78; John M. Murphy, "No End Save Victory: FDR and the End of Isolationism, 1936–1941," in *Making the Case: Advocacy and Judgment in Public Argument*, ed. Kathryn M. Olson, Michael William Pfau, Benjamin Ponder, and Kirt H. Wilson (East Lansing: Michigan State University Press, 2012), 138–139.

35. FDR, "Radio Address—Women's Conference on Current Problems," October 13, 1933, pp. 1–2, box 16, file no. 656, Master Speech Files, Franklin D. Roosevelt Presidential Library & Museum. (Hereafter cited FDRL.)

36. FDR, "San Diego, CA—Address at San Diego Exposition [Good Neighbor]," October 2, 1935, p. 10, box 23, file no. 807, Master Speech Files, FDRL.

37. FDR, "Address at San Diego," 10–11.

38. David Zietsma, "Imagining Heaven and Hell: Religion, National Identity, and U.S. Foreign Relations, 1930–1953" (PhD diss., University of Akron, 2007), 108.

39. "Hull Memorandum," April 1, 1936, FRUS, 1936, 1:652–654; "Memorandum of Conversation Hull and Lindsay," March 28, 1936, FRUS, 1936, 1:649; Hull to Bingham, April 3, 1936, FRUS, 1936, 1:674.

40. Hull, *The Memoirs of Cordell Hull*, 1:525; "Hull Memorandum," October 22, 1936, FRUS, 1936, 1:689.

41. "Statement to Senate Finance Committee," February 10, 1937, in Hull, *The Memoirs of Cordell Hull*, 1:519; Cordell Hull, "International Trade," *Vital Speeches of the Day*, November 19, 1934, 110; Hull, *The Memoirs of Cordell Hull*, 1:391; Proposed Note to Japan, June 29, 1939, *FDRFA*, 16:15.

42. "Address at Chautauqua, N.Y.," August 14, 1936, FDR *PPA*, 1936, 290; Roosevelt to King Leopold II, August 24, 1937, *FDRFA*, 6:371

43. "Annual Message to Congress," January 3, 1934, FDR *PPA*, 1934, 11–12; Gardner, *A Covenant with Power*, 39.

44. Burton W. Folsom Jr. and Anita Folsom, *FDR Goes to War: How Expanded Executive Power, Spiraling National Debt, and Restricted Civil Liberties Shaped Wartime America* (New York: Threshold, 2011), 7.

45. Freidel, *A Rendezvous with Destiny*, 109; FDR to Phillips, May 25, 1934, FRUS, 1934, 1:70; FDR to Hull, November 24, 1934, FRUS, 1934, 1:193; Ninkovich, *Modernity and Power*, 104.

46. Hearden, *Roosevelt Confronts Hitler*, 76; interview with Henry Wallace, 1951, Columbia Center for Oral History Archives, Columbia University, https://oralhistoryportal.library.columbia.edu/document.php?id=ldpd_4075714.

47. Italy represents something of a special case, as Americans were generally optimistic about Mussolini's regime before World War II. "Throughout the 1930s," writes historian Ira Katznelson, public discourse in the United States "broadly admired [Italy's] combination of optimism and commitment to technology." Ira Katznelson, *Fear Itself: The New Deal and the Origins of Our Time* (New York: Liveright, 2014), 93.

48. "Address of the President to the Congress," January 3, 1936, 46–48, box 24, file no. 834, Master Speech Files, FDRL; October 2, 1935, 10, box 23, file no. 807, Master Speech Files, FDRL.

49. John M. Murphy, "No End Save Victory: FDR and the End of Isolationism, 1936–1941," in *Making the Case: Advocacy and Judgment in Public Argument*, edited by Kathryn M. Olson, Michael William Pfau, Benjamin Ponder, and Kirt H. Wilson (East Lansing: Michigan State University Press, 2012), 139.

50. Williams, *Tragedy of American Diplomacy*, 173.

51. Preston, "Franklin D. Roosevelt and America's Empire of Anti-Imperialism," 79.

52. Roosevelt even tried to purge the Democratic Party of its conservative elements in 1938, later writing that "it would be best not to straddle ideas." Robert C. Smith and Richard A. Seltzer, *Polarization and the Presidency: From FDR to Barack Obama* (Boulder, CO: Lynne Rienner, 2015), 30.

53. Murphy, "FDR and the End of Isolationism," 139.

54. Roosevelt to King, December 21, 1937, in FDR, *FDR: His Personal Letters*, 3:735; "Notes of W. L. MacKenzie King on the Permanent Conference on Economic and Social Problems," March 6, 1937, *FDRFA*, 1937, 4:352; press conference, April 20, 1937, *FDRFA*, 1937, 5:87. In one speech, he quoted Dante about the difference between "the sins of the cold-blooded and the sins of the warm-hearted": FDR *PPA*, 5:235.

55. FDR, "Chautauqua, NY—Address [Peace]," August 14, 1936, pp. 5, 7, 1, box 26, file no. 889, Master Speech Files, FDRL.

56. James MacGregor Burns, *Roosevelt: The Lion and the Fox: 1882–1940*, vol. 1 (New York: Harcourt, Brace & World, 1956), 475, 476.

57. G. Thomas Goodnight, "Reagan, Vietnam, and Central America: Public Memory and the Politics of Fragmentation," in *Beyond the Rhetorical Presidency*, edited by. Martin J. Medhurst (College Station: Texas A&M University Press, 1996),142.

58. Reinhold Niebuhr, *Moral Man and Immoral Society: A Study of Ethics and Politics* (New York: Charles Scribner, 1947), 272, 19.

59. Alan Jacobs, *Year of Our Lord 194: Christian Humanism in an Age of Crisis* (Oxford: Oxford University Press, 2018), 3, 52.

60. Reynolds, *From Munich to Pearl Harbor*, 129. Though the concept that would later be widely known as "national security" was emerging as an important theme in political science, "before World War II the term 'national security' scarcely existed": Emily Rosenberg, "Commentary: The Cold War and the Discourse of National Security," *Diplomatic History* 17, no. 2 (April 1993): 277.

61. Dallek, *Franklin D. Roosevelt*, 181; *FDRFA*, 1939, 13:207 (see also 202).

62. Williams, *The Tragedy of American Diplomacy*, 161.

63. FDR to Cudahy, March 4, 1939, in FDR, *FDR: His Personal Letters*, 4:863; press conference, February 27, 1939, *FDRFA*, 1939, 13:335.

64. Hull, *Memoirs of Cordell Hull*, 1:425; "Statement by Cordell Hull," July 16, 1937, *FDRFA*, 1937, 6:161.

65. As the grand theorist of realism Morgenthau himself wrote, "The 'maintenance of the status quo' yield[ed] to the 'maintenance of international peace and security.'" Hans Joachim Morgenthau, *Politics among Nations: The Struggle for Power and Peace*, 5th ed. (New York: Knopf, 1973), 92–93.

66. Ninkovich, *Modernity and Power*, 120.

67. "Fireside Chat on National Security," December 29, 1940, FDR *PPA*, 1940, 638.

68. FDR to Long, June 16, 1933, in FDR, *FDR: His Personal Letters*, 3:352; Frank Burt Freidel, *Franklin D. Roosevelt: Launching the New Deal*, vol. 4 (Boston: Little, Brown, 1952), 377; Kennedy, *Freedom from Fear*, 412. See Micheala Höenicke Moore, *Know Your Enemy: The American Debate on Nazism, 1933–1945* (Cambridge and New York: Cambridge University Press, 2010), 78–87.

69. "Press conference with American Society of Newspaper Editors," April 20, 1939, *FDRFA*, 1939, 14:397.

70. Press conference, June 23, 1939, *FDRFA*, 1939, 15:314, 315.

71. FDR to Norman Davis, January 14, 1936, in FDR, *FDR: His Personal Letters*, 3:545; FDR to Dodd, December 2, 1935, President's Secretary's File, German Diplomatic Files, "Germany: William E. Dodd: 1933–35," FDRL.

72. FDR to William Allen White, December 14, 1939, in FDR, *FDR: His Personal Letters*, 4:967; Roosevelt to Early, January 10, 1939, *FDRFA*, 1939, 13:91; Katznelson, *Fear Itself*, 93.

73. Roosevelt to MacVeigh, September 12, 1934, *FDRFA*, 1934, 2:216; T. H. Watkins, *The Great Depression: America in the 1930s* (Boston: Little, Brown, 1993), 318; "Roosevelt to Hitler and other European leaders," September 26, 1938, *FDRFA*, 1938, 11:214; FDR to Straus, February 13, 1936, in FDR, *FDR: His Personal Letters*, 3:555. See also, e.g., FDR to Bailey, August 29, 1935, *FDRFA*, 1935, 2:628; FDR to Long, February 22, 1936, in FDR, *FDR: His Personal Letters*, 3:560; FDR to Cudahy, June 28, 1938, *FDRFA*, 1938, 10:327.

74. Ninkovich, *Modernity and Power*, 105; FDR to van Loon, March 20, 1939, *FDRFA*, 1939, 14:109.

75. Frank A. Ninkovich, *The Wilsonian Century: U.S. Foreign Policy since 1900* (Chicago: University of Chicago Press, 1999), 107.

76. Francis A. Beer and Christ'l De Landtsheer, "Foreword," in *Metaphorical World Politics*, edited by Francis A. Beer and Christ'l De Landtsheer (East Lansing: Michigan State University Press, 2004), x.

77. William Edward Dodd, *Ambassador Dodd's Diary: 1933–1938*, edited by William E. Dodd Jr. and Martha Dodd (New York: Harcourt, Brace, 1941), 5; FDR to Governor I. C. Blackwood, April 12, 1933, *FDRFA*, 1933, 1:51

78. FDR to Dodd, March 16, 1936, in FDR, *FDR: His Personal Letters*, 3:571; Reynolds, *From Munich to Pearl Harbor*, 51; Hearden, *Roosevelt Confronts Hitler*, 58ff., 88ff., 121; Kimball, *Forged in War*, 24. See the analysis in Thomas J. McCormick, *America's Half-Century: United States Foreign Policy in the Cold War and After* (Baltimore, MD: Johns Hopkins University Press, 1995), 31.

79. Daniel A. Gross, "The U.S. Government Turned Away Thousands of Jewish Refugees, Fearing That They Were Nazi Spies," Smithsonian, November 18, 2015, https://www.smithsonianmag.com/history/us-government-turned-away-thousands-jewish-refugees-fearing-they-were-nazi-spies-180957324.

80. Murphy, "FDR and the End of Isolationism," 132; Dallek, *Franklin D. Roosevelt*, 85, 101–104.

81. Manfred Jonas, *Isolationism in America: 1935–1941* (Ithaca, NY: Cornell University Press, 1966), 1.

82. Lynne Olson, *Those Angry Days: Roosevelt, Lindbergh, and America's Fight over World War II, 1939–1941* (New York: Random House, 2013), 28.

83. Robert D. Accinelli, "The Roosevelt Administration and the World Court Defeat," *Historian* 40, no. 3 (1978): 463.

84. H. W. Brands, *Traitor to His Class: The Privileged Life and Radical Presidency of Franklin Delano Roosevelt* (New York: Random House, 2008), 329.

85. Stephen E. Ambrose, *Citizen Soldiers: The U.S. Army from the Normandy Beaches to the Bulge to the Surrender of Germany* (New York: Simon & Schuster, 1997), 22.

86. Williams, *Tragedy of American Diplomacy*, 168; FDR to Robert Cecil, April 6, 1937, *FDRFA*, 1937, 5:20; FDR to Butler, October 20, 1937, *FDRFA*, 1937, 7:130.

87. Address at Chicago," October 5, 1937, FDR *PPA*, 1937, 409–410.

88. "Address at Chicago," 410.

89. Halford Ross Ryan, "Franklin Delano Roosevelt: Rhetorical Politics and Politi-

cal Rhetorics," in *Presidential Speechwriting: From the New Deal to the Reagan Revolution and Beyond*, edited by Kurt Ritter and Martin J. Medhurst (College Station: Texas A&M University Press, 2003), 28.

90. Ryan, "Franklin Delano Roosevelt," 28.

91. FDR to E. Peabody, October 16, 1937, in FDR, *FDR: His Personal Letters*, 3:716.

92. FDR to John Cudahy, March 9, 1938, in FDR, *FDR: His Personal Letters*, 4:766.

93. FDR to Phillips, October 17, 1938, in FDR, *FDR: His Personal Letters*, 4:818; FDR to Chamberlain, January 1, 1938, FRUS, 1938, 1:120–122. FDR's trusted aide, Sumner Welles, even predicted that the results at Munich might lead to a new world order based on justice and law: FDR, *FDR: His Personal Letters*, 4:817 (note).

94. FDR to Roger B. Merriman, February 15, 1939, Merriman Family Papers, https://www.masshist.org/objects/2010february.php; Reynolds, *From Munich to Pearl Harbor*, 44.

95. Dodd to FDR, August 26, 1937, *FDRFA*, 1937, 6:384; FDR to Dodd, August 30, 1937, *FDRFA*, 1937, 6:399; "Annual Message to the Congress," January 4, 1939, FDR *PPA*, 1939, 12. Mackenzie King urged (and perhaps flattered) FDR to believe that "you more than any other living man, are in a position to save the world situation, and with it, civilization": King to FDR, March 17, 1937, *FDRFA*, 1937, 4:386.

96. FDR to Phillips, September 15, 1938, in FDR, *FDR: His Personal Letters*, 4:810; FDR to King, October 11, 1938, *FDRFA*, 1938, 11:344

97. Entry for April 15, 1939, and White House press release no. 147, April 15, 1939, Adolph A. Berle Diary, Berle Papers, FDRL.

98. Moffatt, "Memorandum of Conversation," September 20, 1938, FRUS, 1938, 1:625.

99. FDR to Hitler, April 14, 1939, *FDRFA*, 1939, 14:303–306.

100. "Press conference with American Society of Newspaper Editors," April 20, 1939, *FDRFA*, 1939, 14:385; press conference, April 8, 1939, *FDRFA*, 1939, 14:290–291.

101. Interview with Herbert Lehman, 4:547, 552, 1957, Columbia Center for Oral History Archives, Columbia University, https://oralhistoryportal.library.columbia.edu/document.php?id=ldpd_4076412.

102. Jonathan Alter, *The Defining Moment: FDR's Hundred Days and the Triumph of Hope* (New York: Simon & Schuster, 2007), 3.

103. "Annual Message to the Congress," January 4, 1939, FDR *PPA*, 1939, 1, 2.

104. Mary E. Stuckey, *Political Vocabularies*, 5.

105. "Annual Message to the Congress," January 4, 1939, FDR *PPA*, 1939, 2.

106. Welles to FDR, March 29, 1939, *FDRFA*, 1939, 14:218–223.

107. Press conference, November 15, 1938, *FDRFA*, 1938, 12:7–9; "Address to Business Advisory Council," March 23, 1940, in Freidel, *Rendezvous with Destiny*, 333; Dallek, *Franklin D. Roosevelt*, 233.

108. FDR to James Roosevelt, January 20, 1938, in FDR, *FDR: His Personal Letters*, 4:751.

109. FDR to Joseph Kennedy, October 30, 1939, in FDR, *FDR: His Personal Letters*, 4:950.

110. Stuckey, *Political Vocabularies*, 160–161.

111. FDR to William Allen White, December 14, 1939, in FDR, *FDR: His Personal Letters*, 4:968.

Chapter 5: The Debate over Intervention

1. "Appeal to Belligerents Against Aerial Bombing of Civilians," 9/1/39, Foreign Relations of the United States, Department of State (Washington, DC: US Government Printing Office), 1939, 1:541 (hereafter cited as FRUS); "Fireside Chat on the War in Europe," in Russell D. Buhite and David W. Levy, eds., *FDR's Fireside Chats* (Norman, OK: University of Oklahoma Press, 1992), 148.

2. Gallup poll, September 26, 1939, in Justus D. Doenecke, *In Danger Undaunted: The Anti-interventionist Movement of 1940–1941 as Revealed in the Papers of the America First Committee* (Stanford, CA: Hoover Institution Press, 1990), 30, 37; Robert Dallek, *The American Style of Foreign Policy: Cultural Politics and Foreign Affairs* (New York: Oxford University Press, 1979), 129.

3. FDR, "Press Conference with Associated Church Press," April 20, 1938, *FDRFA* 1938, 9: 443–445; "Press Conference with American Society of Newspaper Editors," April 20, 1939, *FDRFA* 1939, 14: 394, 397; "Conference with the Senate Military Affairs Committee," January 31, 1939, *FDRFA* 1939, 13: 207.

4. John M. Murphy, "No End Save Victory: FDR and the End of Isolationism, 1936–1941," in *Making the Case: Advocacy and Judgment in Public Argument*, edited by Kathryn M. Olson, Michael William Pfau, Benjamin Ponder, and Kirt H. Wilson (East Lansing: Michigan State University Press, 2012), 147.

5. Doenecke, *In Danger Undaunted*, 37, 30; Dallek, *The American Style*, 129.

6. Leon Surette, *Dreams of a Totalitarian Utopia: Literary Modernism and Politics* (London: McGill-Queen's University Press, 2011), 250.

7. Alan Jacobs, *Year of Our Lord 1943: Christian Humanism in an Age of Crisis* (Oxford: Oxford University Press, 2018), 17.

8. Arthur Schlesinger Jr., "Reinhold Niebuhr's Long Shadow," *New York Times*, June 22, 1992, A17.

9. Jacobs, *Year of Our Lord 1943*, 24.

10. John Bodnar, *The "Good War" in American Memory* (Baltimore, MD: Johns Hopkins University Press, 2010), 1–2.

11. Warren Kimball, asking whether the president believed in 1940 that the United States should and would enter the war, could only answer: "Who knows?": Warren F. Kimball, *Forged in War: Roosevelt, Churchill, and the Second World War* (New York: W. Morrow, 1997), 7.

12. Michael S. Bell, "The Worldview of Franklin D. Roosevelt: France, Germany, and United States Involvement in Europe" (PhD diss., University of Maryland, 2004), 321–323; "Fireside Chat on the War in Europe," September 3, 1939, in FDR, *Public Papers and Addresses of Franklin Delano Roosevelt*, compiled by Samuel I. Rosenman (New York: Macmillan, 1938–1950), 1939, 461–463 (hereafter cited as FDR *PPA*); "President Urges the Extraordinary Session to Repeal the Embargo Provisions of the Neutrality Law," September 21, 1939, FDR *PPA*, 1939, 521. See also Michael

S. Sherry, *In the Shadow of War: The United States since the 1930s* (New Haven, CT: Yale University Press, 1995), 45.

13. Roosevelt pursued opportunities to resupply the British and French with munitions, aircraft, and other military supplies. James MacGregor Burns, *Roosevelt: The Soldier of Freedom* (New York: Harcourt Brace Jovanovich, 1970), 87.

14. Mary E. Stuckey, *Voting Deliberatively: FDR and the 1936 Presidential Campaign* (University Park: Pennsylvania State University Press, 2015), 20–21.

15. William E. Leuchtenburg, *Franklin D. Roosevelt and the New Deal: 1932–1940* (New York: Harper & Row, 1963), 293, 297; Lynne Olson, *Those Angry Days: Roosevelt, Lindbergh, and America's Fight over World War II, 1939–1941* (New York: Random House, 2013), xvi.

16. Simon J. Rofe, *Franklin Roosevelt's Foreign Policy and the Welles Mission* (New York: Palgrave Macmillan, 2007), 85.

17. James A. Farley, *Jim Farley's Story: The Roosevelt Years* (New York: Whittlesey House, 1948), 195.

18. FDR to Morgenthau, May 16, 1940, in Frank Burt Freidel, *Franklin D. Roosevelt: A Rendezvous with Destiny* (Boston: Little, Brown, 1990), 335; interview with Henry Wallace, 5:1011, 1951, Columbia Center for Oral History Archives, Columbia University, https://oralhistoryportal.library.columbia.edu/document.php?id=ldpd_4075714.

19. Sherry, *In the Shadow of War*, 45; David M. Kennedy, *Freedom from Fear: The American People in Depression and War, 1929–1945* (New York: Oxford University Press, 1999), 429; interview with Henry Wallace, 6:1104, 6:1078.

20. FDR to Cordell Hull, 9/19/40, in FDR, *FDR: His Personal Letters*, edited by Elliott Roosevelt, assisted by James N. Rosenau and Joseph P. Lash (New York: Duell, Sloan and & Pearce, 1947–1950), vol. 4, 1065. Roosevelt said that if the Germans wanted to close US consulates, for example in Czechoslovakia, the United States should close German consulates in the United States.

21. Quoted in Michael S. Bell, "The Worldview of Franklin D. Roosevelt: France, Germany, and United States Involvement in Europe" (PhD diss., University of Maryland, 2004), 322–323.

22. Admiral H. R. Stark, "Rough Informal Estimate of the Foreign Situation," March 1, 1940, box 58, folder: Navy: Jan–Mar 1940, Departmental File, President's Secretary's File, Franklin D. Roosevelt Presidential Library & Museum. (Hereafter cited as FDRL.)

23. Entry for July 18, 1940, Henry Lewis Stimson Diaries, 23, microfilm edition, reel 6, Manuscripts and Archives, Yale University Library, New Haven, CT, https://archives.yale.edu/repositories/12/archival_objects/1961444.

24. Speech to New England Council, Boston, November 14, 1940, box 5, Speeches and Writings File, Papers of Frank Knox, Library of Congress, Manuscript Division.

25. FDR to Sen. Josiah W. Bailey, May 13, 41, FDR, *FDR: His Personal Letters*, 1154; Patrick J. Hearden, *Architects: Building a New World Order during World War II* (Fayetteville: University of Arkansas Press, 2002), 24.

26. Robert Dallek, *Franklin D. Roosevelt: A Political Life* (New York: Penguin Books, 2017), 214.

27. FDR to Sen. David Walsh, August 22, 1940, in FDR, *FDR: His Personal Letters,* 4:1057.

28. Walter Isaacson and Evan Thomas, *Wise Men: Six Friends and the World They Made* (New York: Simon & Schuster, 2013), 185; Hearden, *Architects,* 12.

29. Hearden, *Architects,* 12, 16, 14; Godfrey Hodgson, *The Colonel: The Life and Wars of Henry Stimson, 1867–1950* (New York: Alfred A. Knopf, 1990), 219. See also Thomas J. McCormick, *America's Half-Century: United States Foreign Policy in the Cold War and After* (Baltimore, MD: Johns Hopkins University Press, 1995), 31, 32.

30. FDR to Samuel I. Rosenman, November 13, 1940, in FDR, *FDR: His Personal Letters,* 4:1078.

31. FDR, "Address to American Youth Congress," February 10, 1940, p. 17, box 50, Master Speech Files, FDRL.

32. Freidel, *Rendezvous with Destiny,* 329; FDR, Franklin D. *Franklin D. Roosevelt and Foreign Affairs,* edited by Edgar B. Nixon (Cambridge, MA: Belknap Press, 1969–1983), vol. 13, 1939, 213; FDR to Joseph Grew, November 30, 1939, in FDR, *FDR: His Personal Letters,* 2:961.

33. FDR to William Allen White, January 16, 1941, in FDR, *FDR: His Personal Letters,* 4:1106; FDR to Grace Tully, August 1940, in Kimball, *Forged in War,* 58.

34. Burns, *Roosevelt: The Soldier,* 84.

35. FDR to Francis B. Sayre, December 31, 1940, in FDR, *FDR: His Personal Letters,* 4:1095.

36. *Time,* May 27, 1940, cited in Geoffrey Perrett, *Days of Sadness, Years of Triumph: The American People, 1939–1945* (New York: Coward, McCann & Geoghegan, 1973), 27.

37. Perrett, *Days of Sadness,* 28.

38. Wayne S. Cole, *Roosevelt and the Isolationists, 1932–45* (Lincoln: University of Nebraska Press, 1983), 11.

39. "Dewey Warns America: Shun Foreign Wars," *Chicago Daily Tribune,* May 28, 1940, 10; Charles Peters, *Five Days in Philadelphia: The Amazing "We Want Willkie!" Convention of 1940* (New York: Public Affairs, 2005), 19.

40. *Wall Street Journal,* June 12, 1940, from Susan Dunn, *1940: FDR, Willkie, Lindbergh, Hitler—the Election amid the Storm* (New Haven, CT: Yale University Press, 2013), 62–63.

41. Dunn, *1940,* 66–67.

42. Cole, *Roosevelt and the Isolationists,* 14.

43. On Nietzsche and objective inquiry, see Babette E. Babich, *Reflecting Science on the Ground of Art and Life* (Albany: State University of New York Press, 1994), 37.

44. Denise M. Bostdorff, *The Presidency and the Rhetoric of Foreign Crisis* (Columbia: University of South Carolina Press, 1994), 4.

45. Murray Edelman, *Constructing the Political Spectacle* (Chicago: University of Chicago Press, 1987), 4.

46. Olson, *Those Angry Days,* xviii.

47. George Washington, "Proclamation 6—Day of Public Thanksgiving," January 1, 1795, American Presidency Project, accessed February 11, 2023, https://www.presidency.ucsb.edu/documents/proclamation-6-day-public-thanksgiving.

48. Olson, *Those Angry Days*, 98.

49. Zietsma, "Imagining Heaven and Hell: Religion, National Identity, and U.S. Foreign Relations, 1930–1953" (PhD diss., University of Akron, 2007), 148, 150.

50. Dunn, *1940*, 111.

51. "Text of Former President's Address before the Republican Convention," *New York Times*, June 26, 1940, 17.

52. Oswald Garrison Villard, "Foreword," *Our Military Chaos: The Truth about Defense* (New York: A. A. Knopf, 1939), n.p.; *Uncensored* (New York: Keep America Out of War Congress, 1939–1941), June 1, 1940, 6; *Uncensored*, December 21, 1940, 3.

53. Frank Costigliola, *Roosevelt's Lost Alliances: How Personal Politics Helped Start the Cold War* (Princeton, NJ: Princeton University Press, 2013), 138.

54. *Uncensored*, August 10, 1940, 4; Burton K. Wheeler, with Paul F. Healy, *Yankee from the West* (Garden City, NY: Doubleday, 1962), 18; Charles Lindbergh, "Our National Safety," *Vital Speeches of the Day*, May 19, 1940, 484–485. John T. Flynn, "Can Hitler Invade America?," *Reader's Digest*, April 1941, 1–6, offers a good summary of anti-interventionist arguments on this issue.

55. Beatrice Biship Berle and Travis Beal Jacobs, eds., *Navigating the Rapids, 1918–1971: From the Papers of Adolf A. Berle* (New York: Harcourt Brace Jovanovich, 1973), 370; *Uncensored*, January 4, 1941, 2; army ordinance, September–October, 1941, quoted in *Uncensored*, September 27, 1941, 3; *Uncensored*, June 1, 1940, 6.

56. William E. Borah, "Our Imperative Task," *Vital Speeches of the Day*, April 15, 1938, 388.

57. Mary E. Stuckey, *Political Vocabularies: FDR, the Clergy Letters, and the Elements of Political Argument* (East Lansing: Michigan State University Press, 2018), xviii.

58. FDR to Norman Thomas, May 14, 1941, in FDR, *FDR: His Personal Letters*, 4:1156.

59. Cole, *Roosevelt and the Isolationists*, 7., 7.

60. Dallek, *The American Style*, 131.

61. *Uncensored*, December 28, 1940, special suppl.; Stuart Chase, *New Western Front* (New York: Harcourt, Brace, 1939), 136.

62. William McKinley, "President McKinley's Last Public Utterance to the People in Buffalo, New York," September 5, 1901, American Presidency Project, accessed February 11, 2023, https://www.presidency.ucsb.edu/documents/president-mckinleys-last-public-utterance-the-people-buffalo-new-york.

63. William Jennings Bryan, "Imperialism," August 8, 1900, Voices of Democracy, http://voicesofdemocracy.umd.edu/william-jennings-bryan-imperialism-speech-text/. As Elizabeth Gardner points out, "He firmly believed that the American people were exceptional; their history and government, accordingly, stood as a model for other nations to emulate." Elizabeth Gardner, "William Jennings Bryan, 'Imperialism' (8 August 1900)," *Voices of Democracy* 5 (2010): 37.

64. *Uncensored*, May 18, 1940, 1; Norma Thomas, *We Have a Future* (Princeton, NJ: Princeton University Press, 1941), 65.

65. Lindbergh, "Our National Safety," 485.

66. Lawrence Dennis, "The Economic Consequences of American Intervention," unpublished manuscript, last modified 1941, in Doenecke, *In Danger Undaunted*, 22, 205.

67. *Uncensored*, January 4, 1941, 4.

68. Heidi S. Tworek, *News from Germany: The Competition to Control World Communications, 1900–1945* (Cambridge, MA: Harvard University Press, 2019), 205.

69. Micheala Hoenicke Moore, *Know Your Enemy: The American Debate on Nazism, 1933–1945* (Cambridge and New York: Cambridge University Press, 2010), 97; Dallek, *Franklin D. Roosevelt*, 235; David Reynolds, *Munich to Pearl Harbor: Roosevelt's America and the Origins of the Second World War* (Chicago: Ivan R. Dee, 2001), 44.

70. AFC speakers bureau memo, undated, in Doenecke, *In Danger Undaunted*, 153; AFC, "Did You Know," no. 6, July 5, 1941, in Doenecke, *In Danger Undaunted*, 163.

71. Lindbergh, "An Appeal for Peace," 646.

72. *Uncensored*, November 11, 1940, special suppl.; Chase, *The New Western Front*, 180.

73. Olson, *Those Angry Days*, 226.

74. Thomas, *We Have a Future*, 14.

75. Jerome Frank, *Save America First: How to Make Our Democracy Work* (New York: Harper & Brothers, 1938), 105, 146.

76. A. J. Muste, *Non-Violence in an Aggressive World* (New York: J. S. Ozer, 1972), 45. In fact, Nazi leaders had articulated exactly this line of argument since the 1920s, claiming that on the basis of "social justice" Germany deserved an empire like that of Britain or France. Michael Mann, *Fascists* (Cambridge: Cambridge University Press, 2004), 142–147.

77. Thomas, *We Have a Future*, 96.

78. *Uncensored*, March 15, 1941, 4; December 2, 1939, 3.

79. Muste, *Non-Violence in an Aggressive World*, 149, 155; A. J. Muste, *The Essays of A. J. Muste*, edited by Nat Hentoff (Indianapolis: Bobbs-Merrill, 1967), 244; Thomas, *We Have a Future*, 216.

80. "Fireside Chat on National Security," December 29, 40, FDR *PPA*, 1940, 640.

81. *Uncensored*, March 29, 1941, 1.

82. *Uncensored*, January 27, 1940, 1.

83. Thomas, *We Have a Future*, 65, 79.

84. Lindbergh, "An Appeal for Peace," 646.

85. Frank, *Save America First*, 36. Frank eventually rose to be chair of the Securities and Exchange Commission.

86. *Uncensored*, January 4, 1941, 4; December 14, 1940, 5; December 21, 1940, 3.

87. Lindbergh, "An Appeal for Peace," 60.

88. AFC speakers bureau memo, in Doenecke, *In Danger Undaunted*, 119; Villard, "Foreword."

89. See Manfred Jonas, *Isolationism in America: 1935–1941* (Ithaca, NY: Cornell University Press, 1966), 16.

90. Villard, *Our Military Chaos*, 197, 196.

91. Cole, *Roosevelt and the Isolationists*, 377.

92. Zietsma, "Imagining Heaven and Hell," 150, 147.

93. Anne Morrow Lindbergh, *War Within and Without: Diaries and Letters of Anne Morrow Lindbergh, 1939–1944* (New York: Harcourt Brace Jovanovich, 1980), 100; Cole, *Roosevelt and the Isolationists*, 374.

94. *Uncensored*, May 31, 1941, 2; August 10, 1940, 4.
95. Doenecke, *In Danger Undaunted*, 14.
96. Thomas, *We Have a Future*, 96–97.
97. Cole, *Roosevelt and the Isolationists*, 343.
98. Robert E. Sherwood, *Roosevelt and Hopkins: An Intimate History* (New York: Harper, 1950), 126; *New York Times*, December 30, 1940, 7.
99. Michael Fullilove, *Rendezvous with Destiny: How Franklin D. Roosevelt and Five Extraordinary Men Took America into the War and Into the World* (New York: Penguin Press, 2013), 58.
100. Chase, *The New Western Front*, 187.
101. Doenecke, *In Danger Undaunted*, 49.
102. Chester Bowles to Roy Larsen, April 30, 1941, in Doenecke, *In Danger Undaunted*, 286.
103. Chester Bowles to R. Douglas Stuart Jr., July 30, 1941, in Doenecke, *In Danger Undaunted*, 110.
104. Hearden, *Architects*, 28. See also Burns, *Roosevelt: The Soldier*, 37–40.
105. For examples of spring 1941 polls, see Doris Kearns Goodwin, *No Ordinary Time: Franklin and Eleanor Roosevelt: The Home Front in World War II* (New York: Simon & Schuster, 1994), 236.
106. Costigliola, *Roosevelt's Lost Alliances*, 102.

Chapter 6: Roosevelt's Rhetorical Victory, 1940: Arsenal of Democracy

1. Vanessa B. Beasley and Deborah Smith-Howell, "No Ordinary Rhetorical President: FDR's Speechmaking and Leadership, 1933–1945," in *American Rhetoric in the New Deal Era, 1932–1945: A Rhetorical History of the United States*, vol. 7, edited by Thomas W. Benson (East Lansing: Michigan State University Press, 2006), 2.
2. Frank Burt Freidel, *Franklin D. Roosevelt: Rendezvous with Destiny* (Boston: Little, Brown, 1990), 333, 334.
3. Eleanor Roosevelt, *The Autobiography of Eleanor Roosevelt* (New York: Da Capo Press, 1992), 211.
4. "Message to Congress—State of the Union Address," January 3, 1940, 7, box 49, file 1262, Master Speech Files, Franklin D. Roosevelt Presidential Library & Museum. (Hereafter cited as FDRL.)
5. Mary E. Stuckey, "The Great Debate: The United States and the World, 1936–1941," in *World War II and the Cold War: The Rhetoric of Hearts and Minds: A Rhetorical History of the United States*, vol. 8, edited by Martin J. Medhurst (East Lansing: Michigan State University Press, 2018), 15.
6. Frank Costigliola, *Roosevelt's Lost Alliances: How Personal Politics Helped Start the Cold War* (Princeton, NJ: Princeton University Press, 2013), 139.
7. James M. Lindsay, "TWE Remembers: FDR's 'Stab in the Back' Speech," Council on Foreign Relations, June 10, 2013, https://www.cfr.org/blog/twe-remembers-fdrs-stab-back-speech.
8. "'The Hand that Held the Dagger': FDR Delivers Historic Speech in Mem

Gym," *University of Virginia Magazine,* summer 2013, https://uvamagazine.org/articles/the_hand_that_held_the_dagger.

9. James L. Kinneavy, "Kairos in Classical and Modern Rhetorical Theory," in *Rhetoric and Kairos: Essays in History, Theory, and Praxis,* edited by Phillip Sipora and James S. Baumlin (Albany: State University of New York Press, 2002), 62–63.

10. Sharon Crowley and Debra Hawhee, *Ancient Rhetorics for Contemporary Students* (London: Longman, 1994), 45, 48.

11. "Address at University of Virginia," June 10, 1940, in FDR, *Public Papers and Addresses of Franklin Delano Roosevelt,* compiled by Samuel I. Rosenman (New York: Macmillan, 1938–1950), 1940, 261. (Hereafter cited as FDR *PPA.*)

12. "Address at University of Virginia," June 10, 1940, FDR *PPA,* 1940, 261;

13. Samuel P. Perry, "Douglass MacArthur as Frontier Hero: Converting Frontiers in MacArthur's Farewell to Congress," *Southern Communication Journal* 77, no. 4 (2012): 266.

14. Dorsey, "The Frontier Myth in Presidential Rhetoric," 3.

15. Joseph E. Persico, *Roosevelt's Centurions: FDR and the Commanders He Led to Victory in World War II* (New York: Random House, 2013), 36.

16. "Address at University of Virginia," 264.

17. "Full Speed Ahead," *Atlanta Daily World,* June 12, 1940, 6.

18. Richard L. Strout, "Intimate Message from Charlottesville," *Christian Science Monitor,* June 11, 1940, 1.

19. "American Papers Support Roosevelt on Aid to Allies," *Christian Science Monitor,* June 11, 1940, 2.

20. "Full Speed toward What Goal?" *Chicago Daily Tribune,* June 12, 1940, 16.

21. James MacDonald, "Britons Are Told We Insure Victory," *New York Times,* June 12, 1940, 12.

22. Michael A. Genovese, Todd L. Belt, and William W. Lammers, *The Presidency and Domestic Policy: Comparing Leadership Styles, FDR to Obama,* 2nd ed. (Boulder: Paradigm Publishers, 2014), 36.

23. Robert Dallek, *Franklin D. Roosevelt: A Political Life* (New York: Penguin Books, 2017), 247.

24. Ryan Weber, "Stasis in Space! Viewing Definitional Conflicts Surrounding the James Webb Space Telescope Funding Debate," *Technical Communication Quarterly* 25, no. 2 (2016): 89.

25. For an alternative, five-question series, see Jeanne Fahnestock and Marie Secor, "The Stases in Scientific and Literary Argument," *Written Communication* 5, no. 4 (1988): 427–443.

26. FDR to Francis B. Sayre, December 31, 1940, in FDR, *FDR: His Personal Letters,* edited by Elliott Roosevelt, assisted by James N. Rosenau and Joseph P. Lash (New York: Duell, Sloan and & Pearce, 1947–1950), 4: 1093. See David Reynolds, *From Munich to Pearl Harbor: Roosevelt's America and the Origins of the Second World War* (Chicago: Ivan R. Dee, 2001), 13 and 183, on FDR's talk about "a world war": "The 'second world war' was partly an American construction."

27. "Radio Address on Registration Day," October 16, 1940, FDR *PPA,* 1940, 474; "Address on Hemisphere Defense, Dayton, Ohio," October 12, 1940, FDR *PPA,* 1940, 466.

28. John W. Jeffries, *A Third Term for FDR: The Election of 1940* (Lawrence: University Press of Kansas, 2017), 103, 142.

29. Roger Daniels, *Franklin D. Roosevelt: The War Years, 1939–1940* (Urbana: University of Illinois Press, 2016), 93.

30. Donald Bruce Johnson, *The Republican Party and Wendell Willkie* (Urbana: University of Illinois Press, 1960), 127.

31. "Six Hundred and Seventy-seventh Press Conference," September 3, 1940, FDR *PPA*, 1940, 378.

32. Jeffries, *Third Term for FDR*, 141.

33. "Radio Address on Registration Day," October 16, 1940, FDR *PPA*, 1940, 474; "Registration Day Is Proclaimed," September 16, 1940, FDR *PPA*, 1940, 430.

34. "Campaign Address at Boston, Mass.," October 30, 1940, FDR *PPA*, 1940, 517.

35. Julian E. Zelizer, *Arsenal of Democracy: The Politics of National Security—From World War II to the War on Terrorism* (New York: Basic Books, 2010), 48.

36. "Fireside Chat on National Security," December 29, 1940, FDR *PPA*, 1940, 633.

37. "Address at Dayton Ohio," December 12, 1940, box 54, file 1314, Master Speech Files, FDRL.

38. "Address at University of Virginia," June 10, 1940, FDR *PPA*, 1940, 260; "Fireside Chat on National Defense," May 26, 1940, FDR *PPA*, 1940, 239.

39. "Address on Hemisphere Defense," December 12, 1940, FDR *PPA*, 1940, 466. This quote shares a certain similarity to 1 Pet. 5:8, which states, "Be alert and of sober mind. Your enemy the devil prowls around like a roaring lion looking for someone to devour."

40. "Campaign Address at Madison Square Garden," October 28, 1940, FDR *PPA*, 1940, 506; "Fireside Chat on National Security," December 29, 1940, FDR *PPA*, 1940, 639.

41. "Seven Hundred and Second Press Conference," December 17, 1940, FDR *PPA*, 1940, 607, 608.

42. Arthur H. Vandenberg Jr., *The Private Papers of Senator Vandenberg* (Boston: Mifflin, 1952), 10.

43. H. W. Brands, *Traitor to His Class: The Privileged Life and Radical Presidency of Franklin Delano Roosevelt* (New York: Random House, 2008), 580; FDR to Lewis W. Douglas, June 7, 1940, in FDR, *FDR: His Personal Letters*, 4:1038.

44. Norman Thomas, *Hearings before the Committee on Foreign Affairs House of Representatives, Seventy-Seventh Congress, First Session, on HR 1776* (Washington, DC: US Government Printing Office, 1941), 126.

45. According to Kimball and Miscamble, Roosevelt indeed saw "colonialism, not communism, as the -ism that most threatened postwar peace and stability." Warren F. Kimball, *The Juggler: Franklin Roosevelt as Wartime Statesman* (Princeton, NJ: Princeton University Press, 1994), 64; Wilson D. Miscamble, *From Roosevelt to Truman: Potsdam, Hiroshima, and the Cold War* (Cambridge: University of Cambridge Press, 2007), 42.

46. "Fireside Chat on National Defense," May 26, 1940, in Russell D. Buhite and David W. Levy, eds., *FDR's Fireside Chats* (Norman, OK: University of Oklahoma Press, 1992), 154.

47. "Acceptance of Third Term Nomination," July 19, 1940, FDR *PPA*, 1940, 301.

48. Geoffrey Perrett, *Days of Sadness, Years of Triumph: The American People, 1939–1945* (New York: Coward, McCann & Geoghegan, 1973), 124.

49. "Third Inaugural Address," January 20, 1941, FDR *PPA*, 1941, 6.

50. "Third Inaugural Address," 6.

51. "Acceptance of Third Term Nomination," July 19, 1940, FDR PPA 1940, 299.

52. "Fireside Chat on National Defense," May 26, 1940, FDR *PPA*, 1940, 412; "Address at University of Virginia," June 10, 1940, FDR PPA 1940, 264.

53. "Annual Message to the Congress," January 6, 1941, FDR *PPA*, 1940, 666.

54. Walter Isaacson and Evan Thomas, *Wise Men: Six Friends and the World They Made* (New York: Simon & Schuster, 2013), 186. See also Dean Acheson, *Morning and Noon* (Boston: Houghton Mifflin 1965), 216–227.

55. "Fireside Chat on National Defense," May 26, 1940, in Buhite and Levy, *FDR's Fireside Chats*, 160.

56. "Fireside Chat #15—National Defense," May 26, 1940, box 51, file 1283-A, Master Speech Files, FDRL.

57. "Fireside Chat on National Security," December 29, 1940, FDR *PPA*, 1940, 638.

58. "Campaign Address at Madison Square Garden," October 28, 1940, FDR *PPA*, 1940, 510.

59. Radio Address on Registration Day," October 16, 1940, FDR *PPA*, 1940, 474.

60. "Acceptance of Third Term Nomination," July 19, 1940, FDR *PPA*, 1940, 296.

61. "Third Inaugural Address," January 20, 1941, FDR *PPA*, 1941, 4–5.

62. Reynolds, *From Munich to Pearl Harbor*, 177.

63. Reynolds, 142, 140.

64. "Third Inaugural Address," January 20, 1941, FDR *PPA*, 1941, 6.

65. "Acceptance of Third Term Nomination," July 19, 1940, FDR *PPA*, 1940, 301.

66. "Fireside Chat on National Defense," May 26, 1940, FDR *PPA*, 1940, 231.

67. Patrick J. Hearden, *Architects of Globalism: Building a New World Order during World War II* (Fayetteville: University of Arkansas Press, 2002), 16.

68. "Annual Message to the Congress," January 3, 1940, FDR *PPA*, 1940, 6.

69. "Campaign Address at Madison Square Garden," October 28, 1940, FDR *PPA*, 1940, 508.

70. "Fireside Chat on National Security," December 29, 1940, FDR *PPA*, 1940, 634, 637–638.

71. "The President Informs the Congress of the Exchange of Certain United States Over-Age Destroyers for British Naval and Air Bases; and Transmits the Correspondence and the Opinion of the Attorney-General Relative Thereto," September 3, 1940, FDR *PPA*, 1940, 391–392.

72. "Acceptance of Third Term Nomination," July 19, 1940, FDR *PPA*, 1940, 298; "Third Inaugural Address," January 20, 1941, FDR *PPA*, 1941, 6.

73. Dallek, *Franklin D. Roosevelt*, 257.

74. *Life*, December 16, 1940, quoted in Lynne Olson, *Those Angry Days: Roosevelt, Lindbergh, and America's Fight over World War II, 1939–1941* (New York: Random House, 2013), 266.

75. David M. Kennedy, *Freedom from Fear: The American People in Depression and War, 1929-1945* (New York: Oxford University Press, 1999), 463.

76. "Fireside chat, 12/29/40, 5th draft," box 57, file 1351, Master Speech Files, FDRL.

77. "Fireside Chat on National Security," December 29, 1940, FDR *PPA*, 1940, 634.

78. James MacGregor Burns, *Roosevelt: The Soldier of Freedom* (New York: Harcourt Brace Jovanovich, 1970), 45; "Fireside chat 12/29/40," box 57, file 1351, Master Speech Files, FDRL; "Fireside Chat on National Security," December 29, 1940, FDR *PPA*, 1940, 638.

79. "Fireside Chat on National Security," 635-636.

80. "Fireside Chat on National Security," 638-639.

81. "Fireside Chat on National Security," 638.

82. Stephen J. Heidt, "Presidential Rhetoric, Metaphor, and the Emergence of the Democracy Promotion Industry," *Southern Communication Journal* 78, no. 3 (2013): 236.

Chapter 7: Roosevelt's Rhetorical Victory, 1941: The Four Freedoms

1. Roger Daniels, *Franklin D. Roosevelt: The War Year, 1939-1944* (Urbana: University of Illinois Press, 2016), 158.

2. Jerome Seymour, Bruner, *Mandate from the People* (New York: Duell, Sloan & Pearce, 1944), 21; Lee Kennett, *G.I.: The American Soldier in World War II* (Norman: University of Oklahoma Press, 1997), 6.

3. Harvey J. Kaye, *The Fight for the Four Freedoms: What Made FDR and the Greatest Generation Truly Great* (New York: Simon & Schuster, 2014), 86.

4. Robert A. Divine, *The Reluctant Belligerent: American Entry into World War II* (New York: Wiley, 1979), 149-150.

5. "Address on Hemisphere Defense," October 12, 1940, in FDR, *Public Papers and Addresses of Franklin Delano Roosevelt*, compiled by Samuel I. Rosenman (New York: Macmillan, 1938-1950), 1940, 462-463 (hereafter cited as FDR *PPA*); "Fireside Chat on National Defense," May 26, 1940, FDR *PPA*, 1940, 240.

6. Liberal internationalists started to agree that war could be more than just a contest for material advantage between two greedy opponents, which had been the dominant liberal view through the late '30s. Eric Frederick Goldman, *Rendezvous with Destiny: A History of Modern American Reform* (New York: Vintage Books, 1956), 296.

7. Elizabeth Borgwardt, *A New Deal for the World: America's Vision for Human Rights* (Cambridge, MA: Harvard University Press, 2005), 14.

8. Susan Butler, *Roosevelt and Stalin: Portrait of a Partnership* (New York: Alfred A. Knopf, 2015), 8.

9. On aggressive neutrality, see Howard E. Wilson, Nelle E. Bowman, and Allen Y. King, *This America: Our Land, Our People, Our Faith, Our Promise* (New York: American Book, 1942), 196; Michael S. Bell, "The Worldview of Franklin D. Roosevelt: France, Germany, and United States Involvement in Europe" (PhD diss., University of Maryland, 2004), 330; Manfred Jonas, "Robert Shogan. *Hard Bargain: How FDR*

Twisted Churchill's Arm, Evaded the Law, and Changed the Role of the American Presidency," *American Historical Review* 101, no. 5 (1996): 1649.

10. "State of the Union Address," January 6, 1941, sixth draft (labeled "fifth draft"), box 58, file 1353, Master Speech Files, Franklin D. Roosevelt Presidential Library & Museum (hereafter cited as FDRL); "Annual Message to Congress," January 6, 1941, FDR *PPA*, 1940, 672.

11. "Annual Message to Congress," 669.

12. "Fireside Chat on National Defense," May 26, 1940, FDR *PPA*, 1940, 240.

13. "Address at University of Virginia," June 10, 1940, FDR *PPA*, 1940, 261; "Third Inaugural Address," January 20, 1941, FDR *PPA*, 1941, 6.

14. Luke Glanville, *Sovereignty and the Responsibility to Protect: A New History* (Chicago: University of Chicago Press, 2014), 133.

15. "State of Union 1/6/41, Peroration," box 58, file 1353, Master Speech Files, FDRL.

16. FDR, *FDR: His Personal Letters*, edited by Elliott Roosevelt, assisted by James N. Rosenau and Joseph P. Lash (New York: Duell, Sloan and & Pearce, 1947–1950), vol. 2, 546.

17. Eleanor articulated a similar dualism in her own writing, calling on Americans "to fight as a unified nation against the new philosophies arrayed in opposition to Democracy." Eleanor Roosevelt, *Courage in a Dangerous World: The Political Writings of Eleanor Roosevelt* (New York: Columbia University Press, 1999), 47.

18. *Uncensored* (New York: Keep America Out of War Congress, 1939–1941), November 25, 1939, 1.

19. Robert Dallek, *Franklin D. Roosevelt: A Political Life* (New York: Penguin Books, 2017), 284; Patrick J. Hearden, *Architects of Globalism: Building a New World Order during World War II* (Fayetteville: University of Arkansas Press, 2002), 35; Warren F. Kimball, *Forged in War: Roosevelt, Churchill, and the Second World War* (New York: W. Morrow, 1997), 201–202.

20. "Fireside Chat on National Defense," September 11, 1941, FDR *PPA*, 1941, 391.

21. "Annual Message to the Congress," January 6, 1941, FDR *PPA*, 1940, 672.

22. *Uncensored*, November 25, 1939, 1; "State of the Union Address," January 6, 1941, sixth draft (labeled "fifth draft"), box 58, file 1353, Master Speech Files, FDRL.

23. "Six Hundred and Fifty-Eighth Press Conference," June 5, 1940, FDR *PPA*, 1940, 285.

24. James J. Kimble, "Franklin D. Roosevelt, 1941 State of the Union Address ('The Four Freedoms') (6 January 1941)," *Voices of Democracy* 3 (2008): 73.

25. "State of the Union Address, 1/6/41, seventh draft," box 58, file 1353, Master Speech File, FDRL.

26. According to Sherwood, those in the administration were "only interested in seeing that that Goddam sonofabitch Hitler gets licked." Hopkins to Sherwood, March 1941, in James MacGregor Burns, *Roosevelt: The Soldier of Freedom* (New York: Harcourt Brace Jovanovich, 1970), 50; Kimball, *Forged in War*, 78

27. "Annual Message to the Congress," January 6, 1941, FDR *PPA*, 1940, 663.

28. "Annual Message to the Congress," 664, 665.

29. "Inaugural Address," January 20, 1941, box 58, file 1355, Master Speech Files, FDRL.

30. Wayne S. Cole, *Charles A. Lindbergh and the Battle Against American Intervention in World War II* (New York: Harcourt, Brace, Jovanovich, 1974), 131; Duffy, *Lindbergh vs. Roosevelt*, 87.

31. *Uncensored*, April 26, 1941, 4; February 21, 1941, 4; January 25, 1941, 3.

32. Susan Dunn, *A Blueprint for War: FDR and the Hundred Days that Mobilized America* (New Haven: Yale University Press, 2018), 135.

33. Doris Kearns Goodwin, *No Ordinary Time: Franklin and Eleanor Roosevelt: The Home Front in World War II* (New York: Simon & Schuster, 1994), 215.

34. "Proclamation No. 2487 (President Proclaims that an Unlimited National Emergency Confronts the Country)," May 27, 1941, FDR *PPA*, 1941, 195; "Navy and Total Defense Day Address," October 27, 1941, FDR *PPA*, 1941, 438.

35. "A Radio Address Announcing the Proclamation of an Unlimited National Emergency," May 27, 1941, FDR *PPA*, 1941, 181.

36. "A Radio Address Announcing the Proclamation of an Unlimited National Emergency," 190.

37. Kenneth S. Davis, *FDR, the War President, 1940–1943: A History* (New York: Random House, 2000), 173.

38. Richard W. Steele, *Propaganda in an Open Society: The Roosevelt Administration and the Media, 1933–1941* (Westport, CT: Greenwood, 1985), 116.

39. "A Radio Address Announcing the Proclamation of an Unlimited National Emergency," May 27, 1941, FDR *PPA*, 1941, 185, 186.

40. "A Radio Address Announcing the Proclamation of an Unlimited National Emergency," 183.

41. "A Radio Address Announcing the Proclamation of an Unlimited National Emergency," 184.

42. "A Radio Address Announcing the Proclamation of an Unlimited National Emergency," 186.

43. "A Platform," (handwritten document), "Acceptance Speech," July 19, 1940, box 52, file 1291, Master Speech Files, FDRL.

44. Burns, *Soldier of Freedom*, 100.

45. *Uncensored*, May 31, 1941, 1.

46. For more on the "terminological uncertainty" of political states of exception, see Giorgio Agamben, *State of Exception*, translated by Kevin Attell (Chicago: University of Chicago Press, 2005), 4.

47. Goodwin, *No Ordinary Time*, 240; Burns, *Soldier of Freedom*, 101.

48. In fact, in a radio broadcast delivered on the eve of the 1938 midterm elections, FDR stated that support for "Tory Republicanism" would aid the forces of "Fascism and Communism . . . in our land." Harvey J. Kaye, *Fight for the Four Freedoms: What Made FDR and the Greatest Generation Truly Great* (New York: Simon & Schuster, 2014), 70.

49. Albert L. Weeks, *Russia's Life-Saver: Lend-Lease Aid to the U.S.S.R. in World War II* (Lanham, MD: Lexington Books, 2004), 3; Butler, *Roosevelt and Stalin*, 19.

50. Warren F. Kimball, *The Juggler: Franklin Roosevelt as Wartime Statesman* (Princeton, NJ: Princeton University Press, 1994), 35, 38.

51. Divine, *The Reluctant Belligerent*, 91.

52. Oliver Stone and Peter Kuznick, *The Untold History of the United States* (New York: Gallery Books, 2012).

53. Gallup poll, July 13, 1941, cited in David Reynolds, *From Munich to Pearl Harbor: Roosevelt's America and the Origins of the Second World War* (Chicago: Ivan R. Dee, 2001), 136; Raymond H. Dawson, *The Decision to Aid Russia, 1941; Foreign Policy and Domestic Politics* (Chapel Hill: University of North Carolina Press, 1959), 101.

54. FDR to William D. Leahy, June 26, 1941, in FDR, *FDR: His Personal Letters*, 4:1177; Gary Kern, "How 'Uncle Joe' Bugged FDR," *Center for Study of Intelligence* 47, no. 1 (2003): 19.

55. "Press Conference," September 30, 1941, FDR *PPA*, 1941, 401–402.

56. Saleh, "The Just Oppressors: Middle Eastern Victimhood Narratives and New Imagined Communities," Al Jumhuriya, June 9, 2015, https://www.aljumhuriya.net/en/content/just-oppressors-middle-eastern-victimhood-narratives-and-new-imagined-communities.

57. "Fourth of July Address," July 4, 1941, p. 1, box 61, file 1373, Master Speech Files, FDRL.

58. "Message to Congress re Extension of Selective Service Act," July 21, 1941, p. 4, box 61, file 1375, Master Speech Files, FDRL; FDR, "Excerpts from the Press Conference," August 19, 1941, American Presidency Project, accessed February 18, 2023, https://www.presidency.ucsb.edu/documents/excerpts-from-the-press-conference-49.

59. Reynolds, *From Munich to Pearl Harbor*, 136.

60. Mary E. Stuckey, *The Good Neighbor: Franklin D. Roosevelt and the Rhetoric of American Power* (East Lansing: Michigan State University Press, 2013), 50.

61. Tai-chun Kuo and Hsiao-tin Lin, *T.V. Soong in Modern Chinese History: A Look at His Role in Sino-American Relations in World War II* (Stanford, CA: Hoover Institution Press, 2006), 8, https://www.hoover.org/sites/default/files/uploads/documents/tv-soong-in-modern-chinese-history.pdf.

62. "White House Correspondents Dinner Address," March 15, 1941, p. 18–19, box 59, file 1361-A, Master Speech Files, FDRL.

63. William G. Grieve, *The American Military Mission to China, 1941–1942: Lend-Lease Logistics, Politics and the Tangles of Wartime Cooperation* (Jefferson, NC: McFarland, 2014), 9; Jonathan D. Spence, *The Search for Modern China* (New York: W. W. Norton, 1990), 4.

64. FDR, "Report to Congress on the Operations of the Lend-Lease Act," June 10, 1941, American Presidency Project, accessed February 18, 2023, https://www.presidency.ucsb.edu/documents/report-congress-the-operations-the-lend-lease-act.

65. FDR to Churchill, July 14, 1941, Foreign Relations of the United States, Department of State (Washington, DC: US Government Printing Office), 1941, vol. 1, 342 (hereafter cited as FRUS); Dallek, *Franklin D. Roosevelt*, 282; Kimball, *Forged in War*, 99.

66. FDR explicitly disavowed that the charter would apply to the Soviets. FDR, "Press Conference on the U.S.S. Potomac," August 16, 1941, American Presidency Project, accessed February 18, 2023, https://www.presidency.ucsb.edu/documents/press-conference-the-uss-potomac.

67. "Message to Congress on Atlantic Charter," box 61, file 1377, Master Speech Files, FDRL.

68. "Official Statement on Meeting between the President and Prime Minister Churchill," August 14, 1941, FDR *PPA*, 1941, 315.

69. David Kaiser, *No End Save Victory: How FDR Led the Nation into War* (New York: Basic Books, 2014), 273.

70. Reynolds, *From Munich to Pearl Harbor*, 147.

71. Kimball, *Forged in War*, 101, 102.

72. Frank Costigliola, *Roosevelt's Lost Alliances: How Personal Politics Helped Start the Cold War* (Princeton, NJ: Princeton University Press, 2013), 131.

73. Glanville, *Sovereignty and the Responsibility to Protect*, 134.

74. Goldman, *Rendezvous with Destiny*, 301; Blum, *V Was for Victory*, 274.

75. Wayne S. Cole, *Roosevelt and the Isolationists, 1932–45* (Lincoln: University of Nebraska Press, 1983), 495; America First Committee, "Did You Know," no. 21 A & B, September 2, 1941, in Justus D. Doenecke, ed., *In Danger Undaunted: The Anti-interventionist Movement of 1940–1941 as Revealed in the Papers of the America First Committee* (Stanford, CA: Hoover Institution Press, 1990), 342, 331.

76. *Uncensored*, August 16, 1941, 1; November 1, 1941, 2; November 8, 1941, 1.

77. Sumner Welles, "Memorandum of Conversation," August 11, 1941, FRUS 1941, 1:363, 365, 366; see Dallek, *Franklin D. Roosevelt*, 284; Hearden, *Architects of Globalism*, 35.

78. James W. Ceaser et al., "The Rise of the Rhetorical Presidency," *Presidential Studies Quarterly* 11, no. 2 (1981): 164.

79. Kaiser, *No End Save Victory*, 274.

80. "Seven Hundred and Sixty-First Press Conference," September 16, 1941, FDR *PPA*, 1941, 320.

81. Burns, *Soldier of Freedom*, 132.

82. Mary E. Stuckey, "Jimmy Carter, Human Rights, and Instrumental Effects of Presidential Rhetoric," in *The Handbook of Rhetoric and Public Address*, edited by Shawn J. Parry-Giles and J. Michael Hogan (Oxford: Wiley-Blackwell, 2010), 297.

83. "Seven Hundred and Sixty-Second Press Conference," September 19, 1941, FDR *PPA*, 1941, 329–330.

84. Minersville School District v. Board of Education, 310 U.S. 586 (June 3, 1940), http://supreme.justia.com/us/310/586/case.html.

85. Michael S. Sherry, *In the Shadow of War: The United States since the 1930s* (New Haven, CT: Yale University Press, 1995), 51, quoting Walter Millis, *Arms and Men: A Study in American Military History* (New York: Putnam, 1956), 268.

86. Mary E. Stuckey, "The Great Debate: The United States and the World, 1936–1941," in *World War II and the Cold War: The Rhetoric of Hearts and Minds: A Rhetorical History of the United States*, vol. 8, edited by Martin J. Medhurst (East Lansing: Michigan State University Press, 2018), 5.

87. Geoffrey Perrett, *Days of Sadness, Years of Triumph: The American People, 1939–1945* (New York: Coward, McCann & Geoghegan, 1973), 191.

88. Roger Daniels, *Franklin D. Roosevelt: The War Years, 1939–1940* (Urbana: University of Illinois Press, 2016), 193.

89. "Fireside Chat to the Nation," September 11, 1941, FDR *PPA*, 1941, 389, 392.

90. *Uncensored*, September 6, 1941, 2.

91. FDR, "Excerpts from the Press Conference," November 28, 1941, American Presidency Project, accessed February 18, 2023, https://www.presidency.ucsb.edu /documents/excerpts-from-the-press-conference-72.

92. Hadley Cantril, *New York Times Magazine*, "Shooting War," SM21, November 16, 1941; Olson, *Those Angry Days*, 395.

93. *Uncensored*, October 18, 1941, 1.

94. *Uncensored*, August 17, 1940, 1.

95. Carol J. Jablonski, "Resisting the 'Inevitability' of War: The Catholic Worker Movement and World War II," in *American Rhetoric in the New Deal Era, 1932–1945: A Rhetorical History of the United States*, vol. 7, edited by Thomas W. Benson (East Lansing: Michigan State University Press, 2006), 443.

96. H. W. Brands, *Traitor to His Class: The Privileged Life and Radical Presidency of Franklin Delano Roosevelt* (New York: Random House, 2008), 617.

97. FDR to Morgenthau, May 17, 1941, in Dallek, *Franklin D. Roosevelt*, 265; Stimson diary, May 23, 1941, quoted in Cole, *Roosevelt and the Isolationists*, 428; Burns, *Soldier of Freedom*, 91.

98. Dallek, *Franklin D. Roosevelt*, 285; Jean Edward Smith, *FDR* (New York: Random House, 2007), 527.

99. Sherry, *In the Shadow of War*, 63. James MacGregor Burns agreed: "Observers sensed a good deal of apathy among the public, or at least a feeling of fatalism": Burns, *Soldier of Freedom*, 142.

100. Perrett, *Days of Sadness*, 198, 191; Sherry, *In the Shadow of War*, 57, 63.

101. Peter Brown, "Strong and Wrong vs. Weak and Right," RealClearPolitics, January 15, 2007, https://www.realclearpolitics.com/articles/2007/01/strong_ and_wrong_vs_weak_and_r.html.

102. Sherry, *In the Shadow of War*, 60.

103. Robert B. Westbrook, *Why We Fought: Forging American Obligations in World War II* (Washington, DC: Smithsonian Books, 2004), 48.

104. Westbrook, *Why We Fought*, 46; Norman Rockwell and Thomas Rockwell, *Norman Rockwell, My Adventures as an Illustrator* (New York: Abrams, 1994), 338.

105. See Eric Foner, *The Story of American Freedom* (New York: W. W. Norton, 1988), 225–227, and the sources cited there.

Chapter 8: Administration and Public War Aims

1. Doris Kearns Goodwin, *No Ordinary Time: Franklin and Eleanor Roosevelt: The Home Front in World War II* (New York: Simon & Schuster, 1994), 290.

2. "Address to the Congress Asking that a State of War Be Declared between the United States and Japan," December 8, 1941, in FDR, *Public Papers and Addresses of Franklin Delano Roosevelt*, compiled by Samuel I. Rosenman (New York: Macmillan, 1938–1950), 1941, 515. (Hereafter cited as FDR *PPA*.)

3. "Fireside Chat to the Nation Following the Declaration of War with Japan," December 9, 1941, FDR *PPA*, 1941, 528.

4. "Fireside Chat to the Nation Following the Declaration of War with Japan," 522.

5. John Lewis Gaddis, *Strategies of Containment: A Critical Appraisal of American National Security Policy during the Cold War* (New York: Oxford University Press, 1982), 5.

6. Henry R. Luce, "The American Century," *Life*, February 17, 1941, 60.

7. John Morton Blum, *V Was for Victory: Politics and American Culture during World War II* (New York: Harcourt Brace Jovanovich, 1976), 45.

8. Thomas Sanders, *The Last Good War: The Faces and Voices of World War II* (New York: Welcome Books, 2010).

9. Micheala Höenicke Moore, *Know Your Enemy: The American Debate on Nazism, 1933-1945* (Cambridge and New York: Cambridge University Press, 2010), 107.

10. Nigel Hamilton, *The Mantle of Command: FDR at War 1941-1942* (New York: Houghton Mifflin Harcourt, 2014), 358.

11. David Reynolds, *From Munich to Pearl Harbor: Roosevelt's America and the Origins of the Second World War* (Chicago: Ivan R. Dee, 2001), 109.

12. C. A. MacDonald, *The United States, Britain, and Appeasement, 1936-1939* (New York: St. Martin's Press, 1981), 177.

13. For detailed studies of this process see Patrick J. Hearden, *Architects of Globalism: Building a New World Order during World War II* (Fayetteville: University of Arkansas Press, 2002); Carlo Maria Santoro, *Diffidence and Ambition: The Intellectual Sources of U.S. Foreign Policy* (Boulder, CO: Westview Press, 1992); Christopher D. O'Sullivan, *Sumner Welles, Postwar Planning, and the Quest for a New World Order, 1937-1943* (New York: Columbia University Press, 2008).

14. Warren F. Kimball, *Forged in War: Roosevelt, Churchill, and the Second World War* (New York: W. Morrow, 1997), 201.

15. Kimball, *Forged in War*, 243.

16. Robert E. Sherwood, *Roosevelt and Hopkins: An Intimate History* (New York: Harper, 1950), 870.

17. "Speech to Congress," November 18, 1943, cited in Hearden, *Architects of Globalism*, 164.

18. FDR to Joseph W. Alsop Jr., November 11, 1942, in FDR, *FDR: His Personal Letters*, edited by Elliott Roosevelt, assisted by James N. Rosenau and Joseph P. Lash (New York: Duell, Sloan and & Pearce, 1947-1950), vol. 4, 1361.

19. FDR to Robert E. Hannegan, July 11, 1944, in FDR, *Franklin D. Roosevelt's Own Story: Told in His Own Words from His Private and Public Papers*, selected by Donald Day (Boston: Little, Brown, 1951), 418.

20. Robert Dallek, *Franklin D. Roosevelt: A Political Life* (New York: Penguin Books, 2017), 441.

21. Barry Dean Karl, *The Uneasy State: The United States From 1915 to 1945* (Chicago: University of Chicago Press, 1983), 208; Höenicke Moore, *Know Your Enemy*, 105-106.

22. Luce, "The American Century," 62, 64, 65.

23. Stimson biographer Elting Morison quoted in Blum, *V Was for Victory*, 120.

24. Robert A. Divine, *Second Chance: The Triumph of Internationalism in America during World War II* (New York: Atheneum, 1967), 126; Blum, *V Was for Victory*, 302;

Warren F. Kimball, *The Juggler: Franklin Roosevelt as Wartime Statesman* (Princeton, NJ: Princeton University Press, 1994), 200.

25. Brian A. W. Simpson, *Human Rights and the End of Empire: Britain and the Genesis of the European Convention* (Oxford: Oxford University Press, 2001), 183.

26. Luke Glanville, *Sovereignty and the Responsibility to Protect: A New History* (Chicago: University of Chicago Press, 2014), 134.

27. Divine, *Second Chance*, 182.

28. "The Covenant of the League of Nations," December 1924, Avalon Project, accessed February 19, 2023, https://avalon.law.yale.edu/20th_century/leagcov.asp.

29. Martin Sherwin, *A World Destroyed: The Atomic Bomb and the Grand Alliance* (New York: Knopf, 1975), 827.

30. Hearden, *Architects of Globalism*, 166.

31. "Memorandum of Luncheon with Grace Tully and Samuel Rosenman," November 13, 1942, in FDR, *FDR: His Personal Letters*, 4:1366.

32. See Michael S. Sherry, *The Rise of American Air Power: The Creation of Armageddon* (New Haven, CT: University of Yale Press, 1987); Tami Davis Biddle, *Rhetoric and Reality in Air Warfare: The Evolution of British and American Ideas About Strategic Bombing, 1914-1945* (Princeton, NJ: Princeton University Press, 2002), 274-287.

33. Biddle, *Rhetoric and Reality in Air Warfare*, 220.

34. Biddle, 279.

35. Sherwin, *A World Destroyed*, 91,114.

36. "Memorandum for the Secretary of State," September 29, 1944, box 32, "Diplomatic Correspondence Germany: Oct. 1944-45," President's Secretary's File, Franklin D. Roosevelt Presidential Library & Museum (hereafter cited as FDRL). A few months later, in another memo to Stettinius, he wrote cryptically: "In the economic treatment of Germany we should let her come back industrially to meet her own needs, but not to do any exporting for sometime and [read: until] we know better how things are going to work out." Roosevelt to Stettinius, December 4, 1944, box 32, "Diplomatic Correspondence Germany: Oct. 1944-45," President's Secretary's File, FDRL.

37. FDR to Hull, September 29, 1944, in Sherwin, *A World Destroyed*, 285.

38. Kimball, *Forged in War*, 268.

39. "President Urges Immediate Adoption of the Bretton Woods Agreements," February 12, 1945, FDR *PPA*, 1945, 554.

40. Elizabeth Borgwardt, *A New Deal for the World: America's Vision for Human Rights* (Cambridge, MA: Harvard University Press, 2005), 89.

41. Santoro, *Diffidence and Ambition*, 56, 92-94, 186.

42. See Kimball *Forged in War*, 252.

43. Geographer Neil Smith argues that the presumed link between the threat of war and the threat of depression was the driving force behind the UNO plan and emerged from "intense self-interest" on the part of the United States: "The intent was nothing less than the unhitching of specific geographical claims and territorial struggles from the central dynamics of the global economic intercourse. The UN would mediate geographically rooted struggles, conflict, and skirmishes while global commerce proceeded apace." Because, in Smith's analysis, hard borders

that restricted trade appeared to be an impediment to global peace and prosperity, American planners pursued "a self-interested drive to open new markets" to affect an "escape from geography." In his view, the Roosevelt administration pursued free trade to expand American economic largesse—and therefore political leverage—as a method of expanding US power without the inconvenience of maintaining a colonial footprint on the model of the British Empire. Neil Smith, *American Empire: Roosevelt's Geographer and the Prelude to Globalization* (Berkeley: University of California Press, 2003), 377, 373.

44. Smith, *American Empire*, 362.

45. Smith, 357.

46. Gaddis Smith, *American Diplomacy during the Second World War, 1941–1945*, edited by Robert A. Divine (New York: John Wiley & Sons, 1965), 92, 79.

47. Hearden, *Architects of Globalism*, 227.

48. Dallek, *Franklin D. Roosevelt*, 460.

49. FDR to Hull, January 7, 1944, in Hearden, *Architects of Globalism*, 203, 205.

50. FDR to Churchill, July 30, 1943, in Hearden, 79, 313; Dallek, *Franklin D. Roosevelt*, 413.

51. James MacGregor Burns, *Roosevelt: The Soldier of Freedom* (New York: Harcourt Brace Jovanovich, 1970), 384.

52. Sherwood, *Roosevelt and Hopkins*, 714.

53. Dallek, *Franklin D. Roosevelt*, 389.

54. Paul Gordon Lauren, *The Evolution of International Human Rights: Visions Seen*, 3rd ed. (Philadelphia: University of Pennsylvania Press, 2011), 166.

55. Melvyn P. Leffler, *A Preponderance of Power: National Security, the Truman Administration, and the Cold War* (Stanford, CA: Stanford University Press, 1992), 21–22; Lloyd C. Gardner, *Architects of Illusion: Men and Ideas in American Foreign Policy 1941–1949* (Chicago: Quadrangle Books, 1970), ix; Gaddis, *Strategies of Containment*, 4.

56. Thomas J. McCormick, *America's Half-Century: United States Foreign Policy in the Cold War and After* (Baltimore, MD: Johns Hopkins University Press, 1995), 36.

57. "FDR to Secretary of State," September 29, 1944, box 32, "Diplomatic Correspondence Germany: Oct. 1944-45," President's Secretary's File, FDRL.

58. FDR to Cardinal Spellman, September 3, 1943, in Frank Burt Freidel, *Franklin D. Roosevelt: A Rendezvous with Destiny* (Boston: Little, Brown, 1990), 479.

59. Gary Kern, "How 'Uncle Joe' Bugged FDR," *Center for Study of Intelligence* 47, no. 1 (2003): 31.

60. Kimball, *Forged in War*, 335.

61. Dallek, *Franklin D. Roosevelt*, 527, 520, 617.

62. Divine, *Second Chance*, 259.

63. Divine, 217.

64. Divine, 43.

65. FDR to Stimson, August 26, 1944, in Dallek, *Franklin D. Roosevelt*, 473.

66. Divine, *Second Chance*, 120.

67. Divine, 99–103.

68. Divine, 92, 127.

69. Divine, 33.

70. Brinkley, "World War II and American Liberalism," in *The War in American*

Culture: Society and Consciousness during World War II, edited by Lewis A. Erenberg and Susan E. Hirsch (Chicago: University of Chicago Press, 1996), 320–323.

71. FDR to Felix Frankfurter, December 23, 1943, in FDR, *Roosevelt and Frankfurter: Their Correspondence, 1928–1945*, annotated by Max Freedman (Boston: Little, Brown, 1967), 709

72. Frances Perkins, *The Roosevelt I Knew* (New York: Viking Press, 1946), 148.

73. Alan Jacobs, *Year of Our Lord 1943: Christian Humanism in an Age of Crisis* (Oxford: Oxford University Press, 2018), 74.

74. Kimball, *The Juggler*, 196.

75. In the words of one European historian, the US government took an "almost obsessive interest in the future, in stark contrast with the behaviors of nearly every other country, [which] testifies to an American predisposition for organizing reality." Santoro, *Diffidence and Ambition*, 34.

76. Divine, *Second Chance*, 100.

77. Kimball, *Forged in War*, 252.

78. Hearden, *Architects of Globalism*, 313.

79. Freidel, *A Rendezvous with Destiny*, 466.

80. Borgwardt, *A New Deal for the World*, 280.

81. John Lewis Gaddis, "The Insecurities of Victory: The United States and the Perception of the Soviet Threat After World War II," in *The Truman Presidency*, edited by Michael J. Lacey (New York: Cambridge University Press, 1989), 242.

82. Höenicke Moore, *Know Your Enemy*, 110, 111.

83. David M. Kennedy, *Freedom from Fear: The American People in Depression and War, 1929–1945* (New York: Oxford University Press, 1999), 636.

84. Eric Larrabee, *Commander in Chief: Franklin Delano Roosevelt, His Lieutenants, and Their War* (New York: Harper & Row, 1987), 9.

85. Quoted from archival material in Carrie Lee, "Operation Torch at 75: FDR and the Domestic Politics of the North African Invasion," War on the Rocks, November 8, 2017, https://warontherocks.com/2017/11/16075/.

86. Quoted from archival material in Lee, "Operation Torch at 75."

87. Burns, *Soldier of Freedom*, 281; Blum, *V Was for Victory*, 232.

88. James Spiller, 'This Is War! Network Radio and World War II Propaganda in America," *Journal of Radio Studies* 11, no. 1 (2004): 59.

89. John Bodnar, *The "Good War" in American Memory* (Baltimore, MD: Johns Hopkins University Press, 2010), 14.

90. Höenicke Moore, *Know your Enemy*, 107; Dallek, *Franklin D. Roosevelt*, 358.

91. Quoted from archival material in Lee, "Operation Torch at 75."

92. "Rosenman to Roosevelt," December 31, 1943, box 133, "Executive Office of the President: Rosenman, Samuel: General," President's Secretary's File, FDRL.

93. Dallek, *Franklin D. Roosevelt*, 505–506.

94. Freidel, *A Rendezvous with Destiny*, 496.

95. Blum, *V Was for Victory*, 89.

96. Phillip Margulies, *America's Role in the World* (New York: Infobase Publishing, 2009), 40.

97. Bruner quoted in Robert Dallek, *The American Style: Cultural Politics and For-*

eign Affairs (New York: Oxford University Press, 1979), 134. See also Jerome Seymour Bruner, *Mandate from the People* (New York: Duell, Sloan & Pearce, 1944).

98. Blum, *V Was for Victory*, 255; Divine, *Second Chance*, 135; Dallek, *The American Style*, 126, 135.

99. Henry Ware Allen, "Letters to the Editor: Wants Freedom," *Washington Post*, April 7, 1943, 12.

100. Bilge Yesil, "'Who Said This Is a Man's War?': Propaganda, Advertising Discourse and the Representation of War Worker Women during the Second World War," *Media History* 10, no. 2 (2004): 107.

101. Emphasis in original. James J. Kimble, "Mrs. Jekyll Meets Mrs. Hyde: The War Advertising Council, Rhetorical Norms, and the Gendered Home Front in World War II," *Western Journal of Communication* 82, no. 1 (2018): 12; James J. Kimble, "Spectral Soldiers: Domestic Propaganda, Visual Culture, and Images of Death on the World War II Home Front," *Rhetoric & Public Affairs* 19, no. 4 (2016): 545.

102. Eric Sevareid, *Not So Wild a Dream* (New York: A. A. Knopf, 1946), 215; Blum, *V Was for Victory*, 102.

103. Michael C. C. Adams, *The Best War Ever: America and World War II* (Baltimore, MD: Johns Hopkins University Press, 1994), 130. See also Frank W. Fox, *Madison Avenue Goes to War: The Strange Military Career of American Advertising, 1941–45* (Provo, UT: Brigham Young University Press, 1975); Robert B. Westbrook, *Why We Fought: Forging American Obligations in World War II* (Washington, DC: Smithsonian Books, 2004), chapter 2; Geoffrey Perrett, *Days of Sadness, Years of Triumph: The American People, 1939–1945* (New York: Coward, McCann & Geoghegan, 1973), 390.

104. Adams, *The Best War Ever*, 51.

105. William H. Chafe, *The Unfinished Journey: America Since World War II* (New York: Oxford University Press, 1986), 5; Karl, *The Uneasy State*, 191.

106. Carlton K. Matson, "Letters to the Editor: Post-War Economic Planning," *Wall Street Journal*, May 10, 1943, 6.

107. James Bordley Jr., "Letters to the Editor: 'Our Country's War, Not the New Deal's,' This Writer Says," *Baltimore Sun*, August 14, 1942, 10.

108. Bodnar, *The "Good War" in American Memory*, 49.

109. Paul Fussell, *Wartime: Understanding and Behavior in the Second World War* (New York: Oxford University Press, 1989), 138.

110. Blum, *V Was for Victory*, 67.

111. Fussell, *Wartime*, 137.

112. Studs Terkel, *"The Good War": An Oral History of World War II* (New York: New Press, 1997), 5.

113. Terkel, *"The Good War,"* 27.

114. Stephen E. Ambrose, *Citizen Soldiers: The U.S. Army from the Normandy Beaches to the Bulge to the Surrender of Germany* (New York: Simon & Schuster, 1997), 473.

115. See Bodnar, *The "Good War" in American Memory*, 167–172.

116. Bodnar, 50.

117. Blum, *V Was for Victory*, 66; Adams, *The Best War Ever*, 88; Fussell, *Wartime*, 165.

118. Blum, 68; Fussell, 141.

119. Blum, 68, 64; Fussell, 140. On the overriding importance of the soldier's "buddies," see J. Glenn Gray, *The Warriors: Reflections on Men in Battle* (New York: Harper & Row, 1967), 39-51.

120. Bodnar, *The "Good War" in American Memory*, 14.

121. L. D. W., "Letters to the Editor: Citadel of Virtue," *Washington Post*, August 24, 1943, 8.

122. T. Carter Dodd, "Letters to the Editor: The Pitfalls of Lend-Lease," *Wall Street Journal*, August 16, 1943, 8.

123. Bodnar, *The "Good War" in American Memory*, 14.

124. Westbrook, *Why We Fought*, 32, 31.

125. Adams, *The Best War Ever*, 70; Westbrook, *Why We Fought*, 74

126. Burns, *Soldier of Freedom*, 470.

127. "Letters to the Editor: Wife at Home Writes of Duty to Husband," *Boston Globe*, December 19, 1943, B44.

128. Mrs. Elton Chapman, "The Pulse of the Public: Burton," *Atlanta Constitution*, March 19, 1944, 10C.

129. Freidel, *A Rendezvous with Destiny*, 494.

130. Blum, *V Was for Victory*, 104.

131. Alan M. Winkler, "The World War II Home Front," *History Now*, December 2007, http://www.historynow.org/12_2007/historian3.html.

132. Blum, *V Was for Victory*, 70.

133. "A New Way to Make Peace," *Baltimore Sun*, November 1, 1943, TW4.

134. Perrett, *Days of Sadness*, 418.

135. Noah A. Hillman, "Letters to the Editor: Opposing the Proposal to Give the Governor 'War Powers,'" *Baltimore Sun*, January 7, 1943, 10.

136. Fussell, *Wartime*, 181.

137. See Paul Fussell, *Thank God for the Atom Bomb and Other Essays* (New York: Summit Books, 1988), 53-81.

138. Bodnar, *The "Good War" in American Memory*, 34-35.

139. Höenicke Moore, *Know Your Enemy*, 139, 138.

140. "Summary of Public Opinion," November 12, 1941, box 157, "Public Opinion Polls: 1935-41," President's Secretary's File, FDRL. The name "Elmo Roper" is written by hand at the top of the document.

141. Sherwood, *Roosevelt and Hopkins*, 438.

142. Perrett, *Days of Sadness*, 339-340.

143. Perrett, 407; Blum, *V Was for Victory*, 89.

144. Blum, 99.

145. Kennedy, *Freedom from Fear*, 641.

146. Höenicke Moore, *Know Your Enemy*, 138.

147. Bodnar, *The "Good War" in American Memory*, 20.

148. Kenneth Rose, *Myth and the Greatest Generation: A Social History of Americans in World War II* (New York: Routledge, 2008), 251.

149. Adams, *The Best War Ever*, 132.

150. Adams, 115. Chapter 6 of Adams's book documents his summary statement in detail.

151. Dallek, *The American Style*, 134; Perrett, *Days of Sadness*, 425.

152. "Letter to the Editor: Army Officer's Decision," *Boston Globe*, November 7, 1944, 10.

153. Blum, *V Was for Victory*, 258.

154. Leroy G. Dorsey, *Theodore Roosevelt, Conservation, and the 1908 Governors' Conference* (College Station: Texas A&M University Press, 2015), 17.

Chapter 9: Roosevelt's Winning Synthesis

1. John Bodnar, *The "Good War" in American Memory* (Baltimore, MD: Johns Hopkins University Press, 2010), 13; John B. Hench, *Books as Weapons: Propaganda, Publishing, and the Battle for Global Markets in the Era of World War II* (Ithaca, NY: Cornell University Press, 2010), 1–5.

2. Doris Graber, *Verbal Behavior and Politics* (Champaign: University of Illinois Press, 1976), 289–293; Catherine H. Palczewski et al., *Rhetoric in Civic Life*, 2nd ed. (State College, PA: Strata, 2012), 48.

3. Robert Dallek, *Franklin D. Roosevelt: A Political Life* (New York: Penguin Books, 2017), 378.

4. James M. Scott, "The Doolittle Raid Generated More Ripples than Once Thought," *Military Times*, April 18, 2018, https://www.milita.rytimes.com/off-duty/military-culture/2018/04/18/the-doolittle-raid-generated-more-ripples-than-once-thought/.

5. Eric Larrabee, *Commander in Chief: Franklin Delano Roosevelt, His Lieutenants, and Their War* (New York: Harper & Row, 1987), 9.

6. Richard Lanham, *The Economics of Attention: Style and Substance in the Age of Information* (Chicago: University of Chicago Press, 2006), xii.

7. "Speech to Congress 12/9/41, fourth draft," box 63, file 1401, Master Speech File, Franklin D. Roosevelt Presidential Library & Museum. (Hereafter cited FDRL.)

8. "Fireside Chat to the Nation following the Declaration of War with Japan," December 12, 1941, in FDR, *Public Papers and Addresses of Franklin Delano Roosevelt*, compiled by Samuel I. Rosenman (New York: Macmillan, 1938–1950), 1941, 522, 526, 527. (Hereafter cited as FDR *PPA*.)

9. John Morton Blum, *V Was for Victory: Politics and American Culture during World War II* (New York: Harcourt Brace Jovanovich, 1976), 8.

10. Bodnar, *The "Good War" in American Memory*, 14, 18; William L. Bird and Harry Rubenstein, *Design for Victory: World War II Poster on the American Home Front* (New York: Princeton Architectural Press, 1998), 83–84.

11. Geoffrey Perrett, *Days of Sadness, Years of Triumph: The American People, 1939–1945* (New York: Coward, McCann & Geoghegan, 1973), 226.

12. See many examples in Russell D. Buhite and David W. Levy, eds., *FDR's Fireside Chats* (Norman, OK: University of Oklahoma Press, 1992), 209, 215, 219, 231, 238, 263, 292, 293.

13. "Remarks Dictated by the President to be Used in Radio Address," July 11, 1943, box 73, file 1475, Master Speech File, FDRL.

14. "Nine Hundred and Eleventh Press Conference," July 27, 1943, FDR *PPA*, 1943, 324.

15. "Fireside Chat on Progress of the War," February 23, 1942, FDR *PPA*, 1942, 105.

16. Warren F. Kimball, *Forged in War: Roosevelt, Churchill, and the Second World War* (New York: W. Morrow, 1997), 123.

17. Samuel I. Rosenman, *Working with Roosevelt* (New York: Da Capo Press, 1972), 330.

18. Alan K. Hendrikson, "FDR and the 'World-Wide Arena,'" in *FDR's World: War, Peace, and Legacies,* edited by David B. Woolner, Warren F. Kimball, and David Reynolds (New York: Palgrave Macmillan, 2008), 46.

19. "Address to the Congress on the State of the Union," January 7, 1943, FDR *PPA*, 1943, 32.

20. Michael Dobbs, *Six Months in 1945: FDR, Stalin, Churchill, and Truman from World War to Cold War* (New York: Vintage Books, 2012), 6.

21. "Address to the Congress on the State of the Union," 33.

22. "Address to the Congress on the State of the Union," 33.

23. Graber, *Verbal Behavior and Politics,* 289, 290–291.

24. Davis S. Kaufer and Kathleen M. Carley, "Condensation Symbols: Their Variety and Rhetorical Function in Political Discourse," *Philosophy and Rhetoric* 26, no. 3 (1993): 214.

25. Michael Leigh, *Mobilizing Consent: Public Opinion and American Foreign Policy, 1937–1947* (Westport, CT: Greenwood Press, 1976), 111–113; Dallek, *Franklin D. Roosevelt,* 537, 439.

26. Patrick J. Hearden, *Architects of Globalism: Building a New World Order during World War II* (Fayetteville: University of Arkansas Press, 2002), 186. See also Robert A. Divine, *Second Chance: The Triumph of Internationalism in America during World War II* (New York: Atheneum, 1967), 241.

27. "Public Opinion Polls: 1935–1941," November 12, 1941, box 157, President's Secretary's File, FDRL.

28. Divine, *Second Chance,* 137.

29. "Nine Hundred and Fifty-second Press Conference," May 30, 1944, FDR *PPA*, 1944–1945, 141.

30. "Radio Address at Dinner of Foreign Policy Association," October 21, 1944, FDR *PPA*, 1944–1945, 350.

31. Richard Little, *The Balance of Power in International Relations: Metaphors, Myths, and Models* (Cambridge: Cambridge University, 2007), 27.

32. Leigh, *Mobilizing Consent,* 129, 112.

33. Leigh, 121.

34. "Speech to Foreign Policy Association," October 21, 1944, in Robert E. Sherwood, *Roosevelt and Hopkins: An Intimate History* (New York: Harper, 1950), 826.

35. "Address to the White House Correspondents' Association," February 12, 1943, FDR *PPA*, 1943, 74.

36. Willkie, *One World* (New York: Simon & Schuster, 1943); Robert Dallek, *The American Style of Foreign Policy: Cultural Politics and Foreign Affairs* (New York: Oxford University Press, 1979), 138.

37. Dallek, *The American Style,* 134.

38. Perrett, *Days of Sadness,* 418.

39. Elizabeth Borgwardt, *A New Deal for the World: America's Vision for Human Rights* (Cambridge, MA: Harvard University Press, 2005), 81.

40. Divine, *Second Chance*, 83.

41. Leigh, *Mobilizing Consent*, 111–113

42. Perrett, *Days of Sadness*, 284.

43. Neil Smith, *American Empire: Roosevelt's Geographer and the Prelude to Globalization* (Berkeley: University of California Press, 2003), 405, 373.

44. "Day of Infamy Speech," box 63, file 1400, "Day of Infamy Speech," Master Speech File, FDRL.

45. "Fireside Chat to the Nation following the Declaration of War with Japan," December 9, 1941, FDR *PPA*, 1941, 528.

46. "Address to the Congress on the State of the Union," January 6, 1942, FDR *PPA*, 1942, 41, 42.

47. Michaela Höenicke Moore, *Know Your Enemy: The American Debate on Nazism, 1933–1945* (Cambridge and New York: Cambridge University Press, 2010), 117.

48. "Nine Hundred and Sixty-second Press Conference," July 29, 1944, FDR *PPA*, 1944–1945, 212. See John W. Dower, *War without Mercy: Race and Power in the Pacific War* (New York: Pantheon Books, 1986).

49. Edward T. Linenthal, *Changing Images of the Warrior Hero in America: A History of Popular Symbolism* (New York: Edwin Mellen Press, 1982), 113–136, is a good overview of World War II discourse by a historian of religions. Linenthal shows how religious imagery was interwoven with more prosaic images of war and warriors. See also David Zietsma, "Imagining Heaven and Hell: Religion, National Identity, and U.S. Foreign Relations, 1930–1953" (PhD diss., University of Akron, 2007).

50. Gaddis Smith, *American Diplomacy during the Second World War, 1941–1945*, edited by Robert A. Divine (New York: John Wiley & Sons, 1965), 54–57; Barry Dean Karl, *The Uneasy State: The United States From 1915 to 1945* (Chicago: University of Chicago Press, 1983), 213; Warren F. Kimball, *The Juggler: Franklin Roosevelt as Wartime Statesman* (Princeton, NJ: Princeton University Press, 1994), 76.

51. See Russell F. Weigley, *The American Way of War: A History of United States Military Strategy and Policy* (Bloomington: University of Indiana Press, 1973).

52. Smith, *American Diplomacy during the Second World War*, 57, 6.

53. See Dallek, *The American Style*, 132–138.

54. Leigh, *Mobilizing Consent*, 132.

55. Perrett, *Days of Sadness*, 285, citing Jerome Seymour Bruner, *Mandate from the People* (New York: Duell, Sloan & Pearce, 1944), 34–43.

56. Blum, *V Was for Victory*, 323.

57. See Ernest Lee Tuveson, *Redeemer Nation: The Idea of America's Millennial Role* (Chicago: University of Chicago Press, 1968).

58. "Address to the Congress Reporting on the Yalta Conference," March 3, 1945, FDR *PPA*, 1944–1945, 586.

59. "Address to the Congress Reporting on the Yalta Conference," 585.

60. William Kristol, "Is Exceptionalism a Myth? Has it Always Been?" In *American Exceptionalism: The Origins, History, and Future of the Nation's Greatest Strength*, edited by Charles W. Dunn (New York: Rowman & Littlefield, 2013), 99.

61. Divine, *Second Chance*, 47.

62. "3rd draft," box 70, file 1447, "State of the Union, 1/7/43," Master Speech File, FDRL.

63. "Address to the Congress on the State of the Union," January 7, 1943, FDR *PPA*, 1943, 31.

64. David M. Kennedy, *Freedom from Fear: The American People in Depression and War, 1929-1945* (New York: Oxford University Press, 1999), 786.

65. Alan Brinkley, *The End of Reform: New Deal Liberalism in Recession and War* (New York: Alfred A. Knopf, 1995), 67-76; Kennedy, *Freedom from Fear*, 619.

66. Michael Lind, *Land of Promise: An Economic History of the United States* (New York: Harper Collins, 2012), 327.

67. FDR to Mackenzie King, December 29, 1942, in FDR, *FDR: His Personal Letters*, edited by Elliott Roosevelt, assisted by James N. Rosenau and Joseph P. Lash (New York: Duell, Sloan and & Pearce, 1947-1950), 3:1382.

68. FDR to Lilienthal, December 1942, in James MacGregor Burns, *Roosevelt: The Soldier of Freedom* (New York: Harcourt Brace Jovanovich, 1970), 302.

69. "Address to the Nation 7/28/43," box 73, file 1475, Master Speech File, FDRL.

70. "Address to the Congress on the State of the Union," January 7, 1943, FDR *PPA*, 1943, 31.

71. Smith, *American Empire*, 412.

72. "New Year's Day Statement on War and Peace," January 1, 1943, FDR *PPA*, 1943, 3.

73. "3rd draft," box 70, file 1447, "State of the Union, 1/7/43," Master Speech File, FDRL. These lines never made it into the final version.

74. Burns, *The Soldier of Freedom*, 306.

75. Wilson D. Miscamble, *From Roosevelt to Truman: Potsdam, Hiroshima, and the Cold War* (Cambridge: University of Cambridge Press, 2007), 85.

76. "Address to the Congress on the State of the Union," January 7, 1943, FDR *PPA*, 1943, 32.

77. FDR, "Statement on the Second Anniversary of the Atlantic Charter," August 14, 1943, American Presidency Project, accessed February 15, 2023, https://www.presidency.ucsb.edu/documents/statement-the-second-anniversary-the-atlantic-charter.

78. "Address-Signing Agreement Setting up the United Nations Relief and Rehabilitation Administration," November 9, 1943, p. 7, box 75, file 1492-A, Master Speech Files, FDRL.

79. "Excerpts from President's Press and Radio Conference for Release to the Press—'Dr. Win-the-War,' December 28, 1943, p. 6, box 76, file 1499, Master Speech Files, FDRL.

80. FDR, "Statement on the Dumbarton Oaks Conversations," December 9, 1944, American Presidency Project, accessed February 15, 2023, https://www.presidency.ucsb.edu/documents/statement-the-dumbarton-oaks-conversations.

81. FDR, "Message to Congress on the Bretton Woods Agreements," February 12, 1945, American Presidency Project, accessed February 15, 2023, https://www.presidency.ucsb.edu/documents/message-congress-the-bretton-woods-agreements.

82. "Message to the Congress on the State of the Union," January 11, 1944, FDR *PPA*, 1944-1945, 33. See Divine, *Second Chance*, 186.

83. "Message to the Congress on the State of the Union," 41.

84. Cass R. Sunstein, *The Second Bill of Rights: FDR's Unfinished Revolution—and Why We Need It More than Ever* (New York: Basic Books, 2004), 4.

85. Roosevelt, ever the political pragmatist, knew how little chance there was to get new liberal programs approved by Congress. Brinkley, *The End of Reform*, 144, 160.

86. Quoted in Julian E. Zelizer, *Arsenal of Democracy: The Politics of National Security—From World War II to the War on Terrorism* (New York: Basic Books, 2010), 57–58.

87. John Bush Jones, *All-Out for Victory Magazine Advertising and the World War II Home Front* (Waltham, MA: Brandeis University Press, 2009).

88. See David Morris Potter, *People of Plenty: Economic Abundance and the American Character* (Chicago: University of Chicago Press, 1958).

89. Miscamble, *From Roosevelt to Truman*, 85; Kimball, *The Juggler*, 200.

90. Leroy G. Dorsey, "The Frontier Myth and Presidential Rhetoric: Theodore Roosevelt's Campaign for Conservation," *Western Journal of Communication* 59, no. 4 (1995): 3–4.

91. William E. Leuchtenburg, *In the Shadow of FDR: From Harry Truman to Bill Clinton* (Ithaca, NY: Cornell University Press, 1983).

Conclusion: A Still Unfinished History

1. Bradford Vivian, *Public Forgetting: The Rhetoric and Politics of Beginning Again* (University Park: Pennsylvania State University Press, 2010), 79; Dave Siff, "New York Marks Anniversary of Tragedy," CNN, September 11, 2002. http://edition.cnn.com/2002/US/09/11/ar911.memorial.newyork/index.html.

2. Joe Biden, "Remarks and a Question-and-Answer Session at a CNN Presidential Town Hall in Baltimore, Maryland," October 21, 2021, American Presidency Project, accessed March 16, 2023, https://www.presidency.ucsb.edu/documents/remarks-and-question-and-answer-session-cnn-presidential-town-hall-baltimore-maryland; Joe Biden, "Press Release—What They Are Reading in Memphis: 'Our Nation's Infrastructure Is Crumbling. President Biden's Plan Will Repair Our Country,'" July 8, 2021, American Presidency Project, accessed February 11, 2023, https://www.presidency.ucsb.edu/documents/press-release-what-they-are-reading-memphis-our-nations-infrastructure-crumbling-president.

3. Sam Frizell, "Transcript: Read the Full Text of Hillary Clinton's Campaign Launch Speech," *Time*, June 13, 2015, https://time.com/3920332/transcript-full-text-hillary-clinton-campaign-launch/.

4. David French, "In Defense of the Iraq War," *National Review*, March 20, 2019, https://www.nationalreview.com/corner/iraq-war-just-cause-saddam-hussein-threat-stability/.

5. "Why Joe Biden's Instinctive Caution Makes Real Change Possible," *Economist*, July 4, 2020, https://www.economist.com/leaders/2020/07/02/why-joe-bidens-instinctive-caution-makes-real-change-possible; "Joe Biden's Good Pandemic," *Economist*, May 23, 2020, https://www.economist.com/united-states/2020/05/23/joe-bidens-good-pandemic.

324 | NOTES TO PAGES 251-261

6. Vivian, *Public Forgetting*, 77.

7. Winston Churchill, "Prime Minister Churchill's Eulogy in Commons for the Late President Roosevelt," April 17, 1945, ibiblio: The Public's Library and Digital Archive, http://www.ibiblio.org/pha/policy/1945/1945-04-17a.html; also printed in Winston Churchill, *The Great Republic: A History of America*, edited by Winston Spencer-Churchill (New York: Random House, 1999), 364–370.

8. Ole Rudolf Holsti, *Public Opinion and American Foreign Policy* (Ann Arbor: University of Michigan Press, 2004), 26–27.

9. Holsti, *Public Opinion and American Foreign Policy*, 27.

10. W. H. Auden, *The Age of Anxiety: A Baroque Eclogue*, edited by Alan Jacobs (Princeton, NJ: Princeton University Press, 2011); William Graebner, *Age of Doubt: American Thought and Culture in the 1940s* (Boston: Twayne Publishers, 1990).

11. John Bodnar, *The "Good War" in American Memory* (Baltimore, MD: Johns Hopkins University Press, 2010), 60.

12. Mark A. Stoler, "FDR and the Origins of the National Security Establishment," in *The World of the Roosevelts*, edited by David B. Woolner, Warren F. Kimball, and David Reynolds (New York: Palgrave Macmillan, 2008), 81.

13. While FDR generated many of the resources through which his successors would make sense of US foreign policy, it remained up to them to frame the global situation as a "Cold War." As Marty Medhurst writes, "Cold War is, itself, a rhetorical construction. . . . To clarify, I am not arguing that the Cold War was nothing but rhetoric; I am arguing that even in its most material manifestations—armaments, armies, air forces, agreements, et cetera—rhetorical dimensions were necessarily present." Martin J. Medhurst, "Introduction," in *Critical Reflections on the Cold War: Linking Rhetoric and History*, edited by Martin J. Medhurst and H. W. Brands (College Station: Texas A&M University Press, 2000), 6.

14. Medhurst, "Introduction," 3.

15. Thomas B. Farrell, *Norms of Rhetorical Culture* (New Haven, CT: Yale University Press, 1993), 92.

16. Paul A. Chilton, *Security Metaphors: Cold War Discourse from Containment to Common House* (New York: Peter Lang, 1996), 64–65.

17. Robert L. Ivie, *Democracy and America's War on Terror* (Tuscaloosa: University of Alabama Press, 2005), 10–15.

18. For a detailed discussion of this concept of myth applied to American political history and political life, see Ira Chernus, "Essays about America's National Myths in the Past, Present, and Future," Mythic America: Essays, accessed January 17, 2023, https://mythicamerica.wordpress.com/, especially "The Meaning of 'Myth' in the American Context."

19. Warren G. Harding, "Inaugural Address," March 4, 1921, American Presidency Project, accessed February 11, 2023, https://www.presidency.ucsb.edu/documents/inaugural-address-49.

20. Chilton, *Security Metaphors*, 153–154.

21. Chilton, 131.

22. Ivie, "Realism Masking Fear: George F. Kennan's Political Rhetoric," in *Post-Realism: The Rhetorical Turn in International Relations*, edited by Francis A. Beer and Robert Hariman (East Lansing: Michigan State University Press, 1996), 57.

23. Warren G. Harding, "First Annual Message," December 6, 1921, American Presidency Project, accessed February 11, 2023, https://www.presidency.ucsb.edu /documents/first-annual-message-19. See Leroy G. Dorsey, "Sailing into the 'Wondrous Now: The Myth of the American Navy's World Cruise," *Quarterly Journal of Speech* 83, no. 4 (1997): 447–465; and Leroy G. Dorsey, "Woodrow Wilson's Fight for the League of Nations: A Reexamination," *Rhetoric & Public Affairs* 2, no. 1 (1999): 107–135.

24. James J. Kimble, "Franklin D. Roosevelt, 1941 State of the Union Address ('The Four Freedoms') (6 January 1941)," *Voices of Democracy* 3 (2008): 77.

25. Ronald R. Krebs, *Narrative and the Making of US National Security* (Cambridge: Cambridge University Press, 2015), 55.

26. Michael J. Hogan, *A Cross of Iron: Harry S. Truman and the Origins of the National Security State* (Oxford: Oxford University Press, 1998), 2.

27. James T. Patterson, *Mr. Republican: A Biography of Robert A. Taft* (Boston: Houghton Mifflin, 1972), 474–496.

28. Jeff Shaara, *The Rising Tide: A Novel of World War II* (New York: Ballantine Books, 2006), xxxii.

29. Carlton Savage to NSC, February 10, 1953, Foreign Relations of the United States, Department of State, vol. 2.1 (Washington, DC: US Government Printing Office), 1952–1954, 232.

30. Dwight D. Eisenhower, "Radio Address to the American People," May 19, 1953, in Eisenhower, *Public Papers of the Presidents, Dwight D. Eisenhower, 1953*, pp. 307–314, Emmet John Hughes Diary, Emmet John Hughes Papers, box 1, Seeley G. Mudd Library, Princeton University.

31. John F. Kennedy, "Inaugural Address," January 20, 1961, John F. Kennedy Presidential Library and Museum, https://www.jfklibrary.org/archives/other-re sources/john-f-kennedy-speeches/inaugural-address-19610120.

32. Lyndon B. Johnson, "Address Before the General Assembly of the United Nations," December 17, 1963, American Presidency Project, accessed February 11, 2023, https://www.presidency.ucsb.edu/documents/address-before-the-general-as sembly-the-united-nations.

33. George F. Kennan, *American Diplomacy* (Chicago: University of Chicago Press, 1985), 9.

34. Campbell Craig and Fredrik Logevall, *America's Cold War: The Politics of Insecu rity* (Cambridge, MA: Belknap Press, 2009), 11.

35. John Lewis Gaddis, *Strategies of Containment: A Critical Appraisal of American National Security Policy during the Cold War* (New York: Oxford University Press, 1982), 145–151, 202–204, 212–214, 231–235, 282–292.

36. Maureen Dowd, "Who's Tough Enough?" *New York Times*, January 31, 2012.

37. Gary J. Dorrien, *Imperial Designs: Neoconservatism and the New Pax Americana* (New York: Routledge, 2004), 30, 38.

38. "The Vice President Appears on Meet the Press with Tim Russert," White House, September 16, 2001, https://georgewbush-whitehouse.archives.gov/vice president/news-speeches/speeches/vp20010916.html.

39. Ross Douthat, "Baylor ISR—Decadent Societies: A Conversation with Ross Douthat," YouTube, March 5, 2019, 1:06:15–1:06:45, 1:08:20–1:08:25, https:// www.youtube.com/watch?v=ztBCm8myoXw&t=3s.

40. Miranda Green, "Homeland Secretary: People Would 'Never Leave the House' If They Knew What I Knew," CNN, May 26, 2017, http://www.cnn.com/2017/05/26/politics/john-kelly-terror-threat-people-wouldnt-leave-the-house/index.html.

41. This line of analysis is especially well developed in David Campbell, *Writing Security: United States Foreign Policy and the Politics of Identity* (Minneapolis: University of Minnesota Press, 1998); and Ivie, *Democracy and America's War on Terror*.

42. Greg Jaffe, "Lessons in Disaster: A Top Clinton Advisor Searches for Meaning in a Shocking Loss," *Washington Post*, July 14, 2017.

43. Michael Brendan Dougherty, "In Defense of America First," *Week*, May 2, 2016, https://theweek.com/articles/621645/defense-america-first.

44. Jen Kirby, "Why Kirsten Gillibrand's Foreign Policy Plan Is One of the Strongest Yet," Vox, July 26, 2019, https://www.vox.com/2019/7/26/8930265/2020-democrats-kirsten-gillibrand-foreign-policy.

Bibliography

Abbott, Philip. *The Exemplary Presidency: Franklin D. Roosevelt and the American Political Tradition.* Amherst: University of Massachusetts Press, 1990.

Accinelli, Robert D. "The Roosevelt Administration and the World Court Defeat, 1935." *Historian* 40, no. 3 (1978): 463–478.

Acheson, Dean. *Morning and Noon.* Boston: Houghton Mifflin 1965.

Adams, Michael C. C. *The Best War Ever: America and World War II.* Baltimore, MD: Johns Hopkins University Press, 1994.

Agamben, Giorgio. *State of Exception.* Translated by Kevin Attell. Chicago: University of Chicago Press, 2005.

Aldous, Richard, and Heidi J. S. Tworek. "Germany's Quest to Control the News." American Interest, April 9, 2019. https://www.the-american-interest.com/pod cast/germanys-quest-to-control-the-news/.

Alexander, Charles C. *Nationalism in American Thought, 1930–1945.* Chicago: Rand McNally, 1969.

Allen, Henry Ware. "Letters to the Editor: Wants Freedom." *Washington Post,* April 7, 1943.

Alter, Jonathan. *The Defining Moment: FDR's Hundred Days and the Triumph of Hope.* New York: Simon & Schuster, 2007.

Ambrose, Stephen E. *Citizen Soldiers: The U.S. Army from the Normandy Beaches to the Bulge to the Surrender of Germany.* New York: Simon & Schuster, 1997.

Andrews, James R. "Presidential Leadership and National Identity: Woodrow Wilson and National Identity: Woodrow Wilson and the Meaning of America." In *The Presidency and Rhetorical Leadership,* edited by Leroy G. Dorsey. College Station: Texas A&M University Press, 2002.

"A New Way to Make Peace." *Baltimore Sun,* November 1, 1943.

Aoki, Keiko. "A Study of Franklin Delano Roosevelt's Persuasive Communication within the Fireside Chat: An Analysis of Language and Style." *Human Communication* 9, no. 1 (2006): 71–81.

Asad, Talal. *Formations of the Secular: Christianity, Islam, Modernity.* Stanford, CA: Stanford University Press, 2003.

Atkinson, Ann J. "The Rhetoric of Social Security and Conservative Backlash: Frances Perkins as Secretary of Labor." In *American Rhetoric in the New Deal Era, 1932–1945: A Rhetorical History of the United States,* vol. 7, edited by Thomas W. Benson, 211–244. East Lansing: Michigan State University Press, 2006.

Auden, W. H. *The Age of Anxiety: A Baroque Eclogue.* Edited by Alan Jacobs. Princeton, NJ: Princeton University Press, 2011.

Auten, Brian J. *Carter's Conversion: The Hardening of American Defense Policy.* Columbia: University of Missouri Press, 2008.

Babich, Babette E. *Reflecting Science on the Ground of Art and Life.* Albany: State University of New York Press, 1994.

Beasley, Vanessa B., and Deborah Smith-Howell. "No Ordinary Rhetorical President: FDR's Speechmaking and Leadership, 1933–1945." In *American Rhetoric in the New Deal Era, 1932–1945: A Rhetorical History of the United States,* vol. 7, edited by Thomas W. Benson, 1–32. East Lansing: Michigan State University Press, 2006.

Beer, Francis A., and Christ'l De Landtsheer. "Foreword." In *Metaphorical World Politics,* edited by Francis A. Beer and Christ'l De Landtsheer, ix–x. East Lansing: Michigan State University Press, 2004.

Beer, Francis A., and Robert Hariman. "Realism and Rhetoric in International Relations." In *Post-Realism: The Rhetorical Turn in International Relations,* edited by Francis A. Beer and Robert Hariman. 1–30. East Lansing: Michigan State University Press, 1996.

Bell, Michael S. "The Worldview of Franklin D. Roosevelt: France, Germany, and United States Involvement in Europe." PhD diss., University of Maryland, 2004.

Bender, Thomas. *A Nation Among Nations: America's Place in World History.* New York: Farrar, Straus & Giroux, 2006.

Benson, Allan Louis. *Inviting War to America.* Vol. 20. Girard, KS: Appeal to Reason, 1916.

Berle, Beatrice Bishop, and Travis Beal Jacobs, eds. *Navigating the Rapids, 1918–1971: From the Papers of Adolf A. Berle.* New York: Harcourt Brace Jovanovich, 1973.

Biddle, Tami Davis. *Rhetoric and Reality in Air Warfare: The Evolution of British and American Ideas About Strategic Bombing, 1914–1945.* Princeton, NJ: Princeton University Press, 2002.

Biden, Joseph R. "Press Release—What They Are Reading in Memphis: 'Our Nation's Infrastructure Is Crumbling. President Biden's Plan Will Repair Our Country." July 8, 2021. American Presidency Project. Accessed February 11, 2023. https://www.presidency.ucsb.edu/documents/press-release-what-they-are-reading-memphis-our-nations-infrastructure-crumbling-president.

Biden, Joseph R. "Remarks and a Question-and-Answer Session at a CNN Presidential Town Hall in Baltimore, Maryland." October 21, 2021. American Presidency Project. Accessed March 16, 2023. https://www.presidency.ucsb.edu/documents/remarks-and-question-and-answer-session-cnn-presidential-town-hall-baltimore-maryland.

Bird, William L., and Harry Rubenstein. *Design for Victory: World War II Poster on the American Home Front.* New York: Princeton Architectural Press, 1998.

Bisbee, Donovan. "Driving the Three-Horse Team of Government: Kairos in FDR's Judiciary Fireside Chat." *Rhetoric & Public Affairs* 21, no. 3 (2018): 481–521.

Black, Edwin. *Rhetorical Criticism: A Study in Method.* Madison: University of Wisconsin Press, 1978.

Blake, Aaron. "Pack the Supreme Court? Why We May Be Getting Closer." *Washington Post,* October 9, 2018. https://www.washingtonpost.com/politics/2018/10/09/pack-supreme-court-why-we-may-be-getting-closer/?utm_term=.c983931a7745.

Blankfield, Bryan. "'A Symbol of His Warmth and Humanity': Fala, Roosevelt, and the Personable Presidency." *Rhetoric & Public Affairs* 19, no. 2 (2016): 209–243.

Blum, John Morton. *V Was for Victory: Politics and American Culture during World War II*. New York: Harcourt Brace Jovanovich, 1976.

Bodnar, John. *The "Good War" in American Memory*. Baltimore, MD: Johns Hopkins University Press, 2010.

Borah, William E. "Our Imperative Task." *Vital Speeches of the Day*, April 15, 1938, 388.

Bordley, James, Jr. "Letters to the Editor: 'Our Country's War, Not the New Deal's,' This Writer Says." *Baltimore Sun*, August 14, 1942.

Borgwardt, Elizabeth. *A New Deal for the World: America's Vision for Human Rights*. Cambridge, MA: Harvard University Press, 2005.

Bostdorff, Denise M. *The Presidency and the Rhetoric of Foreign Crisis*. Columbia: University of South Carolina Press, 1994.

Bradley, James. *The Imperial Cruise: A Secret History of Empire and War*. New York: Back Bay, 2009.

Brands, H. W. "The Age of Vulnerability: Eisenhower and the National Insecurity State." *American Historical Review* 94, no. 4 (October 1989): 963–989.

Brands, H. W. *Traitor to His Class: The Privileged Life and Radical Presidency of Franklin Delano Roosevelt*. New York: Random House, 2008.

Brantlinger, Patrick. "Kipling's 'The White Man's Burden' and Its Afterlives." *English Literature in Transition* 50, no. 2 (2007): 172–191.

Brinkley, Alan. *The End of Reform: New Deal Liberalism in Recession and War*. New York: Alfred A. Knopf, 1995.

Brinkley, Alan. "World War II and American Liberalism." In *The War in American Culture: Society and Consciousness during World War II*, edited by Lewis A. Erenberg and Susan E. Hirsch, 313–330. Chicago: University of Chicago Press, 1996.

Brown, Peter. "'Strong and Wrong vs. Weak and Right.'" RealClearPolitics, January 15, 2007. https://www.realclearpolitics.com/articles/2007/01/strong_and_wrong_vs_weak_and_r.html.

Bruner, Jerome Seymour. *Mandate from the People*. New York: Duell, Sloan & Pearce, 1944.

Bryan, William Jennings. "Democratic National Convention Address." July 8, 1896. American Rhetoric. Accessed February 22, 2023. https://www.americanrhetoric.com/speeches/williamjenningsbryan1896dnc.htm.

Bryan, William Jennings. "Imperialism." August 8, 1900. Voices of Democracy. Accessed February 11, 2023. http://voicesofdemocracy.umd.edu/william-jennings-bryan-imperialism-speech-text/.

Buhite, Russell D., and David W. Levy, eds. *FDR's Fireside Chats*. Norman, OK: University of Oklahoma Press, 1992.

Burns, James MacGregor. *Roosevelt: The Lion and the Fox: 1882–1940*. Vol. 1. New York: Harcourt, Brace & World, 1956.

Burns, James MacGregor. *Roosevelt: The Soldier of Freedom*. New York: Harcourt Brace Jovanovich, 1970.

Burns, Ken. *The Roosevelts: An Intimate History: The Fire of Life*. Walpole, NH: Florentine Films, 2014.

Butler, Susan. *Roosevelt and Stalin: Portrait of a Partnership*. New York: Alfred A. Knopf, 2015.

Buzan, Barry, and Ole Wæver. *Regions and Powers: The Structure of International Security.* Cambridge: Cambridge University Press, 2003.

Campbell, Alexia Fernández. "Trump's Protectionist Economic Plan Is Nothing New." *Atlantic,* January 9, 2017. https://www.theatlantic.com/business/archive /2017/01/trumps-protectionist-economic-plan-is-nothing-new/512585/.

Campbell, David. *Writing Security: United States Foreign Policy and the Politics of Identity.* Minneapolis: University of Minnesota Press, 1998.

Campbell, Karlyn Kohrs, and Kathleen Hall Jamieson. Presidents Creating the Presidency: Deeds Done in Words. Chicago: University of Chicago Press, 2008.

Cavanaugh, William T. *The Myth of Religious Violence: Secular Ideology and the Roots of Modern Conflict.* Oxford: Oxford University Press, 2009.

Ceaser, James W., Glen E. Thurow, Jeffrey Tulis, and Joseph M. Bessette. "The Rise of the Rhetorical Presidency." *Presidential Studies Quarterly* 11, no. 2 (1981): 158–171.

Chace, James. "The Winning Hand." *New York Review of Books,* March 11, 2004. https://www.nybooks.com/articles/2004/03/11/the-winning-hand/.

Chafe, William H. *The Unfinished Journey: America Since World War* II. New York: Oxford University Press, 1986.

Chapman, Mrs. Elton. "The Pulse of the Public: Burton." *Atlanta Constitution,* March 19, 1944.

Chase, Stuart. *The New Western Front.* New York: Harcourt, Brace, 1939.

Chernus, Ira. *Apocalypse Management: Eisenhower and the Discourse of National Insecurity.* Stanford, CA: Stanford University Press, 2008.

Chernus, Ira. *Dr. Strangegod: On the Symbolic Meaning of Nuclear Weapons.* Columbia: University of South Carolina Press, 1986.

Chernus, Ira. "Essays about America's National Myths in the Past, Present, and Future." Mythic America: Essays. Accessed January 17, 2023. https://mythicamerica .wordpress.com/.

Chernus, Ira. "Franklin D. Roosevelt's Narrative of National Insecurity." *Journal of Multicultural Discourses* 11 (2016): 135–148.

Chernus, Ira. *Monsters to Destroy: The Neoconservative War on Terror and Sin.* Boulder, CO: Paradigm, 2005.

Chesterton, G. K. *What I Saw in America.* London: Hodder & Stoughton, 1922.

Chilton, Paul. *Analysing Political Discourse: Theory and Practice.* New York: Routledge, 2004.

Chilton, Paul A. *Security Metaphors: Cold War Discourse from Containment to Common House.* New York: Peter Lang, 1996.

Churchill, Winston. "Prime Minister Churchill's Eulogy in Commons for the Late President Roosevelt." April 17, 1945. ibiblio: The Public's Library and Digital Archive. Accessed March 26, 2023. http://www.ibiblio.org/pha/policy/1945 /1945-04-17a.html.

Churchill, Winston. *The Great Republic: A History of America.* Edited by Winston Spencer-Churchill. New York: Random House, 1999.

Coats, Daniel R. *Statement for the Record: Worldwide Threat Assessment of the US Intelligence Community.* Washington, DC: Senate Select Committee on Intelligence, 2019. https://www.intelligence.senate.gov/sites/default/files/documents/osdcoats -012919.pdf.

Cohen, Eliot A. *The Big Stick: The Limits of Soft Power & the Necessity of Military Force.* New York: Basic Books, 2016.

Cole, Wayne S. *Charles A. Lindbergh and the Battle against American Intervention in World War II.* New York: Harcourt, Brace, Jovanovich, 1974.

Cole, Wayne S. *Roosevelt and the Isolationists, 1932–45.* Lincoln: University of Nebraska Press, 1983.

Colucci, Lamont. *The National Security Doctrines of the American Presidency: How They Shape Our Present and Future.* Vol. 1. Santa Barbara, CA: Praeger, 2012.

Condit, Celeste M., and John L. Lucaites. *Crafting Equality: America's Anglo-African Word.* Chicago: University of Chicago Press, 1993.

Costigliola, Frank. "Freedom from Fear." In *The Four Freedoms: Franklin D. Roosevelt and the Evolution of an American Idea,* edited by Jeffrey A. Engel. Oxford: Oxford University Press, 2016.

Costigliola, Frank. *Roosevelt's Lost Alliances: How Personal Politics Helped Start the Cold War.* Princeton, NJ: Princeton University Press, 2013.

"The Covenant of the League of Nations." December 1924. Avalon Project. Accessed February 19, 2023. https://avalon.law.yale.edu/20th_century/leagcov.asp.

Craig, Campbell, and Fredrik Logevall. *America's Cold War: The Politics of Insecurity.* Cambridge, MA: Belknap Press, 2009.

Craig, Douglas B. *Fireside Politics: Radio and Political Culture in the United States, 1920–1940.* Baltimore, MD: Johns Hopkins University Press, 2003.

Crowley, Sharon, and Debra Hawhee. *Ancient Rhetorics for Contemporary Students.* London: Longman, 1994.

Dallek, Matthew. *Defenselessness Under the Night: The Roosevelt Years and the Origins of the Homeland Security.* Oxford: Oxford University Press, 2016.

Dallek, Robert. *The American Style of Foreign Policy: Cultural Politics and Foreign Affairs.* New York: Oxford University Press, 1979.

Dallek, Robert. *Franklin D. Roosevelt: A Political Life.* New York: Penguin Books, 2017.

Dallek, Robert. *Franklin D. Roosevelt and American Foreign Policy, 1932–1945.* New York: Oxford University Press, 1995.

Daniels, Roger. *Franklin D. Roosevelt: The War Years, 1939–1940.* Urbana: University of Illinois Press, 2016.

Darsey, Leroy G. "Introduction: The President as a Rhetorical Leader." In *The Presidency and Rhetorical Leadership,* edited by Leroy G. Darsey, 3–19. College Station: Texas A&M University Press, 2002.

Daughton, Suzanne M. "FDR as Family Doctor: Medical Metaphors and the Role of Physician in the Fireside Chats." In *American Rhetoric in the New Deal Era, 1932–1945: A Rhetorical History of the United States,* vol. 7, edited by Thomas W. Benson, 33–82. East Lansing: Michigan State University Press, 2006.

Davis, Kenneth S. *FDR: The Beckoning of Destiny, 1882–1928: A History.* New York: Random House, 1993.

Davis, Kenneth S. *FDR, the War President, 1940–1943: A History.* New York: Random House, 2000.

Dawson, Raymond H. *The Decision to Aid Russia, 1941; Foreign Policy and Domestic Politics.* Chapel Hill: University of North Carolina Press, 1959.

DeAngelis, Tori. "Depression and Anxiety Escalate during COVID." *Monitor on Psychology* 52, no. 8 (2021): 88.

Dewey, John. *The Public and Its Problems*. Athens, OH: University of Ohio Press, 1980.

"Dewey Warns America: Shun Foreign Wars." *Chicago Daily Tribune*, May 28, 1940.

"Disinformation: A Primer in Russian Active Measures and Influence Campaigns." Senate Committee Intelligence Hearing, US Government Publishing Office, March 30, 2017. https://www.intelligence.senate.gov/hearings/open-hearing-dis information-primer-russian-active-measures-and-influence-campaigns-panel-i#.

Divine, Robert A. *The Reluctant Belligerent: American Entry into World War II*. New York: Wiley, 1979.

Divine, Robert A. *Second Chance: The Triumph of Internationalism in America during World War II*. New York: Atheneum, 1967.

Dobbs, Michael. *Six Months in 1945: FDR, Stalin, Churchill, and Truman from World War to Cold War*. New York: Vintage Books, 2012.

Dodd, T. Carter. "Letters to the Editor: The Pitfalls of Lend-Lease." *Wall Street Journal*, August 16, 1943.

Dodd, William Edward. *Ambassador Dodd's Diary: 1933-1938*. Edited by William E. Dodd Jr. and Martha Dodd. New York: Harcourt, Brace, 1941.

Doenecke, Justus D., ed. *In Danger Undaunted: The Anti-interventionist Movement of 1940-1941 as Revealed in the Papers of the America First Committee*. Stanford, CA: Hoover Institution Press, 1990.

Dorrien, Gary J. *Imperial Designs: Neoconservatism and the New Pax Americana*. New York: Routledge, 2004.

Dorsey, Leroy G. "The Frontier Myth in Presidential Rhetoric: Theodore Roosevelt's Campaign for Conservation." *Western Journal of Communication* 59, no. 4 (1995): 1-19.

Dorsey, Leroy G. "Introduction: The President as a Rhetorical Leader." In *The Presidency and Rhetorical Leadership*, edited by Leroy G. Dorsey, 3-19. East Lansing: Michigan State University Press, 2002.

Dorsey, Leroy G. "Managing Women's Equality: Theodore Roosevelt, the Frontier Myth, and the Modern Woman." *Rhetoric & Public Affairs* 16, no. 3 (2013): 423-456.

Dorsey, Leroy G. "Sailing into the 'Wondrous Now': The Myth of the American Navy's World Cruise." *Quarterly Journal of Speech* 83, no. 4 (1997): 447-465.

Dorsey, Leroy G. *Theodore Roosevelt, Conservation, and the 1908 Governors' Conference*. College Station: Texas A&M University Press, 2015.

Dorsey, Leroy G. "Woodrow Wilson's Fight for the League of Nations: A Reexamination." *Rhetoric & Public Affairs* 2, no. 1 (1999): 107-135.

Dorwart, Jeffery M. *The Office of Naval Intelligence: The Birth of America's First Intelligence Agency, 1865-1918*. Annapolis, MD: Naval Institute Press, 1979.

Dougherty, Michael Brendan. "In Defense of America First." *Week*, May 2, 2016. https://theweek.com/articles/621645/defense-america-first.

Dowd, Maureen. "Who's Tough Enough?" *New York Times*, January 31, 2012.

Dower, John W. *War without Mercy: Race and Power in the Pacific War*. New York: Pantheon Books, 1986.

Duffy, James P. *Lindbergh vs. Roosevelt: The Rivalry that Divided America*. Washington, DC: Regnery, 2010.

Dunn, Susan. *A Blueprint for War: FDR and the Hundred Days that Mobilized America*. New Haven, CT: Yale University Press, 2018.

Dunn, Susan. *1940: FDR, Willkie, Lindbergh, Hitler—the Election amid the Storm*. New Haven, CT: Yale University Press, 2013.

Edelman, Murray. *Constructing the Political Spectacle*. Chicago: University of Chicago Press, 1987.

Eisenhower, Dwight D. *The Papers of Dwight David Eisenhower*. Edited by Alfred D. Chandler. Baltimore, MD: Johns Hopkins University Press, 1970.

Eisenhower, Dwight D. "Radio Address to the American People." In *Public Papers of the Presidents: Dwight D. Eisenhower, 1953*, 307–314. Emmet John Hughes Diary, Emmet John Hughes Papers, box 1, Seeley G. Mudd Library, Princeton University.

Eisenhower, John S. D. *Intervention! The United States and the Mexican Revolution, 1913–1917*. New York: W. W. Norton, 1993.

"Employment Fell 3.9% in January." *New York Times*, February 23, 1933, C30.

Engelhardt, Tom. *The End of Victory Culture: Cold War America and the Disillusioning of a Generation*. New York: Basic Books, 1995.

Engels, Jeremy. *Enemyship: Democracy and Counter-Revolution in the Early Republic*. East Lansing, Michigan State University Press, 2010.

Fahnestock, Jeanne. *Rhetorical Style: The Uses of Language in Persuasion*. Oxford: Oxford University Press, 2011.

Fahnestock Jeanne, and Marie Secor. "The Stases in Scientific and Literary Argument." *Written Communication* 5, no. 4 (1988): 427–443.

Farley, James A. *Jim Farley's Story: The Roosevelt Years*. New York: Whittlesey House, 1948.

"Farmers Besiege the Legislatures." *New York Times*, January 22, 1933, N1.

Farrell, Thomas B. *Norms of Rhetorical Culture*. New Haven, CT: Yale University Press, 1993.

FDR to Roger B. Merriman. February 15, 1939. Merriman Family Papers. Accessed February 19, 2023. https://www.masshist.org/objects/2010february.php.

Fisher, Walter R. "Technical Logic, Rhetorical Logic, and Narrative Rationality." *Argumentation* 1, no. 1 (1987): 3–21.

Fitzpatrick, John C., ed. *The Writings of George Washington from the Original Manuscript Sources 1745–1799*. Vol. 35. Washington, DC: United States Government Printing Office, 1939.

Flanagan, Jason C. "Woodrow Wilson's 'Rhetorical Restructuring': The Transformation of the American Self and the Construction of the German Enemy." *Rhetoric & Public Affairs* 7, no. 2 (2004): 115–148.

Flynn, John T. "Can Hitler Invade America?" *Reader's Digest*, April 1941.

Folsom, Burton W., Jr., and Anita Folsom. *FDR Goes to War: How Expanded Executive Power, Spiraling National Debt, and Restricted Civil Liberties Shaped Wartime America*. New York: Threshold, 2011.

Foner, Eric. *The Story of American Freedom*. New York: W. W. Norton, 1988.

Foner, Philip S., and Robert James Branham. *Lift Every Voice: African American Oratory 1787–1900.* Tuscaloosa: University of Alabama Press, 1998.

Fowler, Randall. "'Caliphate' against the Crown: Martyrdom, Heresy, and the Rhetoric of Enemyship in the Kingdom of Jordan." *Rhetoric & Public Affairs* 21, no. 1 (2018): 117–156.

Fowler, Randall. *More than a Doctrine: The Eisenhower Era in the Middle East.* Lincoln: University of Nebraska Press, 2018.

Fox, Frank W. *Madison Avenue Goes to War: The Strange Military Career of American Advertising, 1941–45.* Provo, UT: Brigham Young University Press, 1975.

Frank, Jerome. *Save America First: How to Make Our Democracy Work.* New York: Harper & Brothers, 1938.

Freedman, Lawrence. *Strategy: A History.* Oxford: Oxford University Press, 2013.

Freidel, Frank Burt. *Franklin D. Roosevelt: The Apprenticeship.* Vol. 1. Boston: Little, Brown, 1952.

Freidel, Frank Burt. *Franklin D. Roosevelt: Launching the New Deal.* Vol. 4. Boston: Little, Brown, 1952.

Freidel, Frank Burt. *Franklin D. Roosevelt: The Ordeal.* Vol. 2. Boston: Little, Brown and Company, 1952.

Freidel, Frank Burt. *Franklin D. Roosevelt: A Rendezvous with Destiny.* Boston: Little, Brown, 1990.

French, David. "In Defense of the Iraq War." *National Review,* March 20, 2019. https://www.nationalreview.com/corner/iraq-war-just-cause-saddam-hussein-threat-stability/.

Frizell, Sam. "Transcript: Read the Full Text of Hillary Clinton's Campaign Launch Speech." *Time,* June 13, 2015. https://time.com/3920332/transcript-full-text-hillary-clinton-campaign-launch/.

Fullilove, Michael. *Rendezvous with Destiny: How Franklin D. Roosevelt and Five Extraordinary Men Took America into the War and Into the World.* New York: Penguin Press, 2013.

"Full Speed Ahead." *Atlanta Daily World,* June 12, 1940.

"Full Speed toward What Goal?" *Chicago Daily Tribune,* June 12, 1940.

Furedi, Frank. *How Fear Works: Culture of Fear in the Twenty-First Century.* London: Bloomsbury, 2018.

Furedi, Frank. "Fear Today." First Things, January 2019. https://www.firstthings.com/article/2019/01/fear-today.

Fussell, Paul. *Thank God for the Atom Bomb and Other Essays.* New York: Summit Books, 1988.

Fussell, Paul. *Wartime: Understanding and Behavior in the Second World War.* New York: Oxford University Press, 1989.

Gaddis, John Lewis. "The Insecurities of Victory: The United States and the Perception of the Soviet Threat After World War II." In *The Truman Presidency,* edited by Michael J. Lacey, 235–272. New York: Cambridge University Press, 1989.

Gaddis, John Lewis. *Strategies of Containment: A Critical Appraisal of American National Security Policy during the Cold War.* New York: Oxford University Press, 1982.

Gardner, Elizabeth. "William Jennings Bryan, 'Imperialism' (8 August 1900)." *Voices of Democracy* 5 (2010): 37–56.

Gardner, Lloyd C. *Architects of Illusion: Men and Ideas in American Foreign Policy 1941–1949.* Chicago: Quadrangle Books, 1970.

Gardner, Lloyd C. *A Covenant with Power: America and World Order from Wilson to Reagan.* New York: Oxford University Press, 1984.

Gardner, Lloyd C. *Economic Aspects of New Deal Diplomacy.* Madison: University of Wisconsin Press, 1964.

Gardner, Lloyd C. *Safe for Democracy: The Anglo-American Response to Revolution, 1913–1923.* New York: Oxford University Press, 1984.

Gardner, Richard N. *Sterling-Dollar Diplomacy: Anglo-American Collaboration in the Reconstruction of Multilateral Trade.* Oxford: Clarendon Press, 1956.

Garraty, John A. "New Deal, National Socialism, and the Great Depression." *American Historical Review* 78, no. 4 (1973): 907–944.

Gelderman, Carol. *All the President's Words: The Bully Pulpit and the Creation of the Virtual Presidency.* New York: Walker, 1997.

Genovese, Michael A., Todd L. Belt, and William W. Lammers. *The Presidency and Domestic Policy: Comparing Leadership Styles, FDR to Obama.* 2nd ed. Boulder: Paradigm Publishers, 2014.

Gerstle, Gary. "Race and Nation in the Thought and Politics of Woodrow Wilson." In *Reconsidering Woodrow Wilson: Progressivism, Internationalism, War, and Peace,* edited by John Milton Cooper Jr., 93–123. Baltimore, MD: Johns Hopkins University Press, 2008.

Gillon, Steven M. *Pearl Harbor: FDR Leads the Nation into War.* New York: Basic Books, 2011.

Glanville, Luke. *Sovereignty and the Responsibility to Protect: A New History.* Chicago: University of Chicago Press, 2014.

Goldberg, Jonah. *The Tyranny of Clichés: How Liberals Cheat in the War of Ideas.* New York: Sentinel, 2012.

Goldman, Eric Frederick. *Rendezvous with Destiny: A History of Modern American Reform.* New York: Vintage Books, 1956.

Golway, Terry. *Frank & Al: FDR, Al Smith, and the Unlikely Alliance that Created the Modern Democratic Party.* New York: St. Martin's Press, 2018.

Goodnight, G. Thomas. "Reagan, Vietnam, and Central America: Public Memory and the Politics of Fragmentation." In *Beyond the Rhetorical Presidency,* edited by Martin J. Medhurst, 122–152. College Station: Texas A&M University Press, 1996.

Goodwin, Doris Kearns. *No Ordinary Time: Franklin and Eleanor Roosevelt: The Home Front in World War II.* New York: Simon & Schuster, 1994.

Gosling, Justin. "Mental Causes and Fear." *Mind* 71 (1962): 289–297.

Graber, Doris. *Verbal Behavior and Politics.* Champaign: University of Illinois Press, 1976.

Graebner, Norman A. "Christianity and Democracy: Tocqueville's Views of Religion in America." *Journal of Religion* 56, no. 3 (1976): 263–273.

Graebner, William. *The Age of Doubt: American Thought and Culture in the 1940s.* Boston: Twayne Publishers, 1990.

Gray, J. Glenn. *The Warriors: Reflections on Men in Battle.* New York: Harper & Row, 1967.

Green, Miranda. "DHS Secretary: People Would 'Never Leave the House' If They

Knew What I Knew." CNN, May 26, 2017. http://www.cnn.com/2017/05/26 /politics/john-kelly-terror-threat-people-wouldnt-leave-the-house/index.html.

Grieve, William G. *The American Military Mission to China, 1941–1942: Lend-Lease Logistics, Politics and the Tangles of Wartime Cooperation.* Jefferson, NC: McFarland, 2014.

Groppe, Maureen, and Sarah Elbeshbishi. "Exclusive Poll: Overwhelming Majority Say the US Faces a Mental Health Crisis." *USA Today,* January 8, 2022. https:// www.usatoday.com/story/news/politics/2022/01/08/mental-health-ameri cans-see-crisis-amid-ongoing-covid-pandemic/9135532002/?gnt-cfr=1.

Gross, Daniel A. "The U.S. Government Turned Away Thousands of Jewish Refugees, Fearing that They Were Nazi Spies." Smithsonian, November 18, 2015. https://www.smithsonianmag.com/history/us-government-turned-away-thou sands-jewish-refugees-fearing-they-were-nazi-spies-180957324.

Grove, Eric. "Sea Power in the Asia-Pacific at the Turn of the Millennium." In *Asia-Pacific Economic and Security Co-operation: New Regional Agendas,* edited by Christopher M. Dent. New York: Palgrave Macmillan, 2003.

Haberski, Raymond, Jr. *God and War: American Civil Religion since 1945.* New Brunswick, NJ: Rutgers University Press, 2012.

Hahner, Leslie A. *To Become an American: Immigrants and Americanization Campaigns of the Early Twentieth Century.* East Lansing: Michigan State University Press, 2017.

Hamilton, Alexander. "Federalist No. 1." October 27, 1787. Founders Online. Accessed March 15, 2023. https://founders.archives.gov/documents/Hamil ton/01-04-02-0152.

Hamilton, Nigel. *The Mantle of Command: FDR at War 1941–1942.* New York: Houghton Mifflin Harcourt, 2014.

"'The Hand that Held the Dagger': FDR Delivers Historic Speech in Mem Gym." *University of Virginia Magazine,* summer 2013. https://uvamagazine.org/articles /the_hand_that_held_the_dagger.

Harding, Warren G. "Address Accepting the Republican Presidential Nomination." June 12, 1920. American Presidency Project. Accessed February 11, 2023. https://www.presidency.ucsb.edu/documents/address-accepting-the-republi can-presidential-nomination-2.

Harding, Warren G. "First Annual Message." December 6, 1921. American Presidency Project. Accessed February 11, 2023. https://www.presidency.ucsb.edu /documents/first-annual-message-19.

Harding, Warren G. "Inaugural Address." March 4, 1921. American Presidency Project. Accessed February 11, 2023. https://www.presidency.ucsb.edu/docu ments/inaugural-address-49.

Hasian, Marouf, Jr. "Franklin D. Roosevelt, The Holocaust, and Modernity's Rescue Rhetorics." *Communication Quarterly* 51, no. 2 (2003): 153–173.

Hauerwas, Stanley. *War and the American Difference: Theological Reflections on Violence and National Identity.* Grand Rapids, MI: Baker Academic, 2011.

Hawley, Ellis Wayne. *The Great War and the Search for a Modern Order: A History of the American People and Their Institutions, 1917–1933.* New York: St. Martin's Press, 1979.

Hayes, Jarrod, and Janelle Knox-Hayes. "Security in Climate Change Discourse: Analyzing the Divergence between US and EU Approaches to Policy." *Global Environmental Politics* 14 (2014): 82–101.

Hearden, Patrick J. *Architects of Globalism: Building a New World Order during World War II.* Fayetteville: University of Arkansas Press, 2002.

Hearden, Patrick J. *Roosevelt Confronts Hitler: America's Entry into World War II.* Dekalb: Northern Illinois University Press, 1987.

Hearst, William Randolph. *William Randolph Hearst: A Portrait in His Own Words.* Edited by Edmond D. Coblentz. New York: Simon & Schuster, 1952.

Heidt, Stephen J. "Presidential Power and National Violence: James K. Polk's Rhetorical Transfer of Savagery." *Rhetoric & Public Affairs* 19, no. 3 (2016): 365–396.

Heidt, Stephen J. "Presidential Rhetoric, Metaphor, and the Emergence of the Democracy Promotion Industry." *Southern Communication Journal* 78, no. 3 (2013): 233–255.

Hench, John B. *Books as Weapons: Propaganda, Publishing, and the Battle for Global Markets in the Era of World War II.* Ithaca, NY: Cornell University Press, 2010.

Hendrikson, Alan K. "FDR and the 'World-Wide Arena.'" In *FDR's World: War, Peace, and Legacies,* edited by David B. Woolner, Warren F. Kimball, and David Reynolds, 35–62. New York: Palgrave Macmillan, 2008.

Herring, George C. *From Colony to Superpower: American Foreign Relations since 1776.* Oxford: Oxford University Press, 2008.

Higginbotham, Don. "The American Republic in a Wider World." In *The American Revolution: Its Character and Limits,* edited by Jack P. Greene, 165–170. New York: New York University Press, 1987.

Hillman, Noah A. "Letters to the Editor: Opposing the Proposal to Give the Governor 'War Powers.'" *Baltimore Sun,* January 7, 1943.

Hiltzik, Michael. *The New Deal: A Modern History.* New York: Free Press, 2011.

Hinds, Lynn Boyd, and Theodore Otto Windt, Jr. *The Cold War as Rhetoric: The Beginnings, 1945–1950.* New York: Praeger, 1991.

Hixson, Walter L. *The Myth of American Diplomacy: National Identity and U.S. Foreign Policy.* New Haven, CT: Yale University Press, 2008.

Hodgson, Godfrey. *Colonel: The Life and Wars of Henry Stimson, 1867–1950.* New York: Alfred A. Knopf, 1990.

Höenicke Moore, Michaela. *Know Your Enemy: The American Debate on Nazism, 1933–1945.* Cambridge and New York: Cambridge University Press, 2010.

Hofstadter, Richard. *The Age of Reform: From Bryan to F.D.R.* New York: Vintage Books, 1955.

Hogan, J. Michael. *Woodrow Wilson's Western Tour: Rhetoric, Public Opinion, and the League of Nations.* College Station: Texas A&M University Press, 2006.

Hogan, Michael J. *A Cross of Iron: Harry S. Truman and the Origins of the National Security State.* Oxford: Oxford University Press, 1998.

Holsti, Ole Rudolf. *Public Opinion and American Foreign Policy.* Ann Arbor: University of Michigan Press, 2004.

"Home of Franklin D. Roosevelt." National Parks Service. Accessed March 15, 2023. http://npshistory.com/publications/hofr/index.htm.

Hoover, Herbert. "Address at Madison Square Garden, New York City." October 31, 1936. American Presidency Project. Accessed February 11, 2023. https://

www.presidency.ucsb.edu/documents/address-madison-square-garden-new -york-city-2.

Houck, Davis W., and Amos Kiewe. *FDR's Body Politics: The Rhetoric of Disability.* College Station: Texas A&M University Press, 2003.

Houck, Davis W., and Mihaela Nocasian. "FDR's First Inaugural Address: Text, Context, and Reception." *Rhetoric & Public Affairs* 5, no. 4 (2002): 649–678.

Houck, Davis W. *FDR and Fear Itself: The First Inaugural Address.* College Station: Texas A&M University Press, College Station, 2002.

Houck, Davis W. *Rhetoric as Currency: Hoover, Roosevelt, and the Great Depression.* College Station: Texas A&M University Press, 2001.

Hughes, Emmet John. *The Ordeal of Power: A Political Memoir of the Eisenhower Years.* New York: Atheneum, 1963.

Hull, Cordell, and Andrew Berding. *The Memoirs of Cordell Hull.* Vol. 1. New York: Macmillan, 1948.

Hull, Cordell. "International Trade." Address by Cordell Hull, *Vital Speeches of the Day,* November 19, 1934.

Isaacson, Walter, and Evan Thomas. *Wise Men: Six Friends and the World They Made.* New York: Simon & Schuster, 2013.

Isetti, Ronald. "The Moneychangers of the Temple: FDR, American Civil Religion, and the New Deal." *Presidential Studies Quarterly* 26, no. 3 (1996): 678–693.

Ivie, Robert L. *Democracy and America's War on Terror.* Tuscaloosa: University of Alabama Press, 2005.

Ivie, Robert L. "Realism Masking Fear: George F. Kennan's Political Rhetoric." In *Post-Realism: The Rhetorical Turn in International Relations,* edited by Francis A. Beer and Robert Hariman, 55–74. East Lansing: Michigan State University Press, 1996.

Jablonski, Carol J. "Resisting the 'Inevitability' of War: The Catholic Worker Movement and World War II." In *American Rhetoric in the New Deal Era, 1932–1945: A Rhetorical History of the United States,* vol. 7, edited by Thomas W. Benson, 419–452. East Lansing: Michigan State University Press, 2006.

Jackson, Robert H. *That Man: An Insider's Portrait of Franklin D. Roosevelt.* Oxford: Oxford University Press, 2003.

Jacobs, Alan. *Year of Our Lord 1943: Christian Humanism in an Age of Crisis.* Oxford: Oxford University Press, 2018.

Jaffe, Greg. "Lessons in Disaster: A Top Clinton Adviser Searches for Meaning in a Shocking Loss." *Washington Post,* July 14, 2017.

Jahn, Beate. *Liberal Internationalism: Theory, History, Practice.* New York: Palgrave Macmillan, 2013.

Jefferson, Thomas. "First Inaugural Address." March 4, 1801. Avalon Project. Accessed February 19, 2023. http://avalon.law.yale.edu/19th_century/jefinau1.asp.

Jeffries, John W. *A Third Term for FDR: The Election of 1940.* Lawrence: University Press of Kansas, 2017.

"Joe Biden's Good Pandemic." *Economist,* May 23, 2020. https://www.economist .com/united-states/2020/05/23/joe-bidens-good-pandemic.

Johnson, Donald Bruce. *The Republican Party and Wendell Willkie.* Urbana: University of Illinois Press, 1960.

Johnstone, Andrew. *Against Immediate Evil: American Internationalists and the Four Freedoms on the Eve of World War II*. Ithaca, NY: Cornell University Press, 2014.

Johnston, Henry P., ed. *The Correspondence and Public Papers of John Jay*, vol. 3: *1782–1793*. New York: G. P. Putnam's Sons, 1891.

Jonas, Manfred. *Isolationism in America: 1935–1941*. Ithaca, NY: Cornell University Press, 1966.

Jonas, Manfred. "Robert Shogan. *Hard Bargain: How FDR Twisted Churchill's Arm, Evaded the Law, and Changed the Role of the American Presidency*." *American Historical Review* 101, no. 5 (1996): 1648–1649.

Jones, John Bush. *All-Out for Victory! Magazine Advertising and the World War II Home Front*. Waltham, MA: Brandeis University Press, 2009.

Jones, Mary Harris "Mother." "At a Public Meeting in Charleston." In *American Rhetorical Discourse*, edited by Ronald F. Reid and James F. Klumpp, 619–626. Long Grove, IL: Waveland Press, 2005.

Kabiling, Maria Christina Ana. "World War II in Popular American Visual Culture: Film and Video Games after 9/11." MA thesis, Georgetown University, 2010.

Kaiser, David. *No End Save Victory: How FDR Led the Nation into War*. New York: Basic Books, 2014.

Karl, Barry Dean. *The Uneasy State: The United States From 1915 to 1945*. Chicago: University of Chicago Press, 1983.

Katznelson, Ira. *Fear Itself: The New Deal and the Origins of Our Time*. New York: Liveright, 2014.

Kaufer David S., and Kathleen M. Carley. "Condensation Symbols: Their Variety and Rhetorical Function in Political Discourse." *Philosophy and Rhetoric* 26, no. 3 (1993): 201–226.

Kaye, Harvey J. *The Fight for the Four Freedoms: What Made FDR and the Greatest Generation Truly Great*. New York: Simon & Schuster, 2014.

Keller, Helen. "Strike Against War." January 5, 1916. Gifts of Speech. Accessed March 26, 2023. http://gos.sbc.edu/k/keller.html.

Kennan, George F. *American Diplomacy*. Chicago: University of Chicago Press, 1985.

Kennedy, David M. *Freedom from Fear: The American People in Depression and War, 1929–1945*. New York: Oxford University Press, 1999.

Kennett, Lee. *G.I.: The American Soldier in World War II*. Norman: University of Oklahoma Press, 1997.

Kern, Gary. "How 'Uncle Joe' Bugged FDR." *Center for Study of Intelligence* 47, no. 1 (2003): 19–31.

Kiewe, Amos. "Introduction." In *The Modern Presidency and Crisis Rhetoric*, edited by Amos Kiewe, xv–xxiii. Westport: Praeger, 1994.

Kimball, Warren F. *Forged in War: Roosevelt, Churchill, and the Second World War*. New York: W. Morrow, 1997.

Kimball, Warren F. *The Juggler: Franklin Roosevelt as Wartime Statesman*. Princeton, NJ: Princeton University Press, 1994.

Kimble, James J. "Franklin D. Roosevelt, 1941 State of the Union Address ('The Four Freedoms') (6 January 1941)." *Voices of Democracy* 3 (2008): 77.

Kimble, James J. "Mrs. Jekyll Meets Mrs. Hyde: The War Advertising Council, Rhetorical Norms, and the Gendered Home Front in World War II." *Western Journal of Communication* 82, no. 1 (2018): 1–19.

Kimble, James J. "Spectral Soldiers: Domestic Propaganda, Visual Culture, and Images of Death on the World War II Home Front." *Rhetoric & Public Affairs* 19, no. 4 (2016): 535–570.

King, Martin Luther, Jr. "Letter from a Birmingham Jail." April 16, 1963. African Studies Center. Accessed March 15, 2023. https://www.africa.upenn.edu/Articles_Gen/Letter_Birmingham.html.

Kinneavy, James L. "Kairos in Classical and Modern Rhetorical Theory." In *Rhetoric and Kairos: Essays in History, Theory, and Praxis*, edited by Phillip Sipora and James S. Baumlin, 58–76. Albany: State University of New York Press, 2002.

Kirby, Jen. "Why Kirsten Gillibrand's Foreign Policy Plan Is One of the Strongest Yet." Vox, July 26, 2019. https://www.vox.com/2019/7/26/8930265/2020-democrats-kirsten-gillibrand-foreign-policy.

Knott, Stephen F., and Tony Williams. *Washington and Hamilton: The Alliance that Forged America.* Naperville, IL: Sourcebooks, 2015.

Krebs, Ronald R. *Narrative and the Making of US National Security.* Cambridge: Cambridge University Press, 2015.

Kristol, William. "Is Exceptionalism a Myth? Has It Always Been?" In *American Exceptionalism: The Origins, History, and Future of the Nation's Greatest Strength*, edited by Charles W. Dunn, 95–100. New York: Rowman & Littlefield, 2013.

Kuo, Tai-chun, and Hsiao-tin Lin. *T.V. Soong in Modern Chinese History: A Look at His Role in Sino-American Relations in World War II."* Stanford, CA: Hoover Institution Press, 2006. https://www.hoover.org/sites/default/files/uploads/documents/tv-soong-in-modern-chinese-history.pdf.

Lanham, Richard. *The Economics of Attention: Style and Substance in the Age of Information.* Chicago: University of Chicago Press, 2006.

Larrabee, Eric. *Commander in Chief: Franklin Delano Roosevelt, His Lieutenants, and Their War.* New York: Harper & Row, 1987.

Lauren, Paul Gordon. *The Evolution of International Human Rights: Visions Seen.* 3rd ed. Philadelphia: University of Pennsylvania Press, 2011.

L. D. W. "Letters to the Editor: Citadel of Virtue." *Washington Post*, August 24, 1943.

Lee, Carrie. "Operation Torch at 75: FDR and the Domestic Politics of the North African Invasion." War on the Rocks, November 8, 2017. https://warontherocks.com/2017/11/16075/.

Leffler, Melvyn P. *A Preponderance of Power: National Security, the Truman Administration, and the Cold War.* Stanford, CA: Stanford University Press, 1992.

Lehman, Herbert. "Herbert H. Lehman Project: Oral History, 1957–1962." Columbia Center for Oral History Archives. Accessed March 26, 2023. https://oralhistoryportal.library.columbia.edu/document.php?id=ldpd_4076412.

Leigh, Michael. *Mobilizing Consent: Public Opinion and American Foreign Policy, 1937–1947.* Westport, CT: Greenwood Press, 1976.

"Letter to the Editor: Army Officer's Decision." *Boston Globe*, November 7, 1944.

"Letters to the Editor: Wife at Home Writes of Duty to Husband." *Boston Globe*, December 19, 1943.

Leuchtenburg, William E. *The American President: From Teddy Roosevelt to Bill Clinton.* Oxford: Oxford University Press, 2015.

Leuchtenburg, William E. "The Analogue of War." In *Change and Continuity in Twentieth Century America: The 1920's,* edited by Robert H. Bremner, John Braeman, and David Brody, 81–143. Columbus: Ohio State University Press, 1964.

Leuchtenburg, William E. *The FDR Years: On Roosevelt & His Legacy.* New York: Columbia University Press, 1995.

Leuchtenburg, William E. *Franklin D. Roosevelt and the New Deal: 1932–1940.* New York: Harper & Row, 1963.

Leuchtenburg, William E. "Franklin D. Roosevelt: Life Before the Presidency." Miller Center. Accessed January 17, 2023. https://millercenter.org/president/fdroosevelt/life-before-the-presidency.

Leuchtenburg, William E. "Franklin D. Roosevelt: The American Franchise." Miller Center. Accessed January 17, 2023. https://millercenter.org/president/fdroosevelt/the-american-franchise.

Leuchtenburg, William E. *In the Shadow of FDR: From Harry Truman to Bill Clinton.* Ithaca, NY: Cornell University Press, 1983.

Leuchtenburg, William E. "Keynote Address: The Greenbelt Conference on New Towns." George Mason University Archival Repository Service, May 2, 1987. http://ebot.gmu.edu/bitstream/handle/1920/1887/638_01_01_04.pdf?sequence=1&isAllowed=y.

Levari, David E., Daniel T. Gilbert, Timothy D. Wilson, Beau Sievers, David M. Amodio, and Thalia Wheatley. "Prevalence-Induced Concept Change in Human Judgment." *Science* 360 (2018): 1465–1467.

Lim, Elvin T. "The Lion and the Lamb: De-Mythologizing Franklin Roosevelt's Fireside Chats." *Rhetoric & Public Address* 6, no. 3 (2003): 437–464.

Lincoln, Abraham. "Second Annual Message." December 1, 1862. American Presidency Project. Accessed February 11, 2023. https://www.presidency.ucsb.edu/documents/second-annual-message-9.

Lind, Michael. *Land of Promise: An Economic History of the United States.* New York: Harper Collins, 2012.

Lindbergh, Anne Morrow. *War Within and Without: Diaries and Letters of Anne Morrow Lindbergh, 1939–1944.* New York: Harcourt Brace Jovanovich, 1980.

Lindbergh, Charles. "An Appeal for Peace." *Vital Speeches of the Day,* August 4, 1940.

Lindbergh, Charles. "Our National Safety." *Vital Speeches of the Day,* May 19, 1940.

Lindley, Ernest Kidder. *Franklin D. Roosevelt: A Career in Progressive Democracy.* New York: Blue Ribbon, 1931.

Lindsay, James M. "TWE Remembers: FDR's 'Stab in the Back' Speech." Council on Foreign Relations, June 10, 2013. https://www.cfr.org/blog/twe-remembers-fdrs-stab-back-speech.

Linenthal, Edward T. *Changing Images of the Warrior Hero in America: A History of Popular Symbolism.* New York: Edwin Mellen Press, 1982.

Lippmann, Walter. *Public Opinion.* New York: Penguin Books, 1946.

Little, Richard. *The Balance of Power in International Relations: Metaphors, Myths, and Models.* Cambridge: Cambridge University, 2007.

Luce, Henry R. "The American Century." *Life,* February 17, 1941.

MacDonald, C. A. *The United States, Britain, and Appeasement, 1936–1939.* New York: St. Martin's Press, 1981.

MacDonald, James. "Britons Aare Told We Insure Victory." *New York Times,* June 12, 1940.

Mahan, Alfred Thayer. *The Influence of Sea Power Upon the French Revolution and Empire, 1793–1812.* Boston: Little, Brown, 1892.

Manchester, William. *The Glory and the Dream: A Narrative History of America, 1932–1972.* Boston: Little, Brown, 1973.

Maney, Patrick J. *The Roosevelt Presence: A Biography of Franklin Delano Roosevelt.* New York: Twayne Publishers, 1992.

Mann, James. *Rise of the Vulcans: The History of Bush's War Cabinet.* New York: Viking, 2004.

Mann, Michael. *Fascists.* Cambridge: Cambridge University Press, 2004.

Margulies, Phillip. *America's Role in the World.* New York: Infobase Publishing, 2009.

Marks, Frederick W. *Wind over Sand: The Diplomacy of Franklin Roosevelt.* Athens: University of Georgia Press, 1988.

Marrin, Albert. *FDR and the American Crisis.* New York: Random House, 2015.

Marusic, Damir. "Making Up Monsters to Destroy," American Interest, January 15, 2019. https://www.the-american-interest.com/2019/01/15/making-up-monsters-to-destroy/.

Matson, Carlton K. "Letters to the Editor: Post-War Economic Planning." *Wall Street Journal,* May 10, 1943.

McCormick, Thomas J. *America's Half-Century: United States Foreign Policy in the Cold War and After.* Baltimore, MD: Johns Hopkins University Press, 1995.

McGee, Michael Calvin. "The 'Ideograph': A Link Between Rhetoric and Ideology." *Quarterly Journal of Speech* 66, no. 1 (1980): 1–16.

McKenna, Marian C. *Franklin Roosevelt and the Great Constitutional War: The Court-Packing Crisis of 1937.* New York: Fordham University Press, 2002.

McKinley, William. "President McKinley's Last Public Utterance to the People in Buffalo, New York." September 5, 1901. American Presidency Project. Accessed February 11, 2023. https://www.presidency.ucsb.edu/documents/president-mckinleys-last-public-utterance-the-people-buffalo-new-york.

Mead, Walter Russell. *Special Providence: American Foreign Policy and How It Changed the World.* New York: Knopf, 2001.

Medhurst, Martin J. "Afterword." In *Beyond the Rhetorical Presidency,* edited by Martin J. Medhurst, 218–226. College Station: Texas A&M University Press, 1996.

Medhurst, Martin J. "Introduction." In *Critical Reflections on the Cold War: Linking Rhetoric and History,* edited by Martin J. Medhurst and H. W. Brands, 3–19. College Station: Texas A&M University Press, 2000.

Medhurst, Martin J. "Rhetorical Leadership and the Presidency: A Situational Taxonomy." In *The Values of Presidential Leadership,* edited by Terry L. Price and J. Thomas Wren, 9–84. New York: Palgrave Macmillan, 2007.

Merritt, Richard L. "Woodrow Wilson and the 'Great and Solemn Referendum,' 1920." *Review of Politics* 27 (1965): 78–104.

Michels, Tony. *A Fire in Their Hearts: Yiddish Socialists in New York.* Cambridge, MA: Harvard University Press, 2005.

Millis, Walter. *Arms and Men: A Study in American Military History.* New York: Putnam, 1956.

Milkis, Sidney. "Theodore Roosevelt: Domestic Affairs." Miller Center. Accessed January 17, 2023. https://millercenter.org/president/roosevelt/domestic-affairs.

Minersville School District v. Board of Education, 310 U.S. 586. June 3, 1940. http://supreme.justia.com/us/310/586/case.html.

Miscamble, Wilson D. *From Roosevelt to Truman: Potsdam, Hiroshima, and the Cold War.* Cambridge: University of Cambridge Press, 2007.

Moore, Deborah Dash. *At Home in America: Second Generation New York Jews.* New York: Columbia University Press, 1981.

Morgenthau, Hans Joachim. *Politics among Nations: The Struggle for Power and Peace.* 5th ed. New York: Knopf, 1973.

Murphy, John M. "No End Save Victory: FDR and the End of Isolationism, 1936–1941." In *Making the Case: Advocacy and Judgment in Public Argument,* edited by Kathryn M. Olson, Michael William Pfau, Benjamin Ponder, and Kirt H. Wilson, 127–160. East Lansing: Michigan State University Press, 2012.

Muste, A. J. *The Essays of A. J. Muste.* Edited by Nat Hentoff. Indianapolis: Bobbs-Merrill, 1967.

Muste, A. J. *Non-Violence in an Aggressive World.* New York: J. S. Ozer, 1972.

Niebuhr, Reinhold. *Moral Man and Immoral Society: A Study of Ethics and Politics.* New York: Charles Scribner, 1947.

Ninkovich, Frank. *Modernity and Power: A History of the Domino Theory in the Twentieth Century.* Chicago: University of Chicago Press, 1994.

Ninkovich, Frank A. *The Wilsonian Century: U.S. Foreign Policy since 1900.* Chicago: University of Chicago Press, 1999.

Nugent, Walter. *Progressivism: A Very Short Introduction.* Oxford: Oxford University Press, 2010.

O'Sullivan, Christopher D. *Sumner Welles, Postwar Planning, and the Quest for a New World Order, 1937–1943.* New York: Columbia University Press, 2008.

Offner, Arnold A. "Liberation or Dominance? The Ideology of U.S. National Security Policy." In *The Long War: A New History of U.S. National Security Policy since World War II,* edited by Andrew J. Bacevich, 1–52. New York: Columbia University Press, 2007.

Olson, Lynne. *Those Angry Days: Roosevelt, Lindbergh, and America's Fight over World War II, 1939–1941.* New York: Random House, 2013.

Osborn, Michael. *Michael Osborn on Metaphor and Style.* East Lansing: Michigan State University Press, 2018.

Paine, Thomas. *Common Sense.* Philadelphia: W. & T. Bradford, 1792.

Palczewski, Catherine H., Richard Ice, and John Fritch. *Rhetoric in Civic Life.* 2nd ed. State College, PA: Strata, 2012.

Parry-Giles, Trevor, and Marouf Hasian Jr. "Necessity or Nine Old Men: The Congressional Debate over Franklin D. Roosevelt's 1937 Court-Packing Plan." In *American Rhetoric in the New Deal Era, 1932–1945: A Rhetorical History of the United States,* vol. 7, edited by Thomas W. Benson, 245–278. East Lansing: Michigan State University Press, 2006.

Patterson, James T. *Mr. Republican: A Biography of Robert A. Taft.* Boston: Houghton Mifflin, 1972.

Peek, George Nelson., and Samuel L. Crowther. *Why Quit Our Own?* New York: D. Van Nostrand, 1936.

Perelman, Chaïm. *The Realm of Rhetoric.* Translated by William Kluback. Notre Dame, IN: University of Notre Dame Press, 1982.

Perelman, Chaïm, and Louise Olbrechts-Tyteca. *The New Rhetoric: A Treatise on Argumentation.* Notre Dame, IL: University of Notre Dame Press, 1969.

Perkins, Frances. *The Roosevelt I Knew.* New York: Viking Press, 1946.

Perrett, Geoffrey. *Days of Sadness, Years of Triumph: The American People, 1939–1945.* New York: Coward, McCann & Geoghegan, 1973.

Perry, Earnest. "We Want In: The African American Press's Negotiation for a White House Correspondent." *American Journalism* 20, no. 3 (2003): 31–47.

Perry, Samuel P. "Douglass MacArthur as Frontier Hero: Converting Frontiers in MacArthur's Farewell to Congress." *Southern Communication Journal* 77, no. 4 (2012): 263–286.

Persico, Joseph E. *Roosevelt's Centurions: FDR and the Commanders He Led to Victory in World War II.* New York: Random House, 2013.

Pestritto, Ronald J., and William J. Atto. "Introduction to American Progressivism." In *American Progressivism: A Reader,* edited by Ronald J. Pestritto and William J. Atto, 1–34. Lanham, MD: Lexington, 2008.

Peters, Charles. *Five Days in Philadelphia: The Amazing "We Want Willkie!" Convention of 1940.* New York: Public Affairs, 2005.

Phillips, William. "Reminiscences of William Phillips, 1951." Columbia Center for Oral History Archives. Accessed March 26, 2023. https://oralhistoryportal.li brary.columbia.edu/document.php?id=ldpd_4073373.

Plummer, Brenda Gayle. *Haiti and the United States: The Psychological Moment.* Athens: University of Georgia Press, 1992.

Potter, David Morris. *People of Plenty: Economic Abundance and the American Character.* Chicago: University of Chicago Press, 1958.

Powell, Jim. *FDR's Folly: How Roosevelt and His New Deal Prolonged the Great Depression.* New York: Crown Forum, 2003.

Preston, Andrew. "Franklin D. Roosevelt and America's Empire of Anti-Imperialism." In *Rhetorics of Empire: Language of Colonial Conflict After 1900,* edited by Martin Thomas and Richard Toye, 75–90. Manchester: Manchester University Press, 2017.

Rauschenbusch, Walter. *Christianity and the Social Crisis.* New York: Macmillan, 1913.

Reid, Ronald F., and James F. Klumpp. *American Rhetorical Discourse.* 3rd ed. Long Grove, IL: Waveland Press, 2005.

Reynolds, David. *From Munich to Pearl Harbor: Roosevelt's America and the Origins of the Second World War.* Chicago: Ivan R. Dee, 2001.

Ricard, Serge. "The Roosevelt Corollary." *Presidential Studies Quarterly* 36, no. 1 (2006): 17–26.

Richerberg, Donald R. "The New Deal's 'Revolution' Defended." *New York Times,* December 5, 1937.

Rockwell, Norman, and Thomas Rockwell. *Norman Rockwell, My Adventures as an Illustrator.* New York: Abrams, 1994.

Rodgers, Daniel T. *Contested Truths: Keywords in American Politics since Independence.* New York: Basic Books, 1987.

Rofe, Simon J. *Franklin Roosevelt's Foreign Policy and the Welles Mission*. New York: Palgrave Macmillan, 2007.

Roosevelt, Eleanor. *The Autobiography of Eleanor Roosevelt*. New York: Da Capo Press, 1992.

Roosevelt, Eleanor. *Courage in a Dangerous World: The Political Writings of Eleanor Roosevelt*. New York: Columbia University Press, 1999.

Roosevelt, Eleanor. "Foreword." *F.D.R. Columnist: The Uncollected Columns of Franklin D. Roosevelt*, edited by Donald Scott Carmichael. New York: Pellegrini & Cudahy, 1947.

Roosevelt, Eleanor. "My Day, October 5, 1936." Eleanor Roosevelt Papers, Digital Edition, 2017. https://www2.gwu.edu/~erpapers/myday/displaydoc.cfm?_y=1936 &_f=md054453.

Roosevelt, Eleanor. *This I Remember*. New York: Harper, 1949.

Roosevelt, Eleanor. *This Is My Story*. New York: Harper, 1937.

Roosevelt, Franklin D. "Acceptance of V.P. Nomination." August 9, 1920, box 2, pp. 1–17, Master Speech File, Franklin D. Roosevelt Presidential Library.

Roosevelt, Franklin D. "The Age of Social Consciousness." *Harvard Graduate*, September 1929.

Roosevelt, Franklin D. "Annual Message to Congress." January 6, 1937. American Presidency Project. Accessed February 11, 2023. https://www.presidency.ucsb .edu/documents/annual-message-congress-4.

Roosevelt, Franklin D. "Excerpts from the Press Conference." August 19, 1941. American Presidency Project. Accessed February 18, 2023. https://www.presidency.ucsb.edu/documents/excerpts-from-the-press-conference-49.

Roosevelt, Franklin D. "Excerpts from the Press Conference." November 28, 1941. American Presidency Project. Accessed February 18, 2023, https://www.presidency.ucsb.edu/documents/excerpts-from-the-press-conference-72.

Roosevelt, Franklin D. *FDR: His Personal Letters*. Edited by Elliott Roosevelt, assisted by James N. Rosenau and Joseph P. Lash. New York: Duell, Sloan & Pearce, 1947–1950.

Roosevelt, Franklin D. *F.D.R. Columnist: The Uncollected Columns of Franklin D. Roosevelt*. Chicago: Pellegrini & Cudahy, 1947.

Roosevelt, Franklin D. *Franklin D. Roosevelt: Selected Speeches, Messages, Press Conferences and Letters*. Edited by Basil Rauch. New York: Holt, Rinehart & Winston, 1964.

Roosevelt, Franklin D. *Franklin D. Roosevelt and Foreign Affairs*. Edited by Edgar B. Nixon. Cambridge, MA: Belknap Press, 1969–1983.

Roosevelt, Franklin D. *Franklin D. Roosevelt's Own Story: Told in His Own Words from His Private and Public Papers*. Selected by Donald Day. Boston: Little, Brown, 1951.

Roosevelt, Franklin D. "Fourth Annual Message." December 6, 1904. American Presidency Project. Accessed February 11, 2023. https://www.presidency.ucsb .edu/documents/fourth-annual-message-15.

Roosevelt, Franklin D. "Inaugural Address." March 4, 1933. American Presidency Project. Accessed March 15, 2023. https://www.presidency.ucsb.edu/docu ments/inaugural-address-8.

Roosevelt, Franklin D. "Letter on Additional National and State Parks." May 26, 1937. American Presidency Project. Accessed February 11, 2023. https://www .presidency.ucsb.edu/documents/letter-additional-national-and-state-parks.

Roosevelt, Franklin D. "A Letter on the Improvement of Agriculture." December 8, 1933. American Presidency Project. Accessed February 11, 2023. https://www.presidency.ucsb.edu/documents/letter-the-improvement-agriculture.

Roosevelt, Franklin D. "Letter to the Daughters of the American Revolution on National Defense." April 20, 1936. American Presidency Project. Accessed February 11, 2023. https://www.presidency.ucsb.edu/documents/letter-the-daughters-the-american-revolution-national-defense.

Roosevelt, Franklin D. *Memorable Quotations of Franklin D. Roosevelt.* Compiled by Taylor E. Parks and Lois F. Parks. New York: Thomas Crowell, 1965.

Roosevelt, Franklin D. "Message to Congress on the Bretton Woods Agreements." February 12, 1945. American Presidency Project. Accessed February 15, 2023. https://www.presidency.ucsb.edu/documents/message-congress-the-bretton-woods-agreements.

Roosevelt, Franklin D. "The National Emergency of Peace Times," June 25, 1919. Worcester Polytechnic Institute Archives & Special Collections, Worcester, MA.

Roosevelt, Franklin D. "The Navy Program and What It Means." *Nation's Business,* December 1915.

Roosevelt, Franklin D. "On Your Own Heads." *Scribner's Magazine,* April 1917.

Roosevelt, Franklin D. "Our Foreign Policy: A Democratic View." *Foreign Affairs* 6, no. 4 (1928): 543–586.

Roosevelt, Franklin D. "Press Conference on the U.S.S. Potomac." August 16, 1941. American Presidency Project. Accessed February 18, 2023, https://www.presidency.ucsb.edu/documents/press-conference-the-uss-potomac.

Roosevelt, Franklin D. "Proclamation 2040—Bank Holiday." March 9, 1933. American Presidency Project. Accessed February 11, 2023. https://www.presidency.ucsb.edu/documents/proclamation-2040-bank-holiday.

Roosevelt, Franklin D. *Public Papers and Addresses of Franklin Delano Roosevelt.* Compiled by Samuel I. Rosenman. New York: Macmillan, 1938–1950.

Roosevelt, Franklin D. "Remarks at Watsonville, California." May 11, 1903. American Presidency Project. Accessed February 11, 2023. https://www.presidency.ucsb.edu/documents/remarks-watsonville-california.

Roosevelt, Franklin D. "Report to Congress on the Operations of the Lend-Lease Act." June 10, 1941. American Presidency Project. Accessed February 18, 2023, https://www.presidency.ucsb.edu/documents/report-congress-the-operations-the-lend-lease-act.

Roosevelt, Franklin D. *Roosevelt and Frankfurter: Their Correspondence, 1928–1945.* Annotated by Max Freedman. Boston: Little, Brown, 1967.

Roosevelt, Franklin D. *The Roosevelt Reader: Selected Speeches, Messages, Press Conferences, and Letters of Franklin D. Roosevelt.* Edited by Basil Rauch. Charlottesville: University of Virginia Press, 1957.

Roosevelt, Franklin D. "Shall We Trust Japan?" *Asia* 23, no. 7 (July 1923).

Roosevelt, Franklin D. "Statement on the Dumbarton Oaks Conversations." December 9, 1944. American Presidency Project. Accessed February 15, 2023. https://www.presidency.ucsb.edu/documents/statement-the-dumbarton-oaks-conversations

Roosevelt, Franklin D. "Statement on the Extension of the Automobile Code." January

31, 1935. American Presidency Project. Accessed February 11, 2023. https://www
.presidency.ucsb.edu/documents/statement-the-extension-the-automobile-code.

Roosevelt, Franklin D. "Statement to the Federation of Women's Clubs." December
14, 1933. American Presidency Project. Accessed February 11, 2023. https://
www.presidency.ucsb.edu/documents/statement-the-federation-womens-clubs.

Roosevelt, Franklin D. "Statement on the Second Anniversary of the Atlantic Charter." August 14, 1943. American Presidency Project. Accessed February 15, 2023.
https://www.presidency.ucsb.edu/documents/statement-the-second-anniver
sary-the-atlantic-charter.

Roosevelt, Franklin D. *Whither Bound?* New York: Houghton Mifflin, 1926.

Roosevelt, Sara Delano. *My Boy Franklin.* New York: R. Long & R. R. Smith, 1933.

Rose, Kenneth. *Myth and the Greatest Generation: A Social History of Americans in World
War II.* New York: Routledge, 2008.

Rosenau, James N. *The Roosevelt Treasury.* New York: Doubleday, 1951.

Rosenberg, Emily. "Commentary: The Cold War and the Discourse of National Security." *Diplomatic History* 17, no. 2 (April 1993).

Rosenberg, Emily S. *Spreading the American Dream: American Economic and Cultural
Expansion, 1890–1945.* New York: Hill & Wang, 1982.

Rosenman, Samuel I. *Working with Roosevelt.* New York: Da Capo Press, 1972.

Rozell, Mark J., and William D. Pederson. *FDR and the Modern Presidency: Leadership
and Legacy.* Westport, CT: Praeger, 1997.

Russell, Greg. "Theodore Roosevelt's Diplomacy and the Quest for Great Power
Equilibrium in Asia." *Presidential Studies Quarterly* 38, no. 3 (2008): 433–455.

Ryan, Halford Ross. *Franklin D. Roosevelt's Rhetorical Presidency.* Westport, CT: Greenwood Publishing, 1988.

Ryan, Halford Ross. "Roosevelt's First Inaugural: A Study of Technique." *Quarterly
Journal of Speech* 65, no. 2 (1979): 137–149.

Ryan, Halford Ross. "Franklin Delano Roosevelt: Rhetorical Politics and Political
Rhetorics." In *Presidential Speechwriting: From the New Deal to the Reagan Revolution
and Beyond,* edited by Kurt Ritter and Martin J. Medhurst, 21–39. College Station:
Texas A&M University Press, 2003.

Saleh, Yassin al-Haj. "The Just Oppressors: Middle Eastern Victimhood Narratives
and New Imagined Communities." Al Jumhuriya, June 9, 2015. https://www
.aljumhuriya.net/en/content/just-oppressors-middle-eastern-victimhood-narra
tives-and-new-imagined-communities.

Salmon, William N. "Formal Idioms and Action: Toward a Grammar of Genres."
Language & Communication 30, no. 4 (2010): 211–224.

Sanders, Thomas. *The Last Good War: The Faces and Voices of World War II.* New York:
Welcome Books, 2010.

Santoro, Carlo Maria. *Diffidence and Ambition: The Intellectual Sources of U.S. Foreign
Policy.* Boulder, CO: Westview Press, 1992.

Satia, Priya. "The Defense of Inhumanity: Air Control and the British Idea of Arabia." *American Historical Review* 111, no. 1 (2006): 16–51.

Schiappa, Edward. *Defining Reality.* Carbondale: Southern Illinois University Press, 2003.

Schieberger, Londa. *Has Feminism Changed Science?* Cambridge, MA: Harvard University Press, 1998.

Schlesinger, Arthur M. *The Coming of the New Deal, 1933–1935.* New York: Houghton Mifflin, 1958.

Schlesinger, Arthur M., Jr. "Reinhold Niebuhr's Long Shadow." *New York Times,* June 22, 1992.

Schlesinger, Arthur M., Jr. *War and the American Presidency.* New York: W. W. Norton, 2004.

Scott, James M. "The Doolittle Raid Generated More Ripples than Once Thought." *Military Times,* April 18, 2018. https://www.milita.rytimes.com/off-duty/mili tary-culture/2018/04/18/the-doolittle-raid-generated-more-ripples-than-once -thought/.

Scudder, Vida Dutton. *On Journey.* New York: E. P. Dutton, 1937.

Sevareid, Eric. *Not So Wild a Dream.* New York: A. A. Knopf, 1946.

Shaara, Jeff. *The Rising Tide: A Novel of World War II.* New York: Ballantine Books, 2006.

Sharon, John H. "The Psychology of the Fireside Chat." BA thesis, Princeton University, 1949.

Sherry, Michael S. *In the Shadow of War: The United States since the 1930s.* New Haven, CT: Yale University Press, 1995.

Sherry, Michael S. *The Rise of American Air Power: The Creation of Armageddon.* New Haven, CT: University of Yale Press, 1987.

Sherwin, Martin. *A World Destroyed: The Atomic Bomb and the Grand Alliance.* New York: Knopf, 1975.

Sherwood, Robert E. *Roosevelt and Hopkins: An Intimate History.* New York: Harper, 1950.

Siegel, Katherine A. S. "Technology and Trade: Russia's Pursuit of American Investment, 1917–1929." *Diplomatic History* 17, no. 3 (1993): 375–398.

Siff, Dave. "New York Marks Anniversary of Tragedy." CNN, September 11, 2002. http://edition.cnn.com/2002/US/09/11/ar911.memorial.newyork/index .html.

Simpson, Brian A. W. *Human Rights and the End of Empire: Britain and the Genesis of the European Convention.* Oxford: Oxford University Press, 2001.

Sinclair, Andrew. *The Available Man: The Life Behind the Masks of Warren Gamaliel Harding.* New York: Macmillan, 1965.

Smith, Gaddis. *American Diplomacy during the Second World War, 1941–1945.* Edited by Robert A. Divine. New York: John Wiley & Sons, 1965.

Smith, James K. A. *Awaiting the King: Reforming Public Theology.* Grand Rapids, MI: Baker Academic, 2017.

Smith, Jean Edward. *FDR.* New York: Random House, 2007.

Smith, Kimberly K. "Mere Nostalgia: Notes on a Progressive Paratheory." *Rhetoric & Public Affairs* 3, no. 4 (2000): 505–527.

Smith, Neil. *American Empire: Roosevelt's Geographer and the Prelude to Globalization.* Berkeley: University of California Press, 2003.

Smith, Robert C., and Richard A. Seltzer. *Polarization and the Presidency: From FDR to Barack Obama.* Boulder, CO: Lynne Rienner, 2015.

Smith, Rogers M. *Civic Ideals: Conflicting Visions of Citizenship in U.S. History.* New Haven, CT: Yale University Press, 1997.

Smith, Tony. *America's Mission: The United States and the Worldwide Struggle for Democracy in the Twentieth Century*. Princeton, NJ: Princeton University Press, 1994.

Southard, Belinda A. Stillion. *Militant Citizenship: Rhetorical Strategies of the National Woman's Party, 1913–1920*. College Station: Texas A&M University Press, 2011.

Southern, David W. *The Progressive Era and Race: Reaction and Reform, 1900–1917*. Wheeling, IL: Harlan Davidson, 2005.

Spence, Jonathan D. *The Search for Modern China*. New York: W. W. Norton, 1990.

Spiller, James. "'This Is War!' Network Radio and World War II Propaganda in America." *Journal of Radio Studies* 11, no. 1 (2004): 55–72.

Steele, Richard W. *Propaganda in an Open Society: The Roosevelt Administration and the Media, 1933–1941*. Westport, CT: Greenwood, 1985.

Stoler, Mark A. "FDR and the Origins of the National Security Establishment." In *The World of the Roosevelts*, edited by David B. Woolner, Warren F. Kimball, and David Reynolds, 63–90. New York: Palgrave Macmillan, 2008.

Stone, Jonathan W. "Listening to the Sonic Archive: Rhetoric, Representation, and Race in the Lomax Prison Recordings." *Enculturation: A Journal of Rhetoric, Writing, and Culture* 19 (2015). http://enculturation.net/listening-to-the-sonic-archive.

Stone, Oliver, and Peter Kuznick. *The Untold History of the United States*. New York: Gallery Books, 2012.

Strout, Richard L. "Intimate Message from Charlottesville." *Christian Science Monitor*, June 11, 1940.

Stuckey, Mary E. *Defining Americans: The Presidency and National Identity*. Lawrence: University Press of Kansas, 2005.

Stuckey Mary E. "FDR, the Rhetoric of Vision, and the Creation of the National Synoptic State." *Quarterly Journal of Speech* 98, no. 3 (2012): 297–319.

Stuckey, Mary. E. "Franklin D. Roosevelt, 'Address of the President to the Congress of the United States Broadcast from the Capitol, Washington, D.C." *Voices of Democracy* 12 (2017): 1–15.

Stuckey, Mary E. *The Good Neighbor: Franklin D. Roosevelt and the Rhetoric of American Power*. East Lansing: Michigan State University Press, 2013.

Stuckey Mary E. "The Great Debate: The United States and the World, 1936–1941." In *World War II and the Cold War: The Rhetoric of Hearts and Minds: A Rhetorical History of the United States*, vol. 8, edited by Martin J. Medhurst, 1–51. East Lansing: Michigan State University Press, 2018.

Stuckey, Mary E. "Jimmy Carter, Human Rights, and Instrumental Effects of Presidential Rhetoric." In *The Handbook of Rhetoric and Public Address*, edited by Shawn J. Parry-Giles and J. Michael Hogan, 293–312. Oxford: Wiley-Blackwell, 2010.

Stuckey, Mary E. *Political Vocabularies: FDR, the Clergy Letters, and the Elements of Political Argument*. East Lansing: Michigan State University Press, 2018.

Stuckey Mary E. *The President as Interpreter-in-Chief*. Chatham, NJ: Chatham House, 1991.

Stuckey, Mary E. *Voting Deliberatively: FDR and the 1936 Presidential Campaign*. University Park: Pennsylvania State University Press, 2015.

Sunstein, Cass R. *The Second Bill of Rights: FDR's Unfinished Revolution—and Why We Need It More than Ever*. New York: Basic Books, 2004.

Surette, Leon. *Dreams of a Totalitarian Utopia: Literary Modernism and Politics*. London: McGill-Queen's University Press, 2011.

Terkel, Studs. *"The Good War": An Oral History of World War II*. New York: New Press, 1997.

"Text of Former President's Address before the Republican Convention." *New York Times*, June 26, 1940.

Titcomb, James. "Germany Faces Losing US Intelligence If It Uses Huawei Equipment." *Telegraph*, March 11, 2019. https://www.telegraph.co.uk/tech nology/2019/03/11/germany-faces-losing-us-intelligence-uses-huawei-equip ment/.

Trani, Eugene P., and David L. Wilson. *The Presidency of Warren G. Harding*. Lawrence: University Press of Kansas, 1977.

Thomas, Norman. *Hearings before the Committee on Foreign Affairs House of Representatives, Seventy-Seventh Congress, First Session, on HR 1776*. Washington, DC: US Government Printing Office, 1941.

Thomas, Norman. *We Have a Future*. Princeton, NJ: Princeton University Press, 1941.

Tucker, Robert W., and David C. Hendrickson. *Empire of Liberty: The Statecraft of Thomas Jefferson*. Oxford: Oxford University Press, 1990.

Tugwell, Rexford Guy. *The Battle for Democracy*. New York: Columbia University Press, 1935.

Tugwell, Rexford Guy. *The Brains Trust*. New York: Viking Press, 1968.

Tulis, Jeffrey K. "Revising the Rhetorical Presidency." In *Beyond the Rhetorical Presidency*, edited by Martin J. Medhurst, 3–14. College Station: Texas A&M University Press, 1996.

Tulis, Jeffrey K. *The Rhetorical Presidency*. Princeton, NJ: Princeton University Press, 1987.

Tully, Grace G. *F.D.R., My Boss*. New York: C. Scribner's Sons, 1949.

Tuveson, Ernest Lee. *Redeemer Nation: The Idea of America's Millennial Role*. Chicago: University of Chicago Press, 1968.

Tworek, Heidi S. *News from Germany: The Competition to Control World Communications, 1900–1945*. Cambridge, MA: Harvard University Press, 2019.

Uncensored. New York: Keep America Out of War Congress, 1939–1941.

"US-China Trade War: Causes and Consequences." Foreign Policy Research Institute, April 24, 2019. https://www.fpri.org/event/2019/u-s-china-trade-war-causes-and -consequences/.

"U.S. Invasion and Occupation of Haiti, 1915–1934." Office of the Historian. Accessed February 2, 2023. https://history.state.gov/milestones/1914-1920/haiti.

Vandenberg, Arthur H., Jr. *The Private Papers of Senator Vandenberg*. Boston: Mifflin, 1952.

"The Vice President Appears on Meet the Press with Tim Russert." National Archives and Records Administration, September 16, 2001. https://georgewbush-white house.archives.gov/vicepresident/news-speeches/speeches/vp20010916.html.

Villard, Oswald Garrison. *Our Military Chaos: The Truth about Defense*. New York: A. A. Knopf, 1939.

Vivian, Bradford. *Public Forgetting: The Rhetoric and Politics of Beginning Again*. University Park: Pennsylvania State University Press, 2010.

Wallace, Henry. "Reminiscences of Henry Agard Wallace, 1951–1953." Columbia Center for Oral History Archives. Accessed March 26, 2023. https://oralhistory portal.library.columbia.edu/document.php?id=ldpd_4075714.

Ward, Geoffrey C. *Before the Trumpet: Young Franklin Roosevelt, 1882–1905.* New York: Harper & Row, 1985.

Ward, Geoffrey C. *A First-Class Temperament: The Emergence of Franklin Roosevelt, 1905–1928.* New York: Harper & Row, 1989.

Washington, George. "Farewell Address." September 19, 1796. American Presidency Project. Accessed February 11, 2023. https://www.presidency.ucsb.edu /documents/farewell-address

Washington, George. "Proclamation 6—Day of Public Thanksgiving." January 1, 1795. American Presidency Project. Accessed February 11, 2023. https://www .presidency.ucsb.edu/documents/proclamation-6-day-public-thanksgiving.

Watkins, T. H. *The Great Depression: America in the 1930s.* Boston: Little, Brown, 1993.

Weber, Ryan. "Stasis in Space! Viewing Definitional Conflicts Surrounding the James Webb Space Telescope Funding Debate." *Technical Communication Quarterly* 25, no. 2 (2016): 87–103.

Weeks, Albert L. *Russia's Life-Saver: Lend-Lease Aid to the U.S.S.R. in World War II.* Lanham, MD: Lexington Books, 2004.

Weigley, Russell F. *The American Way of War: A History of United States Military Strategy and Policy.* Bloomington: University of Indiana Press, 1973.

Westbrook, Robert B. *Why We Fought: Forging American Obligations in World War II.* Washington, DC: Smithsonian Books, 2004.

Wheeler, Burton K., with Paul F. Healy. *Yankee from the West.* Garden City, NY: Doubleday, 1962.

"Why Joe Biden's Instinctive Caution Makes Real Change Possible." *Economist,* July 4, 2020. https://www.economist.com/leaders/2020/07/02/why-joe-bidens-ins tinctive-caution-makes-real-change-possible.

Wiebe, Robert H. *The Search for Order, 1887–1920.* New York: Hill & Wang, 1967.

Williams, William Appleman. *The Tragedy of American Diplomacy.* 2nd ed. New York: Dell Publishing, 1972.

Willkie, Wendell L. *One World.* New York: Simon & Schuster, 1943.

Wilson, John F. "Harding's Rhetoric of Normalcy, 1920–1923." *Quarterly Journal of Speech* 48, no. 4 (1962): 406–411.

Wilson, Howard E., Nelle E. Bowman, and Allen Y. King. *This America: Our Land, Our People, Our Faith, Our Promise.* New York: American Book, 1942.

Wilson, Woodrow. "Address on Flag Day." June 14, 1917. American Presidency Project. Accessed February 11, 2023. https://www.presidency.ucsb.edu/docu ments/address-flag-day.

Wilson, Woodrow. "Address to a Joint Session of Congress on the Severance of Diplomatic Relations with Germany." February 3, 1917. American Presidency Project. Accessed February 11, 2023. https://www.presidency.ucsb.edu/documents /address-joint-session-congress-the-severance-diplomatic-relations-with-germany.

Wilson, Woodrow. "Address to a Joint Session of Congress Requesting a Declaration of War Against Germany." April 2, 1917. American Presidency Project. Accessed

February 11, 2023. https://www.presidency.ucsb.edu/documents/address-joint-session-congress-requesting-declaration-war-against-germany.

Wilson, Woodrow. "Final Address in Support of the League of Nations." American Rhetoric, September 25, 1919. https://www.americanrhetoric.com/speeches/wilsonleagueofnations.htm.

Winkler, Allan M. "The World War II Home Front." *History Now*, December 2007. http://www.historynow.org/12_2007/historian3.html.

Wolff, Wendy, ed. *The Senate 1789–1989: Classic Speeches 1830–1993*. Vol. 3. Washington, DC: US Government Printing Office, 1994.

Woolverton, John F., and James D. Bratt. *A Christian and A Democrat: A Religious Biography of Franklin D. Roosevelt*. Grand Rapids, MI: Eerdmans Publishing, 2019.

Wright, Benjamin F., ed. *The Federalist: The Famous Papers on the Principles of American Government*. New York: Metro Books, 1961.

Yesil, Bilge. "'Who Said This Is a Man's War?': Propaganda, Advertising Discourse and the Representation of War Worker Women during the Second World War." *Media History* 10, no. 2 (2004): 103–117.

Zarefsky, David. "Four Senses of Rhetorical History." In *Doing Rhetorical History: Concepts and Cases*, edited by Kathleen J. Turner. Tuscaloosa: University of Alabama Press, 1998.

Zarefsky, David. "The Presidency Has Always Been a Place for Rhetorical Leadership." In *The Presidency and Rhetorical Leadership*, edited by Leroy G. Darsey. College Station: Texas A&M University Press, 2002.

Zelizer, Julian E. *Arsenal of Democracy: The Politics of National Security—From World War II to the War on Terrorism*. New York: Basic Books, 2010.

Zelko, Harold P. "Franklin D. Roosevelt's Rhythm in Rhetorical Style." *Quarterly Journal of Speech* 28, no. 2 (1942): 138–141.

Zietsma, David. "Imagining Heaven and Hell: Religion, National Identity, and U.S. Foreign Relations, 1930–1953." PhD diss., University of Akron, 2007.

Index